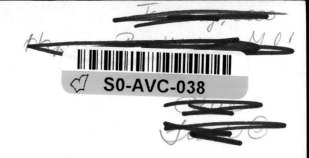

# YESTERDAY'S NEWS

## Why Canada's Daily Newspapers Are Failing Us

# John Miller

Fernwood Publishing • Halifax

To Sandy and Daniel
who understood

and to Irene Isabel Miller
who suggested journalism

Editing: Donna Davis
Cover design: Richard Slye
Design and production: Beverley Rach
Printed and bound in Canada by: Hignell Printing Limited


A publication of:
Fernwood Publishing
Box 9409, Station A
Halifax, Nova Scotia
B3K 5S3

Fernwood Publishing Company Limited gratefully acknowledges the financial support
of the Ministry of Canadian Heritage and the Canada Council for the Arts for our
publishing program.


**Canadian Cataloguing in Publication Data**

Yesterday's news

Includes bibliographical references.
ISBN 1-55266-000-1

1. Canadian newspapers.   2. Journalism -- Canada.   3. Consolidation and merger of
corporations -- Canada.   I. Title.

PN4908.M56  1988              071.'1          C98-950188-4

# Contents

# Foreword

I love newspapers. Since the age of sixteen, all I ever wanted to be, aside from maybe a shortstop, was a newspaperman. I count myself fortunate to have spent twenty years at it, working my way up from a paper boy to acting managing editor of the largest newsroom in Canada, able to assign people to cover news stories anywhere in the world. It didn't bring me wealth or fame, but it gave me something even better: a sense of public service; a feeling that if I could only write something true enough or good enough, I could help people understand the forces shaping their lives, and maybe they could make a difference in the world. I was one of the True Believers.

Newspapers, from the inside, were fun. I loved the musty smell of ink on newsprint. I loved the way a freshly printed paper felt in my hand. I loved everything that went into making a newspaper: the pressure of crafting together the best version of the truth to meet a deadline, and the infectious camaraderie of creative people on high adrenaline. Newspapers mattered, and what we did mattered too. When I left newspapers in 1986 to run a journalism school, I left an industry at the peak of its power and influence. I was sure I'd be training people for the next twenty years to do exactly the same job I'd come to love, secure in the knowledge that newspapers would prosper and grow.

How quickly things changed. In the early 1990s, newspapers came under a wave of unprecedented economic, social and technological pressures, not the least of which was a stubborn refusal to change with the times. They began drawing away from their communities, and we in turn began drawing away from them.

This book is an attempt to identify the factors that made us fall out of love with daily newspapers in Canada, but it is also a good deal more. It is a newspaperman's quest for the survival of his craft; a questioning search for how the press can reconnect with us, how it can learn to serve us better in the twenty-first century; and what we can do to make that happen.

*Yesterday's News* is organized into two parts. Part One documents what I consider to be the blind spots of newspapers: the corporate agenda of a new breed of owners who value profit over public service; the obsession with cosmetic redesign in place of the immensely more difficult task of investing in better and more innovative journalism; the surprising absence of any form of accountability for journalists in spite of growing public distrust for what they do; the failure of newspapers to explain why freedom of the press should matter to us; and journalism's stunning lack of diversity, a factor that has caused newsrooms to fall out of touch with the world that they are trying to cover.

Part Two explores solutions, and I have chosen to seek them out in an unusual way. Impatient with a professional inertia that has prevented editors and owners of Canada's daily press from exploring new ways to cover the news, I returned to my roots in the Ottawa Valley, volunteered as a reporter for a small-town weekly and let my mind open up to the ways in which journalism might once again serve the public interest. My friends were deeply sceptical, since weekly newspapers have a reputation for pandering to both readers and advertisers. But I can say that it was the most educational experience I've ever had as a journalist. There is something very honest about being close to the people you write about and bumping into them the next day on Main Street. What I learned prompted me to question some of the lockstep conventions that have led to the arrogance of daily journalism and, hence, to its tragic decline.

It's ironic that Part One of this book was written in Warkworth, Ontario. Two days before Christmas 1996, the local paper, a weekly that had published faithfully for 104 years, was closed down. It was one of the first death sentences imposed by the profit-driven newspaper empire controlled by Canada's newest lord of the press, Conrad Black. I took time out to write the *Warkworth Journal's* obituary, a nostalgic little piece that recalled the feisty vision of public service expounded by the paper's founder, W.H. Henry. In his very first issue, he urged readers to "help your paper, subscribe for your paper, and give it all the support that it deserves, so that you may always have a paper to keep your town before the world."

I found it telling that Black, writing from England on embossed stationery, was one of the very few people who refused to talk to me as I gathered material for this book. He professes to care about the future of newspapers, and he says that he believes in the value of diverse opinions, yet he wrote that I sounded like a "soulmate of the local Canadian left" and that there was no point in even talking to someone who had criticized him and his company. The man who controls more than half of the country's daily newspapers appears to believe that he should speak only to those who fully agree with him. This is the person we Canadians now have to keep our country before the world.

Luckily, I've been aided in my task by lots of other True Believers, people whose love for newspapers is surely as great as my own. I would like to thank them here. To my early newsroom mentors, who detected signs of creative talent in a rather shy and serious young man: Peter Tomlin; Bob McAleer; Martin Goodman; and Tommy Lytle, one of the best pure newsmen I've ever met, whose famous definition "News is what I say it is" beautifully captures the truth and arrogance of what journalists do.

I am grateful to the wonderful folks at the *Equity,* a community newspaper in Shawville, Quebec, who allowed me to work as their colleague for three months to see how journalism feels when its audience is always just around the corner. Thanks in particular to Heather Dickson; her former editor, Richard Wills; and Ross Dickson, a publisher whose door is never locked.

I am grateful to those who encouraged me to write this book: my close friend Keith Branscombe and my colleagues Stuart McLean, Don Gibb and David Hayes (whose playful gift of a miniature black typewriter sat on the windowsill beside me like a talisman as I plowed on).

Thanks, too, to Ryerson Polytechnic University and my former students who helped in the research—Caroline Nolan, Mark Leger and Kimberly Prince—and to Errol Sharpe of Fernwood Publishing without whom you wouldn't be reading this.

Finally, I thank the many fine journalists who spoke out candidly about what ails their craft. This is all too rare, since the press chooses not to cover itself. I invite others, readers who still care about newspapers and journalists who still believe, to join in contemplating the challenge before us. It is only by facing up to what newspapers are that we can begin to grasp what they might become.

John Gordon Miller
Hope Township, Ontario

# PART ONE

# What's Wrong

# CHAPTER ONE

# Taking the Pulse

Abroad, at home, infirm or stout,
In health, or raving from the gout,
Who possibly can do without
The Paper!

— Poem printed in first edition
of George Brown's *Globe*,
March 5, 1844

Newspapers seldom tell us what they're in business for. Are they here to educate and improve us or merely to entertain? Do they work hard to tell us the truth or only what's in their commercial interest? Do they believe in their own future by investing in better journalism, or are they content to divert us with colour and graphics? If they really know the answers, editors often forget to tell us in their daily rush to cover history on the run. Only in rare moments—usually when something goes very right or very wrong—do they let us glimpse inside their souls.

For readers of Canada's largest newspaper, such a moment came on November 14, 1993. That Sunday the *Toronto Star* launched an ambitious and colourful redesign, which it had hyped for two years with the slogan "The shape of news to come." Perhaps if it hadn't raised expectations impossibly high, the paper would have been admired for its superb colour reproduction and crisp, compact look. Its new $400 million printing plant was capable of turning out the most modern newspaper in North America, and its writers and editors were among the best in the country. With revenue and readers drifting away in a punishing recession, it was time to try something new. But instead of staking out new ground in the journalism of the 1990s, the redesigned *Star* seemed to embrace much of what is wrong with daily newspapers today and why they are failing us in so many ways.

Under a colourful banner of promos to fluffy stories inside the paper, the front page featured the start of a week-long series entitled "What is woman's life like today?" It was a vapid piece of journalism prompted not by any news event but rather by a blatant marketing campaign to win back women readers, who had been drifting away from the paper in large numbers. A column from editor John Honderich introduced the new look in boastful terms: "Our goal has remained constant—to make the *Star* more readable, relevant and renowned." The main changes: narrower pages, more colour pictures, low-rub ink, more charts and graphs, bigger and cleaner type, a news summary on page two for readers in a hurry, and a return to the paper's ribbon-shaped nameplate that had won design awards in the salad days of the 1960s. All of this was supported by hundreds of thousands of dollars of sophisticated market research, which Honderich said gave the paper a solid fix on what its readers really wanted.

What he did not mention seemed more notable: 13 percent less space in the paper; no beefing up of local coverage; no new specialized beats; no substantial additions to editorial content other than a new and short-lived section called FYI that, in the words of its supervising editor, contained "refrigerator journal-ism"—tips, lists, news-you-can-use—for working women and other people who don't have time to read anymore. The shape of news to come was nothing more than a triumph of cosmetics: shorter stories, eye-catching graphics, lots of colour, and a breezy style more suited to the telling of gossip than the significant news of the day. "Readable?" Perhaps to some, but it is not so "relevant" or "renowned" for a newspaper that once sent Ernest Hemingway, Fred Griffin and Ralph Allen to cover wars, Nathan Cohen and Robert Fulford to cover the arts, Peter C. Newman to cover politics, Milt Dunnell to cover sports and Gordon Sinclair, Pierre Berton and Duncan Macpherson to cover life.

The same thing is happening at newspapers across the country. At a time when they should be better than ever and when we most need them to guide us forward in a period of rapid change, too many newspapers have become gaudy and greedy, lazy, elitist and remote, untrusted, out of touch with our lives and filled with information that we somehow value less and less. And although they won't tell us this, the people who actually run them are fearing for the future of ink on newsprint every bit as much as town criers must have when they heard about that man Guttenburg and his printing press. Can an institution so uncertain of its survival in an era of unlimited cablevision and information superhighways be counted upon to reinvent itself before it's too late?

This is a problem that Canadian owners, publishers and editors haven't opened to public debate. They're still stuck in denial and engaged in what I call "lipstick journalism," selling the sizzle of redesign and trying to pander to our elusive tastes instead of investing in what readers really need, which is the substance of quality journalism. Now that cost-cutting has allowed newspapers to once again ring up healthy profits, they're putting their money not into training or hiring or figuring out how better to cover the news, but into marketing, which is a business school concept that treats news coverage as a commodity to be manipulated and sold as cheaply as possible. The job isn't to inquire and inform and give people in your community something that helps them make sense of the world. It's to find out whom you need to deliver to your advertisers, learn what they'd like to read about, give it to them, then go about telling them how valuable it is. Under this model, the audience ultimately determines what news you cover; it's not news coverage that builds the audience. The trouble with marketing is that the right questions aren't always asked and readers don't always know what they want in advance. The greatest newspapers, the ones that endure and prosper, operate the other way around, as rich compendiums of information that we didn't know we needed, written with a style and authority that makes us trust them to deliver it to us every day. Too many of today's newspapers match the unflattering image of a heavily made-up and slightly overweight floozy, too long without love, prowling the streets in a desperate search for something that passes for affection. The marketplace has changed since her salad days; her old charms find no admirers; the competition is faster and younger. Having lost her integrity and her soul, she thinks the answer is more lipstick.

Most certainly, this is the way to oblivion. The new corporate ethos, which puts short-term profit ahead of long-term thinking and which substitutes marketing hype and new technology for editorial renewal, is helping to place print journalism on the endangered list. As the following vital statistics show, its pulse is getting fainter.

Fewer of us are subscribing. Since the recession took hold in early 1990, a disturbing total of 622,000 customers have stopped buying newspapers every day in this country. That's a drop of 11 percent, or 3.7 million fewer papers being sold per week by an industry that depends financially on being able to deliver customers to advertisers.[1] And the papers most vulnerable are the ones most people regard as our best. Canada's ten largest dailies collectively lost a total of 2.2 million sales per week in that period, and not one of them gained. (By contrast, in the United States, where no owner controls more than 11 percent of national circulation and where more money tends to be reinvested in the editorial product, seven of the top ten dailies increased circulation between 1995 and 1996.) Although some large Canadian papers deliberately shed costly circulation to far-flung areas, that doesn't begin to explain the precipitous declines. The *Toronto Star* sells nearly 100,000 fewer copies every Saturday than it did a decade ago. The *Ottawa Citizen*, chosen by Conrad Black to be his Canadian flagship, has seen its weekday circulation drop by one quarter since 1990. Once the proudest gauge of a newspaper's success and featured above the fold on many front pages, circulation figures have suddenly become an embarrassment. Few Canadian dailies print them at all today. The customers, it appears, are telling Canada's publishers something important: "You're not worth our time."

Fewer of us are advertising. For a variety of reasons, big advertisers turned away from daily newspapers in droves during the early 1990s, and smaller advertisers were effectively priced out of the market. The results were devastating. The industry's ad revenues plunged from $2.2 billion a year in 1990 to just $1.6 billion in 1995, a drop of 27 percent. In March 1996, when Conrad Black was about to proclaim his faith in the future of daily newspapers by gobbling up the Southam chain, the industry's *Linage Trends* newsletter showed year-to-date declines in every single category of advertising, in every single circulation group, in every single province.[2] Linage and revenue have rebounded since then, but Canada's daily papers today earn only slightly more from ad sales than they did eight years ago. Some of the new business comes from advertising inserts, a credit not to any renewed faith in newspapers but rather to a vigorous lobbying campaign by the newspaper industry that persuaded the federal government to get Canada Post out of the lucrative door-to-door delivery of flyers. A list of advertisers who by and large ignore newspapers today includes such household names as Procter and Gamble, McDonald's, Seagram's, Ford Motor Company, Coca-Cola, Nissan, Kodak and Campbell's Soup.[3] They are saying something absolutely scary to publishers: "You're not worth our money."

The irony is that all of this is happening at a time when journalists are better trained, newspapers appear to be more professional and the industry is more profitable than ever before. Newspapers have the resources to be great again, and they are still a powerful mass medium, but the mystic bond that once attached us to them has been broken. When I delivered the *Ottawa Journal* door-to-door on my bicycle in the mid-1950s, newspapers sold one copy for every household in Canada and it was an evening ritual to settle in as a family over the sections, Dad usually reading the news first (sustenance for the mind), Mom the recipes (sustenance for the table), and Junior the comics (because they were fun). Sometimes you'd be using yesterday's news to protect the kitchen table from model airplane glue when some headline would catch your eye and you'd put aside the Left Aileron Strut to read about "A-Scarred Jap Girls Fly to U.S." There was a lesson in history, geography or human nature on every page. If the paper boy was unreliable, you'd phone up and tell a real person "My paper is late again," and the poor kid—sometimes, me—would catch heck from neighbours on front steps all down the street. The next week I wouldn't get my twenty-five-cent tip. There was this organic connection between the paper and its customers. And it delivered what we needed most in the emerging post-war consumer society—news and raw information about the world around us.

Today, when our information needs have become much more sophisticated and focused, newspaper sales cover barely half of Canada's households; customers are so spread out that adults must deliver papers in cars, usually before dawn; we pay anonymously by credit card, communicate complaints to voice mail and are seldom surprised when we read the front page because we've often heard the news first on TV or radio. The random access that newspapers provide has become a frustration; we are too weary or too busy to absorb more dots of information and the paper contains too little to connect them up for us. In a recent poll only 34 percent of us said that newspapers are still very important in our daily lives—a huge drop from the 45 percent who said so just ten years ago.[4] And the paper that got me into journalism, the *Journal*, hasn't been published in nearly twenty years.

This decline in popularity and influence has deeply damaged newspapers and, if they are perplexed about what to do about it, they at least know some of its causes. The most obvious is that we *can* possibly do without the paper if we just want to know what's happening in the world. Seventy-one percent of Canadians say that television is our primary source for world and national news, compared to 18 percent who say newspapers. The same poll by Environics Research Group shows that TV is not only more exciting and entertaining, it is "the most informative, educational, frank, believable and useful medium."[5] Even radio has adapted better than have newspapers to this competition, and most major markets have at least one all-news station that can deliver news faster than any paper, some of it written by the paper's own reporters. Even worse, the internet, which 37 percent of Canadians can now access, allows us to create our own information reports and bypass the gatekeepers entirely. This has contributed to what U.S. social critic Neil Postman calls "information chaos,"[6] the paralyzing effect that a revolution in technology has brought to our daily lives since the mid-1960s: too much information, delivered too quickly (by television, photocopier, fax, computer, direct mail), information that comes at us indiscriminately and without context or discernable value, like digital junk food. We feel powerless, confused. Those of us who aren't information junkies yearn today for some interpreter, some travel guide through this jungle of data, but newspapers have not yet taken on this role. They are still obsessed with delivering bits of news or random entertainments, still captivated by what makes events unique, not what connects them.

There is evidence that, in Canada especially, people want newspapers to satisfy deeper needs. In a 1994 poll conducted in eight countries and co-ordinated by the U.S. media giant Times Mirror Co., Canadians were the most likely to regard newspapers as a good influence, as helpful to democracy and as the best source for finding out why events occur. But when questioned about the actual performance of their newspapers in specific areas, it was a different story. Six in ten Canadians believed that news organizations are often influenced by the powerful and therefore are not independent. A similar number said that newspapers tend to favour one side over another in their stories, and half said that they invade people's privacy. One in every three Canadians felt that newspapers can't be relied upon to get the facts straight. This indicates that people value the role that newspapers play in our society, but that they are increasingly holding them up to higher standards and are somewhat dissatisfied with how they measure up. That may be part of the reason why newspapers ranked a poor third behind television and radio among the news media that Canadians said they read or saw yesterday.[7]

Such findings perplex those who run newspapers today. Russell Mills, publisher of the *Ottawa Citizen*, confessed his frustration in a confidential memo to his bosses at Southam in 1995:

> We do our research and listen carefully to what our readers are telling us they want. We design our content carefully around this and still many tell us they have no time to read. We provide a terrific package each day for less than the cost of a cup of coffee and a whole week's worth of papers for less than the cost of a beer in a bar. Many still think we're too expensive.[8]

Consultant Len Kubas, who was commissioned by Canadian publishers to take the pulse of the newspaper industry in 1994, was even more blunt. Of the six factors that he said determine success for daily papers—including circulation, readership, advertising linage and public image—he found four to be in decline. His metaphorical conclusion should send shivers through every newspaper executive's spine:

> The situation with newspapers is analogous to an airplane being "below the power curve"—not being able to climb, no matter how hard the throttle is pushed forward. An airplane can't fly for long in this situation.[9]

Newspapers, of course, *are* businesses, but they are businesses that must perform a public service for their customers. The more profitable the business, in theory, the better able it is to invest in the gathering of the news, which in turn delivers readers, which in turn attracts advertisers. But the business pressures of the early 1990s have caused that formula to unravel. A punishing recession ate into profits at a time when many large newspapers had to invest in new technology, such as presses with high-quality colour capacity. This drove many of them into the clutches of large corporate owners, who were beholden as they never were before to lenders and shareholders. The days of the independent, local, private owner are largely gone, replaced by corporations that are run according to the dictates of the bottom line. To generate enough profit to satisfy the expectations of the market, newspaper managers have reacted as their business training teaches, cutting costs, downsizing, hunkering down, suspending any substantial investment in research and development, resorting to marketing and hype rather than investing in their raw material—information— and redefining the role of newspapers in a multimedia society. The old journalistic role, that of providing a truthful, comprehensive and intelligent account of the day's events in a context that gives them meaning, is suffering from neglect and attrition.

With fewer resources and no incentive to search for a new vision to sustain daily print journalism into the next century, the very heart is going out of the business. In the early 1990s, newsrooms lost some of their most experienced hands to corporate buyouts and early retirements, and stopped up the supply of new young talent through a virtual freeze on entry-level hiring. Journalism, which should be about informing and serving a community, was turned into a cheap consumer product that must be packaged and sold, like dishwashing detergent.

Today, the impenetrable walls that once separated newsrooms from business departments are coming down as executives scramble to rebuild circulation and advertising. Editors are being told to sit down with ad managers and marketing experts to tailor news content in ways that will increase profits. A poll of 339 newspapers in Canada and the United States, done in 1998 by *Presstime* magazine, found that 57 percent of newspapers have marketing committees that include editorial employees, and most of them meet weekly. The arm's length relationship that once protected a newspaper's reporting force from commercial pressures is long gone, and the new way of thinking is expressed best by Stuart Garner, CEO of Thomson Newspapers, which owns the *Globe and Mail* and seven other Canadian dailies. He calls the once-important separation of church and state an "old tribal tradition" that is an impediment to success in today's bottom-line world of newspapering.[10] Southam's Gordon Fisher told *Marketing* magazine that this trend has spread across the industry as newspapers scramble to build circulation. "Those kinds of walls have been blown away in all of our operations," he said. "They just don't exist anymore."[11]

The emphasis on market research and short-term profit caused a thoroughly disenchanted Gillian Steward to walk away from one of the best jobs in Canadian journalism—managing editor of the *Calgary Herald*—in 1990. She'd joined the paper in 1972, when the job was fun and journalism was worthwhile: "I had no inkling that within 20 years the daily newspaper as I knew it would be a thing of the past." As one of the top editors in the Southam chain, she had a front-row seat as the industry's executives made their fateful turn towards profit and away from community. At meetings to discuss declining circulation,

> all they ever talked about was the bottom line, the newspaper as a cash cow whose only value was the milk that could be squeezed out of her. I was still somewhat idealistic then, some would say naive, but I was truly disappointed that none of these people saw the newspaper as a service to the community.[12]

That kind of thinking has since taken firm hold across the industry. Some argue that it's destroying its soul as well. Stephen Ward, former British Columbia bureau chief for the Canadian Press news agency, echoes the concerns of many journalists when he says:

> Today's news executive pines not for the front lines but the bottom

line. His home is the boardroom. His language is the jargon of consultants. Reporters and editors are called "bodies" that provide either "input" or "value-added." News is a product like sausages and the newspaper group is like any other corporate division, devoted to maximum profit through staff reductions, centralization and homogenization of product.[13]

The folly of corporate journalism has been put in even better perspective by one of its most prominent victims. Doug Creighton led a rag-tag group of editorial employees across the street after the *Toronto Telegram* was bought out by the *Star* in 1971 and built his *Toronto Sun* into a media empire that is one of the truly amazing stories of modern Canadian journalism. The brash *Sun* tabloids, heavy on sports, entertainment, photos, opinion and cheek, created a whole generation of newspaper readers. Creighton was idolized by his staff, to whom he was unfailingly loyal, even after control of the company was tendered to media giant Maclean Hunter. He fell victim to a corporate coup in 1992, and he sounded his warning to fellow publishers in a parting shot at the annual Canadian Press dinner. Newspapers are being taken over by the counting-house men and the marketing experts, he said. "Give them a full run to do what they want and we will end up with a Wizard of Oz newspaper industry—no heart, no brains and no courage."[14]

There is little doubt that they've already had their way, and this pessimism has filtered down to those who gather and select the news. Jim Travers, who has edited two of Canada's most prominent newspapers, the *Ottawa Citizen* and now the *Toronto Star*, grieves for the inertia that has gripped many newsrooms. "The single thing that worries me most about the future," Travers said when he left the *Citizen* in 1997, "is that some of the best people in the business are starting to think it's a dying industry. The people who you once would have turned to for the most optimism and the most creativity are now saying ... we're losing this." It's as if newspapers have broken their bargain with democracy in turning away from editorial excellence and public service and towards profit, marketing and cost-cutting. But freedom of the press is not a natural right to protect a private business. It is a privilege accorded in the expectation that journalism will benefit society. Any paper worth anything to society must have some preoccupation with covering people who have the least. And they aren't necessarily the folks whom market research deems important to the commercial future of the paper.

Gillian Steward remembers what happened at the *Calgary Herald* in the late 1980s, when the paper began losing circulation. Instead of following its journalists' instincts and beefing up areas of weak coverage, it commissioned a marketing survey to find out what readers wanted. "Community news" rated so highly it almost went off the scale, and she and her editors looked at each other in amazement. Wasn't that what they were already doing—giving them local news? What all of the editors missed, Steward realizes now, was that readers had a different concept of community than they did. To the readers, it meant fostering common goals, working things out together and sharing values, and they wanted to feel that their newspaper was a partner in that, if not a leader. But the marketing survey didn't pick that up. It wasn't designed to speak to people as members of a community. It was designed to find out what individual consumers wanted to buy, why they wanted it and how much they'd pay for it. It provided editors with quick, superficial, anonymous answers and tended to support simplistic solutions—snazzy new layouts, colour graphics, shorter stories and soft, thumb-sucking features designed to pander to special groups of readers. "Some of us knew that if we had to use professional survey companies to find out why our readers were losing interest, we were in deep trouble," Steward says.

But relying on market research to determine content may have had an even more devastating and long-lasting effect on the industry. "A strong argument can be made that daily newspapers in Canada in the 1980s contributed to the fragmentation of our community life, and in doing so hastened their own demise," Steward says.[15] In other words, newspapers have turned away from their traditional mass market appeal and have begun to cater to certain niches of readers whom advertisers want to reach. The result is that fewer of us can turn to our papers and see what we all have in common, or what our common stake might be if we participate in our democracy. Without that glue to hold our interest, we tend to tune the news out because it's irrelevant.

Such introspection and perspective is sorely lacking in Canadian newsrooms today, thus contributing to the general attitude of denial. When Conrad Black announced plans to start a new national newspaper, the industry suddenly shook off eight years of agonizing about its future and proclaimed a new age of competition, popularity and prosperity for itself. This self-congratulatory binge reached its height when the *Globe and Mail* greeted its potential new rival with an editorial, declaring that "the Cassandras were wrong ... Canada's newspaper industry is prospering, with healthy revenues and good profit margins based on stable readership, rising productivity and—most significantly—improving quality."

This book makes the case that the healthy profits being rung up in the Canadian newspaper industry are temporary and deceptive. There is indeed much to celebrate about the recent return to financial health of most Canadian dailies, but let's not go overboard. One of Canada's leading financial analysts dampened the mood of the 1998 convention of the Canadian Newspaper Association when he described daily newspapers as a "mature industry," no longer able to give sustained growth to investors but a decent short-term buy because profits can still be generated by further consolidation and cost-cutting.[16] Some newspapers are being made better, but it tends to be mere tinkering; what we need is a true revolution. The focus on profits serves to mask a crisis in public confidence and a failure in journalism that grew critical during the recession and should alarm anyone who cares about the future of the free press in our country. My intention is to invite a public and professional debate so that we can fix what is fundamentally wrong with our daily newspapers. It's critical that we act now, when newspapers have the financial resources to invest in their editorial future. I believe that this future depends on what we convince them to do about their seven main areas of failure.

**1. Newspapers behave as if they're serving themselves, not us.** When the motives and agendas of newspapers are hidden from us, when they arrogantly refuse to explain their behaviour or listen to another side, when their sense of independence seems to isolate them from their communities, when they are owned and edited by people without local roots, then we don't have to be malicious to conclude that they are in business to make money and not to serve the public. When reporters spend more time cultivating politicians and business executives than they spend talking to voters and workers, when the news columns are filled with the minutiae of city hall and not the goings-on around the corner, we can reasonably conclude that their values are firmly allied with power, stability and the status quo. Newspapers have lost our trust. And when we think they're just in it for themselves, we stop excusing their faults. We see them as evidence of conspiracy or sloth or worse: the general decline of a service that has become too profitable, too out of touch and too arrogant for its own good. As soon as we start believing that newspapers have crossed over the line to become collaborators with the entrenched and powerful instead of watchdogs for people like us, we feel disenfranchised and distrustful. Just who watches the watchdog when things go wrong? We feel there is no effective way to keep the press accountable because, unlike every other powerful institution in society, it is not subject to daily scrutiny. Newspapers simply choose not to cover themselves.

**2. Newspapers treat us as customers, not as neighbours.** They have lost the ability to connect us with our community. Fifty years ago, that was easier to do. Then our community was closer, more personal, next-door, and newspapers were close enough to us to be able to reflect our values and shared beliefs; we read them to confirm what we thought we were as much as to find out what happened. Today, when most of us live in big cities, when our vital institutions have grown bigger and more remote, when our sense of ourselves may be harder to articulate, newspapers seem to have retreated from us just when we need them most. Instead of showing leadership and helping to define a civic vision, they try to pander to our fickle tastes and treat us as a marketplace for cheaply produced information. Instead of working for our betterment, they are content to be collaborators or cynics, part of the elite that has pushed the average citizen out of politics and community life. They forget that as respect for a community's institutions declines, so does newspaper readership. Whenever problems seem unsolvable and cynicism becomes the political norm, when people feel they can no longer make a difference and withdrawal seems the wisest course, journalists should be the first to be deeply alarmed. For unless a reader also wants to become a citizen, unless she can be made to see a communal obligation beyond her own household, then our free press will soon lose its authority and legitimacy. It will be just another business trying to peddle a disposable product before it spoils.

**3. Newspapers add to complexity, they don't resolve it.** Never has a society been bombarded by so much information, and never have we so needed a filter to tell us what's important among all the gigabytes, infomercials, fear-mongering, entertainment, self-serving hype and crass commercialism being directed our way. The trouble with newspapers is that they're still in the information business, dashing about raising consciousness here, raising consciousness there, then rushing on to raise consciousness somewhere else, leaving all previous crises in our laps, unresolved. Why newspapers have become so one-dimensional is one of the great paradoxes of journalism. At a time when competition from cable news, television, radio, computers, faxes and photocopiers has revolutionized the way people receive information, when their customers are better educated and their own staff are better trained, newspapers are content to cover the easy things. Their sudden bulletins on the odd, the deviant, the discontinuous and the novel aim to produce not understanding, but astonishment. They do a terrific job with hyperbole, posturing, flackery, stereotypes, symbols, conflict, scandal and mayhem, but a poor job at celebrating the successes of everyday life and covering problems that are just over the horizon or a little bit under the surface. It's a sad commentary that newspapers can't obtain and keep new readers when they possess the power to offer us the world for only fifty cents a day.

**4. Newspapers have no vision of their own future.** The people who operate them generally are judged by how well they generate short-term profits, not by what they do to guarantee the future of newspapers. Since many of them are pessimistic about the long-term economic wisdom of what they do every day— cutting down trees to make paper, using petroleum to make ink, printing yesterday's news for delivery tomorrow by truck, car and carrier in all kinds of terrible weather, and all of this at the dawn of the digital revolution—they are achieving their financial goals by short-term solutions. They are downsizing staff, contracting out delivery and printing services, reducing the newshole and trying to attract readership by marketing, price cuts and the cosmetics of redesign. Unfortunately, this does nothing to solve the real problem that newspapers face: the failure to win and keep readers. In their rush to sell subscriptions, newspaper executives have forgotten that their real task is to buy about forty-five minutes of people's time every day. The only way to do that is by spending money to produce stories that will be worth our time to read. Milking out profits by cutting quality instead of investing in the future of ink-on-paper information may turn out to be a self-fulfilling prophecy.

**5. Newspapers pander to our lowest instincts; seldom do they cultivate our highest ones.** Readers believe, with some justification, that "anything goes" to sell newspapers. The old mission upon which freedom of the press is based— to inform the public so that democracy can work—has given way to a marketing agenda that emphasizes shorter stories, crime, violence, celebrity, conflict and other unusual happenings as the surest way to win readers' time. With a recession eating up profits and resources, many newspapers turned away from their traditional strengths—sophistication, depth, complexity, analysis, back-ground, explanation—to copy the strengths of TV—simplicity, hype and ease of use. This was a fatal miscalculation. It ignored the fact that newspapers had already lost the readership that is, essentially, looking only for headlines. They won't get it back, no matter how glibly they display their information. This "dumbing-down" of content is ultimately dangerous to journalism because it underestimates the customer and it cheapens the product, and any fool can tell you where that leads. It is tantamount to asking a patient to seek out the worst doctor in town just because he's entertaining to be with and he won't keep you long.

**6. Newspapers are imperfect mirrors.** Is it any wonder that newspaper circulation has plunged when the daily news is prepared by people who are whiter, more masculine, better educated and better paid than most of their readers? Newsroom demographics are badly out of whack with the public that newspapers are supposed to be serving; they are more reflective of Canadian society in the 1960s than that of the 1990s. Whose truth, then, are we reading? The convenient answer is that journalists today are more professional than those who gathered the news in the past, which is undoubtedly true. They are intellectually better able to interpret today's more diverse, complex society with fairness and balance. But will they know where to look? Are people who earn $60,000 a year going to be good experts on welfare and hunger? Are newsrooms that are 97 percent white going to do a good job covering immigration and race relations? Is an all-male news desk going to value stories that expose problems with breast implants and toxic shock syndrome? Are people who live in suburban bungalows going to stumble onto stories taking place in inner-city slums? Many big-city newsrooms have isolated themselves physically as well as demographically. They are housed in windowless concrete bunkers with security guards and voice mail, virtually impervious to casual daily contact, and those well-trained reporters seldom get set loose unless it's on a specific assignment that another well-off white male has determined to be newsworthy. The mirror that newspapers hold up to society needs to be clearer, and it should be a full-length one.

**7. Newspapers don't have a mission that is worthy of our support.** In no way have newspapers changed so much as in who gets to run them. Joseph Pulitzer, who made a fortune printing sensationalism in his newspapers at the turn of the century in the United States and who then gave some of it away to start his country's most distinguished journalism school, once made an important distinction about newspaper people. A journalist, he said, was "the lookout on the bridge of the ship of state"; he was there to watch over the welfare of the people who trust him, not to fret over the profits of his owners. Pulitzer believed there was a fundamental difference between "real journalists and men [sic] who do a kind of newspaper work that requires neither culture nor conviction, but merely business training." Those "men," the people in the counting rooms, were in the "newspaper business." Reporters and editors were not. They had a higher calling. No one who owns the press in Canada today can articulate this higher calling or even explain to the public why newspapers are important to democracy. They forget that the Canadian newspaper industry was built to greatness by the toil of independent young people who believed, like Pulitzer did, that a healthy future can be built only on a foundation of trust and public service. Thus a 34-year-old self-styled doctor named Edward John Barker established what has become Canada's second oldest continuing daily newspaper in Kingston in 1834, promising to expose corruption and to combat "every incipient encroachment upon the liberties of the people." Canada's most venerable daily, the *Globe and Mail*, was founded ten years later by a 25-year-old Scottish immigrant as a platform for his social reform ideas; George Brown later played a prominent role in creating Canadian nationhood. The *Toronto Star* was rescued from bankruptcy in 1899 by a 33-year-old editor named Joseph Atkinson, who for the next half-century made the paper a crusader for his populist brand of socialism. Such people did not get into the business primarily for profit, and much of what they wrote about was not designed to curry favour with moneyed interests. But the crusading zeal of these editor-proprietors carried the newspaper industry to new heights of popularity, wealth and influence. Their era continued until the middle part of this century, and it was common to talk of them as "giants," people like John W. Dafoe of the *Winnipeg Free Press*, Harry C. Hindmarsh of the *Toronto Star* and Ross Munro of the *Montreal Star,* people who, even if they weren't bona fide proprietors, were of such stature that they enjoyed autonomy from meddling owners who let them put their personal stamp on their papers. By 1970, the report of Senator Keith Davey's special committee on mass media lamented the passing of the "independent" owner-editor, mythologized as "a tough but kindly old curmudgeon who somehow represented the collective conscience of his community." Instead, the Davey commission found, most newspapers were run by "the hired branch-manager for a group of shareholders who typically live somewhere else." There were a few exceptions—like the *Toronto Star's* Beland Honderich, or Doug Creighton—but they have since either retired or been forced out by corporate power-plays. There are only nine small independent daily newspapers left in Canada, and it's only a matter of time before they're gobbled up too. Newspapers in the 1990s are almost invariably run by people who have never written a news story or delivered to a subscriber. They are Pulitzer's "counting-room men," whose souls are stirred by how much profit they can make.

No real debate about the future of newspapers is taking place in Canada, but there should be one. The situation here is far more critical—in terms of concentration of ownership, loss of circulation and advertising, and editorial cutbacks—than in the United States, yet a growing chorus of critics south of the border is warning very publicly that newspapers have lost their way and are being bled dry, operated as declining industries by owners determined to wring the last drops of profit out of an enterprise that has failed to keep up to changing times.

The sense of alarm is so acute that a group of some of the most prominent U.S. journalists have issued a "statement of concern" for the future of journalism. Signed by such writers and editors as David Halberstam, Carl Bernstein, Robert MacNeil and Ellen Goodman, it summons all journalists to a period of national reflection and dialogue with the public, on grounds that new technology, changes in corporate ownership, a lack of consistent standards and the contamination of news judgment by marketing concerns have served to "pull journalism away from its traditional moorings." It declares that "journalists of all generations are concerned about the direction of the profession ... and [that] they want to clarify their purpose and principles." Out of a profound sense of professional concern, U.S. journalists are reacquainting themselves with their readers and trying to work out what their future together might be like.[17]

In a disturbing poll published in January 1998 in the industry's bible, *Editor & Publisher*, newspapers were found to be superficial, too cynical, often inaccurate and not likely to get better. What's alarming is that the verdict comes from the very people who should do something about it: 255 editors and publishers of U.S. newspapers. One of them said: "In a lot of ways, we seem to have lost our way in journalism." Nearly half of them felt that news coverage was shallow and inadequate, and 62 percent believed that newspapers will be no better five years from now.[18]

Unlike in Canada, where media critics tend to be silenced or discredited and where there are no strong professional associations to provide a forum for self-examination, the U.S. newspaper industry has been surprisingly open about its shortcomings. One prominent critic is James Squires, former editor of the *Chicago Tribune*, who has written a kiss-and-tell book called *Read All About It! The Corporate Takeover of America's Newspapers* in which he describes the press as "no longer an institution dedicated to the public interest, but rather a business run solely in the interest of the highest possible level of profitability." The very definition of news has been corrupted by marketing experts so that it no longer matters whether information is important, relevant or delivered in context; it matters whether it is titilating, controversial or entertaining. The motives of the press are suspect and what it delivers, he says, is "no longer journalism at all."[19]

This harsh judgment is echoed by Eugene Roberts, who guided the *Philadelphia Inquirer* to the front rank of U.S. quality newspapers, won seventeen Pulitzer Prizes, and was forced into temporary early retirement by an owner intent on even higher profits.[20] The old mission that sustained newspapers for two hundred years—to act as a check against arbitrary power and to serve the public in the interests of democracy—is being imperilled by a second and third generation of corporate managers who are judged and compensated on the profits they generate rather than on what they do to guarantee the survival of newspapers. Gimmicks, redesigns and marketing-driven features are taking the place of substance, yet Roberts warns that "journalistic history is littered with the corpses of large-circulation newspapers that failed to make long-term and lasting reader relationships and, thus, were viewed as dispensable by their readers and, consequently, by their advertisers."[21]

In Canada, this same pandering to readers has helped undermine the integrity of newspapers every bit as much as Tom Kent's Royal Commission on Newspapers feared when it reported in 1981:

> Readers look to newspapers to tell them what is important. [When] they are met by newspapers conducting market research so that readers will tell them what is important, [this] creates a closed feedback loop in which editors, reporters, readers and advertisers all hold hands in an inward-looking circle.[22]

That's why the 1993 redesign of the *Toronto Star* was such a disappointment. Rather than trust the instincts of its fine journalists, the paper relied on market research provided by Goldfarb Consultants and Minneapolis-based MORI Research to tell it what readers wanted. According to Honderich, they wanted an easier-to-handle format, not any substantial new content. As a result, the *Star* did not follow through on more than seventy-five recommendations for editorial improvements drawn up by a newsroom committee that included three National Newspaper Award winners. Their ideas included a daily local news section, more investigative political reporting and a halt to the paper's knee-jerk practice of tilting news coverage to whatever side was favoured by the editorial page. Unless the *Star* improved its content and its relationship to readers, the committee warned, "We are in danger of becoming like the medieval church, losing the power to awe the ignorant with our magnificent architecture."[23] Despite this explicit warning against the folly of a purely cosmetic redesign, the *Star* did just that, making the same mistake as other newspapers do. Canada's largest daily plunged nearly $30 million into the red by the end of 1993, advertising linage declined by 12 percent and newsroom morale deteriorated. A couple of months later, senior editor Joe Hall, asked to assess the state of the paper after a year away at Harvard University on a Nieman Fellowship, wrote: "We have listened to the advice of people who analyze markets for new and improved dish detergents," and that has caused the paper to turn away from journalism and towards "chrome and fins and do-dads."[24]

It took the paper nearly three more years to invest a similar effort in its content, and then only after more market research was commissioned and Honderich had completed the first phase of his strategic plan, which was rather ominously entitled "Sink or Swim." Canada's largest newspaper, whose superb editorial staff swept an unprecedented nine National Newspaper Awards in 1996, found itself so financially vulnerable that it had to virtually turn itself inside out, shedding eight hundred jobs, sweeping out a moribund advertising department, adding new blood in marketing and finance, and boasting when its advertising revenues finally inched back up to where they'd been ten years before. Not until the end of 1997, with operating profit at a record $90 million and a completely new roster of vice-presidents on its masthead, was the *Star* finally ready to pump extra resources into its writing, editing and photography.

Unfortunately, the process left the *Star's* journalists dispirited and with a deep sense of malaise. An internal staff survey done in May 1997 showed that newsroom morale ranked below the workplace average in thirteen of sixteen categories. The people who gather the news felt that there were few incentives for them to do quality work, few opportunities for mid-career training, no feedback from their editors and no clear direction about the future.[25]

Conrad Black, who has gobbled up 60 percent of Canada's daily newspapers, likes to boast about how he and his associates are creating a "renaissance" of interest in the press. That is typical Black hyperbole, but we certainly must acknowledge the extent of his investment. In the last two years, he's spent $180 million for badly needed new presses to print the *Vancouver Sun* and *Province*, and pledged another $63 million to refit the 39-year-old presses at the *Montreal Gazette*. But aside from the *Gazette*, the *Ottawa Citizen*, the *Vancouver Sun* and perhaps the *Hamilton Spectator*, all of the redesigns of Southam newspapers have been mainly cosmetic and only Vancouver has substantially increased circulation. Even his $2 million a year investment in the *Citizen*—mainly for newsprint to make the paper bulkier—has not managed to attract many more readers. So when Black claims (inaccurately) that he's managed to arrest or reverse the long-standing decline in circulation of Canadian newspapers, he usually talks in classic marketing terms, about how his editors have made "a product less irritating to the average fair-minded reader." Translation: look cleaner and more colourful, but don't stir up trouble. A good example is the *Calgary Herald*, which Black claims to have rescued from being "a newspaper that was antagonistic to the overwhelmingly popular provincial government, antagonistic to the petroleum industry, and represented virtually no one within 500 miles of Calgary."[26] Whenever I pass a newsstand and see Black's major

Canadian dailies spread out on racks, I feel that they are all starting to look very much alike.

There are great expectations for the new national daily—the only paper Black has ever actually created—although no one outside his inner circle can fathom how he will absorb the newly acquired *Financial Post* into it and find loyal readers and advertisers for a fourth general interest newspaper in Toronto, the most competitive newspaper city in North America.Inside Southam, however, there is nothing but hype. Vice-president Gordon Fisher told me well before the new paper's launch that it will revolutionize Canada's newspaper industry. "This company has rediscovered the meaning of journalism. I think we've figured it out—what motivates people to buy newspapers," he said in an interview. But there is a worrisome hubris among Black and his top executives that often turns out, under examination, to be exaggerated and inaccurate. When asked about the robust professional debates about the future of journalism that are taking place in the United States (but not in Canada), Fisher says, quite seriously, that "when you stack our regional newspapers up against theirs, we're just so much better." It's hard to imagine anyone thinking that: the *Calgary Herald* or Regina *Leader-Post* is better than the *Boston Globe* or *St. Petersburg Times?* Similarly, in Southam's annual report, Black paints a rosy picture of the company's circulation gains, saying that its nine largest newspapers all had higher daily circulations in early 1998 than they did earlier—a total increase, he said, of 40,000. In fact, two of those papers (the *Gazette* in Montreal, and the *Windsor Star*) suffered circulation declines in that period, and the total gain was less than 22,000—in other words, almost negligible.[27]

Newspapers have become good sloganeers for themselves, but they're often just finding new ways to sell the same old breakfast cereal. It's a lesson in corporate reality that Harvey Schachter learned in the early 1990s when, as the editor of the *Kingston Whig-Standard,* he was briefly put in charge of marketing. It was quite clear then, he remembers, that circulation decline was so widespread in the industry that newspapers needed to band together to try to persuade people that reading them was an enjoyable and rewarding leisure-time pursuit. He suggested generic ads geared to new readers, but nothing came of it then. Instead, like every other newspaper, he said, "We sold more sports as we cut back sports, sold columnists as better ones drifted away, and sold our lifestyle pages which were vastly inferior to the Toronto competition flooding our town." The Southam-owned *Whig* has undergone two largely cosmetic redesigns in the past three years, and circulation is still going down. The last one was marketed with the ridiculous slogan: "Have you flipped your *Whig* today?"

Even the *Globe and Mail,* the country's most august paper but one spooked to distraction by the prospect of competing against a rival national daily owned by the deep-pocketed Black, is not above stooping to hype to create interest in itself. Large billboards showed the paper's logo superimposed on a picture of a blissful, unclothed beach bunny, above the slogan "Where is a woman's place?"

# Taking the Pulse

Not only is the image of a naked woman with her legs spread apart offensive and sexist, there was virtually nothing in place in the *Globe* at the time to attract women. Its readership was and continues to be the most heavily male of any paper in Canada.

Selling the sizzle and not the steak is what marketing has done for newspapers, and it has turned otherwise serious editors into shills for hype and nonsense. "What we might have described in the past as good newspapering, we now call good marketing," said one Canadian editor who was sent to study marketing for six weeks at the new Jerusalem for such thinking, Northwestern University in Chicago. The editor is Philip McLeod of the *London Free Press,* who, soon after his return, wrote to potential subscribers, offering them a deal that he figured they couldn't refuse. Sign up for home delivery of my paper, he said, and "you'll receive a voucher redeemable for two piping-hot family-size pepperoni pizzas" from McDonald's. "I know you'll enjoy your pizzas," he added, but if you're not happy with the *Free Press*, you can cancel at any time.

Needless to say, such gimmicks don't boost circulation. People are getting out of the daily newspaper habit, and there doesn't seem to be any way to stop it. It's a trend that caught the industry flatfooted in 1989. Until then, almost every Canadian newspaper could take comfort in the fact that its circulation was going up every year. Indeed, figures compiled by the Canadian Daily Newspaper Association (CDNA) in 1990 showed that Canadians were buying 21 percent more newspapers per day than they did twenty years before. But hidden in those figures were some worrisome trends: the population had increased even faster; circulation growth was slowing down; and the number of Canadian households had mushroomed by 58 percent, meaning that newspaper advertisers had missed out on reaching two out of every three new buying units. Much of the growth in circulation, in fact, was due to the enormous boom in Sunday publishing, from a mere 134,500 copies sold in 1971 to more than three million in 1990. This obviously could not continue unless newspapers found an eighth day of the week on which to publish, yet the CDNA blithely announced that its circulation data contradicted the conventional wisdom that the Canadian daily newspaper industry was declining in the electronic age.

The recession knocked a hole in that hucksterism. In 1993, total weekly circulation declined at 62 of the country's 108 daily papers, according to the CDNA. It has since continued to decline. Trying to stretch their dollars, people in competitive markets stopped buying more than one daily newspaper and, if they happened to lose their jobs, stopped buying altogether. Others, able to get their news fix from faster media, cut back their subscriptions to a few times a week. The per-copy price was boosted, largely to compensate for lower advertising revenue and higher costs, particularly for newsprint. Having to fork out up to seventy-five cents for a thinner issue of their local daily gave marginal readers another excuse to stop. And there was an increase in what newspaper circulation departments call "churn"—the problem caused when regular subscribers stop delivery, some permanently because they're moving away or are unhappy with the paper, others temporarily because they're just going on vacation. Some newspapers have to write as many new orders as they have paid home delivery subscribers, and still lose ground year after year.

These fluctuations and decline in circulation have changed newspapers, perhaps forever. One example is the death of the serial cartoon strip. In the 1950s and 1960s, at least one-third of all daily comic strips carried a story line over from day to day, like some illustrated novel-in-progress. Many kids like me developed the newspaper reading habit by following the daily exploits of Big Ben Bolt or Terry and the Pirates. Today almost all comics are stand-alone strips or panels, able to be consumed in a single sitting. The reason, of course, is that newspapers can't count on everyone getting the paper the next day. Another example is the repetitive background information that most newspapers include in their daily reports of continuing stories. This is designed to bring infrequent readers up to speed on those events, but it is starting to alienate the regular customer—so much so that, following sensationalism, repetition or "over-coverage" is the most mentioned complaint that Canadians have about their daily papers.[28]

"Lack of time" is first among reasons that people give for not reading newspapers. We live in a busy society, so it is tempting to believe them despite the fact that it's also quite wrong. Studies done in the United States show that "when people say, 'I don't have time to read it,' what they mean is they don't value it enough to read it," says Peter Francese, president of American Demographics Inc., who has done research on lapsed subscribers. A "time diary" done in 1995 for the *Ottawa Citizen* showed that readers spent an average of ten hours per day participating in leisure activities. Reading newspapers happened to rank sixth among the eight categories, well behind such things as reading books and exercising. On weekends, shopping bumped newspapers to second-last place, ahead only of going to church.[29] The popularity of computer bulletin boards, newsmagazines, targetted consumer magazines and book-buying indicates that people have the time but are increasingly choosy about what they want to read.[30] Newspapers are great for browsers but not so efficient or rewarding for those seeking instruction and depth.

Nor are newspapers adapting to changing demographics. Loyal readers, who still get the paper home-delivered seven days a week, are getting rarer, older and more expensive to keep. Increasingly, they are wealthier and better educated than the average person in society. Advertisers are more interested in reaching younger audiences who have not yet acquired the bulk of their consumer goods and who have more disposable income for things such as entertainment. The trouble for newspapers is that, as older readers die off, they are not being replaced in equal numbers by younger, more cosmopolitan, more mobile consumers who find themselves with more media choices than any generation in history. In a recent survey by Intel Corporation, almost 60 percent of people born after 1971 said that they expect to get their news from the internet. Another 31 percent said that they'll get it from television and radio, leaving fewer than 10 percent who expect to turn to their newspapers.[31] There is also no guarantee that the great bulge of baby boomers, now about to start turning fifty and to enter the prime newspaper reading age, are going to re-acquire a habit that they've let lapse. Women, who traditionally spent the most time with newspapers, are reading them less today, partly because they are participating in the workforce as never before and partly because their time and information needs have become less random.

There is, in all of this, some room for optimism. As powerful an information tool as it has become, the internet is simply not ready to win away readers from newspapers. In fact, judging from how many papers have on-line editions and how people are using them, they may be complementary sources of news, not competitors. As Conrad Black has pointed out (although he has not yet consistently delivered on it): "The serendipitous quality of a well-edited newspaper, with an intelligent selection of news, features, sports, business and comment, becomes more important as the media consumer contemplates the alternatives of swimming upstream against a cascading torrent of undifferentiated transmissions."[32]

Newspapers come with two things that the internet can never deliver: a portable, tactile and user-friendly delivery system, and a lot of reliable information you didn't know you were looking for. Experts can find their own information and will do so elsewhere, but readers will gladly pay for a trusted gatekeeper to do their work for them. And what a bargain! You're paying a staff of hundreds less than half the price of a cup of coffee to deliver a document that is larger than a novel, entirely different each day, able to be saved or taken anywhere and full of information that expands your knowledge of the world. If they can only get things right, newspapers should have a bright future for at least the next generation.

The future of daily newspapers as a mass medium, according to Kristin McGrath of MORI Research, may depend on their ability to capture two key groups of people who now read occasionally but who don't feel a strong commitment to the kinds of newspapers being produced. McGrath, who is based in Minnesota but who has done research in Canada for several papers, including the *Toronto Star*, labels these groups as "at-risk" and "potential" readers and says that they make up one-quarter of the population. Both groups tend to be younger, evenly divided between males and females, usually in two-income households with children, which means they're busy. They tend to plan their leisure time to accomplish something, not necessarily just to relax. But they want two different things. The "at-risk" readers want newspapers to be more efficient and accessible. They don't want three hundred-page Saturday papers piling up unread in the den; they want shorter stories so that they can access information more easily. The "potential" readers, on the other hand, want more depth, explanation and detail than newspapers now offer. Is it any wonder that publishers today feel tugged in different directions as they increasingly rely on market research for their answers?

Faced with evidence that their loyal readers include barely half the adult population in any given market, the industry has responded in a way that is curious and troubling and tells a lot about the nature of its soul. It began to fudge the figures. For years, the *Star* ran circulation figures based on the previous month's sales every day on its front page. The last such figure, 504,000 copies sold each weekday, appeared two days before the 1993 redesign. That Sunday everything changed. A much more upbeat claim of "readership" ran in the bottom corner of page two: More than 1.9 million readers Monday to Friday, 2.2 million on Saturday, and 1.6 million on Sunday. My bullshit detector began to register in the red zone.

My search for an explanation led me to the plushy offices of the Newspaper Marketing Bureau, then just one block away from the *Star* tower on Toronto's waterfront. Its business was to convince more Canadian advertisers to buy space in daily newspapers, and the *Star's* new "readership" numbers came in large part from the bureau's research. A kind of bristly, smile-and-polish optimism hit me as soon as I walked in the door. "There's only one rational reason for not advertising in newspaper," one poster blared. "You've already got more business than you can handle." As an advertising slogan, it's a little wordy for maximum impact, but the message is clear: I had entered the den of True Believers, the very heart of *machismo* about the future of newspapers. All of the promotional literature fanned out on a waiting room table seemed to have an exclamation point at the end of every sentence. Example: "If all of the 1993 Canadian daily newspapers sold were stacked on top of each other, it would be as high as 42,000 CN Towers—now that's reach!"

It's also what journalists call "topspin" or "hype," self-serving puffery usually uttered by political organizers or corporate communications directors. It was a little disconcerting to find it used by an industry association that seemed to be leading Canadian newspapers into new depths of denial. "Readership" has replaced "circulation" on the mastheads of most Canadian newspapers, and they seem to be using this data much as Ben Johnson used steroids—to bulk up their sagging popularity.

What they're certainly doing is substituting a vague, uncheckable figure for a precise, measurable one. Newspapers know how many copies they sell each day, and it's verified by the independent Audit Bureau of Circulations. But when the marketing bureau does its study, called NADBank, short for "Newspaper Audience Databank," it must take people's word for what they read and how often; and the sample size, while an impressive 24,000 nationally, is small in any given city and must be projected to the entire population. This tends to be an inexact science, as evidenced by the Toronto figures that show the *Star,* the *Sun* and the *Globe and Mail* with nearly 2.7 million adult "readers" on weekdays—

a number that falls just short of the total number of adults in the Greater Toronto area. Even the most optimistic circulation director no longer believes that 95 percent of grown-ups in his or her market reads a newspaper every day.

The real danger in giving editorial credence to data compiled to sell advertising is that the extensive demographic data compiled by NADBank is starting to be used to determine what newspapers write about. It is one thing to let advertisers know that two million Canadians renovated their homes in the past two years, but it is quite another to create a Home Repair section as a vehicle for advertisers and then cut back on covering something else, such as the plight of the disadvantaged in our cities. Increasingly, Canadian newspapers are catering to a richer, older and better educated reader for the sake of the bottom line. They are, in short, becoming elitist, programmed by marketing to deliver the "right" kind of readers to advertisers.

This turns off and angers readers who don't happen to fit into the chosen demographic target groups, something the *Star* certainly learned in the mid-1980s with a section it launched specifically to attract upscale fashion advertising. Printed on glossy paper and with an almost unlimited capacity for colour, the section, called "Elegance," was to be inserted only into papers delivered to high-income households. The editorial department wisely refused to have anything to do with it, so the advertising department hired its own editor to commission gushing profiles of the polo-playing and yachting super rich. The section, which went against every one of the *Star's* egalitarian traditions, created such a backlash from advertisers (who were wisely skeptical that a paper that stood for social justice could deliver the carriage trade) and readers (most of whom didn't earn enough to receive it) that it was cancelled after a year. And yet ... the man who championed "Elegance" is now the *Star's* vice-president of new ventures, and Andrew Go says such a section would work today because "there's more cohesiveness between editorial and advertising." The so-called "Chinese wall" that once existed between the two key newspaper departments has been torn down so completely that, when I'm introduced to one of the marketing bureau's executives, he asks if Ryerson teaches marketing to journalism students. I say we do not. He says that that's his "pet peeve" about Canadian editors—not enough of them appreciate who pays the bills.

To such True Believers, everything would be okay if people just stopped talking gloom and doom. Canadian publishers, unfortunately, seem to believe this hype. Nearly two-thirds of them polled in a CDNA survey in 1991 were confident that readership and circulation revenues would increase the following year; in fact, Canadian dailies lost even more subscribers than they had the year before, and that trend is continuing. Len Kubas sees this lasting through the 1990s and warned in his important 1994 report to the industry: "The basic premise of newspapers as a mass medium with broad coverage may have to be re-examined, particularly in larger urban centres."

The decline of newspapers as a mass medium has had a seismic effect on advertising sales, and it is not an exaggeration to say that the whole financial underpinning of the industry has been threatened. How bad is it? When I finally track down ad revenue figures, they paint the bleakest trendline possible: dailies have been losing their share of advertising dollars for twenty years and, from 1989 to 1994, they actually lost revenue, mainly to direct mail, television and weekly newspapers.

As advertising goes, so go newspapers. It provides about 75 percent of any newspaper's revenue, and the information it contains is a major draw for readers. The amount of advertising also determines how much space there is for news, since most papers operate on an advertising-to-editorial ratio of 60:40 or 65:35. In an unguarded moment, Roy Megarry, when he was publisher of the *Globe and Mail,* once said his colleagues should "stop kidding themselves that they are in the newspaper business and admit that they are primarily in the business of carrying advertising messages."[33] If they are, the future looks uncertain. Kubas, who also analyzed the advertising outlook for Canada's newspapers, warned that publishers were dreaming if they expected ad revenue to return to normal when the recession was over. A "sea change" took place that saw many of newspapers' largest advertisers—car dealers, large department stores, shopping malls and supermarkets—declare bankruptcy, merge or become threatened by "power" retailers like Price Club, Super Video stores, Toys R Us and Wal-Mart, who use flyers and direct marketing instead of the mass media. Similarly, a slow-growth economy meant less classified advertising for such things as cars, appliances, real estate and job openings. Newspapers also lost out to more sophisticated marketing techniques that allowed advertisers to target readers by age, income level and neighbourhood; newspapers, by their very nature, cannot deliver precise demographics and, given the decline in household penetration, cannot even deliver enough readers in a given area to satisfy a high-volume retailer. They have tried to adapt to advertisers' preference for flyers by creating expensive "zoning" areas, and distributing only to certain areas, but this brings in less revenue than selling an ad for the general run of the paper. Revenues have been propped up by increased ad rates, but this is pricing many small retailers out of dailies and into the clutches of urban weeklies, which are also poised to capture a lot of the direct mail business because of their greater coverage of the market. After holding that title hands down for years, daily newspapers can no longer claim to be Canada's biggest advertising medium. In the last few years they've been surpassed by television and matched by direct mail.[34]

Although his consulting fees were ultimately being paid by daily newspaper publishers, Kubas didn't hesitate to put the blame where he felt it belonged. Senior newspaper managers, he said, have a more positive view of their products than most advertisers do. "There is ample evidence that daily newspapers should be concerned if not alarmed over the future," he reported.[35] One of his recommendations was for newspapers to start supporting advertisers more strongly with editorial material.

Nothing gets a publisher's attention more than a threat to the bottom line, and they've reacted to Kubas' report in ways that raise profound questions about their commitment to editorial independence and excellence. It's one thing to set up or strengthen marketing departments, but it's quite another to make editors and reporters sell subscriptions by phone, as was done at the *Timmins Daily Press,* and still another to put the paper's editor in charge of the circulation department, as was done at the *London Free Press.* The *Kingston Whig-Standard,* which a few years earlier was boycotted by real estate advertisers who were angered by an article on how to sell your own home, launched a Saturday Real Estate section filled with promotional material about new homes. The *Toronto Star* even sold its entire real estate section front—including the editorial index—to an advertiser. The impetus for these changes is not serving the public, but satisfying advertisers. And advertisers will push it as far as they can. "I'll take the centre of page one if someone will let me have it," one agency executive told *Marketing* magazine. "We're like pigs that way—we can't help ourselves."[36]

Although the trend is by no means new, what became commonplace during the hard times of the early 1990s was for newspaper owners to widely recruit marketing- and business-oriented experts, most of whom believed that their abstract management techniques could be applied without penalty to newspapers. One glaring example is a complicated evaluation scheme that is being used to measure the productivity of editors and reporters at Thomson newspapers across North America. It was devised by Jay Spach, who is titled senior vice-president of re-engineering and organizational development. Dubbed "Pathway to Prime," it uses "process standards" to measure, in percentage terms, how close a journalist comes to fully "earning his hours." Quality becomes the lowest-cost way to get the paper out every day and Spach, in classic business jargon, unashamedly describes the template that he wants to apply to all Thomson newsrooms: "The process standard for a unit of output is the amount of input it takes to produce one unit of output at the average uninterrupted best rate." For example, the suggested "standard" is ten minutes of work for a reporter to write a column inch of type for a news feature. It's like making Picasso punch a time clock.[37]

Publishers will argue that extreme measures are necessary in hard times because, above all, newspapers must earn their own way in the world. This is quite true. The greatest newspaper in the world will fail if its workers aren't productive and if it can't earn enough through advertising to pay its bills. But they've come through the recession with profits even higher than before and have done little to restore the cuts that they had to make to compensate for the last eight years of higher newsprint costs and lower ad revenue. If anything, their eagerness to pander to the readers and advertisers is probably damaging the foundations of their franchise. Kubas' report in 1994 contained "best-case" and "worst-case" scenarios for the Canadian newspaper industry and, in almost every aspect, the worst case came true less than two years later: higher prices turned off both readers and advertisers; high unemployment eroded classified ad linage; and cost-cutting reduced editorial quality. If this is the way of the future, the future cannot be bright.

In the past twenty years, Canadian newspapers have revolutionized themselves in so many ways. They've invented low-rub ink, changed their publishing cycle from evening to morning, made the transition from casting type in lead to spitting it out of computers, gone from paste-up layout to electronic pagination, replaced letterpress with higher-quality offset printing, staked out a tentative position in electronic publishing and even found a way to replace underpaid 12-year-old kids as their front-line sales force. Now if only they could reinvent a journalism that most of us wanted to read.

## Notes

1.  Source: Canadian Daily Newspaper Association circulation data. In 1990, Canada's 108 dailies sold a total of 5.8 million copies per day. In 1996, that figure dropped to under 5.2 million (for 105 dailies). Some individual examples: the *Toronto Star* sold 479,000 copies every Sunday in 1996 (down from 535,000 in 1990); the circulation of *Le Journal de Montreal* was 278,800 every weekday (down from 330,000); the *Winnipeg Free Press* dropped 40,000 copies every weekday; and the *Edmonton Journal* sold 131,000 fewer papers per week in 1996 than it did six years before.
2.  *Linage Trends*, Canadian Daily Newspaper Association, March 1996. Total advertising in Canadian dailies was down by 5 percent from the previous year.
3.  "Newspaper Advertising Expenditures in Canada," Canadian Newspaper Association, 1996.
4.  *The Media Study*, Environics Research Group Ltd., Toronto, 1995.
5.  *The Media Study,* op. cit.
6.  "The Future of Newspapers," speech by Neil Postman to the International Federation of Newspaper Editors, May 1990, Copenhagen, Denmark.
7.  Eight-nation survey done by Times Mirror Center for the People and the Press in Washington, D.C. and published on March 16, 1994. Ten thousand people were polled on their use of the media in canada, the United States, Great Britain, Germany, France, Italy, Mexico and Spain. The Canadian survey was done by Environics Research Group Ltd., which questioned 1,025 adults by phone in English and French in January 1994. The error rate for a national sample of that size is 3 percent.
8.  Memo to Southam CEO Bill Ardell, July 28, 1995.
9.  *Newspapers in the Nineties: Looking Ahead* (Kubas Consultants, Toronto), a report prepared for the Canadian Daily Newspaper Association, April 1994.
10. "Breaching the Wall," by Rebecca Ross Albers, *Presstime* magazine, published by the Newspaper Association of America, April 1998, page 32.
11. "Front of the line," by Justin Smallbridge, *Marketing*, April 20, 1998, page 15.
12. "The decline of the daily newspaper," by Gillian Steward, in *Seeing Ourselves:*

*Media Power and Policy in Canada*, edited by Helen Holmes and David Taras (Harcourt Brace Canada, 1996), page 279.

13. "Journalism in Turmoil," a paper by Stephen Ward, presented at Augustana University College, Camrose, Alberta, on January 14, 1997. Ward, an unusually qualified journalist, holds a PhD in psychology from the University of Waterloo. He spent four months in 1998 as a research fellow at Harvard University's Joan Shorenstein Center for the Press, Politics and Public Policy.

14. "Toronto *Sun* founder blasts those who forced him out," by Alan Harman, *Editor & Publisher,* June 3, 1993, page 17.

15. Steward, op. cit., page 283.

16. The "mature industry" description was made by Doug Kirk, senior media analyst for Nesbitt Burns, speaking on a panel on The Future of Newspapers, April 30, 1998.

17. The statement of concern, and a summary of subsequent deliberations, can be found on the Committee of Concerned Journalists website (*www.journalism.org*).

18. "U.S. press coverage stinks: Startling opinions from America's editors," *Editor & Publisher*, January 17, 1998.

19. *Read All About It!* by James Squires (Random House, 1993), page 210.

20. Eugene Roberts resurfaced as managing editor of the *New York Times*, which hired him from the faculty of the School of Journalism at the University of Maryland. He has since retired.

21. "Nothing succeeds like substance," by Eugene Roberts, *American Journalism Review,* December 1993, page 4.

22. *Royal Commission on Newspapers* (Minister of Supply and Services Canada, 1981), page 172.

23. "Report of the Content Committee," *Toronto Star*, March 1992, page 4. The *Star's* own reporters and editors delivered a broadside that made any outside criticism seem tame by comparison. The paper, their report said, "is in danger of resting on its laurels. At a time when many of the social battles the *Star* has fought for have been won, the paper finds itself too often in a rear guard position, defending the status quo and failing to define a vision for the future."

24. Memo to newsroom, January 27, 1994. Hall also said: "When it comes to new and innovative ways to cover the news, we seem to trust to fate or, worse, to focus groups and readership surveys."

25. *Toronto Star Employee Survey,* Toronto Star Ltd., released October 24, 1997. A survey prepared by consultants from the Hay Group was answered by 204 of the *Star's* reporters, editors and photographers, representing 52 percent of the newsroom.

26. "The Future of Newspapers," an address by Conrad Black to the Spruce Meadows (Alta.) Round Table on Changing Fortunes, September 12, 1997.

27. Publishers' statements filed with the Audit Bureau of Circulation for the six months ending March 31, 1998, show that 90 percent of Southam's big-paper gains came in two cities, Vancouver and Calgary.

28. Times Mirror Survey, op. cit.

29. *1995 Market Report for the* Ottawa Citizen, Vol. I, by MORI Research, September 1995, page 22.

30. In the Times Mirror survey, 56 percent of Canadians said they had books or novels on the go, compared with 51 percent who said they read the newspaper yesterday.

31. The survey was done in 1996 by Intel Corp. It was reported in the *Globe and Mail*, August 26, 1996, page B1: "On-line news on the rise."
32. Black's speech to the Spruce Meadows Round Table, op. cit.
33. Megarry spoke at the 1982 conference of the Canadian Media Directors.
34. "Newspaper Advertising Expenditures in Canada," Nielsen Marketing Research, Toronto, March 27, 1997.
35. *Newspapers in the Nineties: Looking Ahead*, by Kubas Consultants, op. cit.
36. "Front of the line" by Justin Smallbridge, op. cit., page 16.
37. "Managing productivity," by Jay Spach, published in *The Editor*, an editorial newsletter for Thomson newspaper editors. Issue 1, 1998, page 10.

# CHAPTER TWO

# The Arrogant, Imperial Press

I never knew what an asshole I was until I became a journalist.

*— Toronto Star* reporter Nick Pron,
quoted in *Ryerson Review of Journalism,*
Summer 1997

Conrad Black, of all people, once called newspaper reporters "imperial." He said their unchecked power threatens to make them "the rogue elephants of western society" and went on to criticize what he called the Code of Journalistic Self-Government. First, he said, "the overarching journalistic objective is to attract public attention by almost any means, and the appropriateness of those means will be judged by professional journalists and no one else." And second: "There is no such thing as an abuse of press freedom by the press itself. Any attempt to apply this concept to the practice of journalism shall be construed as an attack on the freedom of the press and democracy generally."[1]

Even though we may find it hard to understand Black's lack of respect for the people he must employ to cover the news and marvel at the conceit of his claim that a rich proprietor can act as a countervailing force to ensure democracy, he may have a point about the arrogant and sometimes arbitrary power of print journalists in our society. When a politician, sports figure or business person does something wrong, immoral or dishonest, the press is usually there to shed the strong light of publicity on it. If there is a cover-up or denial, the press pursues it with even greater vigour because sin and weakness are merely newsworthy but lying about it is deplorable. All this changes when the press itself misbehaves, which it does all too often these days. Since newspapers seldom bother to cover themselves, there is no effective watchdog and therefore no compulsion for editors to admit their mistakes. Indeed, they often doubt that any normal person would be interested in reading such "inside" stuff. When challenged with their errors or misjudgments, these editors are apt to react with wounded vanity, hurt pride or abject denial—behaviour so typical it was branded as "notorious" by the 1981 Kent Royal Commission on Newspapers. It is not correct to call this thin-skinned; it's more like scraping an exposed nerve end and watching them yawp. And that's exactly what happened in British Columbia when Chun Chau Wong had her controversial baby.

Tin Wing, seven pounds and eleven ounces, was born five minutes after New Year's at Burnaby Hospital, making him the first baby of 1994 on Vancouver's Lower Mainland. But when the local Welcome Wagon found out that the mother was from Hong Kong, it withheld its traditional gifts. Someone tipped the *Vancouver Sun*, which ran a story on the controversy and said that it was typical of the "several hundred wealthy foreigners" from Hong Kong who fly into B.C. every year to deliver "passport babies," automatically making them Canadian citizens. It added: "Immigration officials are not able to prevent pregnant women from entering the country, even if they suspect they are trying to bypass immigration laws." The story was picked up by Canadian Press and run in several other newspapers, and people telephoned Burnaby Hospital to praise the decision. The *Sun* followed up with an editorial describing the incident as "a sign of how disgruntled Canadians are over the immigration issue" and urging people to direct their concerns to the politicians.

By almost any standard, it was a good story. The only problem was, it was almost completely untrue. Two days later, the father, a 32-year-old business executive, stepped forward to say that he was a landed immigrant who had lived in Burnaby with his wife by for more than two years. He'd been away on business in Hong Kong when the baby was born prematurely. It was all a misunderstanding, probably caused by language and cultural differences. But instead of apologizing for its error, and for linking the mother with an alleged immigration scam, the *Sun* merely published another news story saying that the controversy was over and the parents had "set the record straight," as if it had been their fault from the beginning. This prompted an outraged letter to the editor from city councillor Maggie Ip, who accused the paper of promoting racial disharmony by its negligent reporting. It also sparked a shouting match between *Sun* reporters and members of the Chinese press at a news conference, where hospital officials accused the newspaper of drawing unwarranted conclusions.

The *Sun* had been under fire since 1989 for its alarmist and stereotypical reporting of the "Asian invasion" that was gobbling up downtown real estate and sending prices soaring. To try to blunt charges of racism, the paper set up a multicultural advisory panel, although its members met only sporadically. The paper's editorial staff was still 97 percent white. In the meantime, the Chinese community had grown big enough to support three of its own daily newspapers. One of them, *Ming Pao*, had spoken to Chun Chau Wong in hospital and correctly reported that she was a Burnaby resident, not a rule-bending opportunist as the *Sun* had portrayed her.

Frustrated by the continuing controversy over his paper's coverage, *Sun*

editor-in-chief Ian Haysom told his newsroom to "write the whole thing up."
Some reporters thought that this was simply pandering to the Chinese community. Frances Bula's story, which didn't run until ten days after the initial report,
traced the error to hospital records (as if that was any excuse not to check the
story out further) and said that it was compounded when the reporter leapt to a
wrong conclusion and inserted two paragraphs of background from a story on
passport babies written a few months before by the paper's immigration writer.
That earlier story quoted student nurses who were outraged about queue-
jumping Hong Kongers, and it estimated that 250 to 350 non-residents give birth
in British Columbia every year. This kind of "backgrounding" from earlier
stories is a common practice in newsrooms, but it is often dangerous because the
information may be inaccurate or irrelevant. In this case it was both. Only sixty-
three Hong Kongers gave birth in B.C. the previous year, and in any event this
had nothing whatsoever to do with the case of Chun Chau Wong.

Bula's story quoted Chinese-Canadians who questioned why the province's largest news organization didn't have reporters or editors who understood
Chinese language and culture. She concluded: "Media outlets need an editor
whose job is to question the often-unconscious assumptions reporters make in
their stories." In other words, the whole thing was just one of those accidents that
happen when white people are in a rush to meet deadlines.

The controversy is over, but bad feelings linger in the *Sun* newsroom, where
reporters feel that their paper caved in; in the Chinese community, which still
feels that it is subject to stereotypical coverage; and in a Burnaby household,
where Tin Wing Chung is growing up as a Canadian citizen. The newspaper has
never apologized to his parents for its sloppy and damaging reporting.

To many other people today, newspapers seem to act a lot like rude house
guests. We don't quite know what makes them grind dirt into our rugs or how
to cope with their sullen and hostile behaviour; we can only take comfort in the
fact that they won't be staying long. We spend less and less time with them, then
bundle them out with the recycling. Eventually, we may stop inviting them in.

The Kent Commission wrote:

> The press, which assumes a license to criticize every other institution,
> is the least open of any to criticism of its own performance. It controls
> the principal channel through which criticism can be expressed and
> heard. It is singularly reluctant not only to accept criticism and
> acknowledge error, but even to justify its own conduct when it believes
> itself to be in the right.[2]

This arrogance has helped to break the vital bond that must exist between
newspapers and their readers. We have become cynical about powerful, elite
institutions that don't explain themselves to us, that don't seem to be acting in
our best interests and that seem to be accountable to no one. Because they

seldom tell us, we do not know how they decide what to cover, what justifies their lack of common courtesy or why they say that they operate in the public interest. Consequently, we feel that they no longer seek or merit our trust.

This has shown up in the Gallup Poll since 1982. When Canadians are asked to rate the honesty and ethical standards of people in a variety of professions, doctors and pharmacists have always topped the list, followed by police officers, engineers, university teachers, accountants and members of the clergy. Journalists rank far behind, and in the 1997 poll were actually tied with business executives, who have a net honesty and ethics rating of only slightly above zero.[3]

*Toronto Star* publisher John Honderich says, "Anyone who reads these polls and doesn't get concerned should have their eyes examined. Journalists are not held in high regard. There seems to be a sense that we're part of the problem rather than part of the solution."[4] Kirk LaPointe goes even further. As editor-in-chief of the *Hamilton Spectator*, he bluntly told his colleagues at the 1998 Canadian Newspaper Association convention that it may be time for journalists to reform themselves:

> We are caught up in the thinking that if we haven't gone too far, we certainly haven't gone far enough…. In our newsrooms, we need to ask ourselves the critical questions: Are we overstepping obvious boundaries of decency? Are we setting out to satisfy prurient interests while violating the golden rule? And we must wonder: Are we going to rein in our excesses, or wait for someone to do it for us?[5]

The methods that journalists use to gather the news have certainly contributed to this growing rift with readers, and those methods seem to be getting worse: invasion of personal privacy, justified by highly distorted interpretations of "the public's right to know"; disproportionate reverence for the public statements of powerful people, often accepting them at face value even when contrary evidence is close at hand; outdated and skewed standards of news judgment that value simplicity, personality, entertainment value and wrongdoing over meaning and impact; often turning a blind eye to basic journalistic standards designed to ensure accuracy, balance and fair play; refusing to acknowledge error or to stand accountable to readers, even to the extent of defending reprehensible conduct in the name of freedom of the press; an ingrained cynicism that regards everyone in public life as probably being guilty of something until proven innocent; and an almost blind faith in the value of street-smart guile to dig out the news, when specialized knowledge would almost certainly serve society better. All of this tends to produce in the press an arrogant, almost imperial disdain for the very people it is meant to serve.

It would be a mistake to blame reporters and photographers for all of this. It's their passion for truth-telling that got them into journalism and that keeps them there. It's why some of them die doing their work—so that we will know the truth. If the arrogant imperialism of the press is getting worse, it's because it is worse at the top. The business people who came late to journalism and who now run most of our newspapers have a basic contempt for the people who gather the news. Too many see journalists as a kind of aggravating overhead that brings in no direct revenue and drags down profits. Too little is spent rewarding, training and assisting those who go out each day to tell society's hard truths. Too much effort is spent making newspapers the lowest-cost producers of news in the marketplace. This jeopardizes what American editor Pete Hamill thinks is the primary role of the press: to be "the point of the spear" in the long, heartbreaking process whereby society becomes a better version of itself.[6]

Who then, we might ask, shall watch the watchdog? Who will ensure that all of the news we require is covered, and that it is covered well? Do we leave it to the press itself? Or should we believe the publishers, who say it is the job of the marketplace? Or, if neither of these works, must we invite in the heavy hand of government?

For the past sixty years, Canadian publishers and editors have made a strong and effective case against the state having any business in the newsrooms of the nation. In at least two celebrated cases, they have won support both in the Supreme Court of Canada and in the court of public opinion. In 1938, federal justices ruled unconstitutional the so-called Alberta Press Bill, under which the Social Credit government of Alberta required newspapers to publish, unedited, any statement issued by the government, and to disclose the source of any statement that cast the government in a bad light. If a newspaper refused, it could be shut down. The Supreme Court duly wrote:

> Freedom of discussion is essential to enlighten public opinion in a democratic state. It cannot be curtailed without affecting the right of the people to be informed through sources independent of the government concerning matters of public interest. There must be untrammeled publication of the news .... Democracy cannot be maintained without its foundation: Free public opinion and free discussion throughout the nation of all matters affecting the state within the limits set by the criminal code and the common law.[7]

The press in Alberta, not surprisingly, campaigned vigorously against the repressive law, and the *Edmonton Journal* received the singular honour of being cited for a Pulitzer Prize by admiring American editors. A free and unshackled press and what the court called "the breath of life for parliamentary institutions"—freedom of political discussion—were linked hand in hand. It was a principle that the court again upheld in 1957 when it was asked to rule on the Quebec Padlock Law, Premier Maurice Duplessis' clumsy attempt to clamp down on what he loosely described as Communist propaganda. Any newspaper could be closed if the attorney-general disagreed with what it wrote. The court declared that freedom of thought is as important to people's minds as breathing is to their physical existence, and said that no legislature can suffocate it.

The courts, of course, were right. If governments win the power to regulate the press simply because they disagree with what it writes, we're on the slippery slope to autocracy. Newspapers used those victories to defend themselves against a myriad of threatened state intrusions over the years, most notably in their successful scuttling of federal Consumer Affairs Minister Jim Fleming's proposed *Canada Newspapers Act* in 1983. Responding to the Kent Commission, Fleming moved to set up a national press council and offer federal grants to encourage newspapers to open news bureaus across the country. Although his proposals were far more watered down than Kent's, Fleming's strict limits on ownership would certainly have prevented Conrad Black's takeover of Southam. However, he incurred the righteous wrath of Canada's publishers and his legislation went nowhere. Not only that, he was quickly dropped from the Liberal cabinet and consigned to political obscurity.

The problem today is not that government poses an immediate threat to freedom of the press. The problem is that the questions at the root of the whole debate—just who should the press be accountable to, and how—have not been answered. The press, which doesn't want anyone else to tell it what to do, has not stepped forward to do anything about itself.

This arrogance and hypocrisy troubles a veteran journalist like Clark Davey, retired publisher of the *Ottawa Citizen* and *Montreal Gazette* and a long-time managing editor of the *Globe and Mail*. At a conference of Canadian managing editors in 1995, he criticized the wildly different standards that newspapers adopt when reporting on their own business: they publish the salaries of executives in many other industries but leave out their own; they print glowing obituaries of long-time newspaper employees but ignore the achievements of community leaders; they say that they're accountable but they cut back their means of accountability. He noted that the number of readers' representatives, or "ombudsmen," employed at Canadian newspapers has dropped drastically during the recession. In fact, only the *Toronto Star* and Halifax's *Chronicle-Herald* maintain such positions, down from eight newspapers that dis so in the late 1980s.

Even though the press covers every other important institution in society—some of them, such as business and politics, quite extensively—not one newspaper reporter in Canada is assigned full-time to monitor how the press does its job. Only two do so as part of larger communications beats; Antonia Zerbisias of the *Toronto Star* and Chris Cobb of the *Ottawa Citizen*. Cobb writes only occasionally about the press these days, despite spending six years doing almost nothing but, covering issues of journalism ethics, ownership, improper influence by advertisers and standards used in covering the news. He asked to be taken off the beat because his interests had turned to other things but also because he felt that Black's stranglehold over Canadian newspapers, including his own, meant that the story was largely over. The *Citizen* did not assign anyone else to take over.

It's tempting to conclude that there are no stories to tell, but that's not true. Reporters frequently intrude into the public's affairs, raising issues of privacy, collusion, social responsibility and whether the newspapers they work for are in it for profit or to seek the truth. The Bud Smith case in British Columbia offers a case in point. In the summer of 1990, the province's attorney-general was forced to resign after tapes of several of his telephone conversations were tabled in the legislature. They documented his attempts to plant a story in the media to sidetrack an opposition prosecution into the shady dealings of a former cabinet colleague. As the story unfolded, a disturbing and unedifying series of ethical transgressions committed by reporters came to light: a freelance reporter meticulously used a radio scanner to pick up and tape-record conversations that Smith had by car phone with his wife and his deputy minister; another reporter willingly offered Smith advice on how to manipulate the media; yet another acted as an intermediary in getting the tapes to the political opposition party when her employer wouldn't run her story; and, finally, an entire press gallery used ambush techniques on colleagues to find out just who was involved.

This raised several important questions about reporting practices. Is it legal to tape car phone conversations without consent? Is it ethical or proper for journalists to sneak around like detectives in cheap hotels holding tumblers to the walls? Is it right for a reporter blocked from releasing a story to arrange for the evidence to find its way into the legislature, where it would be privileged and therefore legal to report? Should political reporters engage in cosy relationships with the people they cover? Where is the line between cultivating a source and being co-opted by one? These questions were never properly answered, and none of the reporters involved was ever called before a disciplinary body, even though Bud Smith's reporter-friend had become his virtual agent provocateur, reading her stories to him before they were broadcast, critiquing his speeches before they were delivered, even disrupting a press conference by an opposition politician on his behalf. In doing so, she neglected the most obvious story of all: the attempt by the highest law officer in the province to use the media for political advantage and possibly to subvert justice.

If newspapers, as they so often like to assert, are watchdogs over the public interest, they cannot afford to be seen as partisans or collaborators. You can't cover the parade if you're marching in it. Such blatant conflict of interest dilutes the fragile trust that must exist with the public. Reporters who accept free trips and favours from government, who are paid to act as media consultants to institutions that they may cover and who sit on vital information to cultivate a source run the risk of being seen to serve no public good but only their own private advantage.

The idea that someone should watch the watchdog presupposes that journalists are professional in the way that we think of doctors, lawyers or engineers as being professional. They are not. They may be craftspeople or tradespeople, but journalism has none of the trappings of a true profession. It has no standards for entry, no regulation by peer groups, no licensing body, no penalty for misdemeanour, not even any commonly accepted ethical standards. Richard Harwood, former readers' representative of the *Washington Post*, likes to relate how, a few years ago, his newspaper argued against the professionalism of reporters in a federal court suit involving overtime pay. The *Post* said that reporters are not "learned" people; they are simply "creative" individuals who, like flower arrangers and musicians, are not entitled to overtime pay under U.S. law. The judge in the case, Harwood says, was sympathetic to the argument but was unwilling to concede that all journalists are creative. "He observed that in his own experience he had encountered various reporters who were very pedestrian people."[8]

If that is true, then *someone* should be watching. When the *Toronto Star* established Canada's first readers' representative position nearly thirty years ago, there was some hope that distinguished senior journalists like Borden Spears could act as effective watchdogs for the public inside the nation's newsrooms. Spears certainly did that, and reading a collection of his columns today would educate anyone in the higher principles of journalism. But too many of his successors have been window-dressings for accountability, vested with little real power or inclination to question anything very thoroughly. Most have been long-time newspaper employees, usually editors who'd spent little time outside the newsrooms and were putting in time before their retirements. Now, with much leaner newsrooms, the breed is all but extinct. Perhaps it's just as well. Rocking the boat was not a first instinct with them.[9] A chill seemed to go through the ranks in 1992 when Barry Mullin, readers' representative of the *Winnipeg Free Press*, was forced out of his job by his publisher after he wrote a column mildly criticizing his paper's news judgment. Several readers complained that the paper had buried, on the fifty-sixth page of the fourth section, a news story about the outbreak of race rioting in Los Angeles following the acquittal of four white police officers caught on videotape beating a black man, Rodney King. Wasn't that story more important, the readers asked, than a front-page feature about edible golf tees? Mullin, one of his paper's most experienced journalists, agreed that underplaying such a story "does little to improve our credibility as a newspaper readers can take seriously."[10] He was called on the carpet by his new publisher, Maurice Switzer, and told to apologize publicly for his insubordination and irresponsibility. He quit instead and was never replaced.

Other readers' representative positions, such as those at the *Ottawa Citizen, Montreal Gazette, Calgary Herald, Edmonton Journal* and *London Free Press*, have been downsized out of existence, meaning that they are considered non-essential by today's bottom-line publishers. Readers in those cities have been left to fend for themselves if they have a complaint, trying to reach the right overworked editor in what has become a baffling and inaccessible newsroom bureaucracy. The arguments used to justify the elimination of Canada's readers' representatives are often ridiculous. Jim Stott handled 40,000 complaints during his ten years in that job at the *Calgary Herald*. In his farewell column in 1996, he described himself as the necessary "ham in the sandwich" between readers and editors and said: "All too often there is no real communication. Those who gather the news and those who read it exist in two solitudes."[11] Yet his editor, Crosbie Cotton, said the position was unnecessary and could easily be replaced with a "reader response line." In other words, leave us your recorded message and we may listen to it. Cotton said that the big weakness of readers' representatives is that they can't order an investigation or apology and have no authority over the paper's staff. But rather than give someone those powers, he simply did away with the job. Imagine the same argument being made by a provincial government that decides to eliminate its environment ministry because its regulations are being scoffed at by industry. Newspaper editorials would call for heads to roll and for enforcement to be stepped up. Yet editors are routinely allowed to get away with statements that they would normally mock if others made them. The fact is that they are far too busy putting out tomorrow's newspaper to give a fair hearing to readers concerned about a mistake or omission from yesterday.[12]

Despite the terminal erosion of readers' representatives in this country, Canada's 105 daily newspapers still have the potential to be the most accountable in the world. That's because every province except Saskatchewan has a press council to deal with unresolved complaints about the conduct of newspapers—a degree of oversight that's unmatched on this continent. The idea of press councils was advanced by the 1970 report of the special Senate committee on the mass media, chaired by Senator Keith Davey. It suggested that Canada's newspapers needed to set up a national council with public members and wide-ranging functions to not only receive complaints from the public but to initiate its own investigations of questionable conduct; to draft a set of journalistic standards; to promote the need for training, research and development in an industry where that was notoriously absent; and to be an advocate of open government and freedom of information. Above all, it said, a press council would serve as an important channel for public education about the press. The first provincial council was established in Ontario in 1972, and was quickly followed by councils in Quebec and Alberta as publishers began to worry about government setting up its own. After the Kent royal commission threatened just that in 1981, councils were established in the Atlantic provinces and British Columbia and membership burgeoned all over. Ontario's council now includes all of the province's 39 dailies and more than 240 of its community newspapers.

But Canada's present network of provincial press councils is a pale shadow of what Davey envisioned. They limit themselves to dealing, sometimes not very impartially, with complaints filed by the relatively few members of the public who have the determination and stamina to wait up to six months for a hearing. Most councils do not undertake their own investigations, most deal with complaints on a case-by-case basis instead of drafting a comprehensive code of conduct for the press and publicizing it; none plays a role in training, research or development; nor, judging by the number of complaints and what happens to them, does any council serve as much of a conduit for understanding or dialogue between the press and its public. In fact, they are not often used at all. Only 117 complaints were received from the public in 1995 by the Ontario Press Council, and only 20 received hearings, a steep decline that prompted its chair, Willard (Bud) Estey, to criticize newspapers for not telling readers that they belong to such a thing or how to make a complaint. Estey, a former Supreme Court justice, even speculated that perhaps the council needed to "stage an embezzlement or attract a charge" to get some coverage.[13] Nothing happened, and by 1997 the complaints had dropped even further; only nine were adjudicated that year.

The low level of public participation in Canada's press councils was documented in 1994 by David Hutchison of Edinburgh University, who was attracted by the idea of provincial councils and wanted to see how Britain's national Press Complaints Commission stacked up. What he found surprised him. Readers in Britain, who are dealing with a more remote complaints process, were more than twice as likely to complain about the press as those in Ontario, and nearly four times as likely as those in Quebec and Alberta.[14] Furthermore, Canadians tend to complain about what he called "mild and minor" issues, such as a letter to the editor that wasn't printed, rather than the larger issues of deception, privacy and freedom of the press. One possible explanation was the increased circulation of downmarket tabloids in Britain, but another reason could be that the activities of Britain's Press Complaints Commission receive greater publicity than those of Ontario's provincial council, where complaints are usually heard in private and where many member newspapers don't even tell their readers that they belong to a press council. Seventy-five percent of complaints to the Ontario council are abandoned every year, largely because people get tired of waiting for justice. It's worse in the Atlantic region, where all 72 complaints lodged against newspapers in the three years up to 1996 were either dismissed or abandoned, and in British Columbia, where the same thing happened to all 126 complaints lodged in three years up to 1995.

And here's the fatal paradox for press councils in Canada: it's rare for newspapers to be found guilty in the courts that they largely run themselves, which hardly serves the public very well; yet journalists seem to resent being judged by others, which hardly serves to improve newsroom standards. Michael Valpy once used his national column in the *Globe and Mail* to mock an Ontario Press Council decision that columnists should make sure that their opinions are based on facts. Valpy urged all journalists to ignore such an interference with freedom of the press, just as they ignore anything else the press council does. The fact that no one rebuked him—not his employer, nor the press council, nor any reader—is a frightening illustration that no one really cares. The system protects its own. And whenever it doesn't, most councils in Canada consider the complaint to be lodged against a newspaper, not an individual, and so the culprit is usually spared any public scorn.

This brings us to the Doug Collins case and how press councils, as presently run, are contributing to the imperial arrogance of the press and helping to undermine the public's trust. Collins is a 76-year-old Vancouver journalist who wrote a vitriolic column for the *North Shore News*, a thrice-weekly paper owned by Southam. He proudly bludgeoned readers with rants against "turban lovers," Jews who control Hollywood, and gays and lesbians. Such intolerant, racist and anti-Semitic blather unfortunately found an audience in a city whose population has diversified faster than most. Collins may be entitled to his opinion, but the wonder is that any responsible newspaper would print it, or that any press council would defend it, especially after much of it was unmasked as ridiculous tripe based on a distortion of facts that should alarm anyone who cares about the state of journalism.

Twice in four years, the British Columbia Press Council has defended Collins' right to say that six million Jews didn't actually die in the Holocaust. When a concerned reader objected to one of Collins' 1993 columns on that subject, the press council agreed that Collins had deliberately and selectively distorted quotes from several Holocaust scholars to back up his point, which is a journalistic sin only slightly worse than making up the quotes altogether. But it dismissed the complaint and said that neither Collins nor the *North Shore News* should have to apologize for misleading readers because it's a columnist's right to write opinions that someone might not like. The council even centred out the complainant, a retired university professor, as a man who has waged a war of words with Collins for years. It suggested that the professor had as much right as Collins to speak freely and that the whole dispute was about "different versions of historical truth held by two strong, articulate men." This of course ignored two facts: Collins had no evidence to back up his claim—indeed, all of his experts said the opposite of what he claimed; and the professor wasn't a columnist who enjoyed three-times-a-week access to the public for his opinions. Collins' newspaper bent over backwards to award him the last word, even giving him space on the letters page to shoot back at any readers who wrote in to disagree. The press council took two years to adjudicate this complaint and clearly failed to stand up for the public's right not to be deliberately misled. The *Vancouver Sun* wisely criticized the decision: "Journalists and columnists have a privilege that ordinary citizens don't have when we write for newspapers. It is a privilege that must come with responsibility and accountability. The press council should be the body making us accountable."[15]

It's no wonder that the next complaint about Collins and his anti-Semitism was filed under a higher authority, the B.C. *Human Rights Act,* which grants the power to fine people who expose others to hatred or contempt. Three years of legal wrangling by the Canadian Jewish Congress succeeded in getting Collins before a government-appointed tribunal in early 1997, the first time a Canadian journalist had been put under such scrutiny by a province using its human rights code. It might have been logical to expect that the B.C. press council, having seen itself bypassed as useless, would quietly sit this one out. But no, there it was before the tribunal defending one of its own again. Collins had written another column lambasting the Academy Award-winning movie "Schindler's List"— "Swindler's List" he called it, a clever plot by the Jews in Hollywood to make us accept the "nonsense" that millions died in Nazi death camps. The press council intervened, hiring a lawyer to argue that the law under which Collins was charged is a "political correctness act" and the greatest threat to press freedom in Canada in more than sixty years. Government has no business, the council's 151-page brief said, setting up special bodies to censor the news media, which should be free to act as "public watchdogs." Only authoritarian and shackled societies would permit such action, it said, and went on to compare the B.C. *Human Rights Code,* clause by clause, to South Africa's notorious pro-apartheid censorship laws of 1974 and, even more outrageously, with the Nazi press controls of Josef Goebbels.

Collins was also defended by his paper, which said: "It goes right to the heart of what makes a democracy tick and what keeps it honest: the freedom to express opinions and ideas openly, the freedom to challenge commonly accepted assumptions, the right to be wrong."[16] It's no wonder, with all this support at his back, that Collins was unrepentant. "They're putting me on trial for opinion crime," said the veteran of the Second World War. "I thought I was fighting for the right to say and write what I think when I went to the war to fight for democracy." He's wrong about that, too. It looks like what he was really fighting for was the right to distort, incite, belittle and misrepresent, and to have the people who are supposed to be watching the press look the other way.

The B.C. tribunal ruled that the column in question was offensive, harmful and anti-Semitic, but that it wasn't hateful in the sense contemplated by the *Human Rights Act.* Despite this apparent vindication, Collins' publisher called it a hollow victory that threatened "all British Columbians who value their fragile rights of free expression." He urged editors across Canada to form a united front to fight the law. That was too much for Don Button of the Mission (B.C.) *City Record,* who wrote: "Yes, freedom of the press is important. But with free speech comes the obligation to use it responsibly." Noting that Collins, who has since retired, was being referred to as a professional journalist, Button said: "Sorry. There are hundreds of us out here at community newspapers who don't view racism as professional journalism."[17]

Even if there was a comprehensive code of conduct for the press in this country, and a courageous body to enforce it, it would be effective only if sanctions were attached to it. No journalist or newspaper in Canada today can be fined, disciplined, suspended or forced to redress a wrong, even if a press council finds that he or she or it acted irresponsibly. That is usually left up to the courts (if the transgression is illegal) or individual employers, and of course people have been fired, transferred, disciplined or suspended at the pleasure of editors. But that doesn't happen much. The sole weapon of censure outside the journalistic lodge is publicity—what Ontario's Press Council's Willard Estey once described as "a process of putting the journal or sometimes the journalist into mythical stocks, thereby attracting the passing scorn or disapproval of peer and public alike." This is even too much for some journalists, who argue that professionalism should be a personal goal because journalists cannot agree on common standards and because their very freedom would be compromised if they were licensed or held in check. Don McGillivray, a one-time Southam columnist who served on the executive of the Canadian Association of Journalists, wrote in the Fall 1990 issue of *CAJ Bulletin:*

> An unlicensed press is unruly, untidy and sometimes downright sleazy. But it's on the frontier of freedom. Any attempt to turn journalism into a profession like law or medicine with an enforced code of ethics needs to be fought with all our strength.

I disagree with him. It presumes that a journalist who makes a mistake is actually held up to passing scorn and that newspapers will act ethically and lawfully because it's in their own financial interest to do so. My experience has been that many journalists react to mistakes much as they would had they just dodged a live bullet—with nervous bravado and cynical denial, then on with the job.

*Editor & Publisher*, the bible of the newspaper industry in North America, once foolishly illustrated this objectionable trait when it published an editorial headlined "Stop apologizing." Its premise was that newspapers seem to be doing this far too often, and it asked: "It's true that newspapers need readers in order to survive. But to what lengths do newspapers go in letting readers censor content?"[18]

They react even less well to the recurring and quite legitimate complaint that their coverage is often sensational and intrusive. The best illustration of this was the maelstrom of public outrage over the circumstances leading to the death of Diana, Princess of Wales. When her car, driven by someone who was legally drunk, crashed in a Paris tunnel in 1997, public attention fastened on the paparazzi who were pursuing her at the time. The mercenary photographers, who unscrupulously pursue celebrities by motorbike to satisfy what publishers call the public appetite for news of the rich and famous, personify everything that the public finds offensive about journalists. The unprecedented backlash was transmitted around the world from Diana's funeral, when her brother's eulogy, blaming editors who exist "on the opposite end of the moral spectrum" for turning her into the most hunted person of the modern age, caused hundreds of thousands of mourners to burst into spontaneous applause in the streets outside Westminster Abbey.

Even as it was giving the orgy of grief for Diana an orgy of coverage, the press fumbled around in an effort to redeem itself. In Britain, the chair of the national press council called on the media to voluntarily refrain from subjecting Diana's sons to the same scrutiny. In the United States, the Society of Professional Journalists condemned intrusive newsgathering tactics and reminded journalists that "pursuit of the news is not a license for arrogance .... Avoid pandering to lurid curiosity." Media critic Howard Kurtz wrote in the *Washington Post:*

> What people seem to be saying—and rarely have so many million railed against the media in unison—is that journalists just don't play fair. Not that they should specifically be blamed for Diana's death in a car driven by a speeding drunk, but that they should stop hounding people. That there is such a thing as a zone of privacy, even for the terribly famous. That they're sick of in-your-face, run-over-your-grandmother-for-the-story journalism.[19]

But those who own and control the press, and who have a vested interest in selling as many papers as possible, reacted predictably to the Diana backlash. Typical was the most powerful press lord of all, Rupert Murdoch, whose flashy, mass-circulation tabloids provide the main markets for paparazzi photos. The press must resist any calls for self-restraint, he said, because privacy laws would create "a new privilege for the already privileged." He meant the celebrities who use the press to publicize their causes, not the press itself. In Canada, as elsewhere, the argument most often heard against self-restraint was that the public demanded news of Diana and other celebrities and that news photographers and reporters were only doing their jobs when they went off in hot pursuit. "They love our copy but now they hate us," the *Toronto Sun's* Thane Burnett wrote, accusing the public and do-gooders within the craft of journalism of hypocrisy.[20]

Such arguments, of course, are self-serving and contradictory. The same journalists who say that they are obligated to print whatever people want to read will turn around the next day and ask for protection against anyone telling them what to print, on grounds that their job is to act independently in the best interests of democracy. "The fourth estate can't have it both ways," a perceptive reader wrote the *Toronto Star* at the height of the Diana publicity. "Either it serves the public interest or it serves its own private purse. Which will it be, gentlemen?"[21] The unregulated press, accountable to no one, simply has no answer to that.

Sex and celebrity sell papers. That is undeniable. Such subjects are also easy to cover, since they're all over the supermarket tabloids, the television talk shows and the internet, and are usually presented in such a way as to blur fact with gossip and rumour. The gatekeeping role that editors of newspapers used to perform—deciding what was fact, how important it was and how much could be printed—has been superseded by faster technology and something far, far more dangerous: the corruption of journalism by the culture of entertainment. Of all the sins of journalism noticed over the years by David Shaw, the Pulitzer Prize-winning media reporter for the *Los Angeles Times*, "the most pernicious is the ceding of editorial authority to the purveyors of flash and trash in our society." The standard of what passes for news has fallen. And once a particular story is "out there," no matter who wrote it or how carefully they checked it, it's fair game for all.[22]

A good example is the sex scandal that engulfed Bill Clinton's Washington in early 1998, diverting attention from a major international crisis between the United States and Iraq. The story, that Clinton had tried to cover up an affair with a young White House intern named Monica Lewinsky, was broken—amazingly—by a non-journalist who ran an internet website from his nondescript apartment in Los Angeles. Not so long ago, our news agenda was set by a handful of powerful editors and producers who decided what to print or broadcast using professional standards of investigation and verification. All of that has changed. When someone tipped self-styled "media pirate" Matt Drudge that *Newsweek* magazine had the Clinton-Lewinsky story but was holding it for further verification, he put it "out there" on his website and it was picked up as quickly as if the *New York Times* had broken it. Within a week, the Lewinsky story took up 67 percent of the air time that the three U.S. networks allocate to news. It filled the pages of every newspaper in North America. Suddenly, oral sex had made it to prime time. And all of this happened before it was verified by a single, named source, other than Lewinsky's lawyer.[23]

Why has professional journalism slipped so far away from its roots? While part of the reason is institutional, caused by the strategic allocation of reporting resources or, in the mid-1990s, simply fewer people in the newsroom, a great deal more is the direct result of journalists' own attitudes. On the one hand, there is a sense of cynicism that pervades so much of daily journalism today. By that I mean the reflex on the part of many reporters, photographers and editors to be detached, suspicious and sceptical and to ascribe ignoble motives to those with whom they regularly come in contact—first each other (ink-stained wretches, covering the same things over and over), then those they cover (sleazebag politicians) and finally even the people for whom they are supposed to be writing (whining readers). Part of this is a valuable self-defence mechanism: journalists can scarcely do their jobs effectively if they're too cosy with news sources. Scepticism—or legitimate doubt—can provide the impetus for investigations that expose hypocrisy or disprove conventional wisdom. Most of us, given the choice between a naive reporter and one who is suspicious, would prefer the latter. It is when scepticism drifts into cynicism that journalism suffers. And that is happening to an alarming extent. It was best captured by a controversial article published in 1995 by the *Columbia Journalism Review*. Under the title "A Generation of Vipers," it said:

> Cynicism can be a lazy substitute for curiosity, and in its most corrosive form it can produce journalists who have a diminished view of their profession and of themselves. Worse, it can damage readers and viewers and thus democracy .... Cynicism beckons as a seductive retreat from belief, but it is also a barren spot, one that deprives the soul of sustenance. It produces little that endures.[24]

One of Canada's leading editors, Neil Reynolds, says that the tragic irony of journalism is that it has abandoned its faith in the freedoms that it purports to defend. Journalists aren't only cynical, he says, they're *proud* of being cynical. "Bring me 10 journalists from all of Canada, 10 journalists who have celebrated this democracy in print—without cant or embarrassment or apology—and I will retract every word."[25]

On the other hand, there's an obsession with power and wealth, a sort of fawning clubbiness, whereby journalists subconsciously ally themselves with the priorities, perquisites and attitudes of those in authority whose access they court (while at the same time keeping up the pretense that they are actually in business to represent the public). What newspapers cover, in large measure, is news of important institutions and powerful people. They do this, of course, on the theory that the press should act as a watchdog over public institutions such as the government, the justice system and the stock market. The extent to which they do so, to the exclusion of so much else, often surprises the very editors who direct that coverage. It certainly surprised me. In 1991, I set out to measure the news content of six Canadian dailies to determine how much could be classified more or less as stenography—bare-fact coverage of events clearly on the public agenda, such as a city council meeting, a press conference or speech, happenings in court or off the police blotter, or anything else to which the press was invited. I contrasted this to what I called "initiative" coverage—something that the paper thought of doing itself, even something as simple as taking a picture of people enjoying the fall colors. When I asked the managing editors to guess what I found, they greatly underestimated the percentage of "agenda" news that their staff produced. In fact, between 87 percent and 96 percent of the stories were bare-fact reporting of public events more or less staged for the media. These papers, by and large, showed little interest in poking around where they weren't invited. This raises important questions about the news judgment of today's press. Are journalists too cosy with vested interests? Is traditional news judgment producing stories that are increasingly remote from the day-to-day lives of readers, most of whom don't spend their time getting arrested, participating in city council debate or calling press conferences? What is going uncovered because editors are obsessed with these things?[26]

By so closely following a news agenda set by vested interests, the press is clearly identifying itself with the status quo. This serves to limit the agenda for

public debate, a trend commented upon in 1997 by Justice Rosalie Abella of the
Ontario Court of Appeal:

> If I keep hearing that reducing deficits is government's overriding duty
> to future generations, I may, over time, stop worrying about how a lack
> of resources will affect this one. If I keep hearing the slogan "Can we
> afford to?" I may stop asking "Can we afford not to?"[27]

When powerful politicians, financiers, economists, lawyers and pressure groups
virtually monopolize the ears of reporters, there is less and less opportunity for
the rest of us to be heard. We suspect, sometimes with good reason, that this
closeness leaves the press open to manipulation. Can we believe all that we read?
Are statements made by powerful groups being checked and challenged? Once
we let this filament of doubt get between us and the pages of our daily
newspaper, everything is suspect. Business people are fond of accusing the press
of being anti-business, but the opposite is almost certainly true, given the
frequency with which they are quoted and the fact that almost every newspaper
has a business section that is largely devoted to news made by chief executive
officers. It would never occur to us to expect a section called, say, "Consumers,"
filled with information that might help us to decide which products are worth
buying. It's not hard to feel that the vocal criticisms of the media coming from
the Canadian right—mainly well-heeled conservative institutes, politicians and
corporations—have more to do with their higher expectations of favourable
coverage and greater access than any real grievance about how their views are
being ignored.

   This point was brought home most indelibly to Canadians when a twenty-
eight-page strategy document prepared for the right-wing Fraser Institute was
leaked to *Edmonton Journal* columnist Linda Goyette in early 1997. In it,
executive director Michael Walker boasted about how his institute had managed
to penetrate and co-opt the national media, including the *Globe and Mail*, and
how with a doubled budget of $2.5 million it could maintain "a database of
journalists who respond to our material" and win even greater influence for such
free-market ideas as privatized health care, union-bashing and cuts to social
services. Some of these ideas are alarming, such as Walker's own published
opinion that poverty stems in large part from its sufferers being "dealt an
unlucky intellectual or physical allocation from the roulette wheel of genetic
inheritance."[28] If such views are crowding out more reasoned and informed
theories of poverty in the pages of our newspapers, the Canadian public has a
right to be concerned. And if such verbiage sounds vaguely like something
Conrad Black might say in a weak moment, consider that at Black's *Ottawa
Citizen* two members of the editorial board, including its supervising editor, are
longtime Fraser Institute associates, and that Black's wife, Barbara Amiel, has
served on the institute's board of directors.

It is in this context that we should examine Black's famous complaint that, until he came along, it was practically impossible to find in Canadian newspapers "the slightest derogation" from the politically correct, left-wing, anti-American, socialistic viewpoint. To a leftist like *Globe and Mail* columnist Rick Salutin, this is preposterous. Look at the columnists who for years have enjoyed widespread or national exposure in the press, such as Amiel, Andrew Coyne, Diane Francis and Peter Worthington. "My question is, can you find anyone who is even approximately as far to the left on the spectrum as these writers are to the right?" Salutin asks. It's the same when you look at the discussion of public issues. There are lots of justifications for neoconservative economics and theories such as global competitiveness, privatization, deregulation and paying down the deficit. "But can anyone recall a single example of an argument for a thoroughgoing socialist alternative to capitalism presented anywhere in the Canadian mainstream media?"[29]

Asked once why Southam News, the agency that provides news and commentary to all of the chain's papers, didn't have a columnist writing from left of centre, Kirk LaPointe said that he couldn't find one. That's still the line Southam executives use, forgetting perhaps that Conrad Black once considered those papers so rife with that sort of opinion that he said it ran through their pages like "sludge."

What's wrong with this is that the press is an institution whose public mandate and financial health depend on it being a mass medium. It therefore ought to reflect the society that it tries to observe and interpret. Today, even the most optimistic newspaper executives complain that few editors and reporters are able to identify with their readers. "Of the young people I see coming into the business," says James Bruce, former publisher of the *Windsor Star* who spent his entire career in the newsroom, "I don't get the impression that they're really in touch with people. Are they going to be comfortable walking into a union hall and really getting into the head of an auto worker?"[30] The best example of this detached arrogance is ABC anchor Sam Donaldson, who was once asked in an interview whether top journalists were now so well paid that they have grown remote from ordinary people. Not at all, Donaldson replied. As an example, he said "I'm trying to get a little ranching business started in New Mexico" and talked about how he had to fill out all those government forms just like any small business owner. This "gives me something to be in touch with America about," he said, although he neglected to mention that his little ranch consisted of 27,000 acres.[31]

These and other blind spots have caused Canadian newspapers to miss some of the most important stories of our time. For example, when AIDS activists and hemophiliacs began raising concerns about the safety of Canada's blood supply in the mid-1980s, they were largely ignored by the press. It wasn't until the activists actually did the work for reporters, documenting bureaucratic foot-dragging and cases of people dying from blood that should have been screened for the virus that causes acquired immune deficiency syndrome, that the federal government ordered a judicial inquiry and began unravelling the tragedy in 1993. The press, being good at stenography, finally discovered the story when there were actual meetings to cover. And what a story it was. We learned of the eight-year-old boy who contracted HIV because a well-meaning doctor ordered a two-teaspoon "top-up" of blood at birth. We learned of the four hemophiliac brothers who died of AIDS as a result of getting transfusions of tainted blood. We learned of key documents being destroyed, covering up the fact that Canadian health officials were slow to heed warnings from the United States that AIDS, which was detected in Canada in 1982, could be transmitted by blood transfusions. Those officials knew that 55 percent of the country's hemophiliacs had been infected by 1984, they knew that heat-treating all blood donations could kill the virus, yet they waited eight more months before making that testing mandatory.

The press was not there to blow the whistle when the guardians of our blood supply made mistakes that killed 1,000 innocent Canadians—not until it was too late and amounted to "little more than burying the dead," according to one of the few reporters who seems to have any appreciation of what was missed and why. André Picard, a reporter in the Montreal bureau of the *Globe and Mail*, made his confession at the 1994 convention of the Canadian Association of Journalists.[32] Even though his excellent reporting did much to finally bring the scandal to public attention, Picard said that the press made many mistakes and unfortunately hasn't learned from any of them. Its biggest mistake was trusting the experts: "We were afraid to doubt that they were involved in something as terrible as this—a thousand people who died." He said that reporters were intimidated by the assurances and impenetrable bureaucracy of the thirteen governments that shared responsibility for ensuring the safety of donated blood in the early 1980s—a rare admission from a member of the press that the people we regard as our watchdogs often fail to detect news that is not handed to them. His other criticism is even more telling: "We just didn't see this as a problem. It affected minority segments of our society ... gays, hemophiliacs, drug users." Somehow the denials from politicians and Red Cross officials that anything was amiss seemed to carry more weight with the press than the evidence of people dying of contaminated blood long after the epidemic of AIDS was a documented medical fact.

Clearly, health ranks at or near the top of every Canadian's list of important issues. But few newspapers have reporters covering that beat full time. Witness the almost complete lack of coverage of the debate over Bill C-91, which granted a ten-year monopoly on patents to multinational drug companies when it was passed by the Mulroney Conservatives in 1993. Although the legislation included a mandatory review, Canada's news media paid little attention in 1997 when the Chretien Liberals, who opposed the original bill, reversed themselves without explanation and extended the protection to twenty years. Even though consumer groups claimed that the legislation had pumped billions of dollars into the pockets of the drug companies and deprived Canadians of cheaper generic products, the media did not pick up on it as an issue in the last federal election campaign. No one challenged the government to justify its action or estimate the extra cost to consumers. Much later, an internal study prepared by Industry Canada surfaced, showing that the protection would cost us as much as $663 million by the year 2000.[33] Most Canadians probably do not know that they now pay perhaps the highest prices for drugs in the world, a far cry from the 1980s when they paid the lowest. This is all thanks to billions of dollars of lobbying by the Pharmaceutical Manufacturers of Canada and a press corps that keeps looking the other way.

The essence of journalism is to employ an almost scientific method of discovery, questioning one's own assumptions, debunking all preconceptions, rigorously assailing accepted belief and seeking diverse sources in pursuit of the truth. Yet too many of Canada's elite journalists have stopped doing that. Allan Fotheringham is arguably the country's top-paid print journalist, give or take a Diane Francis or Jeffrey Simpson, but he hasn't done any real reporting in years. He's simply paid to have opinions. The top of the heap for almost everyone else is covering national politics in Ottawa, but too much of news coverage there is shaped by the shared beliefs of fellow journalists, members of the Pack, who are comforted, as Chris Cobb wrote in the *Ottawa Citizen* in 1993, "in knowing that when the newscast goes out tonight or the newspaper comes out tomorrow, they will all have the same story .... The worst thing in the world is to be beaten by the other guy." The irony is that, at a time when newspapers should be better than ever before and when journalists should be better trained than ever before, the best reporters in the country are holding their tape recorders into scrums in the foyer of the Parliament Buildings and simply doing stenography on the most obvious story in town. Since that is what their bosses want, there is little incentive for them to poke around where they aren't invited, even though this would produce news that is far more significant to the lives of ordinary Canadians.

It's a story told again and again in other fields, where criticism of the limited agenda set by newspapers today has contributed to the image of an industry in decline. Evidence of the growing disparity between rich and poor is all around us, yet observers like Ed Finn, of the Canadian Centre for Policy Alternatives, see a press that is full of uncritical reporting of ever-increasing bank profits and grotesque diversions like Canada's ranking by the United Nations as the best place in the world to live. Corporate ownership of the press, he says, convinces us of the "big lie" that mass layoffs, a rise in poverty, underfunding of our schools and hospitals, and lavish tax breaks to businesses are both unavoidable and healthy. For years, Finn has been urging labour unions to start their own newspapers, but none have. And it's not for lack of money. The entire *Sun* newspaper chain was sold a few years ago for $400 million, which is about how much the $40 billion Ontario teachers pension fund generates in interest alone every couple of months. Ironically, the professional managers of that fund, on their own, invested heavily in the papers, enabling a group of employees to retain control and to continue, more often than not, bashing unions in their editorials. Labour must realize that its biggest battle is to win the hearts and minds of the Canadian people, Finn says. "Once people learn why and how and by whom they are being abused, they will become angry enough to rebel and informed enough to direct their anger at their real enemies: at the corporate overlords, not the political figureheads."[34]

Although Finn's call for a press that gives people an alternative to the corporate agenda is clearly self-interested, it does appear to have some merit. Drastic cutbacks by deficit-fighting governments were an important story in the mid-1990s, but few of the country's leading newspapers did a good job of examining the impact or exploring other options. In Alberta, where the Conservative government of Ralph Klein was presiding over the most radical downsizing of social services in recent history, the largest newspaper in the province, the *Edmonton Journal*, did away with its social services beat. The head of that city's Social Planning Council said:

> The average journalist's complete unfamiliarity with the underclass severely hampers adequate reporting. If I was paid a dollar for every time a journalist has called me up over the past fifteen years and asked me to find a poor family, I wouldn't be driving a beat-up truck.[35]

The environment is another neglected area, even though some of Canada's forest management practices have begun to attract international protests and polls show that more people are worried about the health effects of unclean air and water. Perhaps the best example of this was an editorial that the *Globe and Mail* ran in June 1997, calling for the creation of a federal auditor-general for the environment. It was meant to be critical of Prime Minister Jean Chretien, who a few days before had told the Earth Summit meeting of the United Nations General Assembly that Canada would fail to meet its targets for reducing atmospheric pollutants. The day after the editorial appeared, the *Globe's* letters page carried a reply from Brian Emmett, who said he was just the man the *Globe's* editors thought they had invented. As commissioner of the environment in the Office of the Auditor-General, he was responsible for reporting on how all federal departments were meeting their environmental goals. Not only had he been appointed a year and a half before, but the paper had twice before commented on his work (although it had missed reporting on his first annual report when it was tabled in Parliament). Perhaps it's not a surprise that environmentalists have begun turning away from the mainstream media, saying that most stories are being framed as business issues or are being reported by inexperienced journalists. Michael O'Reilly, an Ontario freelance writer who specializes in such coverage, says:

the lack of sound environment reporting is a symptom of the deeper ill in journalism today—lack of depth. It takes time, energy and resources to do good stories .... As the owners of our media reduce their support, by cutting editorial budgets, reducing staff and generally embracing the "more for less" ideology, it is inevitable that the harder stuff will simply not get done.[36]

Jim Fulton, a spokesman for the David Suzuki Foundation, said that something is wrong when most Canadians are not aware that the country's boreal forest has "gone from being a carbon sink of 35 billion tons, to a net emitter of carbon because our forests are coming down at a savage rate." What Canada needs, in his opinion, is a national media foundation that can fund media to report what is really going on in the country.[37]

Blind spots and questionable newsgathering tactics suggest that newspaper reporters and editors may be getting into areas of coverage for which they are socially and ethically unprepared. When a Toronto man dying of amyotrophic lateral sclerosis, or Lou Gehrig's disease, invited the press to his apartment to witness his suicide in November 1993, the wrenching question of whether and how to cover it produced a large and boisterous gaggle of reporters and photographers in his apartment lobby. In this case, the Pack seemed almost paralyzed by the nature of what it was covering. Some felt that they were abetting an illegal act by showing up at such an event. Others felt that they had a duty to watch in case the authorities tried to stop it. Still others cynically derided it as a publicity stunt. But nobody came inside to watch. And nobody felt that the ethical issues themselves were worth discussing in the next day's paper. Erwin Krickhahn was so upset by the indecision and timidity of the press that he called the whole thing off. All he wanted was to end his own agony and shed public light on the important issue of assisted suicide, against which the Supreme Court of Canada had just ruled. When he died naturally three months later, he left a poignant note that said:

> Every extra day that I have been forced to stay alive has been an agony to me. I hope that all those who played a role in frustrating my plans and prolonging my suffering ... will have the decency some day to regret their behavior.

Perhaps mindful that journalists once helped change U.S. foreign policy by reporting how Buddhist monks burned themselves to death to protest the Vietnam war, Krickhahn added: "Are there no reporters with the courage of war correspondents when it comes to human suffering in their own country?"[38]

Newspapers know that they have fallen out of touch. They know that they don't watch themselves as carefully as they should. They know that the public is losing trust in what they do. But they tend to react defensively whenever these things are pointed out to them, much like spouses may argue about how spicy the spaghetti sauce is lately. That's not the issue. The issue is that it's getting to be a bad marriage, and someone should try to fix it.

## Notes

1.  Conrad Black, in his keynote speech to the Canadian Association of Journalists convention in Ottawa in 1994, attributed the list to Herbert Greer, who had written it for *Commentary* magazine.
2.  Royal Commission on Newspapers, (Minister of Supply and Services Canada, 1981), page 175.
3.  The Gallup Poll, Vol. 57, No. 23. In the 1997 poll, 72 percent of Canadians said that they believe pharmacists have very high or high honesty and ethical standards, compared to only 3 percent who think that these standards are low or very low. This produced a net honesty and ethics score of +69. On the same scale, journalists scored +6.
4.  Interview with John Honderich, May 2, 1997.
5.  Kirk LaPointe spoke on a panel examining privacy and a free press at the Canadian Newspaper Association Convention in Toronto, April 30, 1998.
6.  *News Is a Verb*, by Pete Hamill (Ballantine, 1998), page 95.
7.  *A Sourcebook of Canadian Media Law,* ed. by Robert Martin and Stuart Adam (Carleton University Press, 1991), page 26.
8.  "Are We Elitist?" by Richard Harwood, *American Journalism Review,* June 1995, page 29.
9.  Readers' representatives have not helped the press to get better. That verdict was delivered in 1987 by the man whose writings in the *New York Times* two decades earlier inspired the *Louisville Courier-Journal* to establish the first readers' representative—or "ombudsman," as they were called—at a North American newspaper. A.H. Raskin's famous 1967 article "What's wrong with American newspapers" urged newspapers to set up departments of internal criticism. By the late 1980s, more than fifty newspapers had readers' representatives. But Raskin, speaking before the Organization of News Ombudsmen, portrayed an institution that is still affected by hubris, myopia and uncertain ethics. The press, he said, has forfeited its claim to be an effective and accountable guardian for the public good. Source: "Press critic still not satisfied," *Editor & Publisher*, July 4, 1987.
10. "Some subscribers missed front-page L.A. riot story," by Barry Mullin, *Winnipeg Free Press,* May 1, 1992.
11. "After 30,000 calls and 400 columns—that's a wrap," by Jim Stott, *Calgary Herald,* January 28, 1998, page A7.
12. Newspapers still will not admit this. A survey done at Oklahoma State University in 1989 reported that while most editors believe that having a readers' representative improves the paper's image and reduces errors, more than two-thirds wouldn't create such a position. It might lower staff morale and get in the way of editors handling complaints. The survey was done for the Organization of News Ombudsmen, which includes members from the United States and Canada. "How editors view ombudsmen," *Editor & Publisher*, May 13, 1989, page 15.

13. "Chairman's Foreword," *23rd Annual Report,* The Ontario Press Council, 1995.

14. Hutchison's presentation to the Ontario Press Council in June 1996 included the following statistics: in Britain, there is one complaint about the press for every 29,000 people; in Ontario, one for every 71,126; in Alberta, one for every 104,166; and in Quebec, one for every 127,777.

15. "Distortion means not having to say writer is sorry," by Kim Bolan, *Vancouver Sun,* October 21, 1995.

16. "Columnist faces hate charges," by Miro Cernetig, the *Globe and Mail,* May 12, 1997, page A1. The *Globe* quoted both Collins and a six-page news release from the *North Shore News.*

17. "Racism is not professional journalism," letter to the editor, *The Publisher,* newsletter of the Canadian Community Newspaper Association, February 1998, page 5.

18. "Stop apologizing," *Editor & Publisher,* June 11, 1994, page 6.

19. "Public to press: Just play fair," by Howard Kurtz, *Washington Post,* September 15, 1997, page B4.

20. "Throwing mud in our own faces," by Thane Burnett, *Press Review,* Fall 1997, page 9.

21. "Fourth estate can't have it both ways," a letter by Boris Freesman, *Toronto Star,* September 23, 1997, page A23.

22. "Surrender of the Gatekeepers," by David Shaw, *Nieman Reports,* Spring 1994, page 3.

23. The American public registered its strong disapproval of such coverage in a poll conducted in February 1998 by the Media Studies Center at Columbia University, New York. Eighty-one percent said that the coverage was inaccurate, unnecessary and motivated more by the desire to attract a large audience than by any impulse to get to the bottom of the story.

24. "A Generation of Vipers: Journalists and the New Cynicism," by Paul Starobin, *Columbia Journalism Review,* March/April 1995, pages 31–32.

25. "Journalism: The literature of the people," by Neil Reynolds, *The Whig-Standard Magazine,* October 6, 1989.

26. "A hard look at news judgment," by John Miller and Caroline Nolan. The study was presented at Ryerson Polytechnic University in May 1992 at a seminar for newspaper professionals called "Starting the Content Revolution." We studied 3,600 news stories that appeared in a two-week period during the previous fall in the *Calgary Herald, Toronto Star, Globe and Mail, Toronto Sun, Peterborough Examiner* and *Ottawa Citizen.*

27. "The media and the courts," an address by Justice Rosalie Abella to the Canadian Club of Toronto, April 21, 1997.

28. "Fraser Attacks," by Clive Thompson, THIS *Magazine,* May/June 1997, page 19. The article quotes Walker as referring to the media as "second-hand dealers in ideas," and Clive Thompson comments: "It's a wonderful phrase—both derisive and respectful, acknowledging both the power of the press and the grungy, free-market style of modern 'dealing' in ideas. Walker has nailed perfectly the role of the modern press: creators of few ideas on their own, and shoddy purveyors of the ideas of others."

29. "Media bias," by Rick Salutin, *The Owl,* Spring 1993, produced by the Southam Fellows, University of Toronto.

30. Interview with James Bruce, May 31, 1997.
31. "When the Press Outclasses the Public," by Howard Kurtz, *Columbia Journalism Review*, May/June 1994, page 31.
32. "Telling Stories about Bad Blood," *Media* magazine, July 1994, page 26.
33. The Industry Canada study, done in 1996 and based on a basket of fifty-five prescription drugs, was made public by a non-journalist, Ottawa researcher Ken Rubin, who obtained it through the *Access to Information Act*. He turned it over to the *Toronto Star*, which published a small story on it in November 1997.
34. "The War of Words: The left needs its own media outlets," by Ed Finn, *The Canadian Forum*, June 1997, page 9.
35. Edmonton Social Planning Council Director Jonathan Murphy spoke to the 1994 convention of the Canadian Association of Journalists. He asked: "Can a newspaper (the *Edmonton Sun*) which fills its first Saturday front page with an image of the premier wearing its advertising sweatshirt really claim to be independent of government?"
36. Interview with Michael O'Reilly, October 1997.
37. "Canada's Environmental Media Coverage Lowest in Decade," published in *Scan*, the journal of the Canadian Media Guild, December 1996.
38. "Dying man fought for assisted suicide," by Alanna Mitchell, *Globe and Mail*, February 10, 1994, page A9.

CHAPTER THREE

# Black, Inc.

You can't run a business, you know, on the basis of sentiment.

— Kenneth Thomson, on selling to Conrad Black

A procession of business people and workers, all marching in tight, geomet-
ric lockstep, stretches across the facade of the old Toronto Stock Exchange
building at 234 Bay Street. The limestone frieze was designed in 1937 to
symbolize the power of modern industry to rise up from the Depression. Just
above the north door, the figure of a top-hatted financier appears to have his right
hand poised at the pocket of a labourer. Although the artist said the juxtaposition
was unintentional, it became an insider's joke among those who traded stocks
there for nearly fifty years—that the profits of the rich usually come from
exploiting the people.[1]

The old art deco trading floor upstairs has been preserved as a conference
room, and on the afternoon of May 29, 1996, it is packed to the walls with media
and investors gathered for the eleventh annual shareholders meeting of Hollinger,
Inc. Presiding over it like a general surveying the field of victory is Conrad
Moffat Black, who just five days earlier acquired more control over the
information that Canadians get in their newspapers every day than any person
before him.

It's a turning point in the history of the newspaper business in this country,
and the setting is appropriate for the occasion. Behind Black as he mounts the
podium are four of the eight great murals painted by Charles Comfort to
represent the industries whose stocks were to be traded on the new exchange in
the years before the Second World War. One depicts the pulp and paper industry
and shows two newsboys hawking "Extra" editions hot off the printing presses—
a reflection of the time two generations ago when almost everyone read
newspapers and when there was such healthy competition that only the Southam
and Sifton families owned presses in more than one city or controlled any
measurable percentage of national circulation. All of the other giants of the
Canadian newspaper industry at that time were single-paper proprietors like
Joseph Atkinson (*Toronto Daily Star*), Roy Thomson (*Timmins Daily Press*),

# Black, Inc.

John W. McConnell (*Montreal Star*), Rupert Davies (*Kingston Whig-Standard*) and John Bassett (*Sherbrooke Record*).[2]

But now the man standing before us in dark blue pinstripes and gold tie is poised to supplant them all. Although his Hollinger empire spans four continents and controls such prestigious papers as the *Daily Telegraph* in England, the *Jerusalem Post* and the *Chicago Sun-Times*, its holdings in Canada until mid-1995 were limited to a dozen small dailies scattered across the interior of British Columbia and in Quebec. They ranged in size from the 2,000-circulation *Kimberley Daily Bulletin* to *Le Soleil* of Quebec City. But then Hollinger went on a seven-month buying spree, gobbling up twenty-four unwanted dailies in Ontario and the Atlantic provinces from Thomson Corp., adding the Sifton family's Armadale dailies in Saskatchewan, and finally, and most significantly, wresting effective control of the giant Southam chain, Canada's largest in terms of daily circulation.[3]

The lightning blitz made Black the largest newspaper owner in Canada's history, with 58 of the country's 105 dailies under his wing. At 2.4 million copies sold per day, they represent nearly half of the total national circulation, far and away more of our news than has ever come under one person's control. His domain includes 80 percent of the daily papers in Ontario. It includes all of them in three other provinces (Saskatchewan, Prince Edward Island and Newfoundland). And it includes the dominant newspapers in Ottawa and six of the ten provincial capitals.[4]

This is a nightmare long feared by critics of newspaper concentration such as Tom Kent, whose 1981 Royal Commission on Newspapers urged the federal government to set limits. Seventeen years ago, corporate ownership was measured at 77 percent of national circulation, a figure that Kent warned "is clearly and directly contrary to the public interest." Nothing was done. Today, using the same measurement, it has risen to 93 percent, with the lion's share of that under Black's control. The ownership of Canada's daily press is now by far the most concentrated in the western world.

Yet it is fascination rather than fear and loathing that brings the crowds out to the old trading floor to witness Black's first public appearance since the Southam coup. We all want to see how he is going to exercise his newly acquired power. For the first time, he is a publisher of quality dailies in his own country. What will he say to reassure the public that he is prepared to invest in good journalism? How will he answer critics who say that he will surely impose his right-wing views on his new possessions, that he will wring the last profits out of a declining industry and discard newspapers as he earlier discarded such Canadian corporate icons as Massey-Ferguson and Dominion Stores when they could no longer contribute to his bottom line? Will Citizen Black act magnanimous in triumph, or will his venal side want to exact revenge on his real and imagined critics? On a pleasant Wednesday in late spring, this is the best free ticket in town, and no one is going to leave disappointed. As the *Globe and Mail* later wrote: "After the custom of ancient conquerors, Conrad Black amused himself ... by proclaiming the scope of his victory and making sport of the vanquished."

That means making sport of the Southams, the most esteemed newspapering family of them all, and among the Southams present in the audience is 86-year-old St. Clair Balfour, who ran the company for thirty years and is the grandson of William Southam, who bought the dynasty's first newspaper in 1877.[5] Two federal inquiries, Keith Davey's in 1970 and Tom Kent's in 1981, praised Southam's tradition of public service and editorial diversity as models of good ownership in the newspaper industry.[6] But the new owner has a much harsher view. With a respectful bow towards Balfour, who is sitting tightly beside Southam CEO Bill Ardell, Black says he hopes that the Southam executives and directors present "won't take offence," then launches into his tirade. Its twenty newspapers produce "only a handful of pieces a month that would be suitable for publication in some of our better periodicals," Black says, and accuses its management of having "long accepted inadequate returns for the shareholders, published generally undistinguished products for the readers and received exaggerated laudations from the working press for the resulting lack of financial and editorial rigor." He assails what he calls an "obdurate rump" of independent Southam directors for diluting stock in the company, thwarting Hollinger by turning to outsiders for protection and trying to cut the principal shareholders out of decision-making, leaving Hollinger with no choice but to step in and restore order in the company. "If Southam management had been a little more courageous," Black says venomously, "it might still be a family-owned business."

It is an extraordinarily cruel public excoriation, certainly by Bay Street standards and even by Black's, since he says later, in answer to a question, that he has a rule—never make a vendor look bad. But he took pains to make Southam—a company that had served Canadians with distinction by bringing them the news for more than a century—look bad in front of the national media, and my enduring memory is of the stunned silence with which a friendly audience of his own shareholders greeted his remarks. That, and the stoic look on the face of Bill Ardell, who had to endure his own public humiliation in silence and realize that his days under Hollinger were numbered.[7] The only hint that Black felt some moral authority in behaving so outrageously was when he observed that it didn't seem to occur to Southam directors "that we [at Hollinger] have our own shareholders to answer to and serve." And those shareholders, he said, would not thank him for accepting such poor performance from a company in which they'd invested $260 million. No one bothered to point out the disingenuousness of this remark. Hollinger's largest shareholder by a country mile is Conrad Black.

His performance at the Hollinger meeting demonstrated why there is such a furious debate about allowing such a man to control so much of our daily news.

Just how free *is* our free press? How diverse are its voices? What role do we expect newspapers to play in Canada today? Is their primary role public service, or are they businesses like any other, there to make money for their owners? Are they beholden first to readers and the public or to shareholders and lenders? Are reporters and editors truly independent, shining the light without fear or favour on things that need attention in society, or are they merely employees whose first obligation is to please the owner? And what if that owner is Conrad Black, a man with strong right-wing views who has gobbled up most of the significant papers in the country? Are we going to be better informed because he owns so much? Is the future of newspapers more secure?

The great fear is that, at a time when we may need them most, newspapers have been captured by vested interests who see information as power or as a commodity by which to generate great profits rather than as the very fuel of our democracy, a public forum of information and opinion so vital to our well-being that freedom of the press is enshrined as everyone's right in the *Canadian Charter of Rights and Freedoms.* Critics such as columnist Dalton Camp say that Black's stranglehold on the press amounts to nothing less than a crisis for our democratic system because it means more conformity and less dissent. "Will it be possible for journalists to think for themselves," Camp asked in the *Toronto Star,* "or simply more profitable[(for them] to think like Black?"[8]

Even though they had fallen into decline under uncertain leadership that let too much of the journalism get soft and mushy, and even though readers and advertisers were falling away in alarming numbers, the Southam papers at least had a corporate mandate to be excellent and a social mission to provide the best news possible to readers in their communities. Hollinger clearly worships a different god. In its annual report, the company described its business this way: "The Company acquires underperforming newspaper properties with a view to improving the operation and enhancing profitability and value." There are no high-falutin words about the role of the press as a public service or enhancing the free flow of information, just a repeated emphasis on cash-flow and profit. Readership, when it is mentioned at all, is referred to in actuarial terms, as an "asset" necessary to enhance the value of the franchise. There is no specific commitment to editorial excellence, which is surely unusual in a business that runs on the reliability of the information that it gathers. The bottom line is not good citizenship, or service to the community, or the preservation of a free press, or finding a way to deliver information to people in the twenty-first century; the bottom line is profit.[9]

It's fair to say that concentration of ownership is a bigger issue now than it was when Tom Kent measured it nearly twenty years ago. Then, the top two newspaper chains controlled fifty-four papers; now, Black alone controls fifty-eight. Then, corporate control was shared by twelve different chains; now, the number has shrunk to half as many. Some of the smallest and more community-minded owners have sold out, like the Blackburns in London, the Burgoynes in

St. Catharines and the Siftons in Saskatchewan. A change in corporate strategy has caused Thomson to cut its newspaper holdings from forty in this country to just eight, a retreat from its original business into the realm of electronic data bases that has prompted new fears that newspapers may not have much of a future. It's a mark of the lack of competition in newspaper properties that Black was allowed to complete his conquest largely without the bother of competitive bidding. As he said, "We are, as far as I can see, practically the only buyers in Canada of daily newspapers." Forty-four papers sold in eighteen months, and there were few other takers. When Ken Thomson was asked why he was selling the *Timmins Daily Press*, the paper that started his father's newspaper empire and on which young Ken cut his teeth, he uttered a line that illustrates the new corporate ethos that is guiding the industry into the next century. He said: "You can't run a business, you know, on the basis of sentiment."[10] Thomson read the trends and decided that there were more dynamic places to invest than in newspapers. With so many others retreating from the fray, it's no exaggeration to say that the future of newspapers in Canada rests on what kind of owner Conrad Black will be and how long he will stay interested.

Kent's royal commission was prompted by a business arrangement between Thomson and Southam that resulted in the closure of two papers, the *Winnipeg Tribune* and the *Ottawa Journal,* leaving only one paper in those cities. Calling the level of concentration of newspaper ownership "completely unacceptable in a free and democratic society," Kent proposed legislation to prohibit anyone from owning more than five newspapers. The press reacted with outrage, accusing Kent of inviting the government into the newsroom, and the federal government never acted on his main recommendations.[11] Nevertheless, Kent was prophetic. He not only predicted the rise of a mega-owner like Conrad Black, he predicted with eerie precision how and where such a takeover would happen.

Owners like Southam, which emphasized the public service role of newspapering, were more valuable to society than those that measured quality by how much money was made, Kent said. But they were also at a financial disadvantage.

> The service-oriented paper necessarily has a lower financial return, and hence a lower financial value .... A buyer with a business objective can therefore pay what is, for him, a relatively low price for the cash flow that can be realized after he has reduced costs to the minimum consistent with the continued existence of the newspaper.[12]

Kent said that Southam, in particular, was vulnerable to takeover, as indeed it was, although the process was to take more than fifteen years.

The Kent report described newspapers as a five-finger exercise. The editorial department spends money to gather the news and attract potential readers, but it generates no direct revenue. The circulation department gets the paper out to those readers and collects money from subscriptions and single-copy purchases. The advertising department sells those readers to people who want to reach them for commercial purposes, and it brings in the bulk of a newspaper's revenue—nearly 75 percent. The production department gives the circulation department something to deliver, and the administration sees that the other fingers are doing the exercise right.

In 1980, editorial departments across the country spent 15 percent of total newspaper revenues. Kent called this the ratio of output to input—what is spent gathering the news compared to what is generated by advertising and circulation in selling it. It is interesting to note how far below that standard Hollinger operates in 1998. Its American Publishing division at one time gave its publishers a simple piece of paper headed "Guidelines for expense allocation," suggesting that between 10 and 12 percent of total revenue be spent on editorial. The guideline for profits was 25 to 31 percent of revenue—well above the performance of most other companies in the newspaper business and many other sectors of the economy.[13] Hollinger's takeover of Southam was therefore something like the fox being let loose in the chicken coup, and all of the chickens were fat. Once he had a chance to take a look at Southam's books and start cutting jobs, Hollinger's chief financial officer told the *Globe and Mail* in an unguarded moment that he expected most of those papers to one day earn returns of 35 percent or more. Under the Southams, many had never returned half that much.[14]

Now it's not a sin for newspapers to make lots of money, certainly not in the pro-business climate of the 1990s. Under certain circumstances, that may make them better newspapers since they become less beholden to outside interests. But there is clearly a line that marks whether a newspaper is being run for the future or being run into the ground. That line has been drawn best by Jack Fuller, president and publisher of the *Chicago Tribune*, a profitable paper that also is respected for its journalism and commitment to the future. What he says can certainly help us measure Conrad Black's commitment to the future of at least his smaller newspapers:

> If one thinks that newspapers are slowly but inevitably dying, that people's tastes have shifted irretrievably against them, then one would only make very modest investments to keep the enterprise running as it winds down, drawing as much cash as possible from it in order to grow in other areas. On the other hand, if one thinks that newspapers are poised for renewal, that the road ahead seems built for them, then … it would make excellent sense to put money into the enterprise to position it for takeoff. Far from simply using newspapers as a generator of cash for other projects, one would even consider accepting lower returns today to accomplish the things that would create substantially

increased profits later.[15]

What is clear at this point is that no owner has ever set out to draw as much profit out of Canadian newspapers as Conrad Black has. That's been his pattern ever since he sold his first newspaper, the *Sherbrooke Record*, in 1977 for $865,000—which was, as he boasted in his autobiography, "forty-eight times what we paid for it eight years before, and having stripped about a million dollars of profit with which we built our newspaper company."[16] His right-hand man, Hollinger president David Radler, today presides over their international empire with the same parsimonious attention to costs that they learned as young men. Once, early in their careers, Radler and Black visited a newspaper owned by Thomson and were shown a huge ledger documenting every expenditure, right down to the toilet paper. "I thought it was wasteful and silly to have it down to the toilet paper," Radler remembers, "but it was the best system we'd ever seen." So they adopted it themselves. By the end of 1997, with their newspaper buying binge fully digested, Hollinger's net profit more than doubled to $104 million from $42 million a year earlier. Southam, which Hollinger controls, did remarkably better: profits quadrupled, to $185 million from $40 million, in the eighteen months since Black took control of the company. A key reason was the scythe that Southam swept through its workforce.

It is tempting nevertheless to hope that Conrad Black can be the salvation of an industry that is in deep trouble, even though it still sells news to 5.2 million Canadians every day. A twenty-year trend that has seen fewer and fewer households keeping up the habit of a daily subscription ran smack into a punishing recession that shrank the only other source of newspaper revenue—advertising. Most of us look elsewhere for our daily news fix and turn to newspapers only if there's time. Often, there is no time, and the influence of newspapers on our daily lives has declined. Along with it, so has our trust in what they tell us. Instead of investing in making their product better, newspaper chains did what many other industries have done in the 1990s; they downsized, thereby mortgaging their futures on short-term profit goals to keep lenders and shareholders happy. Money was spent on marketing and new presses, but that is only cosmetic; neither makes the content more valuable. Black has the financial resources, the worldwide newspaper experience and the professed love of the written word to carry out an act of editorial salvation. No one else seems to have the opportunity or desire. And so his ascendancy puts the future of Canada's press at a critical crossroads: either it suffers one last greedy hand at the spigot of profit and fades into decline, or else it is led through a redefinition of mission and content that will save it and make it thrive as our tribune, our conscience, our catalyst, our forum of best counsel.

Some years ago, according to Radler, Montegu Black designed an unusual logo for Ravelston Corp., the holding company that he once controlled with his brother and that now manages the Hollinger empire. The logo—playfully reproduced as a hood ornament, which Radler and others used on their cars—showed the image of an eagle devouring a snake. It's fair to wonder which Conrad Black will prove to be for Canadian newspapers—the lord of the skies who soars to prosperity or the predator who squeezes the lifeblood out of a weakened prey. Perhaps he will be both, allowing a handful to achieve journalistic excellence and operating the rest as cash cows for future expansion. Radler gets prickly and evasive when he is challenged to outline exactly what Hollinger is doing to invest in the future. "We're going to bring back the popularity of newspapers as a means of communication in this country," he says.[17] Yet in the next breath he muses about the potential of cutting jobs in darkrooms as soon as digital cameras come on line.

Those who know Black say that we should judge him by what he does, not by what he says. Jim Travers, former editor of Black's *Ottawa Citizen*, offers us the following five benchmarks to measure his performance as Canada's largest newspaper proprietor. Will Black foster debate and insight by welcoming those whose views he disagrees with? Will he put something back into the business through training, hiring and editorial space? Will he give his Canadian papers their own world-wide news service or fill them with generic copy from his other holdings? Will he improve the quality of small papers, or are they primarily profit centres? And do his newspapers do good for their communities? [18]

Black can defend himself on all of these points and frequently does. His ownership of the Southam papers, he says, will ensure a reasonable variety of comment, not just "the overwhelming avalanche of soft, left, bland, envious pap which has poured like sludge" through their pages for years.[19] He pledges that all of his newspapers will be published to the highest standards and that Hollinger is the greatest corporate friend that Canadian working print journalists have. He also declares that he is a patriot whose belief in the future of Canada is second to none.

That is what he says. But what has he done? It is a question well worth asking, given the hyperbolic nature of many of Black's pronouncements and given the propensity of press barons, who after all should know the value of publicity, to put the best spin on their own stories. Writing on that particular subject in the Summer 1996 edition of *Books in Canada*, Scott Disher mentions Lords Beaverbrook and Rothermere in his review of a biography of Black, and says of such men:

> One is never sure whether the job plays an integral role in the creation of the persona or merely serves to attract people previously equipped with the right mix of the requisite bestiary tendencies: deviousness, irascibility, volatility, truculence, restlessness, a childhood marked by fiendish behavior, pathological aggressiveness, paranoia, debilitating anxiety attacks, a cold and foreboding mien, domineering conduct or bumptiousness, tempestuous outbursts, extreme pettiness, erratic ob-

servation of personal and social obligations, unfettered egotism, unbridled arrogance, a casual disregard for factual niceties, hypocrisy, greed, snobbery and capriciousness.[20]

For decades, the ultimate defence used by chain owners to justify their wide holdings of newspapers was that they never used this power to influence what their papers printed.[21] Black makes no such pretense. In fact, he has wasted no time in showing that he is prepared to use his dominant position as newspaper owner to trumpet his own political, social and personal views. Many of his papers have adopted more conservative editorial policies and their opinion pages are dominated by columnists with markedly conservative views. Even more worrisome, journalists who run afoul of Black often find themselves silenced and without any other place to work.

So it was in Montreal at the end of August 1996 when Joan Fraser, one of Canada's most distinguished journalists, decided to resign as editor of the English-language *Gazette*. She left because her opinions on Quebec and Canada were incompatible with those of Conrad Black. Only a few months before, her editorship had been criticized publicly by a Southam director, Montreal investment counselor Stephen Jarislowsky, a close associate of Black. Accusing her of seeking to appease Quebec's separatists, Jarislowsky said "Joan Fraser has to go"—an interference by a member of the board that would not have been tolerated in the days when the Southams ran Southam.[22] The departure of Fraser, winner of two National Newspaper Awards for editorial writing and niece of the legendary journalist Blair Fraser, was roundly condemned by moderate anglophones who feared that stridency from the *Gazette* might drive more francophones into the ballot box to vote Yes to separation. In one of her final commentaries, Fraser argued passionately against anglophone extremism:

> Which do we care more about, a further loosening of the sign laws or the preservation of our country? Which is more important, victory for English rights groups or the maintenance of a civil society that understands that there are legitimate fears and needs on both sides of the language debate?[23]

With her resignation, the strongest voice of reason was lost from the journalism of English-speaking Quebec.

Black and Radler wasted no time putting their mark on the editorial policy of the paper. Five days after Fraser left, they flew in for what newsroom cynics call the "royal visit." All morning they huddled in a boardroom with publisher Michael Goldbloom and his top editors, with Black doing most of the talking. Aware that Black felt that the paper was not defending the rights of the English-speaking minority vigorously enough for his liking, Goldbloom had assembled a log of editorial positions taken by the *Gazette* on just about every issue. He and

# Black, Inc.

the editors were prepared to use it to demonstrate that the paper took a harder line than Black gave it credit for. Instead, what struck the editors in the boardroom that morning was how out of date Black's knowledge of Quebec's language laws was. When he said it wasn't right for the Parti Quebecois government to force non-francophones to take language tests to determine if their children could be educated in English, they had to inform him that the contentious Bill 22 had been written out of Quebec's language laws some years before, thanks mainly to anglophone pressure and a series of *Gazette* editorials. Even so, the editors got the message that they had better stand up straighter in opposing the separatist agenda of the government of Quebec. In his own meetings later with editors, Radler had some suggestions for making the paper more supportive of Israel, a view that he said was widespread in the anglophone community of Montreal.

It was on another subject, however, that Black's displeasure was felt like a chill. In the aftermath of Fraser's resignation, the *Gazette* published a column by Christopher Young, who called her departure a disturbing indication of where the Southam papers were headed. In the course of his argument, he took a sidelong poke at Black for musing about the benefits of closer ties between English Canada and the United States if Quebec left Confederation. It turned out to be the last column Young would write for Southam News, an agency he had once headed during his forty-five-year career as an award-winning writer and editor. Black, who has a habit of using a hammer to swat a fly, ordered the paper to run his overwrought response to what he called Young's "scurrilous on-slaught." In it, he got very personal. Noting that Young had inflicted himself on Canadian newspaper readers for decades, he said: "The animosity of such a failed and trivial partisan is somewhat gratifying."[24] But that wasn't the end of it. Now, in his first meeting with the paper's editors, Black had a question that hung for a second in the air, like a bully's threat that no one in the schoolyard wanted to acknowledge. Who, he said, made the decision to run Chris Young's column? The editorial page editor, Jennifer Robinson, was just about to say that the decision was hers, but before she could, all of her colleagues pointed the finger at her in the sycophantic way the meek often behave in the company of the powerful. "Did you interpret it as saying don't run anything like this again?" Robinson says. "I suppose you could."

The *Gazette* certainly refused to run Young's rebuttal to Black's attack on him, an odd response from a newspaper that professes to believe in dialogue and diversity of opinion. It was worth publishing, if only because Young docu-mented what he said was Black's worrisome vision of Canada. He quoted from a largely overlooked speech that Black had given at the University of Alberta a week before the October 1995 Quebec referendum. In it, Black speculated on the choices facing Canada if Quebec voted to leave. "We could also draw officially closer to the United States, with whom, if we chose, we could make a much more rewarding arrangement than we have had with an unappreciative

Quebec." He referred specifically to negotiated arrangements that would "preserve our regional distinctiveness as Texas and New England have preserved theirs," raise our standard of living, lower taxes and reduce our debt burden:

> Just 220 years after its founding the most conceptually and materially powerful country would be virtually born again geopolitically by gaining access to Canadian resources and population. Any U.S. president consummating such an arrangement would be the greatest builder of the American Republic since Jefferson bought much of the south and midwest from Napoleon.[25]

Those are certainly not thoughts that most of us would utter if we proclaimed ourselves Canadian patriots. But perhaps it is understandable that Black is sensitive about personal views that have been described as verging on paleoconservatism. Both he and Radler have long memories when it comes to criticism of themselves or their causes. Chris Young has felt it before. A gentle, courtly man, he is hugely respected in journalistic circles for his integrity and ability. In 1982, he found himself walking through the Palestinian refugee camps of Sabra and Shatilla in Beirut, Lebanon, hours after Israeli-backed Christian militias had exacted their bloody revenge for the assassination of prime minister-elect Bashir Gemayel. Hundreds of men, women and children were slaughtered. Young's powerful story, filed under deadline pressure, won a National Newspaper Award and pointed the finger of blame at the Israeli army, which had encircled the camps and had at least given tacit approval of the massacre.

Ten years later, in 1992, Young found himself assigned to do a story on Hollinger buying into Southam and placed a call to Radler in Vancouver. As soon as he heard Young identify himself, Radler unleashed a torrent of obscenities and personal abuse, accusing Young of never being in the refugee camps and of inventing the story about Israeli complicity. Even today, Young is amazed by the vehemence of the attack on his integrity by Radler, an avowed supporter of the right-wing Likud party in Israel. Certainly no one who follows history or who has read Young's magnificent story would doubt that what he describes did in fact occur, and that he saw it. In Andrew MacFarlane's book *Byline: The 1982 National Newspaper Awards*, Young describes in ten pages how he got into the camp, adding "I have never seen anything like that in my life and I hope I never do again."[26] The massacre was a pivotal event in the recent history of the Middle East. It led to the resignation of Israeli prime minister Menachem Begin and the introduction of U.S. troops in Lebanon. An Israeli inquiry headed by the president of the supreme court documented and accepted Israel's share of responsibility: its cabinet had let the vengeful Falangists enter the camps, its army provided maps and lit the camps with flares, and its generals did nothing to stop the slaughter once they knew what was going on. What is almost as disturbing is that David Radler, the man who helps run more than half of Canada's daily papers, doesn't seem to know the difference between reading great journalism and believing hard-line Israeli propaganda.[27]

Black's willingness to use his newspapers as a bully pulpit was demonstrated again in the fall of 1996, after the CBC broadcast a two-part documentary called "The Paper King." Narrated by Joe Schlesinger, it was a chronicle of Black's rise to power, including some critical interviews with biographer Peter C. Newman and old adversaries like Chris Young, Charles Bury and Tom Kent. Black refused to be interviewed for it, but Hollinger's side was vigorously put forward by Radler. The documentary was so balanced that it was difficult to know what it meant to say. Black, however, once again launched himself into high editorial dudgeon, and all of his newspapers were instructed to run his reply on the same Saturday and with the same headline. Thus, 2.4 million readers were able to read his rebuttal to a documentary that fewer than 800,000 CBC viewers could have seen—a margin of overkill that presumably satisfied Black's aggrieved ego. Besides calling the documentary crude and unprofessional and denying that his ownership of most of the county's newspapers constitutes a menace to freedom of expression, Black said: "No editors of ours have ever retired because of interference from my associates or I." More than one reader found his arguments—to use a favourite Black expression—a bit rich: "There's a delicious irony in Conrad Black's order to his editors to publish a letter informing the public that Black never tells his editors what to do," one person wrote to the *Toronto Star*.[28] Another found it curious for Black to proclaim his own sense of moderation yet fill his article with phrases like "febrile adversaries" and "smear job" and "televised kangaroo court." No one seemed to notice that Black's 700-word tome took up the lion's share of letters space that day and ran on pages that warned readers not to submit form letters or any views longer than 200 words.[29] It's doubtful that any other Canadian, from the prime minister on down, would have received such an uncritical and widespread circulation of his or her views in the country's major newspapers.

Black may say that he seeks no more than a fair hearing for a range of intelligible views, but he boasts about "burying" most vestiges of left-wing comment in his newspapers.[30] He has ensured that the most prominent views his papers print are narrowly ranged on the right, not so much by direct order but by indirect suasion, and not by controlling the selection but rather the supply. Southam News distributes syndicated columns and wire services to all of the chain's member papers. It has always prided itself on developing home-grown talent, plucking promising columnists and journalists from its papers and giving them a wider audience. That changed when Black began to exert his control. Three new national columnists were recruited from outside of the chain, and they happened to include his wife, Barbara Amiel, writing about foreign affairs.[31] The others were Andrew Coyne, recruited from the *Globe and Mail* to write about national politics, and Giles Gherson, formerly of the *Globe* and fresh from the staff of a Liberal cabinet minister who was directing a critical review of Canada's social programs, who was hired to write about economics. All have what Black likes to call "gravitas" but, more importantly, all write from a right-of-centre perspective. A good example was a controversial Amiel column defending spousal abuse, in which she said: "In a private relationship between two adults—spouses, lovers, friends, drinking acquaintances—any kind of conflict they have including a physical conflict is nobody's business until one of them lays a charge and calls in the authorities."[32] In other columns, she has written in favour of "ethnic cleansing" to cure Canada of multiculturalism, railed against hordes of "anxious, pushy Orientals with outstretched palms and camp smarts, trying to worm their way into the West," and likened black activists to Nazis.

The pressure on all Southam papers to run these columns is enormous. First of all, they're paying for them, whether they use them or not, and in the new Hollinger universe it's difficult to justify spending more to retain other views. Second, Black is a man of decided views and immense power, and he had already signalled his desire to righten the editorial policies of the *Ottawa Citizen* and *Montreal Gazette*. If you think defiance might cost you your job, you tend to go along. As the *Windsor Star's* Jim Bruce told me: "If you want to be gainfully employed, you play the game. And if someone decides that a certain column deserves to be put on the Southam wire, you run it." Most Southam editors went along and allowed the Hollinger influence to extend to the op-ed or opinion pages as well. The company pressured the editors of its bigger papers to dump supplementary wire services from the *Guardian* and *Observer*—competitors in Britain to Hollinger's *Daily Telegraph*—and instead run stories from the chain's other papers around the world. Plans were announced almost simultaneously to cut back on foreign correspondents posted abroad by Southam News. Bureaus were closed in Hong Kong, Africa, Moscow and the Middle East, leaving only Washington and London active. Slowly, a different kind of perspective began to dominate the news pages and weekend commentary sections. There were fewer Canadian eyes on the world, less written about holes in our social safety net and more about the need to cut the deficit.

Two motives—profit and influence—have tended to fuel the acquisition of Canadian newspapers during the past thirty-five years of rapid concentration. It's an understatement to say that newspapers are profitable. Practically every newspaper organization in the country had a record year for profits in 1997. They have consistently outperformed most other businesses and have rewarded their owners with fabulous dividends. Ken Thomson's annual salary of $1.5 million is dwarfed by the $220 million or more that he earns in stock dividends. Conrad Black and David Radler each earn about $3 million in salary and bonuses, but Black, who controls nearly half of the common shares of Hollinger, earns upwards of $20 million per year in dividends. The company has tripled its dividends per share since 1988, taking care of its owners quite tidily even as it has downsized its workforce in the face of a punishing recession, falling advertising linage and higher newsprint prices. The best example of this is the "special dividend" Hollinger awarded its shareholders in May 1997, which put $70 million in cash directly into Black's own hands.[33]

Part of the hostile public reaction to Black no doubt has to do with the perceived hypocrisy of someone who profits so handsomely from owning the main vehicle by which the public can inform itself, yet who uses it selfishly to bellow against real or imagined critics. This is not new. The Kent inquiry noted fifteen years ago that

> in a country that has allowed so many newspapers to be owned by a few conglomerates, freedom of the press means, in itself, only that enormous influence without responsibility is conferred on a handful of people. For the heads of such organizations to justify their positions by appealing to the principle of freedom of the press is offensive to intellectual honesty.[34]

Perhaps the most fundamental characteristic of a democratic society is that those exercising power are generally believed to do so legitimately, thus earning some consensus of public confidence. Kent felt that wasn't true of the press in 1981, and it certainly hasn't improved since. Unlike the owners of most other Canadian industries, newspaper proprietors enjoy protection and subsidies from government that leave them largely free to do as they please and carve up $3 billion a year of business among themselves. Yet they continue to say that it's not so. The industry's brief to the Kent commission said that dailies "are published freely and independently ... of subsidization of any sort." This is patently false. Newspapers have successfully lobbied for lower postal rates and exemptions from excise taxes, and against any measures to toughen up Canada's notoriously weak anti-combines and competition laws. Canadian Press, the national newsgathering service, was launched in 1917 thanks to a $50,000-a-year subsidy from the federal government. Today, when the government is encouraging foreign companies to compete against Canadian firms in other fields, including the airline and telephone industries, Canada's newspaper proprietors enjoy total protection. The *Income Tax Act,* passed in 1965, allows advertisers to deduct the cost of placing ads in publications only if they're 75 percent Canadian-owned. That's enough to keep the door shut to foreigners.

Such protection may have made sense thirty years ago but is scarcely credible today. More information than anyone can use is available by simply flicking on a computer, and the nationality of an owner means little in today's global economy. Black's Hollinger is, by and large, a foreign company controlled by someone who may have been born in Canada but who chooses to live in England and is therefore remote from the interests of those who read and work for his newspapers. If, as Black himself says, Hollinger is the only remaining buyer of newspapers in this country, aren't we badly served by a law that keeps out other bidders? Would Knight-Ridder or the New York Times Company be worse proprietors than Thomson or the Peladeaus or Black? Having already secured their stranglehold in a protected market, Hollinger executives like Radler now actually welcome opening the door to foreign competition on the grounds that it would enhance the value of their newspaper investments. In fact, it is impossible to find anyone in Canadian journalism who would fight hard to preserve the protection.[35] Tom Kierans, president of the C.D. Howe Institute and a board member at Southam before he was replaced by Black, blames the tax laws for creating the present levels of concentrated ownership.

This brings us back to the subject of influence. Black clearly relishes the cachet that his proprietorship of the *Daily Telegraph* gives him in England. Perhaps it makes sense then, in view of the political, economic and social levers of power available for him to pull, that the newspaper he initially chose to be his Canadian flagship happens to be located in Ottawa.

The *Citizen*, with a circulation of 140,000, has consistently been one of the most profitable money spinners in the Southam chain. Under publisher Russ Mills, it achieved annual operating margins of nearly 20 percent by pursuing a strategy of containment against an upstart rival tabloid, the *Ottawa Sun* (circulation: 55,000). Mills tried to check the *Sun's* growth by shifting his most talented writers to sports and entertainment and by emphasizing local news coverage. Whenever he asked his newsroom about a story, it was usually some car accident or police story he'd heard on the radio. This put him a little out of step with his top two editors, both of whom had covered Parliament and served as foreign correspondents with Southam News. It certainly put him out of step with Black, who said publicly that the *Citizen* didn't really have "the air of a newspaper of the capital of a G7 country."[36] The message that the new majority owner sent to the *Citizen* at the beginning of September 1996 was that the paper just wasn't taken seriously by the decision-makers in government, and he wanted it to be.

Fair enough. It's an owner's prerogative to set the mission for his newspaper. But he wanted more, including a new, more conservative editorial policy, and he didn't think that the people running the paper could carry it out. Southam's new president Don Babick, who called himself "merely a messenger," delivered Black's message for him. Editorial page editor Peter Calamai remembers asking editor Jim Travers, "Well, have we still got jobs or haven't we got jobs?" and Travers said, "Yes, but we're going to have to fight for those jobs." They began preparing a case to convince Black that the *Citizen* published a variety of political opinions and often took editorial positions that were conservative enough for his taste. Yet everyone knew that the man whose head was probably first on the block was Mills.

Advanced survival skills are part of every Canadian publisher's job description these days, and Mills has more than his share. He also has an important connection with Babick, a brilliant executive and Mills protégé who was named publisher of the *Edmonton Journal* when Mills headed Southam's newspaper division. Together they arranged for Mills to fly down to New York for an audience with Black at his Carlisle Hotel apartment. Mills went armed with a plan to turn around the *Citizen* to Black's liking. In the course of preparing it, however, he made a convenient discovery: many of the paper's editorials were indefensible.

Calamai, perhaps the most intellectual and innovative editorial page editor in Canadian journalism, certainly felt that the dossier of editorials that he prepared for Mills and Black to review would pass muster. Russ Mills, after all, was a member of the editorial board and regularly attended the morning meeting held by Travers and Calamai to discuss what the paper should say. He saw proofs of all editorials before they were published. The paper had always been fiscally conservative, even endorsing cutbacks in the federal civil service—an unpopular position to take in Ottawa. But when Mills began leafing through three years of his paper's editorials about the Ontario government of Mike Harris, he realized that "it was pretty hard to defend .... We were just focusing on this cut is bad, this cut is bad. It didn't really show any understanding for the situation the government is in."[37] Mills had discovered what some might call his "General Boyle defence." The paper's "soft left" performance was going to be hung around the necks of Travers and Calamai.[38]

This was a virtual *fait accompli* when Mills flew down to meet Black at the Carlisle. Travers had been approached about taking the vacant editorship of the *Hamilton Spectator*, but was not keen on moving his family for such a clear demotion. Calamai, still unaware that it was all unravelling, was in Reston, Virginia, as the only Canadian journalist attending the American Press Institute's prestigious Montgomery Curtis seminar on the future of newspapers.[39] Black had flown in from Israel the day before and chatted with Mills about the Mideast, and Canadian and British politics. It was a friendly meeting, Mills remembers: "He was aware of the fact that when I was its editor, the *Citizen* was a different newspaper ... we always endorsed the Tories (even Brian Mulroney at the depths of his unpopularity)." Carefully briefed in advance about what Black's concerns were, Mills presented an ambitious plan to turn the *Citizen* into a paper, as he put it, that would be respected "among the people who are significant to him, who are people in high levels of government and business." That meant a new, more conservative editorial policy and beefed up national and business news. It represented a U-turn away from the kind of paper that Mills had run and towards the kind of paper that Travers had been hired to produce by Mills' predecessor as publisher, Clark Davey. But Black had someone else in mind to be editor of his Canadian flagship—Neil Reynolds, an innovative editor who had transformed the *Kingston Whig-Standard* and later the Saint John *Telegraph-Journal* in New Brunswick into intelligent and prize-winning papers. Without waiting for the niceties of replacing Travers or informing Mills, Black had already spoken to Reynolds. All that remained was for Mills to fly down and hire him.

Back in Ottawa, the dirty work happened quickly. Travers posted his resignation on the newsroom bulletin board, saying that it was partly due to differences of opinion on "significant issues" with Conrad Black.[40] Mills officially regretted his departure, noting his twenty-three years of experience with Southam and saying that Travers "brought a depth of experience that probably nobody else in the country had. This is a better paper because of it." The same day, Calamai, just back from Reston and Baltimore where he had worked on arrangements for the *Citizen* to host the 1998 meeting of the National Conference of Editorial Editors, was called in by Mills and handed his termination notice. Unlike Travers, he was offered no other work, either at the *Citizen* or elsewhere in the twenty-seven-paper Southam chain. This meant that Calamai's newspaper career was cut short at the age of fifty-three. In his thirty years with Southam, he'd built one of the most remarkable resumes in Canadian newspapering: three National Newspaper Awards for reporting; experience in six national and foreign news bureaus; citations from UNESCO and a Michener Award for a forty-part series that measured the state of literacy in Canada; and a research study that caused nine provinces to change the rules to allow reporters to tape record evidence at trials. He is precisely the kind of intelligent, inspired journalist that Canadian newspapers need to win back lost readers. But although he offered to relocate and take a lower-paid writing position, Mills told him there was nothing open.[41]

Within weeks, Calamai saw the *Citizen's* editorial policy change "about 160 degrees." There was a tougher line taken against Quebec separatists and a friendlier line towards the Mike Harris government. Mills cleaned out his editorial board and replaced it with writers, some of them non-journalists, whose resumes spoke of work for the Fraser Institute and the Harris government. Calamai was replaced by William Watson, a conservative McGill University economist whose last column for the *Financial Post* expressed the hope that history would judge Mulroney to be one of the great prime ministers. Mills said:

> I'm making sure that the things that are published in the *Citizen* are things that I personally agree with. I have to be able to defend them because Conrad may be on the phone saying "Why did you do that?" It hasn't happened yet but that can happen.[42]

Black clearly was putting Mills on probation, and he didn't help his publisher's credibility when he told *Maclean's* magazine that he'd considered asking for his resignation as well. He changed his mind, he said, because Mills "satisfied Don Babick and myself that he was not entirely responsible for the shortcomings of the *Citizen*, and that he had undergone what, in ecclesiastical matters, is called grace of conversion."[43] The bully in Black had struck again.

Attracting an editor of the stature of Reynolds is a strong signal that Black is serious about improving the quality of the *Citizen*. Although more enigmatic and remote than Travers and Calamai, Reynolds has a proven ability to inspire writers to do their best work and often takes chances with young talent. He won the 1996 President's Award from the Canadian Association of Journalists for his "commitment to excellence, leadership and dedication in journalism" and the first Excellence Award from the Canadian Journalism Foundation. Doug Fetherling, who wrote adoringly of Reynolds' fourteen years as editor of the *Whig-Standard* in his 1993 book *A Little Bit of Thunder*, says that the 56-year-old editor's arrival at the *Citizen* is "the most hopeful thing that's happened in the dreary world of Canadian newspapers for quite some time." Typically, in his first talk with his new editorial staff, Reynolds quoted C.S. Lewis. Canada's most imaginative newspaper editor finally found his way to Narnia.

Today, nearly two years later, the *Citizen* is a fatter and better paper thanks to Black's investment in talent and newsprint. He has made a handful of others better too, notably the *Hamilton Spectator*, *Montreal Gazette* and *Vancouver Sun*, although none has been allowed to approach its staffing levels of ten years ago and Gordon Fisher, Southam's vice-president of editorial, vows that "we are being very rigorous about not getting fat again." What's changed at the big regional papers controlled by Southam is a return to journalistic basics and "a CEO who gets up in the morning, and you know he's reading your paper."[44] The chain's new national paper, which Fisher boasts will revolutionize Canadian journalism, has attracted a who's who of talent—Christie Blatchford, Allen Abel, Roy MacGregor, John Bentley Mays and others—and created an elite class of writers who, for the first time in their careers, are earning six-figure salaries. The excitement at the top ranks of Canadian journalism is palpable.

It's a different story almost everywhere else in Black's Canadian domain. In his first year as majority owner, he replaced publishers at ten of Southam's thirty-two papers. Most of those people had roots in their communities and came from editorial backgrounds. Most of their replacements were outsiders with business, marketing and accounting skills, people who understood and could deliver Black's bottom line without a lot of fuss. As we will see in Chapter Four, editorial staff at some smaller papers have been cut by as much as 30 percent. At one, all staff cars have been sold and cost-conscious editors refuse to allow underpaid reporters to claim for mileage, forcing them to do most interviews and research by phone. The *St. Catharines Standard*, once a good, aggressive small paper, has been turned into a boneyard of broken dreams by Southam's penny pinching. The publisher of another small paper told friends that he quit because he got tired of David Radler phoning from his private jet to ask why last quarter's profit ratio was so low. Such remote, bottom-line management pays no heed to what smaller newspapers still mean to their communities.

It is this attitude, as well as Black's desire to be influential in high circles, that cause people like Peter Calamai to worry about his influence over so many Canadian newspapers. Changing editorial policy without explanation, as the *Citizen* did, is not only intellectually dishonest, Calamai says, it also betrays an attitude that the general public doesn't count. He sees Black as a power broker rather than as a believer in *civitas*—the idea of a properly informed society acting together to produce what's best for everyone.

> Black is a person who thinks what matters is speaking directly to the people who have influence, speaking directly to the people who have their hands on the levers. So you write your editorials for the governor of the Bank of Canada and the deputy minister of finance ... and they therefore take you seriously. The fact that you haven't helped most of your readers one iota to understand what the issues are is immaterial because *they don't count*. They're merely to be brought along, to be manipulated and taxed.[45]

Neil Reynolds is at least candid about who he's editing the *Citizen* for. While most editors say they are in business to serve readers, Reynolds says his job is to connect with "certain key groups in the community." First on his list is Conrad Black. Second are government officials and public policy-makers. Third priority goes to business people and professionals. Then, finally, come ordinary readers who want to read good stories.[46]

Other critics say that Black is investing in the ownership of Canadian newspapers but isn't acting as if he believes in their long-range future. In the short term, it seems like a smart strategy, and Black and Radler are smart entrepreneurs: borrowing rates are at a historic low, newsprint prices are in another cyclical decline, and the leading edge of the baby boom is approaching the age of fifty and entering the bifocal zone, which has been a traditionally strong demographic group of newspaper readers. If newspapers can be excellent enough and give them relevant information in a form that suits their needs, these readers could very well make circulation go back up. Hollinger says that it wants to make all of its papers better. As Amiel told a convention of women journalists,

> I'm not afraid to suggest it is time for newspapers to turn into cultural, literary and public affairs experiences for those large number of sophisticated readers who want that experience .... The newspapers that will survive and prosper are those we take up-market.[47]

The trouble with this is that it's expensive. It requires money to hire journalists, provide more space for them to write in, set up training programs to retool outdated skills, and sustain a commitment to developing new products for new markets. At most of its papers, Hollinger is doing the opposite. Radler, who runs the company's worldwide stable of 142 daily papers from a nondescript two-storey office building without a sign in West Vancouver, cannot name more than one or two papers that have increased their editorial staff under Hollinger. They've usually been cut back. There is no mid-career training for journalists in this country, mainly because Hollinger and Thomson used their clout to get the Canadian Newspaper Association's editorial division to drop that function from its agenda. Hollinger's vice-president in charge of editorial matters is Amiel, who spends most of her time writing columns and has never worked as a reporter in a newsroom. As for research and development, almost as soon as Black gained effective control of Southam, he cut its New Media division, which was beginning to develop a new market for information using CD-ROM technology.

The reason for these cutbacks is simple: to fuel its rapid expansion, Hollinger has gone heavily into debt, which puts it at the mercy of lenders, shareholders and investment analysts—three groups whose vision seldom extends beyond the next quarterly profit. The pressure that this puts on newspapers to perform is often contrary to their long-term strategic interests, because at the end of the day if you've let the product get too shabby you've destroyed the investment. To grasp the doomsday scenario, consider what would have to happen at scores of already-lean Hollinger newspapers if either interest rates or the price of newsprint were to rise sharply. It would be like having to renew your mortgage several percentage points higher while on a fixed or declining income.

The lesson of over-extending themselves in uncertain times has already been learned painfully by other ambitious Canadian business people, such as the Reichmanns and Robert Campeau. Black's record shows that he is not likely to wait around to share their fate. In 1997, he was the largest single seller of newspapers in the United States, dumping more than eighty of them in small markets and setting his sights on something bigger, perhaps eventually in Los Angeles and New York. In fact, Black sometimes jokes about his good timing and good fortune. In February 1995, he found himself sharing a table with then fellow co-chair of the Southam board Paul Desmarais at a luncheon marking the inauguration of the *Ottawa Citizen's* new presses. Black noticed Desmarais hadn't touched his dessert, a calorie-rich lemon chiffon concoction with lots of whipped cream, and his interest was obvious to everyone at the table, including the U.S. ambassador. "Paul," Black finally said, "aren't you having yours?" Whereupon Desmarais reached for Black's empty plate and scraped his dessert onto it in a lump. Black scarcely missed a beat. "Ahhh, it's the story of my life," he said. "Scraps from a rich man's table."

An admirer of Napoleon, Duplessis, Charles de Gaulle, Thatcher, Nixon and Reagan, Black is a kind of brute-savant with still mysterious ambitions. His old teacher at Upper Canada College, Laurier LaPierre, says: "In the James Bond and John LeCarre stories, there is always some weird genius who has a nuclear bomb and is threatening to use it to sanctify mankind. Conrad is like that:

he will apply his economic clout politically to repress what he considers the moral wrongs of the world."[48] One of the leading media analysts on Bay Street, Jeremy Burge of TD Securities Inc., says Black is in the newspaper business for two reasons—"to make money and for his ego. He's not in it for the good of the country. He's in it for profit, and if he finds he can't get profit out of it, say by cutting costs, he'll sell."[49] As Black himself said when he bailed out of another flagship business, Massey-Ferguson, he simply chose to transfer his flag to "a more seaworthy vessel."

For now, Black has the newspapers to carry out his mission; a voracious appetite for more; and the bully's ability to intimidate, second-guess and silence journalists who get in his way. It's not a new habit. Ottawa writer Rosa Harris Adler remembers working for Black as one of his earliest newspaper employees, shortly after he, Radler and Peter White bought the *Sherbrooke Record* in 1969. One day Black strolled by her desk with a rolled-up newspaper in his hand and spotted a French-language press release sitting on her desk. "What's this?" he bellowed. "Seppy literature? Seppy literature?" Adler says, "The rolled up paper came lightly down upon my head. Then he was gone. It took me some time to recognize the 'seppy' was Black-talk for separatism."[50]

Why should we care about all of this? There are five reasons. We should care because Black himself once said we should care. In 1969, the 24-year-old entrepreneur appeared before Keith Davey's Senate committee as the co-owner of a single paper. It was there that he coined his most famous putdown of journalists, whom he called "ignorant, lazy, opinionated and intellectually dishonest." But what escaped notice at the time was his warning about the menace of press conglomerates and monopolies. Both are reprehensible and undesirable, he said, referring in particular to the giant Power Corp., which owned the biggest papers and controlled most of the printing contracts in Quebec at the time. He called on the government to restrict the number of newspapers any corporation can own: "Diversity of opinion and aggressive news gathering tend to disappear with the disappearance of competition, and public opinion could thereby become more of a hostage to private interests than a master to public policy."[51] Among the ways even the best chains do that, he added, is by sharing correspondents and combining feature services, thus reducing the diversity of press opinion—all things Black is doing now at his Southam newspapers.

We should care because, as the great Prairie editor John W. Dafoe once said, we need journalists who can operate with "a kind of reckless courage" if they are to serve us properly. Editors and writers in the employ of such a strong personality as Black, who has shown a willingness to fire whomever he dislikes, can easily develop a propensity for intimidation, fear and doubt. In these uncertain economic times, the ability of journalists to withstand illegitimate influences on their editorial judgments is decreasing.

We should care because we cannot as a society afford to let our newspapers be sacrificed on the altars of either ideology or excess profit. They are too vital—as the chief information providers in our democracy, as our watchdogs against abuse, as our way of learning about ourselves, as our faces to the world—for us to allow them to be run as just another business. When a newspaper cuts its news staff, we all suffer, because there are fewer footsoldiers to search out the truth and set the agenda for public debate. All of the other media and all of our other democratic institutions depend on newspapers to do that basic spade work. Because of its reliance on newspapers for information, society can quickly be thrown off balance if it is distorted or shaped by a corporate, or any other, agenda. As U.S. publisher Joseph Pulitzer said almost a century ago: "A cynical, mercenary, demagogic press will produce in time a people as base as itself."

We should care because it is ultimately up to us to determine if the social contract that gives the press its unique place in our society is working. As a privately owned, public enterprise, the press answers to the dictates of the constitution as well as to the will of the marketplace. In return for advancing democratic values, we grant it the liberty to investigate, advocate, dissent and make profit. When the press trumpets its freedom but neglects its duties, it loses our trust and we as citizens must demand better. The lowest point in the recent history of Canadian newspapers may well have been when Matthew Barrett, chair of the Bank of Montreal, told the 1998 CNA convention: "Thank-you for being a role model." The successful concentration of ownership of Canadian newspapers, he argued, should reassure Canadians that bank mergers will not be bad for them either.

We should care because it's risky if the future of such a vital and fragile institution as the press is allowed to rest in the hands of just one person.

## Notes

1.  *Designing the Exchange*, edited by Nelda Rodger (1994, The Design Exchange), pages 57–61. The Toronto Stock Exchange moved to more modern quarters in 1983. The facade of the old building is preserved, but is surrounded by the modern black windows of the Ernst & Young Tower, part of the Toronto Dominion Centre. The sewer in front of the entrance is a favourite sleeping place for the city's homeless.
2.  Things have changed a lot since Carlton McNaught wrote in 1940 that "the control of Canada's newspaper press has remained largely decentralized." As he shows in his book *Canada Gets the News* (Ryerson Press), Southam controlled 12.5 percent of Canadian daily circulation by owning six papers (the *Ottawa Citizen, Hamilton Spectator, Winnipeg Tribune, Calgary Herald, Edmonton Journal,* and *Vancouver Province*) and the Siftons controlled 5 percent (*Winnipeg Free Press, Regina Leader-Post* and *Saskatoon Star-Phoenix*). The rest of the country's ninety-seven papers were mostly independent.
3.  Hollinger paid $294 million to buy out rival shareholder Paul Desmarais and double its stake in Southam to 41 percent. By the end of the year, it had raised that to 51 percent and majority control.

4. By mid-1998, after Hollinger swapped four southwestern Ontario dailies to Sun Media to secure control of the *Financial Post*, the ownership picture for the country's 105 daily newspapers looked like this, according to the Canadian Newspaper Association: Hollinger (58), Sun Media (15), Thomson (8), Quebecor (4), Power Corp (4), Irving (4), Annex Publishing (2), Torstar (1) and Independent (9).

5. "How an empire was lost," by Patricia Best, *Toronto Star*, June 9, 1996. Balfour's son-law, Walter Bowen, is quoted as once saying: "The spiritual force of the company is an 80-year-old man who has immense authority but no successor." Since 1992, there have been no direct Southam heirs in any positions of influence in the company, and even Balfour has sold most of his shares.

6. *Royal Commission on Newspapers,* (Minister of Supply and Services Canada, 1981), page 177. The Kent report calls Southam "the Canadian exemplar" of a media conglomerate, noting that its investment in editorial content is above the industry average. In contrast, Thomson runs "a lacklustre aggregation of cash-boxes" and Conrad Black's infant Sterling Newspapers, with eleven dailies at the time, is dismissed as "a smaller version of Thomson."

7. Ardell's dismissal was announced on August 8. He told the *Toronto Star* that he was terminated and that David Radler and Black had decided to "make a change." Radler said Ardell quit on his own: "There are differences in our styles. There is the Southam style as opposed to the Hollinger style. He probably measured those differences and said to himself, 'I'd rather not participate.'" Either way, Ardell's golden parachute was worth $2.9 million, on top of his annual salary of $311,000.

8. "Our democracy's quiet crisis," by Dalton Camp, *Toronto Star*, March 12, 1997, page A23.

9. If that was the story, everyone missed it. News stories of the meeting focused entirely on Black's attack on Southam and ignored his company's dreadful financial performance. The annual report that Hollinger released to the meeting showed net operating earnings of $10 million for 1995, a drastic tumble from $118 million earned in 1994, a result that Black himself called "unsatisfactory."

10. "Timmins paper Roy's favourite," by John Saunders, *Globe and Mail*, May 1, 1996, page B6.

11. Kent's recommendations seem draconian and unthinkable by today's standards. They would have barred ownership of an existing daily by any company whose other assets are worth more than its newspaper holdings; required Thomson to sell either the *Globe and Mail* or all its other newspapers; taxed any newspapers whose spending on editorial fell below the industry average; and set up a Press Rights Panel to screen any sales and monitor the written contracts that all newspaper owners had to draw up with their editors, guaranteeing them full control over all content.

12. *Royal Commission on Newspapers*, op. cit., page 102.

13. *Shades of Black*, by Richard Siklos (Reed Books, 1995), page 169. David Radler categorically denied in an interview that American Publishing has any such guideline, but Siklos says the memo was given to him by Peter White, who is a founding partner and board member of Hollinger.

14. "Hollinger unit's profit soars," by Casey Mahood, *Globe and Mail*, February 27, 1997, page B1. Hollinger's vice-president Jack Boultbee said that the 1998 goal was for the Southam group of newspapers to show an operating profit of 25 percent.

15. *News Values*, by Jack Fuller (University of Chicago Press, 1996), page 208–09.
16. *A Life in Progress*, by Conrad Black (Key Porter Books, 1993), page 81.
17. Interview with David Radler, March 25, 1997.
18. "Readers will decide if Conrad Black's right," *Toronto Star*, November 6, 1996, page A23. Travers notes: "Canada's previous failed attempts to control media ownership suggest no penalties would be attached to missing those benchmarks.... Despite some government discontent, action is unlikely now. Governments are far less interventionist than they were fifteen years ago and no political party picks a fight with a press baron just before an election."
19. "Turning the page at Southam Inc.," *Globe and Mail*, October 2, 1996, page C1. Black is quoted as saying that commanding editors to take certain positions in news stories or editorials isn't meddling. "These are straight questions of the maintenance of high professional standards."
20. *Books in Canada*, Spring/Summer 1996, page 30.
21. Kent didn't believe them. "They make their disclaimers in the morning but they go to bed knowing their trusted agents keep their papers on their lines." *Royal Commission on Newspapers*, op. cit. page 233.
22. The long-standing rule of non-interference was broken again when Southam director and long-time Black associate Peter White published an editorial manifesto for the *Gazette* on its letters page. The paper, he said, should be an uncompromising defender of minority rights—especially language rights.
23. Joan Fraser's column appeared on the *Gazette's* editorial page on August 10, 1996.
24. "Black responds to scurrilous onslaught," a letter to the editor by Conrad Black, *Montreal Gazette,* September 4, 1996, page B3.
25. Quite wrongly, Black said Young had accused him of advocating the annexation of English Canada by the United States. Young had not used that word in his column but, after quoting Black's speech in his unpublished letter, asked: "Is this annexation or what? Perhaps as a noted wordsmith, the author of these ideas can find a sweeter term for his 'rewarding arrangement.'"
26. *Byline: The 1982 National Newspaper Awards,* by Andrew MacFarlane (Methuen, 1983), page 148.
27. Radler confirmed to me his run-in with Young, and said of Sabra and Shatilla: "What happened was Gentiles killed Gentiles and Jews got blamed"—a remark strikingly similar to Menachem Begin's famous "Goyim killing Goyim" slur in 1982. Radler said Young "represents the worst of Canadian journalism." Interview with David Radler, March 25, 1997.
28. "CBC may be on to something," a letter to the editor by Brian Bucknall, *Toronto Star,* November 1, 1996, page A28.
29. Most newspapers publishing his letter on Saturday, October 26, 1996, identified the writer as chairman of Hollinger Inc. and CEO of Southam. But the *Leader-Post* in Regina ran the letter signed just "C.M. Black, Toronto," as if it had been submitted by just another reader.
30. The *Globe and Mail* quoted Black as saying at Southam's annual meeting on May 5, 1997, that for many years it was impossible to find in Canada's newspapers "the slightest derogation from the most rigorous adherence to a politically correct, left-wing, anti-American, socialistic, feminist and, in respect to anybody who actually achieved anything, envious viewpoint, and that's what we've buried."
31. "I did not want to write a column for Southam," Amiel told the Canadian

Association of Journalists Women in the Media convention in Ottawa in November 1996. She was approached to do so when her husband was a minority shareholder, and said no. "I felt very uneasy about it .... If I had been going to do it I should have done it then, before we had the major control, because the timing looked even worse when I did." Her national column was announced in August 1996, and every Southam paper began running it.

32. *Vancouver Sun*, November 12, 1996, page A13. Her column prompted a flurry of letters from outraged readers, one of whom said, "I have no doubt that at least one more woman will be hit today by a man who felt his actions have been given an affirmation by Ms. Amiel."

33. The hypocrisy of this was pointed out by Andrew Willis, in his *Globe and Mail* business column. He called the special dividend an "abrupt about face," since Black had earlier promised to use the cash to pay down Hollinger's debt. Around this time Black scolded former Southam executives for the "astonishingly generous" severance packages that he was forced to pay to get rid of them. They amounted to only $7 million—10 times less than his self-administered bonanza.

34. *Royal Commission on Newspapers*, op. cit. page 217.

35. "It should stop," Radler said of the tax protection. "I'm a firm believer in a free press, and if you believe in a free press you believe that anyone should be allowed to come in and own it." Interview with David Radler, March 25, 1997.

36. "Black sees Southam editors staying," *Globe and Mail*, October 9, 1996, page B7.

37. Asked to explain his turnaround, Mills told me in an interview on November 5, 1996, "What happened is that, aahh, I guess I was delegating a lot of stuff? Under the old [Southam] regime, there was so much focus on other things that the content of the newspaper was pretty far down the list of priorities .... As long as we had opinions in there that were reasonably well formed and thought out, and would stimulate debate, I wasn't down there every day insisting that everything reflect my point of view."

38. Before General Jean Boyle quit as chief of Canada's defence staff in October 1996, he suggested that he was the victim of a conspiracy of his subordinates. Ironically, the *Citizen's* editorial ("General relief," October 9) said that Boyle could have departed more honourably if he'd taken responsibility for his own actions. Soldiers, the editorial said, "need a leader they can follow, trust and respect, not one who shoves them out of the trenches and then slinks back beyond the line of fire."

39. Calamai was in pretty fast company. Seats at the API's famous oval table are by invitation only, and this seminar attracted such American grandees of journalism as Eugene Roberts, managing editor of the *New York Times*, and Tom Winship, former editor of the *Boston Globe*.

40. One of those issues was Black's opinion of journalists. As Travers later told the CBC radio program "Now the Details" (October 13, 1996): "I don't think the general population of newsrooms is as frightening as Mr. Black seems to think. I don't think they are a bunch of leftists out to undermine the system. I think they are people very much like our readers." One of those readers wrote: "Three cheers for Jim Travers. It is truly a great and rare act of integrity to put yourself and your job on the line for what you believe in .... I fear that Ottawa may now have lost its last mainstream refuge of moderate local opinion." Travers was also loved in his newsroom, and Ric Davey, head of the *Citizen* unit of the Ottawa Newspaper Guild, wrote to Russ Mills on October 9, 1996, saying: "It makes us angry to see a journalist of his stature, with

boundless enthusiasm for the craft and many years of loyalty to the company, dismissed in such a cavalier way." Mills replied the next day: "I can assure you that Jim's resignation was as gut-wrenching at my end of the building as it has been in the newsroom."

41. Publicly, Mills praised Calamai as "the most effective editorial page editor I have seen during my time in newspapers." Privately, he told me that Calamai was a better writer than administrator and hadn't been offered another job because he didn't ask for one. Calamai said that he feels betrayed by his publisher. "I think he went down [to New York] and pleaded his own case," he said in an interview.

42. Interview with Russell Mills, November 5, 1996.

43. "Winds of Change: Black orders a shakeup at the *Ottawa Citizen,*" by Jennifer Wells, *Maclean's,* November 11, 1996, page 62.

44. Interview with Gordon Fisher, April 22, 1998.

45. Interview with Peter Calamai, November 4, 1996. Calamai has met Black only once, after he successfully pestered the Hollinger boss into delivering the keynote speech at the 1994 Canadian Association of Journalists convention in Ottawa. Black seemed irritated by Calamai's repeated phone calls and letters, and he told *Citizen* reporter Chris Cobb, who was interviewing him on another matter: "You can tell your Mr. Calamai ... that I'm unlikely to forget his name because, after all, it's the same as the name of the man who was captain of that ship." He pointed to a picture in his office of the *Andrea Doria,* an Italian liner that sank in the Atlantic in 1956. An obviously impressed Calamai says, "There are probably only five people in the world who know that the captain of the *Andrea Doria* was Pietro Calamai."

46. Reynolds spoke of this on a panel at the Canadian Newspaper Association's annual meeting in Toronto, April 17, 1997.

47. Amiel spoke at the CAJ Women in the Media convention in Ottawa, November 1996.

48. LaPierre's quote to Peter C. Newman was cited in *Books in Canada,* Spring/Summer 1996, page 30.

49. I interviewed Burge after he spoke to journalism students at Ryerson Polytechnic University's Floyd Chalmers Lecture on October 3, 1996.

50. "Blacksmith's Apprenticeship," by Rosa Adler Harris, *Ottawa Business Quarterly,* Winter 1994, page 21.

51. *The Big Black Book,* by Maude Barlow and James Winter (Stoddart, 1997), page 2.

# CHAPTER FOUR

# Drowning the Kittens

We used to have a daily newspaper in this town.
Now we have a profit generator.

— a Saskatoon reader

Bushwakker's pub is a favourite watering hole for journalists in Regina. Dim lights and thick wooden pillars encourage secrecy and private conversation, but it's also the kind of place where a writer can be kept honest by regular exposure to darts and socialists. On the evening of March 1, 1996, most of the editorial staff of the *Leader-Post* booked off early, pushed through the pub's saloon-style doors and gathered grimly around several hardwood tables. No one ordered the house special, Saskatchewan Hot Plate (pyrogies, cabbage rolls and Ukrainian sausage). They were there to drink the beer and curse Conrad Black.

Just the day before, Black's giant Hollinger Inc. completed its purchase of the *Leader-Post* and *Saskatoon Star-Phoenix* from the Sifton family, which had owned the newspapers for three generations. There was no fanfare; a brief note announcing the change in ownership was pinned to bulletin boards in the mid-afternoon. Despite repeated assurances from young Michael Sifton and his publishers that it would be "business as usual" after the sale, Hollinger's reputation for cutting jobs at new acquisitions was well-known. Pessimists in the Regina and Saskatoon newsrooms feared the worst, even though hiring freezes and early retirements were already part of the corporate culture at the two Armadale papers, and Regina hadn't hired a full-time reporter for six years. Optimists placed their faith in the paternalistic Siftons and the fact that the two papers were turning a profit even though rising newsprint prices were knocking most newspaper bottom lines into the red. Some even thought that the *Leader-Post* might become the flagship of Black's Sterling newspaper chain, and that for commercial reasons he might not want to stir up any more opposition to the sale from Saskatchewan's New Democratic Party government, which no doubt was concerned that the testosterone capitalist now owned every daily newspaper in the province.[1] In its only editorial comment on the sale, the *Leader-Post* said that it was a natural step in the paper's evolution and that the community should welcome it. Under Black, it said, the paper would have access to "further resources and opportunities."

Bill Doskoch, the *Leader-Post's* 36-year-old health reporter, was one of the pessimists. A forestry graduate from the University of Alberta, he drifted into journalism for $300 a week in Fort Saskatchewan and went on to develop a reputation beyond the West as an advocate of computer-assisted reporting and a board member of the Canadian Association of Journalists. He was distrustful of chain ownership, which he said means "run it as cheaply as you can, and milk it for as much as you can." He was also a bit of a burr under the saddle of those who saw the modern press as a business serving shareholders rather than readers. At the 1995 CAJ convention in Vancouver, he was the only journalist to stand up and challenge Southam's then chief executive Bill Ardell to talk about the public service role of newspapers, which he had neglected to mention in his upbeat forecast of the future of newspapers as a business. Looking forward to celebrating his ten-year anniversary as a journalist, Doskoch had fallen in love with a second-hand Ford Ranger XLT with 80,000 kilometres on it, a gorgeous truck but at the upper end of his price range. Known for his facetious and deadpan sense of humour, Doskoch barged into the office of John Swan, his editor-in-chief, and told him, "John, if you're going to fire me, please do it now." Swan looked startled until Doskoch explained the reason for his outburst. "Nahh, Billy, we won't be firin' ya," Swan said in his light Scottish brogue, a little joke between colleagues. Yet here it was just six months later, and Doskoch and the others who gathered at Bushwakker's had good reason to fear what the morning would bring.

He'd been on the phone taking a story tip from a source earlier that afternoon when Swan came by and slipped an envelope into his hand. Everyone in the small newsroom was getting one. Inside was a letter signed by the publisher asking all of the *Leader-Post's* 350 employees to gather for a highly unusual meeting at a Regina hotel on Saturday morning, their day off. "Important information" about the company's restructuring would be announced, the letter said. It didn't say that anyone would be fired, but Doskoch had his suspicions. "I thought I was a dead man because Swanny wouldn't look at me." Reporters and editors waved their letters around nervously and resorted to gallows humour to mask their fear. When chief photographer Ian Caldwell said that he was going down to the cafeteria for a smoke, a colleague said, "Hell, smoke it here. What are they going to do—fire you?"

On his way out of the newsroom two hours later, Doskoch found himself reminiscing about his eight years there—the great stories, the boisterous games of nerf football the reporters played after their editors went home, the precious collection of souvenir snow bubbles that reporters brought back from trips in the days when the *Leader-Post* still had a travel budget. "This is the last time I'll ever walk out of here," he thought, and noticed someone carrying empty cardboard boxes into the newsroom and dumping them on the floor.

It didn't take long at Bushwakker's for someone to start the dead pool. In the grim, cynical mood journalists sink into when they're drinking together, everyone started guessing the size of the purge. Estimates ranged from 0 to 126, Doskoch being second highest at 125, which was about one-third of the paper's employees. Most reporters guessed at the low end or thought that the meeting would just provide details of the sale to Hollinger, which had never been spelled out. In fact, there had been no communication to employees from Hollinger in the three months since the sale was announced, although David Radler was spotted during a brief visit to Saskatoon. Lori Allan-Wiens, a communications aide to the provincial Liberal party, which hasn't held power in Saskatchewan since 1971, stopped by the *Leader-Post* tables on her way out and said that maybe there wouldn't be any layoffs. Doskoch said, "Yeah. And maybe you guys will form the next government."

Someone suggested extending the pool to naming names, but no one had the stomach for that. There was real fear in the air, and most people drifted off home before nine p.m. Doskoch drank beer until eleven with entertainment editor Pat Davitt and Lyse Thompson, who worked in classified advertising. They agreed that even if you were lucky and kept your job, your friends were probably going to lose theirs. "No matter what happens in the morning, it's going to be sad," Doskoch said as they left.

He and his colleagues spent a sleepless night wondering where they'd go and what they'd do if they lost their jobs since one man, Conrad Black, now owned all of the daily newspapers for a day's drive in any direction. But no one was prepared for the bloodletting and callousness that occurred on what came to be called Black Saturday. It's worth recounting in detail here, partly because everyone—victim and survivor alike—was so intimidated that a proper account of the carnage did not appear in the press at the time, and partly because how it happened tells a lot about the morality, greed, expediency and short-sightedness of those who own the press in Canada today.

Purging a newspaper of editorial talent to juice up profits may serve the bottom line in the short term but it ultimately undermines the franchise, depriving a paper of loyal employees who will work for its betterment and stripping a newsroom of the means to improve quality and thereby to attract both new readers and advertisers. "Drowning the kittens" is apparently Black's word for it. The phrase is attributed to him in Richard Siklos' 1995 biography, *Shades of Black,* and describes his marching orders at Britain's *Daily Telegraph* when he took it over in 1986.[2] Within seven years, the workforce of 3,900 was cut to 1,000. The phrase evokes the chilling image of an unwanted litter writhing inside a burlap sack as it is lowered into the water, but it is certainly apt. The events of Black Saturday were so unprecedented in Canada, so over the top, that Black himself felt the need to refer to them at the heavily covered Hollinger annual meeting in Toronto three months later. He said that the "demanning" of his recent acquisitions in Saskatchewan was absolutely necessary and would have been done by any serious proprietor, but that it had been handled in a "somewhat inelegant" fashion. "Had we been the domineering meddlers we are occasionally taxed with being, the issue would have been handled with more finesse."

His kind of evasive, bullyboy jingoism fails to capture the wrenching emotions and sense of betrayal felt by those on the receiving end. The Saskatchewan victims worked for years for a family-owned company that boasted no layoffs, not even during the Great Depression. The previous owner, Michael Sifton Sr., who died the year before, had claimed to know all of his employees by name. One victim, Wilf Popoff, worked for thirty years for the *Star-Phoenix*, serving as reporter, news editor, managing editor and associate editor. He was fifty-four, a few months away from a chance at early retirement. Over the years he'd taken up collections for colleagues who'd retired, and he'd attended the going away parties, laughing over the witty cards and funny speeches, usually hearing a word of thanks for long and faithful service from the proprietor. "It was all part of the civility that affected our lives," he wrote later in the *Globe and Mail*.

> I can only attribute my sudden firing, within several months of possible retirement, a dignified retirement I had seen so many others receive, to a total abandonment of common civility, a phenomenon more and more prevalent today. You see, I was fired not because of anything I did or didn't do, but because of the need to cut costs in the quest for fantastic profits. Scores of others went with me. And how the affair was stage managed tells more than one wishes to know about the uncivil environment surrounding contemporary capitalism.[3]

Popoff and the other 300 employees of the *Star-Phoenix* gathered as directed at the Bessborough Hotel in Saskatoon at 11 a.m., exactly the same time that Bill Doskoch and 350 *Leader-Post* colleagues were driving through the clear Prairie morning to the Queensbury Centre, a convention hall on the Regina racetrack grounds. There were no Hollinger people to greet them, only strangers operating a registration desk who turned out to be employees of Deloitte & Touche, the management firm hired by Michael Sifton Jr. to cut staff at the papers that his ancestors had built. Sifton, who said that he was selling to Hollinger because a larger organization could improve the newspapers and take better care of their employees, was retained by Hollinger as president of Sterling Newspapers as part of the deal, but he didn't show up to say goodbye. It was a sad end to the era of family-owned daily newspapers in the province, the finish of the Sifton dynasty, and there was little left of the paternalistic spirit that prevailed when powerful individuals, not corporations, ran newspapers.

Young Michael's great-grandfather, the legendary Sir Clifford Sifton, bought the old *Regina Leader* and *Saskatoon Star* in 1928 to add to his *Winnipeg*

*Free Press* and to cement his influence over the West that he had built as Wilfrid Laurier's minister of the interior at the turn of the century. As a politician, he directed the vast influx of eastern Europeans that shaped the Canadian West, and as a newspaper publisher, he hired strong editors like John W. Dafoe to shape the political and economic future. Now his heirs had sold his legacy to a man, Conrad Black, whose connection to the West consisted of a few mediocre papers in British Columbia. The 66,500-circulation *Leader-Post* and 62,300-circulation *Star-Phoenix* were now the second and third largest papers that Hollinger owned in Canada, but no one expected Black to treat them anything like his international flagship, the *Daily Telegraph*. They were just two more small-town monopoly papers to generate cash flow for him to buy more. Asked once why he was such an optimist about the future of newspapers, Black said: "There is one more mighty cycle of newspaper profits left, at least."[4] That, more than any desire to uplift editorial quality, explained what was happening at almost every small paper that Hollinger acquired during its Canadian buying spree of late 1995 and early 1996.

"Downsizing" had become almost a corporate religion in Canada and was especially popular in the newspaper industry, which was under assault on the revenue side because of declining circulation and advertising linage and was suffering through a cyclical increase in newsprint costs. Companies like Hollinger, which had to borrow to finance their purchases or invest in new technology to keep up with the times, found themselves beholden to lenders or shareholders who demanded a fair return on their investments, and a fair return on an investment in newspapers ran upwards of 15 percent, even in the midst of a punishing recession. The result was that a lot of cash flow was being plucked out of newspapers to satisfy Bay Street, and very little was being invested in talent to ensure that they enjoyed a healthy future. Hiring freezes and early retirement incentives were in vogue not only at Hollinger, which was quickly gaining a reputation as a bottom-feeder able to take extra bites out of even hard-swimming Thomson papers, but at larger organizations that Black had interests in, like Southam, whose profit completely disappeared in 1995 because it spent $80 million to eliminate 700 employees.[5] Even so, no newspapers in Canada had ever fired 27 percent of their employees in a single morning. But that's exactly what was about to happen in Regina and Saskatoon.

At Regina's Queensbury Centre, 350 *Leader-Post* employees stood in line, their names were checked off alphabetically and each was given one of four room numbers. There were nervous jokes about slaughterhouses and "being next in the chute," and darker, more exaggerated allusions to Belsen and not knowing if you're being sent to the gas or the showers. Doskoch was sent to Salon D, where he ran into Al Rosseker, the paper's director of information services, standing by the door. "Wrong place to be, pal," Rosseker said, pointing to the backs of a lot of grey heads in the room. Doskoch felt shivers come over him as he took his place among the others. Rosseker remembers: "It was rather chilling, like watching animals caught in the headlights of a vehicle as more people filed into the room. Dead Men Walking, I thought, as workers with thirty or forty years with the company entered our gulag." Eventually, eighty-nine people filled nearly every chair in the meeting room. A Deloitte & Touche employee read out everyone's name and said, "If you're not on this list, please leave." It took ten minutes to read.

Bob Hughes, the publisher, came in and quickly read a prepared statement, although he had trouble getting all the words out. He talked about "unprecedented conditions," including the rising cost of newsprint and declining advertising revenue, and when the time came to fire a whole roomful of his colleagues, he seemed to falter. "Every person in here has done a good job for this company," he blurted, then turned on his heels and left. Human resources manager Janice Dockham handed out the plain brown envelopes. Each one contained a letter from Hughes that began: "This is formal notice of the termination of your employment with Hollinger Inc., effective May 25, 1996. You will remain an employee of Hollinger Inc. until that date, but you will not return to work at the *Leader-Post*."

Doskoch remembers reading his letter and looking around and seeing the stunned disbelief on the faces of his friends. One of them was the agriculture reporter, D'Arce McMillan, who the night before at Bushwakker's had chosen eighty-nine in the dead pool, and now realized that he'd won it at the expense of his own job. Everyone had questions—What about my pension? When do our health benefits run out?—but no one had answers. One of the Deloitte & Touche minions went to a microphone and told the crowd: "You've all just gone through a very traumatic experience here." Someone called out: "Thanks for validating us." Janice Dockham got into a bizarre argument with Don Curren, the assistant city editor, whose termination letter was addressed to "Andrew." She kept calling him Andy, refusing to believe him when he said that it wasn't his name. Curren said that they were probably confusing him with city editor Andy Cooper. "Who do we fire, Andy or Don?" Curren said finally. "I know—let's split the difference."

That's what bothered Doskoch most—the hamhandedness and the indignity of it all. He particularly resented the fact that they'd chosen Salon D for the death room. Most of the east wall was glass, leaving those who were fired with no private area to grieve together. On the other side of the glass, looking in at them, were most of Black Saturday's survivors, who had spilled out of the other three rooms. It was a fishbowl of the dead.

Deloitte & Touche (quickly nicknamed Toilet and Douche) had been hired to run the operation with military precision, but there were glitches that, to those most affected, made things worse. Swan, the editor, found himself assigned to deliver the news of what was happening to a roomful of survivors down the hall. But after he read out his prepared statement and left without answering questions, as he was instructed to do, one of his editors ran after him down the hall, calling his name three times to get him to stop. "Swanny, are we all fired or not?" Realizing the statement was unclear, he had to pop his head back in the room to tell everyone that no, it was the people down in D; all you people still have jobs.

Doskoch, after eight years on staff, got severance of $15,100. Together with about $10,000 that he'd managed to put into RRSPs, he estimated that his "Fuck You Fund" would be empty in a few months. It probably meant giving up the truck. Including him, the *Leader-Post's* editorial department lost seventeen of its sixty-eight employees. The paper was left with only seven reporters to cover the news in a city with a population of 180,000.

In Saskatoon, a similar scene was being played out in Ballroom A of the Bessborough Hotel, where eighty-four were fired, including more than a third of the *Star-Phoenix* editorial department. "It was sad to see them coming out holding their brown envelopes," a colleague says. They included Popoff, whose editorial page seven months before had warned readers in Moose Jaw and Prince Albert to expect worse journalism once Hollinger took control; Deanna Herman, an editorial writer and women's issues columnist who was seven months pregnant; and Verne Clemence, the book editor, who was in a wheelchair because of childhood polio and had twenty-five years at the paper. His wife, the paper's librarian, had been sent to another room and was spared, although she quit three weeks later because the staff cuts left her without any help. "Not only were we finished," Popoff wrote in his *Globe and Mail* article,

> our place of work a few blocks away had been locked up, incapacitating our entry cards, and was under guard. We could never go back, except to retrieve our personal belongings, and this under the watchful eye of a senior supervisor and one of the newly retained guards. I felt like a criminal .... I couldn't be trusted not to snitch a pencil or note pad.

The mass firing of loyal and blameless workers has become almost a ritual of Canadian corporate life, and it's not always done because the business is failing. Between 1988 and 1994, five of the country's top "job killers" also ranked among the top in sales revenue.[6] Terminating people once caused public relations nightmares in their communities, but now such companies find themselves rewarded for it on the stock market. In fact, it's become a favourite tactic to spike shareholder value. This loyalty to short-term profit ignores the fact that employees who depend on a company for their livelihood have a far bigger stake in its future than shareholders whose investment may be fleeting and represents but a tiny portion of their net worth. It also ignores the importance of investing in talent to help build market share for the future. A survey of American businesses done in 1996 by the Society for Human Resource Management found that layoffs produced less profit and productivity than expected, and often yielded a harvest of resignations, absenteeism and bad morale.

Downsizing can be likened to heavy dieting. It's done to make yourself leaner, but the risk is that it can easily become obsessive and self-destructive, leading to corporate anorexia. The only healthy way to fitness is to nourish and exercise your muscles. Good companies traditionally turn to, rather than on, their workers, and find new ways to get business growing again. Downsizing doesn't attack the underlying problem; it just demoralizes the remaining employees, whose loyalty and innovation are vital to turning things around. Lesson after lesson in the corporate world tells us that if you let employees know that you need their help to lift the company out of difficulty, and provide training and incentives, they'll give all that they have.

Michael Sifton sold his great-grandfather's papers to Conrad Black for $94 million, much higher than the price that was rumoured at the time. He'd become an object of some mirth in the Regina newsroom during the year he'd run Armadale following his father's death. One joke about the sale had Sifton staring down at his hand and saying, "Okay, I didn't get much for the paper, but these magic beans that David Radler gave me, if I plant them in spring ...." He was seldom seen in his newsrooms and was known mostly for his advocacy of the Quality Improvement Process, a loopy and manipulative management theory that tried to achieve efficiencies by empowering groups of employees to meet regularly and root out "non-conformances." (The QIP motto is "Quality isn't goodness; quality is conformance to requirements.") People were sent off to seminars and encouraged to do quality charting at home. The consensus about young Michael was that he just wasn't a *newspaperman* like his dad.

At the press conference called in Regina to announce the firings, Sifton was asked how much money the papers were losing to justify such a drastic reduction in staff. He said rather tellingly: "Armadale has not lost money. It has made money. It has not made enough money."

He did not communicate with any of the 173 fired employees, but he did send to the survivors a form letter, addressed to "Dear Colleague" and containing spelling mistakes, mainly to dispel rumors of a second wave of firings. "Some people have spread this rumor ... based on popular myths about Hollinger and some of its principle [sic] shareholders. To this rumor I say 'don't believe all that you hear.'" Sifton added:

> I would like to take this opportunity to personally thank you for your support in these very difficult days following our announcement. I know the sun will come up again tomorrow and it will be brighter here on in. I would also like to ask you to help your friends who are no longer part of our team. My heart goes out to each and every one of them and their families.

After invoking the image of family to describe life at his newspapers, Sifton wrote: "I hope I never have to go through such an event ever again—anywhere."

The *Leader-Post*, which Sifton pledged would continue to excel editorially despite the loss of a quarter of its staff, had to entrust the story of the purge to a journalism student intern, who was ordered not to quote any of those let go.

Conrad Black himself later defended the staff cuts in an exchange of letters in the *Globe and Mail* with Bruce Wark, a Canadian Association of Journalists board member who challenged the financier to assure Canadians that he cared about building newspapers, not just wringing profits out of them. Black bristled at the suggestion and wrote that the Saskatchewan newspapers "employed half the work force of the London *Daily* and *Sunday Telegraphs* to produce six-day newspapers of 12 per cent of our London circulation and a fraction of the *Telegraph's* quality by any measurement."[7] He went on to say that "any owner of those newspapers ... would have had to reduce the work force by approximately one-fifth, as we reluctantly did." (Actually, he got his sums wrong: his 20 percent was really 27 percent.) Black later changed his story somewhat and told *Maclean's* magazine that "if we had the faintest idea that it was going to be handled like that we would have intervened."[8]

Yet Hollinger president David Radler was briefed about the layoffs in advance and, as Michael Sifton says today, his new Hollinger bosses knew enough to have 173 severance packages ready for Black Saturday. Radler is snappish when asked about it. "Look, the number that counts is that 170 of the 173 severance packages were accepted within a day. That's how good they were." In fact, most weren't snapped up that quickly. They were accepted grudgingly after lawyers said that they weren't worth the cost of fighting in court. Hollinger showed little willingness to settle with the three who did sue, leading us to either question Hollinger's sincerity or wonder how much in control its top executives are over the important business dealings in their far-flung empire. The fact is that Sifton, the actual author of the bloodletting, has since been put in charge of most of Hollinger's and Southam's smaller papers in Canada, many of which are now also being downsized.

The impact of Black Saturday on the two Saskatchewan newspapers was predictable. Having fewer journalists to gather the news meant that there was a visible decline in editorial quality. A study conducted by the University of Regina journalism school examined the news content of the *Leader-Post* for the three weeks immediately before and after the firings. It showed that both the size of the paper and the number of locally written news stories had declined.[9] Most of the decline, naturally, came in the areas where staff was cut. Beat reporters covering agriculture, health and civic affairs were among those let go, and that coverage dropped precipitously. Only 86 agriculture stories were counted in the study during the three weeks after the firings, a fraction of the 392 that appeared in the three weeks before the beat reporter lost his job. John Swan admitted that morale in the newsroom was low but that most remaining reporters had stepped up production. The reason, one of his reporters said, was that they're all "scared shitless." Another said that the paper is now unable to do longer, more in-depth projects. He gave the following example. Some colleagues were about to start a long project on poverty in Regina, a subject that many felt the paper had been ignoring. But on the Monday after the firings, the city editor called it off. "Hollinger doesn't care if they burn us out and we move on," the reporter said. "They'd love that. If you get a new guy and he leaves after two years, you never have to worry about paying him the top rate." Seven months later, when the University of Regina did a follow-up study, the *Leader-Post* was found to be carrying 5 percent less local news than it had before the takeover. Its pages were filled mainly with cheap wire copy. Instead of the "further resources and opportunities" promised as a result of the Hollinger takeover, the study concluded: "The opposite happened. The newspaper was, in effect, raped."

Make no mistake about it: Conrad Black is one of corporate Canada's true believers in the merits of downsizing to create value for shareholders. He is an open admirer of the king of all job-cutters, Al Dunlap, who as CEO of Scott Paper Co. turned around the money-losing U.S. company by firing eleven thousand workers and then selling it at a huge profit to a competitor in 1995. This was enough for even the *Globe and Mail's Report on Business* magazine to brand Dunlap "a blight on the corporate body politic ... a walking, bragging argument for government regulation."[10] Black, however, was quick to spring to Dunlap's defence when *Toronto Star* columnist Dalton Camp criticized Dunlap for profiting so handsomely for doing nothing more than firing 35 percent of his workers. In one of his most overwrought letters to the editor, Black scolded the paper for printing such rubbish, criticized Camp personally as a "quavering and spavined personification of political failure," and defended Dunlap as a corporate hero. Pointing out that the stock value of Scott Paper had more than doubled, Black said that the man who had achieved that should be honoured for bringing benefit to those who are truly most deserving—the shareholders.[11]

Such bloodthirsty efficiency in pursuit of corporate profit can take your breath away. Black Saturday will live in infamy as a textbook example of the cold-blooded, mid-90s corporate purge, which values greed over kindness and financial success over human achievement.[12] In Saskatoon, one of the careers it claimed was that of Eric Burt, not a brilliant journalist by any standard but a man who'd given fifty years of service to the *Star-Phoenix* and was kept on long past retirement to write a column and lay out the religion pages part-time. That's the way paternalistic family newspaper owners like the Siftons often treated loyal employees, helping them top up pensions that may be insufficient. No similar sentiment beats in the heart of the new breed of capitalist owners, or those who fall under their employ. Less than a week after he was fired by Hollinger on Black Saturday, Eric Burt's wife died. Steve Gibb, editor of the *Star-Phoenix* and the man who wrote Eric Burt's name down on his list, defends the mass firings as necessary to ensuring the future of the paper:

> If it's got to happen, there's something to be said for doing it the way

we did. We've speculated 'How would it have been done if the decision had been left up to us?' If you have to fire 84 people at once, the newspaper is a different kettle of fish than any other business. If you were running a meat packing plant, where everyone comes to work at 8 a.m., you'd just stand at the gates and hand out pink slips to everyone. But here people work different shifts, and you have to get the paper out the next day.[13]

Of Burt's double loss of his job and his wife, Gibb says simply: "Bad timing."

A decade or so ago, such monopolistic control of one province's daily press would have prompted an outcry and led to a royal commission of inquiry. Today it's passed off as a normal business activity, even in Socialist Saskatchewan. One of the few political leaders there to express any concern was Ron Osika, the interim Liberal leader. Six days after Black Saturday, he accused Hollinger of trying to drive several central Saskatchewan weekly newspapers out of business by undercutting ad rates. "Hollinger has been a corporate citizen in our province for exactly one week," he told the Legislature. "In that time it has not only put a quarter of its own work force on the streets, it now threatens the very futures of ... papers that have been around for six, seven or eight decades."[14] Since there was no independent press left to expose this threat, he urged the NDP government of Roy Romanow to step in. "I know it's scary for politicians to take on men who buy their paper by the roll and ink by the barrel. But we must in order to ensure the future of independent publishers in this province." Osika's speech was barely reported in the Conrad-owned daily press, and the government said nothing.

Black is fond of describing the state of most Canadian journalism as deplorable; he has also boasted that papers under his control often improve. It was difficult to see this when I picked up copies of the *Leader-Post* and *Star-Phoenix* six months after Black Saturday. There were no local opinion columns on the editorial page of the *Leader-Post*, and the *Star-Phoenix* devoted an entire back page of its Weekend Extra section to a wire service feature and colour picture of the Oktoberfest celebrations in Kitchener, Ontario. What made this worse was that the title of the page was "Weekend Destinations," as if residents of Saskatoon out for a Sunday drive in the country might just want to drop in to southwestern Ontario for a beer and bratwurst. Too much of the journalism seemed shallow, uninspired and indifferently written, as if it was being churned out to fill space by an overworked staff.[15]

David Radler, the tough-minded Hollinger president who is often called Black's "human chain saw," admits that reductions are taking place at many other papers in the Hollinger empire but says that almost all are confined to production and distribution staff. "Very few journalists have been let go," he told me.[16] This no doubt comes as news to people at the Cornwall (Ontario) *Standard-Freeholder*, a perennially profitable paper that Hollinger bought from

Drowning the Kittens

Thomson in late 1995. A year and a half later, it fired seventeen employees, leaving the daily with just thirty-six people to cover the news, sell the advertising, keep the books, print the paper and distribute it. The newsroom lost one-third of its staff, including its managing and city editors, and was left to be run by the sports editor. Publisher John Farrington blamed a drop in circulation and said that the 160-year-old paper needed to beef up its local news coverage to survive. Asked how he could do that with less news staff, he replied: W-o-r-k." A few months later, after he had imposed an eight-inch limit on news and feature stories and chosen a classified advertising salesperson to edit the weekend magazine, Farrington boasted that "the readers are the winners." It's the same story almost everywhere else at Hollinger's smaller papers, and the carnage in newsrooms is causing a malaise that is driving many others out of the business.

Sharon Burnside walked out the door of the *Ottawa Citizen* in April 1997 after serving for six years as managing editor. She was only forty-three, one of the freshest thinkers in the business and in charge of Conrad Black's flagship newsroom in Canada, but she was suddenly fed up. The job absorbs you, and it's great fun, but to put out that kind of effort you need to be working for people you believe in, for principles you believe in, and for values you believe in." After Black's takeover of Southam, she said, "No attention was being paid to the development of staff, or training, or how do we get better at what we do. All the emphasis is in the other direction—how do we do more with less."[17]

The many casualties of Conrad Black's first year of majority control of Southam were obvious when the best journalists in Western Ontario gathered for their forty-third annual awards dinner in Waterloo in April 1997. It's usually a friendly and upbeat gathering, drawing together writers, editors and photographers from Windsor, Hamilton, London, Kitchener, Sault Ste. Marie, North Bay and sixteen other papers in between. But this time there was a dark cloud over the prime rib, and the opening remarks included a euphemistic reference to the "incredible amount of change" that has led to the departure of so many old friends. Indeed, six popular publishers and editors had just been fired or replaced by Southam, several award-winners or finalists had taken downsizing buyouts and several others, including the young writer chosen as Journalist of the Year, were leaving for better jobs. There was drinking, but it was subdued, more or less fitting for a reunion of survivors. The dinner was co-sponsored by Southam, and its top news executive, Gordon Fisher, spoke briefly and glowingly about his organization's new emphasis on editorial quality. Several of his editors in the audience, including Dave McLellan, barely were able to restrain themselves. "One of the things I find really irritating is this lip-service they pay to the reader," McLellan said later, referring to people like Fisher and Conrad Black. "They keep talking about improving editorial, about how that creates readers, and advertisers will follow readers. If I hear that one more time I'll start tearing my hair out. That's not what's happening."[18]

McLellan, who is only forty, abruptly quit as editor of Southam's *North Bay*

*Nugget* rather than carry out the third downsizing ordered by head office in three years. This reduced his editorial staff from twenty-seven to eighteen—a 33 percent cut with the last stage of it being approved by Michael Sifton. McLellan, who spent his entire twenty-year career at the *Nugget*, has won several awards for his editorial writing and columns and used to love the newspaper business, said: "I had a hard time accepting that we had to put more people out of work in order to improve the profit of a very, very profitable paper." He plans to try his hand at a second career, managing a doughnut franchise, on the theory that Canadians will always eat doughnuts, but may not continue buying mediocre newspapers.

Mediocre news coverage is what readers of Hollinger's smaller papers may have to settle for these days. In some cases, the news just isn't being covered at all, such as the 1997 funeral of a 2-year-old murder victim that was held about one hundred metres from the front door of Hollinger's *Niagara Falls Review*. One thousand mourners attended, making it one of the biggest local stories of the year, but the paper sent no reporters or photographers to cover it. A small item on the funeral appeared the next day, but it was provided by Canadian Press, the national newsgathering co-operative, which had to send in a reporter from another city. The *Review* is a profitable paper but its editorial staff has been cut in half because Hollinger wants to wring even more profit out of it.[19]

Hollinger's cost-cutting stranglehold has been felt even more acutely at Canadian Press, which Black now controls because he owns so many of its client newspapers. CP gathers or distributes most of the news Canadians get about themselves in newspapers and radio broadcasts, yet pressure from Southam and Hollinger has forced the agency to cut 40 percent of its staff since 1990. This means fewer eyes and ears to bring us our news every day. The cost was spelled out candidly by Jim Poling, the outgoing general manager, who told CP's stakeholders that the service was "perilously close to a level unacceptable to members .... The overall news report is now smaller, less comprehensive and not as well edited as in the past. There are fewer voices being heard ... and less coverage of life beyond the urban areas."[20] It didn't help that Hollinger used its clout to get Michael Sifton, who is rapidly becoming the grim reaper of Canadian newsrooms, chosen as chairman of CP.

Hollinger's pare-to-the-bone strategy is no secret. It's how it goes about doing business and declares as much in its annual filings to the U.S. Security and Exchange Commission:

> The company's strategy for achieving growth in its newspaper business is based on achieving two principal objectives: improvements in the cash flow and profitability of its newspapers, principally through cost reductions, and growth through acquisitions .... The most significant source of savings is labour costs.[21]

The bottom line? Southam's labour costs as a percentage of revenue have declined from 50 percent in 1993 to 37 percent today.

Unfortunately, there is a pattern in Canada of newspapers being subjected to radical downsizing and then going in the wrong direction as businesses. Southam does not give financial results for its individual papers, but there are few doubts that its *Kingston Whig-Standard* is a lesser paper since "the Sweep" happened in 1994. On one Tuesday morning, twelve of the paper's best and most experienced writers and editors were summoned to Room 532 in the local Holiday Inn and fired. Gordon Fisher, who had just moved in as publisher, said that the quality of the paper wouldn't suffer, even though the cuts left him with such a shortage of senior staff that the chain had to fly in two editors from Alberta to help get the next day's edition out. Those let go included editor Harvey Schachter and city editor Anne Kershaw, who had brought the *Whig* uncommon journalistic recognition: two National Newspaper Awards for editorial writing, one for special project reporting, a Michener Award for meritorious public service and a couple of National Magazine Awards. The paper, once described by Peter C. Newman as "the model of what a daily newspaper should be," had gained a national reputation for quality and intelligence. Now, it was going to be a paper exactly like too many others in the Southam chain, redesigned full of short stories and the kind of "Chicken McNugget" journalism that former editor Neil Reynolds and the strong editorial team he'd assembled (which included many of those let go) used to deplore. This very term, Reynolds once said, was a libel on a commercial product "that provides more nourishment for the body than formula journalism provides for the mind." The new-look *Whig* was not a success. One reader exploded in a letter to the editor: "Get out of town, Gordon Fisher, you pathetic little Southam toad, and give us back our paper."[22] As it happened, Fisher did get out of town—promoted to Southam's head office in Toronto as its first vice-president of editorial, personally approved by Conrad Black and one of the very few executives who survived when Hollinger secured majority control in 1996. But circulation of the *Whig* just kept going south, from 40,000 in its heyday under Reynolds to 27,000 today.

The same brutal downsizing happened at the *Hamilton Spectator*, another Southam paper that in 1994 was ordered to cut $2 million out of its $9 million editorial budget. It eliminated 22 of the newsroom's 140 jobs, which meant that every reporter hired in the previous six years was let go. One of them was 33-year-old Norman DeBono, who'd just won a Western Ontario Newspaper Award for his writing. He had a mortgage, a new baby, a wife on maternity leave and, suddenly, no job. Although he is still in newspapers, as an award-winning education reporter for the *London Free Press*, he says:

> If you're a young person, you've really got to be worried about the future of this business. When they get rid of jobs they're getting rid of their younger and more productive workers. All of a sudden you walk

into that newsroom and all you see are a bunch of old white guys. You need a core of young people if you're going to have a quality newspaper in five or ten years. And newspapers don't have that now and that's really dangerous.[23]

What made things worse for Canada's daily papers during the early 1990s was that, at the same time that they were cutting reporting staffs, they were raising their prices—an incredible double whammy that helped speed the drastic declines in circulation. David Radler had it at least half right when he told the *Financial Post* in July 1997 that "the prices are too high" and announced a three-year freeze on any more increases in the Southam chain. What he missed, or chose not to say, was that it was beginning to dawn on readers that they were getting a lot less for their money. Newspapers were thinner and had fewer people to cover the news. But somehow this did not seem to occur to Canada's publishers. Given the economic realities of escalating newsprint costs and declining advertising revenues, they set about trying to shift more of the burden over to readers. The median price for a single copy of a Canadian newspaper shot up from forty cents in 1990 to seventy-five cents in 1997, an astonishing increase of 86 percent.[24] Moreover, the biggest increases came in smaller markets, where the cost-cutting guillotine of Hollinger dropped hardest. A confidential report prepared by the Canadian Newspaper Association in 1997 showed that big papers in large markets sold for significantly less than their smaller counterparts. A reader in Calgary or Toronto, where the newspaper markets were competitive, could buy a weekday paper for fifty cents. But a reader in Penticton, or Chatham, or Moncton, had to pay seventy-five or eighty cents.

Kirk LaPointe, brought in by Black to rescue the *Spectator*, calls the previous Southam strategy "a classic miscalculation." Making the paper thinner and charging more for it made circulation plunge so much that "the bottom was dropping out. The best journalists were not coming to the city because it wasn't a major paper anymore."

Another folly of downsizing is that companies deprive themselves of the capacity to react when market conditions change. That happened in Saskatchewan just eight months after Black Saturday, when all of a sudden the *Leader-Post* and *Star-Phoenix* had serious competition. Sensing an opportunity, former *Star-Phoenix* publisher Bill Peterson launched a pair of twice-weekly competitors in Regina and Saskatoon. With financial support from a venture capital company and moral support from Premier Roy Romanow, the Free Presses began eating Hollinger's lunch. The two dailies "seemed a bit lazy before we got here," Peterson says, but he noticed the change: more space, Regina's sudden shift to morning home delivery after years of hesitating and the hiring of more journalists so soon after they had fired so many. All of a sudden, there was a newspaper war, but there was only one trouble: the two Hollinger papers chose to recruit an inexperienced and cheaply paid army to fight it for them. None of the veterans who were fired on Black Saturday were hired back, even though David Radler promised to do so if there were openings. Saskatoon editor Steve Gibb says, "We haven't made any conscious decision not to .... But there's no question there would potentially be problems in doing that. You're obviously going to carry a lot of baggage, having gone through something like that." And a lot of baggage can slow you down when you're rushing about trying to gussy up the bottom line.

To Bill Doskoch, life became a race to find a job in a downsized industry before his Fuck You Fund ran out. The people whom he thought he could count on for help turned away. It took the *Leader-Post* library a month to send him photocopies of his clippings—which he needed immediately to accompany his resume. He asked for his Rolodex of contacts, but it was declared company property and he had to get a friend to snitch it. Meanwhile, his files documenting four years of health reform in Saskatchewan were simply dumped in the garbage because the paper had no plans to fill his beat. He sold his truck at a loss of $1,500 and moved about as far away from Conrad Black's newspaper empire as you can get, accepting a job as foreign editor of the *Cambodia Daily,* an English-language paper published in Phnom Penh. But bad luck can sometimes turn even worse. Doskoch herniated a disk in his back shortly after getting there and had to return home, unable to work for seven months. When he did find another job, it was as an editor with the Southam New Media Centre in Edmonton, whose ultimate proprietor became ... you know who. He started his job on June 16, 1997. Three weeks later, Southam announced the closure of the centre. Doskoch still doesn't believe it: Conrad Black managed to downsize him twice in little more than a year.

## Notes

1.  Black owned all four dailies, thanks to his purchase in the previous October of the 9,800-circulation *Prince Albert Herald* and 10,150-circulation *Moose Jaw Times-Herald* from Thomson.
2.  Black, being a student of history, would have borrowed the phrase from an earlier time. Alfred Harmsworth, later Lord Northcliffe, launched the *Daily Mirror* in 1903 as a paper for women, edited and written by women. The idea was a flop, largely because many of the female staff were inexperienced and had to be sacked, a task the new editor, Hamilton Fyfe, likened to "drowning the kittens."
3.  "One day you're family; the next day you're fired," by Wilf Popoff, *Globe and Mail*, Facts & Arguments page, March 14, 1996. A rebuttal published five days later by Cheryl Tibbetts, who described herself as a "corporate restructuring specialist," generated a debate among *Globe* readers about corporate morality. Tibbetts derided Popoff for casting aspersions on the character of the family that employed him for his entire career and said that people like him "expect the System to provide them with a job, and they have simultaneously lost the gumption to create

one." People who don't understand being downsized don't understand "what a free market is all about," she added. "Every cent drained from shareholders by retaining employees who are no longer economical assets ... is one cent less that the shareholders will have available to spend to boost the economy elsewhere." Reader Benjamin Stein said that Tibbetts illustrates the "cutthroat attitude that has become the norm in corporate culture" in the 1990s. Another reader, Bryce Erickson from Saskatoon, wrote, "We used to have a daily paper in this town. Now we have a profit generator."

4. *Shades of Black*, by Richard Siklos (Reed Books, 1995), page 323. Black's profit expectations are high, even for an industry used to high profits. Papers that he acquired in the United States in 1988, which were already generating a fairly impressive gross operating profit of 16 percent, earned an average of 23 percent in 1993. Those acquired in 1990 improved from 20 percent to 30 percent.

5. Southam spent another $64 million on downsizing in 1996.

6. They were General Motors, Ford, Alcan, Ontario Hydro and Imasco. "The Job Killers," by Tony Clarke, *Canadian Perspectives*, Autumn 1996.

7. "Black advises therapy for print journalists," letter to the editor, by Conrad Black, *Globe and Mail,* May 8, 1996, page A15.

8. "The Prince of Papers," by Jennifer Wells, *Maclean's*, November 11, 1996, page 60.

9. "The *Leader-Post* is a leaner, meaner and nastier place," University of Regina content analysis, June 1996. The *Leader-Post* published a total of 716 pages of news during the three weeks before March 2, 1996, and 700 pages during the three weeks after. Locally written news stories dropped from 2,618 in the period before the firings to 2,470 afterwards.

10. "The Ugly Executive," by David Olive, *Report on Business Magazine*, December 1996, page 17. The article pointed out that Dunlap pocketed $100 million for the sale, and the understaffed company subsequently lost market share in all three of its core businesses.

11. "Dishonorable hypocrisy," Letter to the Editor, *Toronto Star*, August 5, 1995, page D3.

12. To his credit, Southam CEO Bill Ardell condemned the Saskatchewan firings in an interview a few days later with the *Montreal Gazette*. Even though he was under pressure by Black, who at the time owned 20 percent of Southam, to cut staff and costs, Ardell said that Hollinger shouldn't have done it. "Anybody can want things to move faster. But to throw a grenade into a building is unfair to people ... and it may harm the property."

13. Interview with Steve Gibb, October 18, 1996.

14. Osika spoke to the Saskatchewan Legislature on March 8, 1996.

15. The date chosen at random was September 28, 1996. One of the few local columns left in the *Star-Phoenix* was by Les Macpherson, and it struck me as one of the silliest that I've ever read. His research consisted of looking up words in the newspaper's database to see how often they appeared. "Good," for example, appeared 1,888 times since June, compared to 605 mentions of the word "bad." Macpherson says "on balance, I think we can definitively say that the paper contains much more good than bad." After noting that the word "woman" appeared only 607 times, compared to 1,134 times for the word "man," he wrote: "I hereby give feminists my solemn undertaking to do all that I can to correct this imbalance.

Woman, woman, woman. There's three more for the database."

16. Interview with David Radler, March 25, 1997. Radler told author Peter C. Newman in 1992: "I visit the office of each prospective property at night and count the desks. That tells me how many people work there. If the place has, say, forty-two desks, I know I can put that paper out with thirty people, and that means a dozen people will be leaving the payroll even though I haven't seen their faces yet." When I talked with him, Radler denied it. He said that it happened only once, in Prince Rupert, B.C. "It was after the last ferry left and I asked the publisher how many people worked there and he said he didn't know. So we went around and counted the desks." I concluded that Radler cannot be believed on this matter.

17. Interview with Sharon Burnside, April 11, 1997.

18. Interview with Dave McLellan, May 7, 1997. McLellan said that the perception of the small Southam papers is that the editorial improvements of the *Ottawa Citizen* are "being done on our backs." In contrast to previous Southam management, Michael Sifton just gives smaller papers a number, and that's the profit margin that he wants the paper to meet; and it's always "significantly higher."

19. Carol Wall, a negotiator for the Communication, Energy and Paperworkers Union, says that readers notice the difference when a paper cuts reporters: "I say to publishers at the bargaining table, 'So you wonder why circulation's going down?' They insist that the papers have improved and can cut staff further, then they remind us of what happened in Saskatchewan. Do we want that to happen again?"

20. General manager's report, Canadian Press annual meeting, April 18, 1997.

21. Hollinger International Inc. annual report, SEC file number 001-14164, submitted March 31, 1997.

22. "Southamizing the Whig," by Jamie Swift, *Canadian Forum*, April 1994, page 9. The article points the finger of blame at Conrad Black who said, at the first Southam board meeting he attended in 1993, that 2,500 of Southam's 7,800 newspaper employees were superfluous and "shouldn't have been there." The increased number of Southam dailies has rendered those figures meaningless, but the company's annual report shows that 8,446 people were employed in 1997, nearly 500 fewer than a decade earlier when the chain consisted of thirteen newspapers. It now has thirty-five.

23. Interview with Norm DeBono, June 23, 1995.

24. "Southam plans long-term price freeze," by Brenda Dalglish, *Financial Post*, July 30, 1997, page 9. The story said that a five-cent-per-copy circulation increase translates into extra revenue of $29 million for Southam, which sold 1.6 million papers per day.

# CHAPTER FIVE

# Freedom of the Press: 2(b) or not 2(b)

The most passionate and effective defence made for freedom of the press in this country took place more than 150 years ago, in a courtroom. A young editor named Joseph Howe, whose *Novascotian* was campaigning against abuse in local government, published a letter signed "The People" that accused magistrates and police of stealing thirty thousand pounds from the pockets of the poor and distressed. Refusing to recant or identify the letter writer, Howe was accused of seditious libel and hauled into court in 1835. His case was hopeless. Under the law, he could not call witnesses or introduce evidence to prove the accusations were true. The fact that he had published something that could damage the reputation of a public man was enough in itself to convict him. Lawyers urged him to throw himself on the mercy of the court, but Howe, who had spoken only twice in public and had a bad stammer, courageously chose to defend himself. "The newspaper press," he wrote in his paper, "must be the great medium of instruction to the people." He placed his fate in the hands of the twelve jurors.

This was the dawning of the age of representative government in British North America, and Howe was guided more by a spirit of vigorous independence than by any reasoned philosophy of journalism. No doubt his lack of legal training gave him some latitude, and he certainly took advantage of it, telling the packed courtroom to remember who his accusers were: "I know them, as you know them, to be the most negligent and imbecile, if not the most reprehensible body that ever mismanaged a people's affairs."

That set the tone for the power of his remarks. He mixed high principle with sarcastic humour, saying of one grafting magistrate's family that "even the melody of Miss Roach's canary was breathed through cages manufactured at the public's expense." He described horrid conditions of neglect, which made one of the jurors break down and cry. Joseph Howe spoke for more than six hours without a note. It has been called one of the greatest orations in Canadian history, and his closing words rang with conviction: "Will you, my countrymen, permit the sacred fires of liberty, brought by our fathers from the venerable temples of

# Freedom of the Press: 2(b) or not 2(b)

Britain, to be quenched and trodden out on the simple altars they have raised? I conjure you ... to leave an unshackled press as a legacy to your children."

Although the presiding judge was a man whom Howe had attacked in print for nepotism and meddling in politics, and although he directed the jurors to find Howe guilty as charged, they took just ten minutes to find him innocent. A biographer tells what happened next:

> It was impossible for the bench to keep order. The excitement spread to the corridor, down the broad steps and out into Granville Street, and when Joe emerged the crowd swept down on him, shook his hand, hugged him, clapped him on the back, and some cried. Then, hoisting him on their shoulders, they bore him through the cheering, laughing crowd to his front door.[1]

Howe succeeded in justifying the libertarian principle that the government is the servant of the people, not its master. "Be sure," he told his supporters, "to teach your children the names of the twelve men who have just established freedom of the press in Nova Scotia."

When I walked into Courtroom One on the second floor of Toronto's Osgoode Hall on the last day of January 1994, I hoped to hear the modern version of Howe's eloquence and conviction. The issue at stake was no less important: the right of the public to learn details of one of Canada's most sensational murder cases and to decide for themselves whether justice was being done. Instead, the high-vaulted and windowless chamber almost seemed to sag under the weight of jurisprudence and legal precedents. Lining the aisles were cardboard boxes containing copies of the fifty-three legal depositions, some hundreds of pages thick. Perhaps soured by what one lawyer called "our paper problem," the mood of the five Ontario Court of Appeal justices on the bench was feisty and impatient, especially that of the acerbic Chief Justice Charles Dubin, who acted as if something foul, foreign and faintly disreputable had crept into his domain.

Before him, filling most of the courtroom, were two Crown prosecutors and sixteen lawyers representing the heavyweights of the Canadian media—the biggest newspaper, the *Toronto Star*; the most prestigious, the *Globe and Mail*; the largest television network, the CBC; the new colossus of cable television, Rogers Communications Inc.; the giant Thomson newspaper chain; and the tabloid *Toronto Sun*. This unlikely alliance was gathered in a common cause to argue for the lifting of a six-month-old court order that dropped a veil of secrecy over details of how two Niagara-area teenagers had died, and how one of their killers had been dealt with. Twenty-five reporters, hungry for the right to write what many of them already knew, leaned forward to catch every legalistic word. There were only eight seats left in the small courtroom to accommodate the public, which everyone in the room—the judges, the media, the lawyers and the government—purported to represent.

There was a carnival atmosphere about the proceedings. In the hallway outside, Gordon Domm, a former police officer who was campaigning against the media ban, handed out copies of a *Newsweek* article in defiance of the law. An Ontario Provincial Police sergeant and two commissionaires turned a blind eye, although Domm was later tried and convicted for distributing banned material. Nearby, author William Deverell had to line up for scarce spectator tickets because *Saturday Night* magazine, which flew him up from Costa Rica to cover the hearing, forgot to arrange press accreditation. None of Joseph Howe's journalistic descendants, no publishers or editors, bothered to show up, except for *Toronto Star* editor John Honderich, who slipped in twice briefly to watch.

Two and a half years had passed since June 15, 1991, when Grade 9 student Leslie Mahaffy failed to come home from school in Burlington, Ontario. Two weeks later, a man fishing in Lake Gibson discovered her body, which had been cut up with a power saw and encased in concrete. On that same day a wedding occurred in Niagara Falls, joining Paul Bernardo and Karla Homolka in holy matrimony. They would later be charged with Leslie Mahaffy's abduction and killing, as well as the death, in April 1992, of 15-year-old Kristen French, who was abducted on her way home from school in nearby St. Catharines. Her raped and nude body was found in a ditch. The brutal killings of the two young girls shocked their communities and led to unprecedented and competitive media coverage—so much, in fact, that Mr. Justice Francis Kovacs banned the public from the trial of Karla Homolka in July 1993, and ordered the Canadian media not to report on the key details of her plea, the description of evidence and the statements of the victims' families. His reason was that "widespread, massive and repetitive coverage" of the case would jeopardize the subsequent trial of Paul Bernardo. The press called the judge's reasons absurd and launched an appeal of the order.

In the meantime, international media excluded from Kovacs' courtroom began to publish and broadcast details of Homolka's trial, raising the very real question of whether any ban on publicity could be effective in an age of instant electronic communications. These stories were available to anyone with a computer and a modem. The ridiculous efforts required to police the ban—including cable-TV producers zapping out offending American signals and officials confiscating extra copies of U.S. newspapers at the border—raised a public debate that quickly spread to other provinces.

So now, when Canada's most sensational and controversial murder case was surfacing finally in open court, it wasn't a defendant named Homolka or Bernardo who was on trial. It was the media. If there was any doubt about that, it was dispelled when Chief Justice Dubin interrupted Ian Binnie, the lawyer for the CBC, a few minutes into his argument on behalf of "the right of other people—the people of Canada—to know the basis of how the case was handled." Dubin, coiled like a skilled counter-puncher and peering through thick round glasses, asked if Binnie was sure that the media had the right to represent the public. This of course was a key argument of the provincial Crown attorney's office, which said "the media are not elected" (perhaps forgetting that neither judges nor Crown attorneys are either).

In choosing this case to mount such a vigorous constitutional challenge on behalf of press freedom, the media were guilty of some of the excesses and lack of proportion that they often exhibit in their news judgment. Bernardo and Homolka were murderous monsters, and the public was much more interested in seeing them brought to justice than in reading or viewing more lurid details about how they did it. One letter writer criticized the *Vancouver Sun* for editorializing against the ban, saying that if "Bernardo's lawyer were successful in finding one technicality that allowed a guilty man to walk free, then what value is there to media scrutiny? I would rather have results than a story."

The judges, particularly Dubin, seemed to be using the Crown's 140-page factum as something of a script with which to question the media lawyers, particularly concerning its assertion that the power of the mass media was a dangerous force in society since they had "the ability to control others while remaining resistant to control by others." Allowing the press to pursue commercial advantage without limit would be unacceptable, it said, and urged the judiciary, on behalf of the public, to "watch the watchdog" by imposing control. This ran counter to the centuries-old libertarian theories of philosophers such as John Stuart Mill, who argued that the free exchange of information was a far better safeguard to truth than intervention by the state, which may have vested interests itself. That undoubtedly was true in this court, since Chief Justice Dubin administered the very judicial system whose judgment was being questioned.

It quickly became clear that the media lawyers, representing an all-star team of rich and prosperous law firms, were not up to the job of successfully defending their clients' constitutional rights before such a hostile court. If ever there was a time when newspapers had to mount a convincing rationale for freedom of the press, this was it. After all, Judge Kovacs' ban violated the spirit and letter of section 2(b) of the *Canadian Charter of Rights and Freedoms,* which guarantees "freedom of thought, belief, opinion and expression, including freedom of the press and other media of information." Canada's courts have recently chosen to override that right in an alarming number of instances in order to protect a competing right, such as a defendant's privacy, business dealings or right to a fair trial. To win this case, the media would have to convince these judges that freedom of expression was the basis for all other freedoms and was too vital to be trumped in a case such as this where Karla Homolka's swift, silent trial and light sentence—twelve years for manslaughter, with possibility for parole in four—suggested a plea-bargain deal that the public should have the right to scrutinize. That they failed utterly to do that tells volumes about the sorry state our press is in. It has, almost by default, made itself vulnerable to the argument that, as a commercial business, its interests are more concerned with the marketplace than with the public's right to know; that it does not seek the public's consent for acting as its surrogate and does not explain how it decides what should be on the public's agenda; that it insists on operating without self-restraint or accountability; and that there are no commonly accepted standards of responsibility to ensure that its freedom is properly executed. By not being able to articulate why freedom of the press is important to us, and by not living up to the responsibility that should go with it, the press is in danger of losing the public support so necessary for its preservation.

All of us have a stake in this. The limits of our freedom of expression are largely defined by the battles that the mass media fight on our behalf. Thus, if the Canadian government were to resort to arbitrary measures, such as interning a group of citizens in time of strife, as it did with Japanese-Canadians and Quebec separatists, we would want to know so that we would have a chance to debate it. Censorship and control are the enemies of democratic debate; Canadians cannot be fully informed unless a wide spectrum of ideas is presented for public consideration. We cannot direct our elected representatives to make laws on our behalf if we are denied information, even if it is upsetting or objectionable to some of us. If vital public institutions, such as our system of justice, are to work fairly, they must be scrutinized on our behalf. Too many Canadians are ignorant of the seventeen words in section 2(b) that give constitutional protection to various types of "fundamental" freedoms. Because of its commercial nature, freedom of the press is in many ways the most vulnerable of those freedoms. Too often it is invoked as a shield to protect journalists who invade our privacy or newspapers that make huge profits out of publishing the results. It is almost never brought up as a public value until there is a juicy story to cover that might sell more papers.[2]

In Courtroom One, the CBC's Binnie and a parade of other lawyers argued that, while freedom of the press is not absolute, it should not be curtailed until the Crown proves that it would prejudice a fair trial. Indeed, section 1 of the *Charter* says that any limit to such freedoms should be both "reasonable" and "demonstrably justified," implying some onus on the Crown to prove its case for a publicity ban. Instead, Binnie argued, Judge Kovacs relied on an "eyeball judgment" that Bernardo's jurors might be influenced by what they read beforehand. There is, he said, no evidence that this has ever been so, and no legal basis for arguing that the right of an accused to a fair trial is automatically more important than the "public interest in knowing what happened in that courtroom .... Was justice done and, if it was done, was it done fairly?"[3] Dubin interrupted, agreeing with the Crown's contention that coverage of Homolka's trial wasn't banned but simply delayed until after Bernardo's trial, which might take two years. "That's available," Dubin told Binnie. "Not today, maybe, but it will be." Binnie replied: "We submit that the right to know is the right to know now."

This exchange brought to mind Patrick O'Callaghan's famous dismissal of attempts to get the newspapers that he once published to hold off printing something that they knew in order to protect someone. Such attempts, he said, are usually self-serving and accompanied by some pledge to provide the full facts eventually, which he likened to "the empty promises a billion virgins have heard just before the lights go out in the bedroom."[4]

Dubin and the other justices had trouble understanding why the media objected to what the Crown called Judge Kovacs' "publicity deferral order." It would take more than empty rhetoric to persuade them that rendering a "contemporaneous" report was a key role of the news media. But nothing else was offered. On the final day, poised and confident Crown Attorney Casey Hill pointed across the courtroom and declared, quite correctly, that the legion of media lawyers had not identified one issue connected with Homolka's trial that couldn't be debated "later."

You'd think the media would have learned something from the increasing number of court-imposed publication bans suffered in recent years. In some of the cases, real harm was done that media scrutiny could have prevented. In 1992, when police in Saskatchewan laid 170 charges against nine members of an alleged child-abuse cult—including a town constable, two former police chiefs and an RCMP constable—the small town of Martensville was traumatized. Publication of all testimony was banned to protect the young witnesses and to ensure a fair trial for the accused. What was suppressed came out only nineteen months later when only two people had been convicted on fifteen charges; all other charges were dropped, including those against the four police officers, whose reputations and careers were nevertheless damaged. The publication ban had kept secret the questionable testimony of the chief Crown witness, a boy of seven, who claimed that one of the defendants (a woman, who was one of those freed) cut off the nipple of one child and swallowed it. Yet no child with a missing nipple was found. The same boy said that he had been molested on a waterbed in a storage shed, but there was no waterbed and no shed. Nor was there any medical evidence that an axe handle and a vibrator had been shoved into several of the boys or that acid had been poured on anyone's face. Expert witnesses (whose testimony at the trial could not be reported) said that the police questioning of the young boys was unprofessional and that it had probably coerced them into making the sensational allegations. Despite all evidence to the contrary, Saskatchewan Justice Minister Robert Mitchell, whose crown attorneys had requested the publication ban in the first place, refused to call a judicial inquiry to find out how the law had gone wrong. The issue is public scrutiny of the courts, and if justice is to be served, it can't wait for "later."

The increasing concentration of ownership has been one factor in cutting away the moral high ground from newspapers in such cases. David Lepofsky, a brilliant constitutional lawyer working for the Ontario Attorney-General's Ministry, challenges the very idea of the corporate press being a surrogate for the public. "News organizations will appear in court, from time to time, to assert

... that they are attempting to enforce the public's rights," he wrote prophetically in 1991.[5] "Yet they secure no prior authorization from the public before doing so. Many members of the public may well not agree with the position purportedly being advanced in their name." Lepofsky decided that "news outlets, like the producers of any product or service consumed by the public, can be properly seen as private operations" that have no special rights and over which the public has no effective control. And this came up again and again as the five judges peppered the media lawyers with questions. Dubin, for example, interrupted counsel for Thomson Newspapers by observing: "Sometimes I wonder if the press acknowledges self-interest.... It's not altruistic." In other words, the press is as much interested in selling newspapers and in making a profit as it is in defending the public's right to know. And no one sitting before him, certainly not a gang of lawyers paid $350 an hour by Canada's largest media owners, was in a position to argue.

But there was another reason that the media were in trouble in Courtroom One. The Crown's bulky factum put them squarely on trial for what it called a significant quantity of coverage that "departed from lawfully accepted standards." Media restraint in the Homolka case, it said, had been abandoned.

> Much of the reporting was grossly sensational and reprehensible and obnoxious to the *sub judice* principle in its prejudicial impact. Some of the media, apparently operating upon the misconception that the public's right to know is exhaustive and inalienable, purported to advance freedom of expression by such coverage as a bidding war for the Bernardos' wedding pictures.

A supplement to the factum contained 394 pages of news reports from such papers as the *Toronto Star*, the *Toronto Sun* and the *St. Petersburg Times*, news services such as the Canadian Press and Reuters, and broadcasting outlets such as the CBC and CITY-TV. Much of this collection had been tabled as Exhibit One before Mr. Justice Kovacs, and it was the chief reason that he decided to put a stop to such saturation coverage. It was no less influential at the Court of Appeal, where Dubin and others leafed through the supplement, citing articles that concerned them (topics included the *Toronto Sun's* successful bid of $10,000 for the wedding pictures and an analysis of Paul Bernardo's handwriting). Dubin, who openly sympathized with Kovacs for issuing the gag order, said that the media were very close to advocating trial by media instead of trial by jury. He interrupted Peter Jacobsen, counsel for the *Globe and Mail*, and stated: "The nature of the stories, I thought, should be of concern to responsible media people." When Bert Bruser, representing the *Star*, tried to argue that the coverage was neither prejudicial nor constituted contempt, he was cut off and told to sit down.

The effect of all of this left Exhibit One—six months of laboriously collected news coverage of the Homolka-Bernardo case, and its indictment by the Crown—unchallenged as an example of how the media abused their power and forfeited the right to freedom of the press. Even though it was available to them, no newspapers wrote any articles casting a critical eye on Exhibit One's findings. When I examined it later, I was alarmed at the scurrilous exaggerations in it. For example, the Crown charged that the *Toronto Star* ran a story linking Paul Bernardo's arrest to 110 unsolved slayings of women in southwestern Ontario in the last twenty years. This was disturbing enough to make me look up the story, and it was not what it was made out to be. Bernardo's arrest was featured in the lead of the twenty-eight-paragraph story. The second last paragraph quoted the founder of a victim's rights group. And the very last paragraph contained background on the group, which had been formed out of concerns about a twenty-year history of unsolved slayings. If a reporter and not the Crown attorney's office had written such an irresponsible summary of this article, he or she might have been fired.

I had my own problems with some of the news coverage of the Bernardo case and in fact was quoted approvingly in Exhibit One: "It is respectfully submitted that Professor John Miller accurately depicted the coverage as 'a circus.'" This I did, more or less, in an article published in the *Globe and Mail* immediately after Kovacs issued his order. My opinion piece began: "Anyone who knows anything about how a newsroom works must now realize that, in losing its right to report fully on the trial of Karla Homolka, the press probably got what it deserved."[6] I criticized what I saw as a "media free-for-all," which produced "some" coverage that violated both the basic legal presumption of innocence and the policies of the news organizations involved—for instance, rules covering the use of anonymous sources, mainly police officers, who were quoted frequently and who painted an unflattering picture of Bernardo's character. Between February 1993, when he was named as the prime suspect in the Mahaffy-French slayings, and May of that year, when his name finally appeared on a murder warrant, Paul Bernardo's life was laid bare in the press. We were told that he had declared bankruptcy, that he had been charged with beating his wife, that he drank heavily and chased women, that his father had a criminal record, that he once killed an animal in revenge (his pet iguana, for biting him), that his wife might testify against him, that seven hundred pieces of evidence were taken out of his rented home and that police with other unsolved murders on their hands were reopening their investigations. The *Toronto Sun* ran his picture under the caption "Crime of the Century," three months before he was charged in the case. Whenever such coverage was criticized, I found the press to be typically snappish, thin-skinned and unrepentant, and after my article appeared I got a taste of that defensiveness myself. At a wake for a former colleague, a reporter involved in the coverage angrily berated me and said that he was ashamed that I, the chair of the journalism school from which he had graduated, was so uninformed.

There is simply no way that the press should have tried to defend some of that coverage. While it did not technically constitute contempt—media lawyers would argue that publicity so far in advance of trial was not likely to influence prospective jurors—some stories amounted to unbridled pack journalism of the worst kind, each newspaper and broadcast outlet tripping over the other to get the latest morsel to feed what it saw as a voracious public appetite. The public interest and the noble aim of scrutinizing the justice system took a back seat to the furious competition to sell newspapers, especially in Toronto. "This is a very competitive news town," said the managing editor of the *Sun*, defending his coverage. "Our readers have a very high interest in this story." In the process, the Canadian media lost what had always been their moral high ground—that at least they're not like *American newspapers*. The extra protection afforded the news media there under the First Amendment to the U.S. constitution—that "Congress shall make no law ... abridging the freedom of speech or of the press"—has produced excessive coverage of crime, which the Canadian media have always condemned. Yet on June 8, 1993, the *Buffalo News* punctured that myth forever. It found newsworthy the Ontario media stampede for lurid details of the Homolka investigation, and its story began:

> ST. CATHARINES—It is Monday afternoon. Alex Urosevic is stand-
> ing on Dundonald Rd., holding what appears to be a small cannon on
> the end of a pole. But it isn't a cannon, it's a camera with a 600 mm lens,
> powerful enough to read a street sign from a block away. Or, in this
> case, photograph a murder suspect from across the road.
>
> Urosevic, who works for the tabloid *Toronto Sun*, has been here
> since 7.30 a.m. He will stay until 4 p.m. It is sunny, it is hot, he is not
> moving.
>
> Urosevic is pursuing the Holy Grail of southern Ontario journal-
> ism, at least for this week—a clear photo of Karla Homolka ....
>
> Many, maybe most, people think the media is too intrusive. They
> see reporters run like lemmings after a subject, crowd someone into a
> corner, stake out an accused murderer's house. The method is repel-
> lent. But Alex Urosevic knows if he gets a clear photo of Karla
> Homolka, the *Sun* will sell a lot more papers than usual.

The *Buffalo News* piece was unusual in its candor. It had no equivalent in the Canadian media, which never covered what it was doing and instead lashed out (as the *Ottawa Citizen* did) against critics such as Ontario attorney-general Marion Boyd for using her "bully pulpit" in a "clumsy attempt to frighten the media into political correctness." In the end, both the *Toronto Star* and *Sun* did print pictures of Homolka in a bathing suit in the backyard of her parents' home, and the *Star* privately boasted that it had a topless picture but decided not to use *that*, as if it was to be admired for its restraint. I wrote a letter to the editor of the

*Star* in which I questioned the paper's judgment. These extreme measures were taken not to get news that society might need but to titillate readers and to get them to buy the paper. "Similar behavior by the British tabloid press," I said in the letter, "has led to calls for privacy laws to protect people from journalists. Keep up your good work and we'll have that here, too."

By the time Casey Hill got up to make his summation for the Crown in the Court of Appeal, the five justices had roughed up the media lawyers so thoroughly that they were commiserating with each other grimly in the hall-ways. "There's one advantage to being up last," a lawyer for Rogers Communications said to a colleague. "It's that there are enough bodies already on the floor to cushion the blow." Hill, young, vigorous and poised, said that both the quantity of the coverage and its nature had persuaded Mr. Justice Kovacs that there was a substantial risk to Paul Bernardo's fair trial. Although Hill said that he was not trying to put the media on trial, he quickly added that "a substantial number of stories ... do make a mockery of fair trial rights and do have the effect of stripping the presumption of innocence to little more than a hollow label." It was an argument that the media might have rebutted by citing a Southam-Angus Reid poll that showed that 74 percent of people in Ontario claimed to have no knowledge of banned details of Homolka's trial, and that it was probably still possible to empanel an impartial jury. But no one did so, and it was probably an argument that the media weren't going to win. Clearly, the overriding public interest in the Bernardo case was in bringing the murderer to justice. Any suggestion that the race for news might jeopardize this in any way was going to render meaningless all of the high-minded rhetoric offered by the media lawyers—that freedom of the press is being threatened, that the public has a right to know, that justice must be seen in order to be done. The behaviour of the media called these principles into question. It was simply the wrong case, argued the wrong way, before the wrong court.[7]

To fight such battles on behalf of the public, the press first needs a sound argument for why freedom of expression and the press should matter to all of us. Empty and self-serving rhetoric will not do the job. The Ontario Press Council's Willard Estey certainly had much to contribute to this. "Arbitrary power," he told a conference of Canadian managing editors in April 1994, "is the enemy of the community." There is a high degree of potential for manipulation of the justice system by provincial politicians and bureaucrats, he said, and the only safeguard against it is to expose it to "hourly, daily, weekly surveillance."

Estey wrote in 1990 that the press has "a duty and obligation and right" to allow the democratic process to work by supplying accurate facts and opinions on all public matters.[8] It must act as "a bulwark between the people and the state; and between the individual in his enjoyment of life and statism." He added that "it is a discovery of the 20th century that the democratic state can become a tyrant in much the same way as can the totalitarian state." Surveillance by the press is needed because the power of the state manifests itself in the tiniest details of our daily lives, telling us when and how fast we can drive, how much we are paid to work, when we have to retire, how much noise we can make, when we can shop, how often we can water the lawn, whether we can improve our property and how the clothes on our back are made. Virtually the only check against "the over-exuberance of the bureaucrat" is the free and independent press. At the same time, Estey wrote, the press must be responsible. The public must be assured that it is behaving with fairness, independence and integrity. Defamation laws are one such check on the press. So are codes of ethics, press councils and other forms of self-regulation. "Thus," Estey said, "we see a finely balanced set of machinery with mingled sources of authority and fibres of discipline all in delicate balance and offsetting one another. The end product is democracy itself; the immediate product is a free press useful to the community."

If only things worked as effectively as Estey said they do. It is fair to argue that the press failed to regulate itself in covering the Homolka case, but that is to miss the point. Despite the fact that we have had two extensive examinations of the conduct of the press in the last twenty-five years—the Davey Committee in 1970 and the Kent Royal Commission in 1981—neither produced any document that defines the nature, the importance and the responsibility of the press in Canadian society. We desperately need one, to help set the proper balance of competing rights in our post-*Charter* public life.

In simple fact, it's more important than ever before that Canadians have newspapers that they can trust and respect. More than any other news media, newspapers decide what the public will know. They even decide, by how they frame news events, what we *feel* about what we know. At a time of rapid globalization of so much of our economic, political and cultural life, the unique gatekeeping role that newspapers play is vital to the healthy working of our democratic society. It therefore follows that we, as responsible citizens, must begin to hold newspapers to ever-higher standards, not only for the accuracy, completeness, scope and tone of their reporting, but for the social responsibility of their mission. Pointing out that today's society cannot afford to leave the media entirely to their own devices, Allan Hutchison once said: "While it is essential that we have a free press in a democratic society, we must equally strive for a democratic press in a free society."[9] He meant that the public has a stake in how the media are run and in whose interest they operate.

One of the most thoughtful justices on the Ontario bench, Justice Rosalie Abella of the Court of Appeal, calls this relationship between public and media "a kind of fiduciary" one and says that media that keep their motives secret cannot inspire any more confidence than judges who mete out justice in private. In their influence over public opinion, the media are far more powerful than even the judiciary, she said, and therein lies a problem:

The courts operate according to accepted legal standards and principles and can be judged accordingly; the media, which regrettably under-reaches by treating itself (sic) as a trade rather than a profession, operates according to no overriding governing code and cannot as easily be held to account .... The courts judge only those disputes before them; the media judges anything and anyone it wants. Judges, ever since the Magna Carta, have been truly independent, and can only be removed from office for manifest breaches of public confidence; the independence of journalists, on the other hand, is frequently circum-scribed by the philosophies and economies of their owners.[10]

Newspapers do not make a habit of explaining what freedom of the press means to Canadians, and there is little evidence that they've actually even thought deeply about it. There are those, in the media, in government, in business and in private life, who invoke it for selfish ends, such as freedom to make money, freedom from offensive ideas or freedom to be left alone, even if that requires immunity from discussion altogether because of past inequities. It is here that the press, with its financial interest in appealing to the greatest number of readers and advertisers, is sometimes content to let its higher duty get left behind in the race for commercial approval. Freedom is like muscle: use it or lose it. The press may be concerned that the system of justice is increasingly being closed to public scrutiny, but it has failed to make us care except when it can't get in to cover a sensational trial. It may be concerned that freedom of expression and the press is at risk, but it has failed to monitor the little battles in everyday life that weaken it. It may contend that it exercises its freedom responsibly, but it has done little to hold its standards up to public scrutiny, and of course it has made a point of not covering itself.

Estey's idea of balancing press freedom with press responsibility is a precarious task. Too much freedom can lead to arrogant self-interest, just as too much responsibility can limit the scope of "truths" that we have to debate. Since print journalists are not licensed or regulated in Canada, other than by the law, the balancing act must be largely self-administered, and this is where the problem lies. For us to believe ourselves well-served by our press, we need to understand the standards by which they gather the news. Yet this concept is as foreign to the minds of Canadian publishers and editors as the quaint notion that newspapers are, above all else, a public trust. They go to extraordinary lengths to hide what they do from public scrutiny.

I learned this first hand when I was asked to sit on the editorial committee of the Canadian Daily Newspaper Association in 1993, the first outsider so honoured. At the time, the seventeen-member committee of editors was wres-tling with how to update the organization's Statement of Principles, which was drawn up in 1977 and offered at least the pretence of ethical and practical rules by which the performance of the press could be measured. When it was adopted, it was intended as a high-minded declaration that would raise the standards of

Canada's newspapers and hold them accountable to the public. It said, for example, that "the newspaper keeps faith with its readers by presenting the news comprehensively, accurately and fairly, and by acknowledging its mistakes promptly." This meant that facts should not be distorted by over-emphasis, that quotations should always be in context, that headlines should not go beyond the facts in the story. Newspapers, it said, should respect the right to privacy, not endanger anyone's right to a fair trial and "give expression to the interests of ... the less powerful elements in society." All outside interests that could affect, or appear to affect, the newspaper's freedom to report the news impartially should be avoided. Above all, the chief obligation of the press was "fidelity to the public good."

There was nothing in these principles that the publisher of your local newspaper would hesitate to put in a public speech, but there were nevertheless two problems that nobody had foreseen when they were drafted by two great editors of the *Toronto Star*, Martin Goodman and Borden Spears. The first was that few people outside of publishers' offices were aware of them. I spent almost ten years as a newspaper editor in blissful ignorance, even though many of the principles directly affected the way in which I should have been doing my job. I learned of their existence only when I began to draw together and update the *Star's* editorial policy manual in 1985. The first sentence of the Statement of Principles stated: "Newspapers have individual codes of ethics and this declaration of principles is intended to complement them in their healthy diversity." I knew this to be untrue as soon as I'd read it. After all, there I was working at the biggest newspaper in the country, and we had no code other than a few yellowed sheets that I had retrieved from the bottom of somebody's drawer. Not many other newspapers have written codes of conduct even today, as a show of hands at the 1994 Canadian managing editor's conference indicated. More than forty editors attended, but only five put up their hands when the question was asked.

The second problem was that, if you write down your principles, someone might expect you to live up to them. This appears to scare the hell out of some people, especially the lawyers who have to defend the conduct of newspapers in court. So, at a meeting of the legal affairs subcommittee of the CDNA early in 1994, its members voted 4–3 to abolish the 1977 Statement of Principles and come up with a substitute that wouldn't cause any legal embarrassments. This move was led by the three lawyers on the subcommittee, representing Southam, Thomson and the *Toronto Sun*. Minutes of the meeting said: "They were concerned that some of the principles could be challenged in court and reflect negatively on a newspaper's position." This concern was hypothetical; nobody could recall a newspaper losing a libel case because it had failed to live up to its written principles. Nevertheless, the motion to abolish them was sent on to the editorial committee together with a brief four-point substitute drafted by the CDNA's legal counsel, Stuart Robertson. Its language was legalistic rather than noble, full of what lawyers like to call "weasel words." It began: "Each daily newspaper in Canada should make every reasonable effort at all times to maintain its integrity." The part about "fidelity to the public good" was replaced with the phrase "Each daily newspaper ... should determine its own method of conducting its own business." Instead of "every person has a right to privacy," the new statement said that newspapers should ensure that those who prepare the content "are cognizant of the interests of those persons who might be affected by the publication of information in the newspaper." There wasn't a lot on which to hang your hat, let alone the credibility of a newspaper.

When the editorial division committee met, with me as its newest member, this new draft was described as "our watered-down version" by John Honderich. I was horrified. It was like watching doctors sit down in a room and vote to abandon the Hippocratic oath on grounds that it could get them in trouble someday. I said that abandoning the principles would send a poor message to the industry and the public, but the discussion veered off into public relations and damage control. Alan Allnutt, managing editor of the *Montreal Gazette*, said that any move to abandon the principles would have to be done carefully so as not to give the impression that the association is dumping it. After some discussion, it became clear that many of the editors had problems with certain phrases in the 1977 Statement of Principles and wanted to abandon it, but there was no enthusiasm for Stuart Robertson's substitute. Several expressed their uneasiness with abolishing such an important document and having nothing to put in its place, no matter how symbolic. So, having reached both an impasse and the limit of our attention spans, we put the matter over to the next meeting.

A few weeks later, I learned about a decision of the Ontario Press Council that seemed to demonstrate the value to the public of written codes of conduct by newspapers. It partially upheld a complaint against the *Kitchener-Waterloo Record* because its editors did something that breached the rules in their own internal ethics code and certainly offended the spirit of the CDNA principles. The complaint was from a Kitchener woman who was held hostage with her two young children in a terrifying sixteen-hour ordeal. She reluctantly gave an interview to a *Record* reporter and was shocked to discover two months later that the reporter had sold her photograph and story to the sensationalist supermarket tabloid *National Enquirer*. This was done privately, even though the *Record's* written code of conduct required the reporter to get the newspaper's approval. The woman told the press council: "Can you imagine having pictures of yourself, along with your two very young children, in such a trashy publication? I trusted my local paper to be ethical. People actually believe that I sold my story to the *National Enquirer*." Although the *Record* at first tried to defend itself by saying that the *Enquirer's* story was, after all, accurate, it agreed to toughen up its own policy on resales. The fact that any fair-minded member of the public would agree with the press council's decision is beside the point. Newspapers were seen to have rules of fairness that they could be held accountable for, and that could serve only to improve their credibility. I made up my mind not to let the Canadian newspaper industry deprive the public of explicit guidelines for how it goes about its business.

When the editorial committee met on January 27, 1995, in the windowless, eleventh-floor boardroom of the association's downtown Toronto offices, we were presented with a new motion, one that proposed doing away with the 1977 Statement of Principles altogether because it is "out of date, has been superseded by events and recent decisions of the Supreme Court of Canada, and is prejudicial to members of the CDNA." It would be replaced by nothing. Newspapers would be mailed a fill-in-the-blanks letter encouraging them to voluntarily commit themselves to meeting certain expectations, the first of which was to "represent the public's curiosity." There was no mention of the importance of accuracy, the need to avoid conflicts of interest, the limits of freedom of the press or the importance of balanced and fair reporting. Michael Doody, counsel for Thomson Newspapers, described the 1977 statement as dangerous because it put responsibilities and liabilities on each of the association's eighty-two member newspapers. "It's like begging people to sue you," he told us.

To my alarm, most of the editors present seemed to be willing to go for it. They represented such prestigious news organizations as the Canadian Press, *Globe and Mail*, *Ottawa Citizen*, *Toronto Star*, *Winnipeg Free Press*, *Kitchener Record* and *Windsor Star*, and they were sitting there and abandoning the principles that had guided their industry for eighteen years. Some just seemed tired of talking about it. Others, like Rick Laiken of the *Ottawa Citizen*, asked why the newspaper industry should have a list of principles since it had no power to enforce them—nor should it, he said, because the CDNA was primarily a lobby and resource group. Earle Gill of the *Globe and Mail*, who had moved to abolish the statement, made the somewhat disingenuous point that newspapers are responsible to their readers directly, not through an association. He neglected to mention that his paper has no written code of conduct to help readers measure the *Globe's* performance. When I objected that abolishing industry-wide principles would be a retrograde step and that other bodies, including the courts, might be tempted to fill the void by setting our standards for us in legal judgments, the editors stopped talking about the main issue—how newspapers can best stand accountable to their readers—and began talking about spin control and public relations. Laiken said that the CDNA could inform the public that, since most newspapers had their own codes of ethics, there was no need for the newspaper industry to have one anymore. That's when I knew we were in trouble. After less than an hour's discussion, the vote was decided 6-1 to abolish. I was the only person there who felt that Canadian newspapers still needed to have industry-wide standards.

For the next month, I had a long wrestle with my conscience. There was no doubt in my mind that the publishers who sat on the CDNA board would quietly endorse the decision at their April meeting. Publishers are even more squeamish than editors at being exposed to potential legal problems, and Doody would be on hand to argue that the 1977 statement was dangerous. I also had no confidence that the public would ever find out about it. After all, none of the editors who had voted to abolish the principles had found it newsworthy enough to assign one of their reporters to write about it. Perhaps they felt that the deliberations of the editorial committee were confidential, perhaps they didn't want to break ranks with the "club," or perhaps they realized that their decision would be difficult to justify in public. I felt all of those things, but I felt something even more keenly: that it was wrong for newspapers to retreat from the little public accountability offered their readers and that they should be strengthening, not weakening, the standards agreed to eighteen years earlier. Using the hypothetical example of doctors abolishing the Hippocratic oath, I began asking friends for their reactions. Those who had no connection to the media said that they'd be outraged. Those who did said that it would be one hell of a news story. So I decided to make it a news story.

I wrote an opinion page article describing the vote and questioning its wisdom, saying that it raises questions about the professionalism and accountability of the press in Canada. I quoted Clark Davey, former publisher of the *Ottawa Citizen* who helped approve the 1977 statement, as saying that abolishing it was an act of madness. And I informed readers: "Now you have a vote, too. You can cast it by writing a letter to the editor of your favourite newspaper."

The first paper that I approached to run it was the *Globe and Mail*, but it refused on grounds that the subject "concerns the newspaper" and editor William Thorsell wanted to run a more balanced account.[11] Instead, I faxed the article to all of the other newspapers represented at the editorial committee meeting. It was published by four of them, and almost before the ink was dry two important things happened: there was a strong public reaction against the decision, which was gratifying, and I felt the chill of thin-skinned disapproval from my friends in the newspaper business, which was hardly surprising. The *Ottawa Citizen* followed up my column with one from Laiken, its assistant managing editor, accusing me of shoddy ethics and saying that the principles were just a collection of "motherhood pronouncements." A reader disagreed, saying that he was alarmed to learn that "our press freedoms are at stake" and that the editors who voted to abolish the 1977 statement "must drop their monumental arrogance towards their readers .... If our national press resists any commitment to ethics, then we can no longer tolerate the existence of newspaper monopolies."[12] *Winnipeg Free Press* editor Duncan McMonagle felt the need to point out to his readers that the six votes to abolish the principles were cast by hard-working newspaper editors, while the only vote against was from "a Toronto university teacher." This catty attitude was typical of the editors whose closed-door vote I had just exposed. Jim Poling, vice-president of the Canadian Press, wrote to accuse me of unethical conduct, betrayal of confidence and dirty journalism. I wrote back to say that a public debate about newspaper standards was clearly helpful and necessary and wouldn't have happened any other way. "The fact I made it happen shouldn't be the issue," I said. "The issue is what responsibilities we have toward the public. I happen to think this should matter a lot to all of us." The CDNA got enough calls of protest from people to realize that it had a hot potato on its hands, and when the board of directors met in May, it quickly voted to overturn the decision of the editors. We were told bluntly to update and approve a new Statement of Principles.

The lawyers were outraged by my end-run. Blair Mackenzie, counsel for Southam newspapers, wanted the CDNA to discipline me for going public before the final vote. "It is very difficult for our subcommittee to give advice to CDNA, let alone for any member of the board of CDNA to discharge his or her duties adequately, if conduct of this kind is to be accepted as routine," Mackenzie said.[13] Members of the editorial committee were no more charitable when we met in May. Old friends gave me the cold shoulder and I half expected to be kicked off the committee. What I didn't expect was a 180-degree change in attitude about the value of industry-wide standards. Southam editors, including Ian Haysom of the *Vancouver Sun* and Jim Bruce of the *Windsor Star*, said that their organization now felt that the CDNA should have a strong Statement of Principles and that the proposed draft resubmitted by Stuart Robertson would not stand up to public scrutiny. I agreed, saying that any new statement should articulate the value of freedom of the press to the public and the responsibility of newspapers to their communities. It should also have some stirring language and poetry about it. I moved that we appoint a committee to spend the summer redrafting the 1977 statement. I agreed to recruit its members but demurred when someone nominated me as head of the group. I felt that the role should be performed by an active newspaper editor, and Duncan McMonagle volunteered. This was accepted by a vote of 11–1. Ian Haysom said that this controversy should serve as a lesson for newspapers to let the public know more often that freedom of the press is buttressed by commonly accepted principles of reporting.

The first person recruited to join our committee was Clark Davey, who served as a link to the group of visionaries who drafted the 1977 statement.[14] At one of our first meetings he brought a document that was a sobering reminder of just how far Canada's publishers had strayed from their idealism of two decades earlier. It was drafted in 1977 by Cleo Mowers, publisher of the *Lethbridge Herald*, and it was entitled "The People and Their Press":

> Free people must know. Self-government cannot be sustained on ignorance. Democracy requires understanding of each other's concerns and aspirations. Communication is essential.
>     The daily press is the chief medium of communication, for it puts the news in context, in detail, and on the record. In a country as diverse

and complex as Canada and in an age as confused and frustrating as this, the Canadian daily press is particularly critical to the health of the nation and of society.

A free people's press must itself be free. Its allegiance is to the news alone, as discerned by honest journalists. It cannot be the voice of a government or a party, a sect or a class or a union, a corporation or a philanthropist.

It follows that a subsidized press is less than a free press. Newspapers must be self-sustaining, and in the long run they must be profitable for their owners. Otherwise they cannot afford the independence expected of them by their readers.

Dependence upon advertising revenues does not compromise the essential independence of the press. Advertisers have learned the value of buying space in a good newspaper, and they know with that purchase they have acquired no rights or influence on the news and editorial function of the press.[15]

Today's proprietors would consider this statement hopelessly idealistic and faintly Marxist, particularly the notion that newspapers should hold allegiance to the news alone (not to shareholders) and that a profit should be achieved only "in the long run." However, we knew the main opposition would come from the lawyers, and that happened as soon as we showed them a first draft of our update of the 1977 Statement of Principles. A new preamble stated that the document "expresses the commitment of Canada's daily newspapers to operate responsibly and in the public interest." The lawyers objected. What does "responsibly" mean? What is "the public interest"? Why make any commitment? A new section establishing for the first time that newspapers realize that they have responsibilities to their communities drew the heaviest fire. It said that "the operation of a newspaper is a public trust and its overriding responsibility is to the society it serves." (The lawyers objected that this was vague and could haunt newspapers in court.) It also said that a paper "should strive to paint a representative picture of its diverse communities, to encourage the expression of disparate views and to be accessible and accountable to all readers, whether rich or poor, weak or powerful, minority or majority." (The lawyers objected that it isn't a newspaper's job to do that; its job is to cater to the interests it believes its readers share.) Another major change was to include a statement saying that a newspaper "should treat the people it covers with courtesy and fairness. It should respect the rights of others, particularly every person's right to a fair trial." (The lawyers said that conceding that people have rights could backfire in court.) We made some minor changes in wording, but still were unable to get the lawyers' endorsement and decided to do without it. But at least the lawyers cared enough to give us their input. Only three publishers and two managing editors bothered to do so, despite the fact that we distributed a draft to executives at eighty-four daily newspapers across Canada and asked them to comment.[16]

When our revised Statement of Principles was unanimously endorsed by the CDNA in September 1995, I felt vindicated, and not only because I had largely drafted two of the document's six sections; those concerning Freedom of the Press and Community Responsibility. I was happy because the newspaper industry had agreed on a statement of its values and beliefs, and it was planning to make this public for the first time. The CDNA board endorsed a suggestion from McMonagle and me that every daily paper in the country should print the full statement on October 14, which was Newspaper Carrier Day. At the same time, I wasn't naive about what we'd achieved. Our list of principles was a general one and certainly neither courageous nor poetic. The mere act of writing it all down and publishing it wasn't going to restore the public's trust in newspapers. That could happen only if the behaviour of journalists changed, something the code itself could not achieve since the newspaper industry had no mechanism to enforce it. Nevertheless, the very act of publishing a statement of first principles was bound to open up a dialogue with the community and to create more understanding for the role of the press in our modern society.[17]

This mass publication didn't happen, of course. Typically, many newspapers exercised their right to ignore any direction from their professional organization. A few big papers, including Montreal's *La Presse* and *Gazette,* the *Calgary Herald* and the *Ottawa Citizen*, published the six-paragraph statement, but none of the three dailies in Toronto did, nor did any of the thirty-eight dailies owned at the time by Thomson. That may have been because they all got a letter from Michael Doody warning them that they might increase their legal liability if they did so. In an ironic twist, the publisher of Thomson's *Winnipeg Free Press* slapped Doody's letter down on the desk of his executive editor, McMonagle, and ordered him not to run the same Statement of Principles that he had done such a good job of revising.

It is not easy to edit a newspaper these days. The credibility of journalists is at an all-time low. The dismal economy has meant fewer resources to cover issues that seem to be getting more and more complex. Competing interest groups in society, including some that have traditionally been excluded from public debate, clamour for attention. The basic raw material that newspapers sell—information—can be received faster elsewhere. The corporate ownership of much of our press has raised concerns about its independence and its value as a public service. Although no such research exists in Canada, a 1993 poll by the *Los Angeles Times* showed that only 17 percent of Americans believe that the media do a very good job, down from 30 percent in 1985. Reporting the news is further complicated by the fact that members of the public don't understand much of the work journalists do: journalists seem to have little respect for privacy, and their tradition of keeping at arm's-length from their communities is often misconstrued as arrogance. But credibility depends above all on

# Freedom of the Press: 2(b) or not 2(b)

accountability, and this is something American editors seem to understand better than their Canadian counterparts. Faced with revising their own outdated ethics code,[18] the Associated Press Managing Editors organization in the United States didn't pass the buck or wimp out; it consulted eighty other codes written for individual newspapers or journalistic organizations, then held four town meetings to get public input. The resulting five-page code toughens up existing guidelines, establishes new ethical rules against computerized photo manipulation, and lists specific performance standards, sometimes in painful detail. A main theme of the code is public disclosure: if you're going to do something controversial, like quoting an unnamed source, explain clearly to readers why it's necessary. Although the attorney for the Associated Press expressed alarm at the code, saying that it provides complainants with too many "hooks and advantages" to prove journalistic malpractice, the chair of the committee that wrote it, David Hawpe, editor of the *Louisville Courier-Journal*, said, "I think it would be fairly irresponsible not to have some fairly specific set of guidelines at a newspaper."

Even British editors, whose guilt in some of the worst excesses of the civilized press is evident on the front pages of their downmarket tabloids, have shown themselves to be capable of defining their standards—although the government had to bludgeon them into action. In 1993, they adopted a code of practice that would be enforced by a Press Complaints Commission, sort of a national press council to which complainants can turn. Canada's provincial press councils operate on a case-by-case approach and most have never attempted to define any standards for the press to measure up to, possibly because they were created and paid for by newspapers. But the British code is a model of toughness and is as specific as any such document can be.[19] One can quibble with its loopholes, and one can certainly question whether the British tabloid press honestly intends to comply with it, but it is a code written down and held up to the public as a test of newspaper performance. For journalists, it is a standard to be strived for in their daily conduct.

In our courts, in our society, in our universities, freedom of expression and the press are under attack as never before. Perhaps this is healthy. Freedoms are made by public consensus, and if they can no longer be defended to us, if they do not seem to serve us very well, they will be unmade.

It has been 150 years since Joseph Howe changed men's minds with his call for an unshackled press. Today, regrettably, the natural and traditional champion of press freedom—the press itself—is unable or unwilling to argue persuasively on its own behalf. It has failed to educate us to understand that disturbing words or images are a small price to pay for the right to write, speak and believe as we wish. It has failed to convince us to relinquish a little of our privacy to win the wider justice and understanding that can be achieved by making our circumstances public in a fair and responsible press. It has failed to demonstrate to us that it considers its duty to inform the public to be at least as

123

important as its duty make money for its shareholders. In sum, it has failed to satisfy us that it really does operate in the public interest.

## Notes

1. Kay Hill, *Joe Howe: The Man Who Was Nova Scotia* (McClelland and Stewart, 1980), pages 78–79.
2. The democratic tradition recognizes the right of all citizens to know, to speak and to express opinions without first seeking the permission of authorities and without the risk that the law will be used to suppress ideas. The understanding is that free expression is so fundamental to democracy that it can be limited only for clear and pressing reasons. Freedom of the press was recognized as a fundamental right in the *Canadian Bill of Rights* passed in 1960, although it wasn't part of the constitution. It was an ordinary law subject to repeal and limited to laws enacted by the federal Parliament. It wasn't until the *Constitution Act* established the *Canadian Charter of Rights and Freedoms* in 1982 that a free press was enshrined in our constitution. Ref: *A Sourcebook of Canadian Media Law* (Carleton University Press, 1989) by Robert Martin and Stuart Adam, page 70.
3. It wasn't until December 8, 1994 that the Supreme Court of Canada put the public's right to know what goes on in criminal trials on an equal legal footing with the right of an accused to a fair trial. The 6–3 decision in *Dagenais* v. *Canadian Broadcasting Corp.* was written by Chief Justice Antonio Lamer and said that "publication bans are not available as protection against remote and speculative dangers." Before they are granted by a court, the Crown must show that publication would pose "a real and substantial risk to the fairness of the trial." The ruling voided a lower court judge's ban on a CBC docudrama called *The Boys of St. Vincent*, a fictional story of sexual abuse at a Christian Brothers orphanage. At the time, some trials of real-life Christian Brothers were about to take place in Ontario. The *Dagenais* ruling stands as one of the most important legal decisions affecting the press in this country. Ironically, several lawyers representing newspapers initially criticized the CBC for taking the case to the Supreme Court.
4. O'Callaghan, the late and irascible former publisher of the *Calgary Herald* and *Edmonton Journal*, made the remark in a speech to Canadian managing editors meeting in Saint John, New Brunswick, in June 1989.
5. "The Role of the Press in Freedom of the Press," by David Lepofsky, presented at the Cambridge lectures, Queen's College, Cambridge University, July 1991, page 40.
6. "Circus-style news had it coming," by John Miller, *Globe and Mail,* July 8, 1993, page A25.
7. The Ontario Court of Appeal never ruled on the media's attempt to overturn the Homolka ban. Later that year, the Supreme Court of Canada ruled that it had sole jurisdiction to review all provincial court publication bans. By that time, the trial of Paul Bernardo was about to start.
8. *18th Annual Report* (Ontario Press Council, 1990), the Chairman's Foreword, page 2.
9. "How free should the press be?" by Allan Hutchison of Osgoode Hall Law School, *Globe and Mail*, June 1, 1989, page A7.

10. "The Media and the Courts," an address by Mme. Justice Rosalie Abella to the Empire and Canadian Clubs, Toronto, April 21, 1997.

11. Conversation with associate editor Sarah Murdoch, February 22, 1995. She said that she had asked Thorsell why she hadn't heard about the decision to abolish the newspaper industry's Statement of Principles. "He said, 'I haven't heard about it either.' We discussed it and he said, 'Say to John thanks for the opinion but we prefer to do a news story on it first …. You have a particular take on it, and some people might want to write from the other side.'"

12. "Freedoms at stake," letter to the editor by Terry Cottam, *Ottawa Citizen*, February 28, 1995, page A8. He said, "I'm outraged at the editors who voted for this cowardly action, for thinking that even a pretence of ethics can be dispensed with."

13. Memorandum from Blair Mackenzie to Michael Doody, July 13, 1995.

14. Other members were Bryan Cantley, editorial director of the CDNA; Mel Sufrin, executive secretary of the Ontario Press Council; Marcel Desjardins, editor of *La Presse*; and Raymond Brassard, managing editor of the *Montreal Gazette*.

15. "The People and Their Press," by Cleo Mowers, sent as a suggestion to Martin Goodman in 1977.

16. One of the publishers, Bill Peterson, then of the *Kingston Whig-Standard*, wrote: "It may sound silly, but I think we need to be able to hang this statement on the wall as a reminder of why we come to work each day." Another publisher, Paul Willcocks, then of the *Victoria Times-Colonist*, said that we shouldn't waste our time. The old statement, he said, seems sound, "and in any case is little consulted. I fear some good work will be done on a project which is not too relevant."

17. An *Ottawa Citizen* reader, Mark Templin, wrote to congratulate the CDNA for its decision to maintain its Statement of Principles. "In declaring themselves not only participants but leaders in community opinion, it is incumbent on newspapers to take this lead with integrity," he wrote Bryan Cantley. "To let the market solely determine the values and content of newspapers, without the guidance of solid ethical principles, is to shirk these responsibilities."

18. The need for a written code was illustrated by a survey answered by more than 500 U.S. editors. Seventy-one percent of them said corporate pressure for profits has affected news coverage in adverse ways, and it's harder to avoid giving advertisers special treatment. "Legislating Ethics," by Alicia Shepard, *American Journalism Review* (January/February, 1994).

19. For example, the section on privacy in the British code of practice says, "intrusions and enquiries into an individual's private life without his or her consent are not generally acceptable and publication can only be justified when in the public interest. The public interest would include: (a) Detecting or exposing crime or serious misdemeanour; (b) Detecting or exposing seriously anti-social conduct; (c) Protecting public health and safety; (d) Preventing the public from being misled by some statement or action of that individual."

# CHAPTER SIX

# Out of Touch

For the first eleven years that I worked at the *Toronto Star*, I had only one black colleague. One out of 350 of us. Canada's largest newsroom was white and it was going to stay white. In the late 1970s, after a series of racial incidents involving the police, the paper came under pressure from the black community to have some reporters who reflected the city's diversity. As far as anyone could recall, non-whites just never applied for jobs at the *Star*. The publisher said we had to do something, so some of us began spreading the word in the black community that it might be time.

One day the managing editor came to me with the name of a candidate. I was organizing a Sunday feature series called "Going Home"; I'd assigned several senior writers to return to their home towns and do stylish and nostalgic personal stories on what they found. Now my boss wanted me to add another writer to the assignment—this new applicant, who'd been born in Jamaica. It wasn't the usual routine chore that the paper gave out to see if a greenhorn could hack it as a general assignment reporter, but my boss wanted it done. I'll never forget his final words: "He's going to be one happy nigger."

That's the way things were in newsrooms as recently as twenty years ago. Blacks and other visible minorities were lucky just to get a foot inside the door, and editors were in the habit of tossing racial slurs about as freely as obscenities. It wasn't right but it was expected, like an all-white exclusive club whose members sit in their leather armchairs and make sport with each other about the unfortunate masses outside. Hamlin Grange, the young journalist in question, was hired on my recommendation and stepped into this alien, hostile world. Although grateful for the chance to bring a new voice to the paper, he got the message from day one that he'd better check his blackness at the door. A note went up on the bulletin board mentioning that he'd grown up in Toronto and gone to journalism school in Colorado, where he'd worked for the *Rocky Mountain News*. No mention was made of his more recent and far more senior experience as managing editor of *Contrast*, the newspaper that then served Toronto's black community. "It sent a very strong message to me that experience on a black paper didn't count, that the only way you're going to fit in here is to be part of the fraternity," Grange remembers. "You worked at a white paper."

Grange spent three frustrating years at the *Star* and left, he told me, because his career was going nowhere. By then the paper had attracted a couple of other black reporters, but all of them frequently found themselves working together at some remote suburban bureau, not at the main newsroom downtown where most of the action was.

Now a veteran news anchor for CBC television, Grange can look back nearly twenty years and still feel the sting of racism and rejection that he experienced in the *Star's* newsroom. It offended his deep sense of professionalism and was instrumental in his decision to help found the Canadian Association of Black Journalists (CABJ), a networking organization designed to help other blacks achieve equality in their chosen field. The CABJ has nearly one hundred members, a far cry from a decade ago when Grange remembers sitting down at a table in Toronto's Underground Railroad restaurant with all the other blacks employed in print or television in the city. They were a group of seven.

Things have changed, but you don't have to look far to realize that our newspapers really haven't kept pace with the dramatic changes in society. In Toronto, Canada's most multicultural city where one in every three residents is a person of colour, the four competing daily newspapers employ only two staff columnists who are non-white: Royson James of the *Star* and Jan Wong of the *Globe and Mail*. There is no black sports columnist, no Asian business columnist and no one on staff writing about lifestyles from a diverse perspective. The blind spots are glaring, even disturbing, and one wonders why, when circulation is declining, newspapers are not reaching out more aggressively to the fastest growing segments of their population. Why is race covered so negatively and stereotypically, and racism—the polite, silent Canadian variety—covered hardly at all? Why do the images seen in the pages of our newspapers fail to match the images of the people we see in the streets around us?

The answers start at the top, where Canadian publishers and editors have not committed themselves to equity like their American counterparts did more than twenty years ago. After race rioting devastated several U.S. cities in the 1960s, the National Advisory Commission on Civil Disorders (the Kerner Commission) reported that the U.S. media had "failed to report adequately [on] ... the underlying problems of race relations." This prompted American newspaper publishers to take action to correct this by putting diversity at the top of their agenda, by hiring more minorities and by making their coverage more diverse. Thanks in large part to this initiative, which was supported by a full-time diversity director hired by the American Society of Newspaper Editors, the percentage of minority professional journalists working at U.S. newspapers has tripled to more than 11 percent.

I had the opportunity to find out how differently Canada's newspaper managers feel about this issue when I joined the Canadian Daily Newspaper Association's editorial committee in 1993. Some of the country's top editors were trying to turn it into a forum for them to exert professional leadership in areas like training, hiring and building readership. I volunteered to chair a subcommittee to examine diversity in newsrooms, having come to believe that lack of diversity in hiring and coverage is putting newspapers badly out of step with the society they're trying to serve. I embarked upon this, thinking that if newspapers had the facts in front of them and understood the opportunities that they were missing to build readership and better reflect their communities, they'd change how they do things. I should have known better.

The CDNA then was a rather poorly funded professional association dominated by publishers who used it mainly as a central marketing and lobbying group. Taking care of business was their number-one concern. They spent most of their time and money on market research, lobbying the government to get Canada Post out of the advertising flyer business and keeping abreast of legal issues that could end up costing them money. Editorial matters took a back seat. Managing and covering diversity, for instance, ranked nineteenth on a list of twenty-one problems facing the industry in 1993, according to a CDNA poll of its member publishers.[1] Ahead of it were improving advertising effectiveness and value, coping with reduced staff and circulation cost control. Getting publishers to care about making their papers better for readers was going to be an uphill struggle, and so was getting anyone who knew about diversity to join my subcommittee. The first person whom I asked to volunteer, a black columnist for a newspaper in Nova Scotia, turned me down. He said that he'd lost hope that the industry could ever change.[2]

Amazingly, the CDNA had never polled its members to find out how many *people* worked in newsrooms, let alone how many of these might be minorities. So my small volunteer subcommittee decided to find out. Forty-one daily newspapers, from Victoria to St. John's, returned my questionnaire, and the results were dismal: 40 percent of them still had an all-white staff, and most didn't see that changing. One editor wrote across his questionnaire: "Frankly, I am finding these questions somewhat insulting." Another said, "Journalists who are members of racial minorities may not be interested in coming to our area." The bottom line was that, of 2620 professional jobs in those 41 newsrooms, only 67 were held by people of colour. This works out to 2.6 percent, at a time when aboriginals and visible minorities constituted 13 percent of Canada's population. We could identify only four native Canadians and sixteen blacks working in newsgathering jobs across the country. Despite these abysmally low numbers, one editor said that non-whites were unlikely to be hired due to "backlash from white staff."

In the final analysis, minority representation in Canadian newsrooms in 1994 was five times lower than their share of the country's population. Population forecasts commissioned by the Canadian Advertising Foundation indicate that by the turn of the century, 18 percent of Canadians will be non-white, with the proportion as high as 45 percent in Toronto and 39 percent in

Vancouver. In my report to the 1994 annual meeting of the CDNA, I said that publishers and editors do not appear to recognize either the opportunities or the urgency of improving coverage and hiring, and I urged them to "begin understanding diversity and setting specific and measurable goals for action." This was delivered to a half-empty room. One Ontario publisher said later, "[Having someone tell me who to hire] really sticks in my craw." I was urged to not get people's backs up by talking about measurable goals, even though Ontario's NDP government was about to promulgate equity legislation—later rescinded by the Tories—that required all of the province's employers to do just that or face fines of $50,000.

Responsible journalism surely requires fairness and thoughtfulness in news decisions. If most of those decisions are made by middle-aged white men, there are going to be blind spots. That certainly happens regularly in newspapers across the country. In both their newsroom staffing and in how they depict minorities in print, Canada's dailies are nearly as white as the paper they're printed on.

Noting that editors and publishers just don't feel any urgency to promote diversity in their midst, columnist Irshad Manji wrote in the *Ottawa Citizen* in 1994:

> They insist it's not the reporters who matter to the public. It's what they report—and how accurately—that counts. Stop the presses; there's a story here somewhere. Accuracy is precisely why the public deserves to be reflected in their media. How can any paper claim to give their readers an accurate picture of the world when that picture is sketched, refined and reprinted by one group [middle-aged white guys] with a limited set of experiences?[3]

Nowhere is this more evident than in the way newspapers often gratuitously link race and crime, a phenomenon that anthropologist Frances Henry of York University has called "racialization." That is to say, criminal behaviour committed by whites is treated as an aberrant individual act, which it usually is, but when it's perpetrated by blacks or Asians it's often seen as a form of "group crime" for which an entire minority community is held responsible.[4] How newspapers can stir up these harmful and inaccurate attitudes was demonstrated in Toronto in April 1994, when a point-blank blast from a sawed-off shotgun tore into the chest of an elfin, 23-year-old part-time hairdresser, and a whole city temporarily went nuts.

Georgina (ViVi) Leimonis was eating cake at a trendy midtown cafe on the edge of exclusive Forest Hill when three robbers broke in and lined patrons up against the wall. As they were helping themselves to wallets and purses, one of them panicked and opened fire. The random and savage death of Leimonis shocked an entire city, especially when police released video shots of her black assailants and said that they came from "The Jungle," an area of public housing in suburban North York. It might have been a useful time to debate gun control or even the economic disparities of a city where 75,000 children ate at food banks every month. But that didn't happen. Columnists mourned the city's loss of innocence, especially the *Globe and Mail's* Michael Valpy, who said. "The barbarians are inside the gate"—an unfortunate and inflammatory comment that implied that this was not a random act at all but rather an invasion of civilized society by the underclass. Stirred up by the media coverage, 3500 people turned out for the young woman's funeral, and the cafe where she was shot became a shrine filled with flowers and messages in her memory. One note appealed for people not to pin the crime on the black community, but it was quickly defaced. Someone wrote across it: "Kill your own. Leave us alone."

The problem was that the city's two biggest newspapers, the *Star* and the *Sun*, had entered into an unseemly competition for news and indignation that took readers far away from the central issues and exacerbated racial tension in Canada's most cosmopolitan city. Both papers splashed grainy, security-camera photos of the suspects across their front pages. The *Star* quoted the head of the homicide squad as urging citizens to cut out the photos, "tape them to your car's visor, so that you will recognize them when you see them." It took editors three days to realize what kind of vigilante justice this might provoke. An editorial admitted that the images were so fuzzy they could be almost anyone— any young black man, that is. It asked: "How many law-abiding black youths will feel the suspicious glances of passers-by, or police officers, who may wonder: *Are they the monsters?*"

The *Sun* never did get it. An editorial using the most incendiary language said: "Find these SOBs and get them off our streets. Now!" When a black suspect was named by police, the paper published his criminal record, including details of fourteen charges either withdrawn or dismissed. It's against the law for anyone other than police to have that information, but that didn't seem to matter. When the suspect surrendered peacefully a week later, the *Sun's* three-inch-deep headline said "GOT HIM." And when a second man turned himself in, the paper blared "TWO DOWN." Quite apart from the harm done to the presumption of innocence of two men, it raised the temperature of black-white fear in Toronto to the bubbling point and served to stereotype this tragedy as a "black crime." The owner of Just Desserts, the restaurant where Leimonis was killed, was quoted as saying: "What if *they* start going to the parks, to the skating rinks, everywhere else where there are children? How do we stop them?"

"They" became the enemy. And the news coverage made clear that the enemy was black, violent, probably on drugs and now ready to emerge from suburban ghettos to launch random attacks on "good" (meaning white and middle-class) neighbourhoods. The barbarians, as the columnist said, were indeed inside our gates.

As if the flames weren't being fanned high enough, the city's two most prominent local columnists—the *Sun's* Christie Blatchford and the *Star's* Rosie DiManno—used their columns to wage a war of words with each other on the morning after the young woman's funeral. Both are superb reporters, but instead of trying to shed light on what happened, they diverted everyone's attention by attacking each other's newspapers for trying to capitalize on the tragedy (something that had been obvious to the rest of us for days). Blatchford accused the *Star* of giving away plans for a police raid in the Jungle neighbourhood; DiManno countered that the *Sun* was designed for people who move their lips when someone reads the paper to them and "wouldn't know ethics if it up and bit 'em on the ass." This sort of silliness served to feed the wrong co-ordinates into the city's sophisticated media guidance system, and for days other columnists, including the *Star's* readers' representative in a front-page justification for the story in question, fired back and forth at each other. Even Valpy got back into the act, although he couldn't decide which was worse—such a crime happening within a twenty-minute walk of the financial district or the fact that "our robbers and teenagers aren't supposed to behave this way." You got the feeling that all of the opinion leaders of the Toronto media were firing their guns off in the dark against an imaginary enemy.

And if *that* wasn't bad enough, the *Sun* tried to turn ViVi Leimonis into a marketing stunt. "This is our baby," assistant managing editor Jane Van Der Voort said at a meeting of Canadian editors, holding up a "Turn in Your Guns" sign with the paper's logo and the crest of the Metro Toronto police. The *Sun* was offering free tickets to the Blue Jays, concert passes or gift certificates from Pizza Hut and Burger King to anyone who turned in firearms to the police. A few guns trickled in, but the stunt turned into a fiasco when a police commissioner, under fire for his extensive collection of semi-automatic weaponry, bought a cheap rifle and turned it in for the publicity. That was too much even for the *Sun's* Blatchford, who criticized her own newspaper for knowing about this and covering it up. She didn't mention that the whole idea of a gun amnesty organized by a paper that strongly opposes any form of gun control on its editorial page smacks of opportunism and hypocrisy.

It was not until three weeks after the shooting that any newspaper even bothered to visit the Jungle neighbourhood that had been so badly stereotyped in the Leimonis coverage. The story was by a young freelancer, and it ran in the *Globe and Mail*, not the more locally-oriented *Star* or *Sun*. It said the neighbourhood's nickname originated with taxi drivers who got lost in the winding roads, not as a slight against the low-income, mainly black, residents. It also said that contempt for the name is almost as widespread as contempt for the media. "My girls are always outside at night playing and I'm not worrying about getting them back," a woman who has lived there sixteen years said. "You call that a jungle?"

Public reaction mirrored the media coverage: deport the criminals; lower immigration quotas; give us back our city. It was the classic, unthinking white backlash. As journalist Margaret Cannon explained in her 1995 study of racism in Canada: "From our perspective, those of us who have lived here for decades, we have not changed and so the problems must be someone else's fault. It must be the newcomers, the Other."[5] After newspapers printed letters from blacks saying that the media's Leimonis frenzy was imposing a "collective guilt" on their community, the *Sun* countered with a ridiculous and crypto-racist editorial. It said the blanket coverage wasn't prompted by race, but by class—"the simple economic reality that most of our readers (as is the case with all our competitors) are middle class." The implication was that blacks were not.

Almost lost in the rush to judgment were the comments of two cooler-headed commentators. Antonia Zerbisias, the *Star's* media columnist, wrote that "lack of understanding breeds not only fear, but more trouble." Instead of titillating audiences by playing up crime to sell papers, newspapers have a responsibility to report more on the inner-city neighbourhoods where crime begins. She asked: Why in most big-city newsrooms are there more reporters covering crime than health, education and social justice stories put together? Her colleague Thomas Walkom asked an even better question: Why did the shooting of a middle-class white woman in 1994 provoke such an outrage, when the killing three years earlier of another innocent bystander, who happened to be Chinese, did not? When Tin Wah Lui was killed outside a downtown karaoke bar in 1991, it was dismissed as another Chinese gang shooting and didn't even make front page. But the killing of Leimonis, he said, "invaded the middle class soul of the city."

Cecil Foster, one of the very few black journalists who has had a platform in Toronto's mainstream press over the past decade, said that media coverage turned the Leimonis case into a symbol of "all the ills black men can inflict on white women." Instead of treating it as a tragic, random event, newspapers made it appear that the entire city had become lawless—black youths with ski masks were running rampant throughout the city, and anyone, especially whites, could get slaughtered. Similar random killings in the black community hardly merited mention in the newspapers and certainly did not generate any outpouring of sympathy, Foster noted. "As long as blacks were killing blacks, the city was still safe."[6]

Nor did the mainstream media devote many resources to covering the tortuous legal ordeal of the four black men arrested in the Leimonis slaying. The case has consumed nineteen judges and more than $1 million in legal aid, and legal maneuvering by lawyers has delayed their trial by four years. Three of the suspects are still in custody. The fourth was freed in January 1998, after it was belatedly discovered that there was no reliable evidence against him. Even though coverage is restricted by a publication ban, it's clear something is very wrong. Would the media be so timid if the suspects were white?

Haroon Siddiqui, who used to edit the *Toronto Star's* editorial page and was a prominent member of my diversity subcommittee, wonders if the stereotypical coverage of minorities in the media is the result of outright racial prejudice or of the institutional flaws of the business. It's probably a bit of both. The press, Siddiqui once wrote, too often serves as a willing conveyor belt for unsubstantiated and damaging assertions about minorities:

> When some police officers pass on their personal prejudices, or offer ethnic scapegoats for their own failures to control crime, reporters often fail to ask: What proof is there that black kids are committing proportionately more crime than others? Even if they are in a certain neighbourhood, are they any more inherently criminal than other poor, unemployed kids in similar circumstances? If an Asian Triad is out on the prowl, what are the police doing about apprehending the criminals as opposed to invoking their ethnicity? If a Sikh is a suspect in a crime, why is his religion relevant? Why is a missing suspect's Jamaican accent important?[7]

Siddiqui listed other institutional sins, such as the propensity of reporters to take a black-and-white view of the world, often quoting angry, flamboyant extremists as representing a certain community. If a black or Chinese Canadian receives coverage, the focus is usually on some issue involving race, not on larger issues affecting everyone. Even race relations does not receive ongoing coverage, and so it is usually reactive, negative and lacking context when it appears. Although people of colour are often treated as foreigners, they're anything but. They're Canadians by choice, educated, productive, assertive and confident consumers paying high taxes and asking equality in return. This reality is rarely reflected in the media, mainly because newsrooms remain overwhelmingly white. It's time for that to change, Siddiqui believes, "not only because it is in our long-term business interest but because this is a moral matter—of being fair, balanced, ethical and Canadian."

No one really wants to talk about this. Editors either moan about hiring freezes and the unfairness of non-existent affirmative action "quotas," or they deflect responsibility down to Canada's journalism schools, accusing them of training too few. It's a fair accusation, up to a point. When I came to Ryerson in 1986, I was struck by the lack of diversity among journalism students. There were only a couple of dozen non-whites in a total enrollment of 350. The dean of another university journalism school told me that he couldn't recall the last visible minority student he'd had. I felt that Ryerson, located in the middle of the most diverse city in Canada, had to take the lead. Thanks to the co-operation of the Ontario Human Rights Commission, which authorized us to conduct an anonymous survey of applicants, we were able to determine that recruitment wasn't the problem; minorities were applying to our school in numbers that roughly corresponded to their share of the population. So we addressed the selection process. At the time, up to 1,600 students had applied for just 160 first-year places in our program, and we screened them according to experience and performance on entry tests. Without changing our policy of admitting the best qualified students, the faculty and I agreed to broaden the range of experience that we considered meritorious. We'd long accepted the notion that an applicant's knowledge of sports or business or work on a high school newspaper should be counted as a qualification for entry, but now we recognized that facility in another language and activities in the community should be considered as well. Our percentage of minority students slowly began to rise. At the school's 1993 convocation, I counted 35 minorities among the 140 new journalism graduates. Several were among our most promising.

Many graduates and students who are also members of a minority run into hiring practices that seem caught in some redneck time warp. Three interviewers from one of Canada's major dailies, for instance, grilled a Muslim student on whether she'd be unbiased enough to cover a speech at a synagogue. They didn't seem to want to assess her other qualifications. Another student, also a Muslim, had to endure a job interview with a weekly newspaper in which the editor asked how "radical" she was about her religion. Was she aware that the Ku Klux Klan had been active in the area? Did she think she'd be comfortable here? Such questions are not only intimidating and irrelevant, they're against the law.

If newspapers want to hire minorities, they're going to have to take down the "Do not apply here" signs. Unfortunately, that's not going to happen soon in Canada. Even though minorities are so poorly represented in newsrooms that they can scarcely be counted, editors say there's nothing they can do about it. Edmonton, for example, is a city with a population that is 18 percent non-white, yet in 1995 only two of the *Edmonton Journal's* sixty-eight news reporters were minorities, and there were none at the rival *Edmonton Sun*. The reaction of Michael Cooke, who was then managing editor of the *Journal*, was typical: What do you want me to do? Start firing veterans so we can hire a lot of new people?[8]

Even when minorities do manage to get into newsrooms, they often find a chilling environment. The National Association of Black Journalists, which is the largest organization of minority journalists in the United States, polled its members on this subject in 1995, and 67 percent said that their newsroom managers were not committed to retaining and promoting blacks in the newsroom. Ninety-seven percent of the managers claimed that blacks were more likely than other journalists to be given the chance at career advancement, but only 24 percent of blacks agreed. Moreover, more than one-third of blacks felt that their careers might be put on hold if they even raised racial issues in their newsrooms.[9] There aren't enough minority journalists working in Canadian newsrooms to do a statistically valid poll, but indications are that conditions here are just as bad.

All those years ago, Hamlin Grange made it a point to challenge what he saw as the *Toronto Star's* insensitive or outright racist portrayals, and he's convinced his career there would have been different if he'd just kept quiet and been one of the crowd. But he says stereotypes and institutional racism need to be confronted, and it won't be done successfully until there is a critical mass of reporters from diverse cultures in the newsroom. It will take more time, and a change of thinking, to achieve that. Editors won't start hiring differently until they realize that there may be a commercial advantage to reflecting diversity in their newsrooms. "Historically, people tend to hire people they're comfortable with, or people they admire," Grange says. "And I'll tell you, there aren't too many white guys who'd like to be black."

Since coming to Canada from Barbados twenty years ago, Cecil Foster has managed to work with distinction in practically all forms of journalism. His resume lists his achievements as a newspaper reporter, editor and columnist, a radio talk show host, a television news writer, and the author of several books and magazine articles. Few Canadian journalists could match those qualifications, yet Foster says, "I do not believe I have ever been fully accepted into mainstream journalism." He does not feel sorry for himself; rather, he laments the lack of progress non-whites have made in penetrating white, middle-class newsrooms. Not much has changed at the *Globe and Mail* since he was its only black reporter in 1989. When he left the *Financial Post* four years later, he commented, "100 percent of the black editorial staff went with me." In such newsrooms, Foster says, there is limited understanding of what should be the full public agenda, of what stories need to be related to Canadians to tell them about themselves. If there was diversity in newsrooms, one group would not automatically have the first and last word about what matters, why it matters and what it means.[10]

The battle for inclusion in Canada's "old-white-male" newsrooms has been fought before—by women—and their experience is instructive in assessing the prospects for increased racial diversity today. Although women now occupy about a third of the desks in any large newsroom, many still complain that equality is a distant dream. They do so with good reason. Of Canada's fifteen largest papers, only the *Edmonton Journal* has a woman as its publisher (Linda Hughes) and only five have women managing editors. All of the others are published and edited by white males. In hundreds of subtle and not-so-subtle ways, women are told the door is closed. Until a few years ago, the Christmas "piss-up" for newsroom managers at the *Hamilton Spectator* was held every year in the men's room of a nearby hotel. At a few other big papers, female journalism students lucky enough to be hired as summer interns often find themselves "hit on" by senior editors who ultimately decide whether to hire them full-time. And when you look at who writes the stories that get on the front page—the traditional sign of who's covering the hot news beats at any paper—women come out far behind. A Ryerson study done in 1993 found that, at six of nine Canadian dailies studied, women had a much poorer chance of getting their stories on page one than their numbers in the newsroom might suggest.[11]

This situation didn't sneak up on newspapers. It hit them in the face, hard, as readership among women—a traditional strength at most papers—began to decline markedly and as women entering newsrooms in larger numbers began to demand a fairer shot at executive positions. In 1989 at Southam, Canada's largest newspaper chain, only 6 of the chain's 126 senior managers were women, and all 33 of the people promoted to those ranks that year were men. Faced with this dismal situation, Paddy Sherman, progressive president of the Southam Newspaper Group, organized a task force of his top editors and human resources executives to recommend solutions. The findings of the Southam Task Force on Women's Opportunities, distributed to all of the chain's publishers in 1990, made ten recommendations. Some were just common sense, like a statement from the top saying that full equity for women was company policy and asking member papers to provide more day care and job-sharing. Others were controversial, like the infamous "bucks for broads" proposal to evaluate publishers according to how many women they recruited, promoted and trained each year. This was ridiculed in public by *Vancouver Sun* columnist Trevor Lautens, who called it "Kafkaesque" and said: "It's straight from Big Sister's manual. No thumbscrews. No electrodes on the genitals. Just a smile, a kindly hand on the manager's shoulder, and a reminder that if he or she doesn't go along, it'll cost them."[12]

Even though the report was received politely by Sherman's successor, Russ Mills, nothing much happened. Three years later, when another task force reviewed what had happened to the ten recommendations, it found that only two had been carried out. Southam's employment equity manager declared that there was "a complete lack of progress" in advancing women into executive positions and added, in an interview shortly after she left the company, that the report was shelved and that she doubted the existence of a single copy anywhere in the corporation.[13] Another Southam executive, Tim Peters, said that the promotion of women "is not the critical issue it once was" and that there are no plans to implement any more of the proposals. Ironically, one of the suggestions in the 1993 review was for Southam's president to broaden his as-yet-unwritten employment equity commitment to cover not only women but other traditionally excluded groups, such as disabled people and visible minorities. That has never been done either, and Southam lags behind most other private-sector companies in its commitment to equality in the workplace.[14] The alarming thing is, Southam is probably more advanced than most other Canadian newspaper organizations.

Despite decades of progress, the record of Canadian newspapers in hiring and promoting women is dismal. A 1997 survey conducted by McGill University and Université de Sherbrooke showed that women filled 44 percent of jobs in the Canadian workforce but just 28 percent of full-time newsgathering positions in Canada's dailies. Most occupied lower-ranking positions as reporters and junior editors, despite the fact that women were more eager to be promoted than men and seemed to have values and ideals that newspapers need most in the 1990s. Women journalists surveyed had higher ethical values than men and tended to be in journalism for nobler reasons—to foster new ideas or to call attention to social problems. They were more likely than men to value journalism for its role as a public educator and less likely to see it as a platform for entertainment. Instead of being promoted, however, they were marginalized, and 60 percent of them told researchers that they'd been sexually harassed on the job.[15]

This head-in-the-sand attitude and the lack of diversity in newsrooms should concern us all, because newspapers exert a powerful influence over how we see the world around us. If few women or visible minorities are in positions where they can determine what newspapers cover and how, issues affecting them are probably not going to receive proper attention or get on the agenda for public debate. And like the wonky mirrors in the fun house at the fair, our newspapers can reflect a dangerously distorted view of our society. Sociologists like Augie Fleras have concluded, after studying the way newspapers depict minorities, that:

> Generally speaking, aboriginal and racial minorities exemplify a "social problem" as far as the media are concerned. They are described in the context of having problems in need of solutions that expend an inordinate amount of political attention or a disproportionate slice of national resources .... The cumulative effect of constant negative messages may be to marginalize minorities as irrelevant or as a threat to society.[16]

It doesn't take an academic study to tell us how the public will perceive aboriginals if they're constantly being portrayed as a threat to Canada's social order (the Oka blockade), an economic liability (cost of the massive land claims), a burden on our criminal justice system (there are more natives in prison than their percentage of the population seems to warrant) and a medical problem (drunkenness and suicides). Nor is it a surprise that Canada's immigration policy, which should be a matter of national pride, is constantly under fire. Immigrants are frequently covered in the press as troublemakers, criminals, frauds and a burden on our social services instead of who they most often are: people who bring wealth to our shores; who create jobs; who add diversity to our culture; and who are better educated, pay more taxes and are less likely to collect welfare than the average person born in Canada.[17]

Racial stereotypes fit neatly into the culture of Canada's predominantly white newsrooms. News stories can, and often do, produce inaccurate reporting, which serves only to feed popular prejudices. A case in point was a story that the *Toronto Sun* ran in March 1994 in an attempt to show that Canada's immigration laws could be sidestepped by liars and criminals. It revealed that a woman from Somalia, who was seeking refugee status in Canada, was in fact an international welfare cheat. The story quoted unnamed sources as saying that Amina Farah was on the dole both here and in Britain and is the kind of "asylum shopper" that Canada should immediately send packing. Amina Farah sued, claiming that the story was completely untrue and was concocted for the *Sun* by her estranged husband, who wanted to see her deported. The newspaper, which at the time was on a campaign to tighten up Canada's immigration rules, staunchly stood by its story, and said that the plaintiff, as a cheat and a fraud, had no reputation to damage. There was only one problem: the paper couldn't back anything up. When he was questioned by the plaintiff's lawyer at examination for discovery, the *Sun* reporter could not point to any documents proving that Ms. Farah had ever received refugee status in Britain or that she had ever collected welfare there. He had made no attempt to corroborate what he'd been told by his main source, her former husband, nor did he interview Ms. Farah. An attempt was made to phone her, but it was belated, and the writer did not discuss with his editors the possibility of holding off publishing the story until he could get her side. The story was so grievously wrong and stereotypical that, when I was asked to provide expert witness testimony on behalf of the plaintiff, I agreed to do it for free. The *Sun*, I believed, published this story without regard for many of the standards of accuracy commonly accepted in the Canadian newspaper industry. It couldn't prove what it wrote, it made only a half-hearted attempt to contact the subject of the story, and it shielded the identity of the main source of the story even though there was no reason to do so. Indeed, the ex-husband's troubled relationship with Ms. Farah and his possible motives for snitching on her should have rung alarm bells of caution at the paper. It was a shocking journalistic performance and a good example of how newspapers let stereotypes influence their reporting. The *Sun* agreed to an out-of-court settlement with Ms. Farah, perhaps realizing it was defending the indefensible.

Such reporting is not only wrong, it's stupid, because immigrants of racial and religious minorities are the fastest growing segment of the Canadian public. Newcomers do not come with high expectations of favourable cover-age, but if the type of coverage given them is full of stereotypes, slurs and ignorance, they stand little chance of becoming regular readers of mainstream daily newspapers.

Newspapers also have a higher moral responsibility to combat stereotypes in news coverage. Teun A. van Dijk, an expert in racism and discourse at the University of Amsterdam, notes in his 1991 book *Racism and the Press* that most citizens rely on newspapers to provide all of their knowledge of ethnic affairs. Stereotypical coverage tends to strengthen prejudices, produce emo-tional reactions and impair public policy initiatives designed to promote tolerance in society. Van Dijk and others argue for what they call integrated coverage, where minorities are represented in all types of news, not only in crime or conflict, but they note that this is almost totally lacking in coverage examined in Europe and the United States.

# Out of Touch

How are Canadian minorities depicted in their newspapers? To find out, Ryerson graduate student Kimberly Prince and I did a "content audit" of the major newspapers in five of the country's most cosmopolitan cities in 1993. We examined 2,141 photographs and 895 local news stories carried in a random week's editions of the *Vancouver Sun, Calgary Herald, Winnipeg Free Press, Toronto Star, Toronto Sun* and *Montreal Gazette*. We wanted answers to three questions: Are non-whites in each city receiving the amount of news coverage that their numbers seem to warrant? Are their pictures appearing in representative numbers throughout the papers? Is this coverage positive, negative or neutral? We based our study on "audit" techniques developed by the American Society of Newspaper Editors. We were looking particularly for gaps in coverage that might reinforce stereotypes or exclude potential readers. We found that people who read those papers can easily reach three general conclusions about visible minorities: that half of them are either athletes or entertainers; that if they're in the news otherwise, they're in trouble of some sort; and that few make any contribution to business or have noteworthy lifestyles. I have divided our specific findings into the following three categories: local news coverage, photographs and tone of coverage.

**Local news coverage.** Only 128 of the 895 local news stories in those papers mentioned minorities or were about issues that directly affected minorities. Only the *Montreal Gazette* published a higher percentage (18 percent) of local news stories about minorities than their share of the local population. By contrast, only 11 percent of the news stories in the *Vancouver Sun* concerned minorities, whereas the local non-white population is well over two times bigger.[18]

**Photographs.** Thirty-six percent of all minority photographs appeared in sports sections. Another 12 percent were pictures of entertainers. Non-whites, however, were nearly shut out of business and lifestyle sections. When six of English Canada's largest newspapers can publish a total of only twelve photos of minority business people in a week, they are not reflecting their communities. One paper, the *Winnipeg Free Press*, published no pictures of minorities in either its business or lifestyle section in the seven days selected for our study.

**Tone of coverage.** The generally positive tone of the photos—45 percent of the pictures of minorities were positive and only 19 percent negative—was influenced by the large number of sports and entertainment photos. The tone of minority news content, on the other hand, was more negative (49 percent) than positive (42 percent), and there were great discrepancies. The *Calgary Herald's* margin was 75 percent negative to 19 percent positive; the *Toronto Sun's* margin was 61 percent negative to 21 percent positive. By contrast, the *Montreal Gazette* wrote positively about minorities 72 percent of the time, and negatively 17 percent. The *Toronto Star, Vancouver Sun* and *Winnipeg Free Press* tended to be more balanced.

A story was considered positive if it was about a person of colour achieving something, or if the angle tended to represent a minority viewpoint. This included, for example, a *Toronto Star* article about an aboriginal director winning a film award, and a *Vancouver Sun* story on an Asian-Canadian launching a human rights discrimination suit against a private school that wouldn't admit her son. Examples of negative stories included a *Calgary Herald* report on an Alberta cabinet minister suggesting that youth gangs are strictly an immigrant problem, and a feature the same day on native sons of alcoholic parents; a *Toronto Sun* column deriding Asian-Canadians for campaigning against racism in immigration policy; and a *Vancouver Sun* story on how unilingual signs in Chinese stores are upsetting shoppers.

It's no accident that the *Montreal Gazette* showed the most diverse coverage in the Ryerson study. The paper, then under editor Joan Fraser, had wisely targeted ethnic minorities as important potential readers in a city where English-speaking white Canadians were a minority themselves. "We simply made it a priority," she told me. "And it has to be kept uppermost in people's minds, otherwise it will slip back down into limbo again." That meant assigning responsibility and committing resources. Ashok Chandwani, assistant managing editor for news and one of only four non-whites in the *Gazette's* 167-person newsroom, ensured that all assignment editors, reporters and photographers bore in mind the need for minority coverage. He also wrote a weekly column about the minority experience. One of the best reporters on staff was assigned to do real stories on minorities, not what Fraser called "Ukrainian-easter-egg and Chinese-new-year-dragon predictable stuff." It was hard work, but it paid off in the long run. Few other newspapers have made such a sustained commitment, largely because they seem to share the opinion expressed by Russ Mills, publisher of the *Ottawa Citizen*, when I asked him why newspaper circulation across Canada has suffered such steep declines in the 1990s. Multiculturalism, he said, has made the country more interesting, but "it may be that they don't have as much in common with all of their fellow citizens as they used to. Certainly our readership among visible minorities is pretty dismal." In other words, it's *their* fault. The language and culture of recent arrivals from Asia and Africa, not stereotypical coverage by the newspapers, may be keeping them away. This, of course, is hogwash.

Minorities tend to be good newspaper readers and express their loyalty to Canada more readily than many native-born citizens, who arrived here by chance rather than by choice. Many newcomers use newspapers to teach themselves colloquial English or to learn about Canadian customs, and some immigrants from Hong Kong, where dozens of mass-circulation newspapers thrive, wonder why Canadians are such poor subscribers. Studies in the United States show that newspaper readership among minorities tends to match their percentage of the population.[19]

By the middle of 1995, I was growing frustrated. Despite the best efforts of CDNA editorial director Bryan Cantley and the volunteers on my diversity initiative, the country's publishers and editors by and large still didn't get it. Some of them were beginning to worry that the CDNA's diversity research was giving the industry a black eye. Why beat ourselves up in public? Why pander to people who probably weren't going to read us anyway? My subcommittee decided to lay some more facts on them.

Surprisingly, no research had ever been done in Canada about race and newspaper readership. My inquiries even prompted an angry outburst from Charles Dunbar, the CDNA's director of research, who said that a study on this subject was impossible to do because minorities were unreliable and seldom identified themselves honestly. Despite such opposition, I decided to do it and managed to winkle $20,000 out of several newspapers to pay for some preliminary research. Haroon Siddiqui and I used the money to hire John Laschinger of Goldfarb Consultants and commissioned him to do several focus-group conversations with minority readers across the country. What do they think of newspapers? How do they read them? How do they see themselves covered there? If there's a problem, how can it be fixed?

Laschinger got an earful. When he asked a group of Toronto blacks to describe newspapers in human terms, these are the words they used: "Sloppy, vindictive, propagandist, not professional, demagogue, threat, danger, self-serving, manipulative, mean, narrow-minded, distorted and ignorant." Two focus groups conducted in Vancouver with South Asians and Chinese also expressed more negative than positive attitudes towards newspapers. In fact, the only group he talked with that had a strongly positive image of newspapers was a control group of white readers in Hamilton. His report concluded that newspapers have a readership problem with many members of key visible minority groups, and that most of the people he talked with felt that they treat visible minorities like foreigners, stigmatize them as criminals, ignore their cultural events and practice discrimination when they cover their communities. Fifty-seven percent of the participants said that daily newspapers help reinforce the feeling that visible minorities are not part of mainstream Canada.[20]

A modest list of recommendations was forwarded to the publishers, including the need to review crime coverage, if necessary by opening a dialogue with readers about it, and to educate newsgathering staff about the changing demographics of their communities. We got absolutely no response.[21]

Despite the Goldfarb report's finding that visible minorities are avid readers and constitute a growing potential market for daily newspapers, the industry apparently wasn't interested in changing its ways and going after them. So I wasn't surprised a few weeks later when my local dailies showed me once again that ill-informed and stereotypical reporting about minorities is ingrained in the culture of newsrooms and won't disappear soon without a strong commitment from the top.

Eight days before Christmas 1995, three men were shot while leaving a restaurant in an area of downtown Toronto that is sometimes called "Chinatown East." Cut down in a fusillade of two dozen shots fired from an AK-47 assault rifle, 24-year-old Chanh Thong Vo bled to death on the sidewalk at 3:30 a.m. outside of the Jun Jun Seafood Restaurant. His two friends were wounded. Thirteen police cars and eight emergency vehicles turned the area into a virtual war zone, and police rounded up the restaurant's sixty patrons at gunpoint, searched them and—largely because few officers working the overnight shift in Toronto know how to converse in Mandarin, Cantonese or Vietnamese—bused them off to the police station for questioning. The shooting happened too late to make any of the Sunday newspapers, but by Monday the story had been filled out by reporters and photographers who, like the police, could not speak to witnesses or neighbours in their own languages. Instead of just treating it as the city's fifty-fifth homicide of the year, the *Sun*, *Star* and *Globe and Mail* chose to make unsupported links to a crime wave fomented by Asian gangs; they depicted "Chinatown" as one geographic area instead of several and as a place rife with gambling, extortion, robberies and execution-style murders; and they raised the spectre of an Asian invasion of potential criminals who deserved to be thrown into work camps.

The tabloid *Sun* devoted its entire front page and two inside pages of Monday's paper to "Ambush at Chinese restaurant." Despite the fact that police refused to speculate on a motive for the slaying, the *Sun* depicted it as the city's "first gangland-style murder this year" and said that it "echoed previous Chinatown slayings in Metro." A story by reporters Ian Robertson and Rob Lamberti referred to an "assassin" instead of a mere killer. An accompanying story was headlined "Gang slaying fits pattern," even though it could dredge up only two other slayings in the last five years that had anything to do with Asian gangs. The very last sentence of the story said that "the motive for yesterday's slaying and woundings remains unknown," but that didn't stop the *Sun*. Next day, the banner spread across the top of the tabloid's front page read: "Inside Metro's Asian Underworld: How extortion and guns for hire spawned Chinatown shootings." The only evidence that such a link was warranted was an unattributed statement, buried in the sixteenth paragraph of the story inside, that "police are investigating Vo's links to extortion as a possible reason for his slaying." The story quoted unnamed "sources" as saying that Vo was "a gangster who sold protection to bawdy houses and illegal gambling dens" and was known by the street name "No Dick" since shooting off half his penis with a .45-calibre handgun he kept stuffed down inside his belt. Vietnamese hoodlums like Vo, the *Sun* said, are often hired by Chinese gangs to be their muscle in collecting debts, although police find it difficult to make links among Vietnamese "because of their lack of loyalty."

This over-the-top coverage had its inevitable sequel the next day when a popular *Sun* column written by Bob MacDonald was headlined "Immigrant gangs out of control," with a subheading that read "Bring back capital punishment, work camps." This was printed despite the fact that the paper quoted a police detective as saying that Asian turf wars and crime weren't getting worse. Nevertheless, MacDonald sounded the alarm and tied it all to the liberalization of Canada's immigration laws in the late 1960s. "The word went out that Canada was a sucker nation. It was an easy place to get into, no matter what your criminal past, and a great place for providing tons of social welfare monies, often with few questions asked."[22] It was the worst type of inaccurate, stereotypical reporting, and MacDonald offered not one fact to back it up. He did offer lots of solutions, though. "Demand that our gutless politicians tighten our immigration and criminal laws," he wrote. "Reinstating capital punishment and creating compulsory work camps wouldn't hurt at all."

The *Star* and *Globe and Mail* were careful to avoid any mention of Asian gangs in their first-day stories on the slaying, although the *Star* declared on Tuesday that "it appears Vo may have been the victim of a gang-style hit." The only evidence for this was a rather lame paragraph that read: "His attacker or attackers appeared to have been waiting outside the restaurant, a technique that has been used in gang-related violence." The story quoted the son of the owner of the Jun Jun restaurant as saying that the shooting was likely a result of someone wanting to settle a personal score, but the reporters clearly put more stock in their own theories because that quote appeared in the sixteenth paragraph of an eighteen-paragraph story.

Headlines during the four days that this story got play could easily have caused readers to assume that the Chinese community was crime-ridden. *Star* headings included "Chinatown killing sparks manhunt," (December 18, 1995); the *Sun* blared "Ambush at Chinatown restaurant" (December 18); "Crime gangs head north: Cops fear influx of Asian thugs" (December 20) and "Chinatown victim hit by 22 slugs" (December 20). Coupled with this, the *Star* chose to run a front-page story headlined "More Chinese settling in GTA" two days after the slaying. The story was based on Statistics Canada figures from the 1991 census, and an accompanying chart showed the percentage of Chinese in the population of the Greater Toronto Area rising from 1 percent in 1971 to 7 percent in 1991. It made no mention of the slaying but the link was inescapable: we should be on our guard; the problem's getting worse.

Four days after the slaying, all three of the papers reported the dramatic arrest of a 20-year-old suspect, who was not Chinese but Vietnamese like his victim and who lived far from Chinatown in North York. But that wasn't what ended the orgy of stereotypical coverage that dominated the local pages of the city's newspapers for most of the week. What caused them to drop the story like a hot potato was the fact that the slaying turned out to have little or nothing whatsoever to do with Asian gangs. It appeared to be "personally motivated," the police said, the result of an argument earlier in the evening at a Scarborough karaoke bar. Only the *Star* story, however, quoted a detective as dismissing the gang theory. The *Sun*, clearly with too much newsprint invested in the idea of an Asian gang "hit," once again described the victim as an extortion and protection racketeer who loved violence and labelled the karaoke bar as a club "favoured by Metro's Vietnamese underworld." It quietly dropped any reference to "gangland slaying," but the implication was still there.

The arrest of a suspect caused even greater problems at the *Globe and Mail*, which had its multicultural reporter, Isabel Vincent, looking into the background of the victim, Chanh Thong Vo, and using his slaying as a peg to examine Asian crime gangs. Instead of reporting what the police were now saying—that the slaying wasn't gang-related—the *Globe* ran Vincent's story, front page, on December 21, headlined "Man's life of violent crime led to death." It contained what in newspaper jargon is called a "nut graph," one paragraph that tries to tie together all the threads of the story. Vincent's was particularly apocalyptic, improbable and, in light of the facts reported elsewhere, dead wrong:

> The killing of Mr. Vo, coupled with a recent increase in the number of home invasions and extortions of Oriental small business people in major Canadian cities, has many Asian crime experts worried that Vietnamese and Chinese gangs are striking with greater force and brutality.

The story gave no statistics to show that crime of any sort in the Asian community had increased, and when it quoted exactly one Asian crime expert by name—a staff sergeant in Vancouver—he expressed no fear that gang violence was more prevalent or brutal. It was a story spun of the thinnest yarn and, lacking hard facts, it resorted to innuendo and stereotypes to try to make its points: that Asian gangs are recruiting heavily in junior and senior high schools; that Vietnamese—many of whom formed criminal networks in refugee camps and imported them to Canada—are particularly violent; and that they appear to have stricken fear into areas like Chinatown, where people are reluctant to talk to reporters for Canada's national newspaper. The story was filled with images that portray Chinese and Vietnamese Canadians as secretive, fearful and primitive. In Vo's neighbourhood, according to the *Globe*, shoppers haggle over plastic bags of frozen chicken parts while the owner uses an abacus to calculate prices.

A letter to the editor of the *Toronto Star* a few days later managed to make the point that all of the newspapers missed. Winnie Ng noted the differences between how the police and media responded to the killing of the Vietnamese in Chinatown and the killing of Leimonis in Just Desserts a year and a half earlier. The Chinese and Vietnamese patrons of the Jun Jun restaurant, many of them in shirtsleeves, were rounded up and searched in sub-zero temperatures, then hustled off to police headquarters for questioning. The media made no issue of this. But after Leimonis was killed on a warm April night, "the police did not round up the obviously shocked patrons and force them to stand outside with their hands up against a wall." Police and media response to the Chinatown slaying, Ng said, shows two things: that both institutions still have stereotypical notions of the Chinese community—"you can't tell who the criminal is"—and that they both still have a long way to go in securing the community's respect.

Despite all of the damning facts and useful suggestions for change that my subcommittee put on the table for Canada's publishers during the three years we were allowed to operate, we got back suspicion, anger and resentment from most of the people who were in a position to do something about it. It was the most frustrating and futile education project that I've ever been associated with.

The newspaper industry closed its door on diversity when the CDNA merged with the Newspaper Marketing Bureau in the spring of 1996 and became the Canadian Newspaper Association. At one of their last meetings, the CDNA publishers—quite hypocritically and with absolutely no discussion—endorsed the recommendations of the Golfarb report and declared diversity an important priority for the country's newspapers. But there was no public announcement of this and, when the new association got under way, diversity was deliberately left off its agenda. In my note of thanks written to members of the subcommittee, I called the CDNA's deathbed endorsement an empty gesture that committed Canadian newspapers to nothing at all, and I expressed the hope that the industry would receive more enlightened leadership in future. None of us should hold our breath about this. In my experience, most of the people who run newspapers in this country are quite happy with the imperfect mirror that they're holding up to our society.

## Notes

1. "Members' responses to 1993 questionnaire on issues facing the Canadian daily newspaper industry," CDNA. Seventy-one publishers from the organization's eighty-two papers answered the survey.
2. My diversity subcommittee began with eight members besides me: Betty Ann Adams, a Dene reporter from the *Saskatoon Star-Phoenix;* Adrian Cloete, a black editor from the *Guelph Mercury;* Haroon Siddiqui, the South Asian editorial page editor of the *Toronto Star;* three white editors from Southam papers, Joan Fraser, Ian Haysom and Michael Cooke; and two outsiders, Elyse Graff, executive director of the Canadian Council of Christians and Jews, and Dennis Strong, a black business consultant from Toronto who specializes in diversity training.
3. Irshad Manji's column in the *Ottawa Citizen* appeared April 19, 1994.
4. "The Racialization of Crime," from *The Colour of Democracy: Racism in Canadian Society*, by Frances Henry, Carol Tator, Winston Mattis and Tim Rees (Harcourt Brace & Company, 1995).
5. *The Invisible Empire: Racism in Canada*, by Margaret Cannon (Random House,

1995), page 15.

6. *A Place Called Heaven: The Meaning of Being Black in Canada*, by Cecil Foster (Harper Collins, 1996), page 207.

7. "Media and race: Failing to mix the message," by Haroon Siddiqui, *Toronto Star*, April 24, 1993, page D1.

8. "Equity in Edmonton's newsrooms," by Sheila Hallett-Kushniruk, *First Reading*, March/April 1995, published by the Edmonton Social Planning Council. Population projections done for the Canadian Advertising Foundation say that Edmonton's population will be 25 percent non-white by the year 2001.

9. *Muted Voices: Frustration and Fear in the Newsroom*, published in 1995 by the National Association of Black Journalists. The poll was answered by 537 black journalists and 100 managers.

10. Foster, op. cit., page 193.

11. "Women's byline study," by John Miller and Kimberly Prince, School of Journalism, Ryerson Polytechnic University, 1994. Overall, men wrote 67 percent of front-page stories. More than one-half were stories about crime, economics or government, and three times out of four those stories were written by men. Women at *Le Devoir*, the *Montreal Gazette* and the *Whitehorse Star* have a better than average chance of getting their stories on the front page. Those at the *Toronto Star, Calgary Herald, Vancouver Sun*, Halifax *Chronicle-Herald, Globe and Mail* and *Windsor Star* have a poorer than average chance.

12. "Shades of Kafka," by Trevor Lautens, *Content* magazine, July/August, 1990, page 26.

13. Mary Jane Handy left Southam in 1996 for a job with Abitibi-Price, thoroughly frustrated with the lack of progress towards full equality for women in the Canadian newspaper business. The report she co-authored, *Review Committee Report; The Southam Newspaper Group's Opportunities for Women Task Force*, February 1993, notes that two U.S. newspaper groups, Gannett and Knight-Ridder, have won recognition for hiring, training and promoting women and minorities by setting annual goals for their publishers.

14. Clark Davey, then publisher of the *Ottawa Citizen*, wrote to the head of the review committee in 1992 to express his dissatisfaction that it "did not shine a hard, bright questioning light on the lack of progress toward gender equality" at Southam. He added that he was embarrassed when about thirty senior Southam managers sat down to brainstorm solutions for the future, and "there was only one senior female executive in the room."

15. "Women's Participation in the Canadian News Media: Progress since the 1970s," by Gertrude J. Robinson, McGill University, and Armande Saint-Jean, Université de Sherbrooke, May 1997. The authors conclude: "Recruitment barriers to women remain strong in daily journalism."

16. "Please adjust your set," by Augie Fleras, in *Communications in Canadian Society*, 4th edition (Nelson, 1995).

17. Statistics Canada, *Canada's Changing Immigrant Population*, (Prentice-Hall, 1994). The report states that people who immigrated to Canada since 1961 are harder working, better educated and more likely to marry than people born here. For instance, 14 percent of adult immigrants held university degrees, compared to 11 percent for the native born; and 66 percent of immigrants were married, compared to 52 percent of the native born.

18. *The Imperfect Mirror*, by John Miller and Kimberly Prince, School of Journalism, Ryerson Polytechnic University, April 1994.

| News stories | % of minority news stories in newspaper | % of minorities and aboriginals in population * |
|---|---|---|
| *Toronto Sun* | 20 | 26.8 |
| *Toronto Star* | 15 | 26.8 |
| *Montreal Gazette* | 18 | 12.8 |
| *Vancouver Sun* | 11 | 26.7 |
| *Winnipeg Free Press* | 10 | 17.7 |
| *Calgary Herald* | 11 | 17.0 |

*Source: Statistics Canada, 1991 census

19. "The myth of the minority reader," by Gilbert Cranberg and Vincent Rodriguez, *Columbia Journalism Review*, January/February 1994, page 42.

20. *Tapping into a Growing Readership: Visible Minority Research Project*, a report by Goldfarb Consultants for the Canadian Daily Newspaper Association, August 1995.

21. Although the Goldfarb report urged newspapers to do more research, particularly on crime coverage, this has not happened. A group of journalism students at Ryerson, under the supervision of Professor Dan David, did a follow-up study in February 1996, analyzing one week's worth of crime coverage by Toronto's three largest daily newspapers and three top-rated television news programs. Nearly half of the crime stories published in the three papers mentioned the race of either the suspect or victim, and 81 percent of the TV coverage did so also. Only two of the more than two hundred stories mentioned race or national origin when the suspect was caucasian. *Murder, Mayhem and Minorities: The Toronto Media and Crime*, School of Journalism, Ryerson Polytechnic University, 1996.

22. "Immigrant gangs out of control," by Bob MacDonald, *Toronto Sun,* December 20, 1995, page 40.

# PART TWO

# Solutions

# CHAPTER SEVEN

# A Pilgrimage to Main Street

The price of this paper is one dollar per year
They'll issue on Thursday—once a week—never fear
No blots, blotches or scars on it, you will see
They print common sense in the *Equity*.

— Poem in first issue of the *Equity*, June 7, 1883

It's rare these days to feel compelled to buy any newspaper, but it's almost impossible to walk through the town of Shawville, Quebec, without stopping in to pick up a copy of the *Equity*. The paper's gray, wooden, two-storey office building hugs the main street so tightly there's no room for a sidewalk, and as soon as you walk in the front door, you're eye to eye with the circulation manager.

The daily life of a town of 1,500 flows past the newspaper's windows like a living story that it can capture in little bits every week. Just as there's a Main Street in every small town, there should be one in every journalist's heart. It's the place where you come face to face with the people you are supposed to write for, and they allow you to begin to understand their needs and dreams and fears. Big-city newspapers long ago moved away from their Main Streets to concrete suburban bunkers or inaccessible towers with security guards on the other side of expressways. But here in Shawville, the town literally trips over its paper.

A few steps away, at the intersection of Centre and Main, the only stoplight in Pontiac County halts traffic on the spot where mischievous town boys used to burn outhouses every Hallowe'en, and although the lights have been there for more than thirty years, friendly people still get out of their cars to chat while waiting for them to change. The irony strikes me almost immediately: in this unhurried and unpretentious little town, I am hoping to find some of the answers for what troubles Canada's multibillion-dollar daily newspaper industry.

I once wrote the first chapter of a novel about the Ottawa Valley that began:

"J. Ollie Pemberton's cream and green Plymouth swooped down into Trillium like a great, wounded bird, sprung rear door flapping in the night, a bald tire spanking Main Street." I never finished it because I had been too long away from the Valley, where I was born, and perhaps I had nothing very important to say. All writing must stem from a need, and my need became far from fictional. After a career that took me from paper boy to second-in-command of Canada's largest newsroom, and then to a journalism school where I was training others to do what I'd done, I needed to reassure myself that the craft I love has a future that works.

In my eighteen years as one of the top editors of the *Toronto Star*, I directed coverage of such events as Watergate and the Vietnam war. I loved the daily rush of covering world-shaking events. I felt that what I was doing was vital to society. It was only when I left to run the journalism program at Ryerson, in 1986, that the doubts began to set in. I became just another reader, albeit a very informed one. And I began to notice that there was something missing. Newspapers were not delivering what I needed, and every indicator said that they were not delivering what most Canadians needed. Years of success had made them arrogant, they had fallen out of touch with the concerns of their readers and they had let themselves be hopelessly bound by traditional ways of identifying and writing the news. They'd lost the art of storytelling and description that had once been their passion. They assumed the role of remote critic instead of community collaborator. They were being run as businesses out for profit instead of what we always depended on them to be: explainers of change and watchdogs for the public interest. What I was feeling was not so different from that which hundreds of thousands of readers and a few of Canada's more thoughtful journalists were thinking: newspapers would have to change, or die.

So I decided to embark on a quest: I would try to find answers in a place where the newspaper is still trusted, profitable and read by almost everyone; where it is regarded as such a part of its community that its loss would be like a death; and where news is measured not by the rhythms of important people or earth-shattering events but, well ... by the beat of bald tires spanking Main Street.

My colleagues and friends were sceptical when I told them of my plans, especially when I booked the winter off work. But the idea excited me professionally as nothing ever had—not because I hoped to find a better sort of newspaper out there (our dailies are the best there are and no one is foolish enough to argue that small-town weeklies have anything to teach them about great journalism), but because I wanted to see what covering the news again at the level of Main Street would teach me about how big papers might start to rebuild the trust they seem to have lost with their readers.

The problem with dailies is that too many of their publishers and editors, and an increasing number of their reporters and photographers, have fallen out of touch with the street. They've forgotten that good newspapers are written for their communities and that you can only understand those communities if you take the time to listen to them. How many daily publishers take public transit to work? How many big-city editors stop in at the corner store for a chat? How many reporters know the back streets of the poorest neighbourhoods? What they miss is how the city is changing, which is the starting point for finding the news. Who's moving in, who's moving out? What's got people scared, what's got them excited? What sounds and smells and passions add texture and compulsion to ordinary lives? That, it seems to me, is the first thing daily newsrooms need to win back.

I began my search with four requirements. First, the paper had to be locally owned, not part of a chain with most of its interests elsewhere. That criterion narrowed my research considerably, since most dailies and an increasing number of community papers have been gobbled up by absentee owners who have no organic connection to the cities and towns they are serving. Second, the paper had to be free of all hint of art direction or design. Cosmetics had prettied up dailies but had served to mask a failure in content, and I wanted honest wrinkles and blemishes, not lipstick. Third, it had to devote considerable space to Social Notes, those charming chronicles of who's visiting whom and who else is in hospital. Names still make news, and a paper that digs for them is working hard for its readers. Fourth, it had to avoid pretense and hype. My test was that it had to run lots of pictures of people looking straight at the camera, in that trusting way they always do when you take family snapshots.

That's why I find myself driving from Ottawa up the north side of the Ottawa River into Pontiac County, an English enclave of western Quebec located across the river from Renfrew. As soon as I walk in to the *Equity's* office, I know I have to work here. A reader is deep in conversation with the editor, and they are laughing. The most interesting local story in the paper is the death of fiddler Dominic Curley, not the crisis in Bosnia. And in her award-winning Social Notes column, correspondent Hermonie Sharpe observes: "As we go into January and all the fuss and excitement of Christmas and New Year's is over, many people get quite depressed." She offers a refreshing suggestion: "One thing we can do is keep our outside lights on for a while to brighten things up."

Editor Richard Wills and his publisher, Heather Dickson, are happy to accept an unpaid second reporter for the winter. As we shake hands on it, Heather says: "We don't actually have anyone on staff who's been trained in the field of journalism. You'll be our first."

Small-town journalists face many frustrations and obstacles: low pay; long hours; publishers who frequently bow to the wishes of advertisers and fellow Rotarians; small budgets that restrict time for indepth reporting; and the other subtle and not-so-subtle pressures telling you that if the news involves your neighbour or something unpleasant, it's often easier to look the other way. Still, according to a 1994 Angus Reid poll, 10.4 million Canadians read a community paper every week, and their interest is intense and growing because those papers cover issues and events that affect them most directly. They're written and edited by people who seem to care about their communities. A successful community publisher once told *Marketing* magazine: "It's like showing up with an apple pie at someone's door."[1]

News that matters and that you can understand. News that tells you what's happening around the corner rather than on the other side of the world. News that involves people you know. News that you can do something about. It's an attractive formula, no matter whether you're a reader in a small town like Shawville or in a neighbourhood in the middle of a large city. Big-city dailies, once dominant in their appeal to readers and advertisers, are wising up to this competition and, in places like Toronto, Montreal and Vancouver, are buying those upstart community papers to protect themselves. In its unsuccessful Supreme Court challenge to Southam's purchase of thirteen weeklies in the Lower Mainland area of Vancouver, the federal Bureau of Competition Policy tried to show that those papers posed a direct threat to the chain's two Vancouver dailies, the *Sun* and the *Province*. A consultant's report even said that daily newspapers in Canada were becoming, "in the cruel jargon of marketing, a discretionary product" for many advertisers, who were impressed by the lower distribution costs and higher household coverage of community papers.[2]

Newspapers traditionally measure their readership for advertisers by how many households they "penetrate" in the area they serve. For daily newspapers, that figure is now barely 50 percent. For the *Equity* in its home town of Shawville, it's 115 percent. In Pontiac County as a whole, the paper's total circulation of 4,600 reaches 83 percent of households. So confident is the paper of its hold on its community that it raised the price of each issue from fifty cents to seventy-five cents in the middle of a recession. Circulation wasn't affected at all, and on some weeks it's hard to find a paper to buy three days after it's published. So I start work with many important questions to answer. What kind of news fuels such intense interest? How can big-city dailies find their Main Streets again? Is it possible to be both a good journalist and a good citizen? If you go too far in telling the truth, what happens to friendships and advertising? If you don't go far enough, what happens to your credibility with readers?

Richard Wills is one of those calm and precise people who always seem to work well surrounded by clutter. He has a watchful, resourceful, owl-like look about him, like a man who notices things that others do not and never throws anything important out. His small metal editor's desk is piled with letters, old newspapers, bits of lunch and pages of notes to himself done in neat, all-capital blue printing. From here he looks out through open shelves to where the *Equity* sells Blueline record books; Avery office labels; Bildemup paper fasteners; Rexel Taurus staplers; Carter's stamp pads; Staedtler Mars plastic erasers; Berol Dart Markers; and Grumbacher Harmony Medium Weight Cold-Pressed Watercolour Sheets, fifteen to a pad. Here the people of Shawville buy their children's school supplies, the logs that let them calculate how much their farms lost last year and, yes, even the stationery that allows them to write letters of complaint or commendation to the editor of the *Equity*. To a visitor from Toronto, this seems to make him foolishly vulnerable. Richard's only protection against crazed and angry readers storming in is that he would first see them coming from his perch behind the office supplies. Much more often, they come in to tell him about the news happening in their community that ought to be in his paper.

"Welcome to the *Equity*," he says, shaking hands. He's in his early forties but looks younger, a lean, chiselled, clean-cut man who talks as if he's carefully thought out every word first, so his sentences progress in logical lockstep, exactly like his editorials do. There's something inescapably reliable about a man who comes to work every day in blue jeans and talks like he writes. As we sit down to get acquainted, he adjusts his horn-rimmed glasses, kicks off his Kodiak-style boots and hoists his feet up on the corner of his desk. This relaxed informality is deceptive, because the more we talk the more Richard strikes me as a man who prefers to keep a tight reign on his emotions, lest all his horses bolt. I may have just doubled his entire reporting staff by walking in the door, but I am an outsider, and his guard is up.

The newspaper reflects these proper aspects of his character. In the pages of the *Equity*, the people of Shawville and Pontiac County win curling bonspiels; get elected to the Fair Board; are runners-up in the Miss Snow Queen contest; graduate from the Office Specialist Course at Pontiac High School; beat the Timberwolves Atoms in two games; become managers of the Canadian Tire store; win public speaking competitions, 4-H awards, Athlete of the Week and euchre or whist jackpots; and are made Lions, Rotarians, Kinsmen and Oddfellows. Its pages chronicle the rites and rituals of daily life, the kind of things that seem so ordinary as not to be newsworthy until you realize that they are the things that bring people together, the things that make a community a community instead of a concentration of real estate. More kids win essay prizes at S.E. McDowell Elementary School than deal drugs or get in trouble with the law; more families have reunions or go to the Lion's bingo than have domestic disputes; more folks volunteer in service clubs or at the hospital than complain about the mayor. Isn't that what most of our lives are like anyway? The *Equity* merely reflects that life in its pages.

A "mission statement" I once read in another small-town paper captured this spirit admirably:

> While the high and mighty strut and stamp across the world's stage, six women go out to visit the elderly. A small boy scores the winning goal in a soccer game. An amateur theatre group produces a smash hit. A town council passes an important new law. The real lives of real people. Stories that should be told. And I tell those stories every week.

# A Pilgrimage to Main Street

Because I am a community newspaper.

The thirst for this type of news is amazing to an outsider, who isn't used to seeing such things in his daily newspaper. Ordinary people don't often make news in big cities, except as statistics. Daily journalism's infatuation with conflict and the inner workings of government, with the cosmic meaning of economic indicators and the antics of millionaire athletes has crowded out the ordinary with the extraordinary, smothered the familiar with the foreign, displaced the common interest with the vested interest. Dailies are more often sowers of discord than promoters of consensus. They worship conflict. They cover the institutional and ignore the individual. They are suspicious of success, abnormally intrigued by failure and spend little time with the great in-between. Their fatal flaw is their lack of compulsion to explore common humanity and the deeper meaning of things. People say they can no longer see themselves in the pages of metropolitan dailies, and editors across Canada wonder why. There's no mystery. No one says that about a paper like the *Equity*, where almost every page carries a picture of familiar-looking people looking straight out at us, all ready to be clipped and pasted in a scrapbook. Editors of such papers, unlike their daily cousins, understand that a newspaper is ultimately judged by how close it comes to giving readers a record of their daily lives that they can believe in.

A daily newspaper might define news as what went wrong yesterday. I ask Richard how he defines it. He seems lost for a second, then remembers I'm a journalism professor and should know that myself.

"How are you supposed to define it?" he asks. "I'll take a picture of some ribbon cutting, and write down all the names for the cutline, then stop and say 'I know everyone here. Most people in town do. So is this really news—if everyone knows?'"

"But you print it."

"Of course I print it."

"And nobody complains?"

"People generally complain about what isn't in the paper, rather than what is. I guess that's different from a big-city paper. I've never worked on one of those. Maybe what didn't make it is a picture someone passed on from their grandfather's estate, or maybe a new litter of kittens."

"So what do you tell them?" I ask.

"Oh, that we'll try to get it in next week. Usually we find a way, if they keep calling."

The *Equity* looks like one of those old newspapers that turns up yellowed and curly in your basement during spring cleaning. Its pages are sixteen inches wide, one of the broadest broadsheets still printed. This means lots of room for ads. Chugg Electric is in every week, and so is Salon Chez Lise (Wet and Cut for $6.00). Geo. H. Froats & Sons Monuments is tombstoned beside a punnish

155

come-on for the Cobden Farmers Market ("Lettuce entertain you; just turnip Saturday!"). Across the top of the front page, proudly in red, is exactly the same nameplate, in exactly the same typeface, that ran in the very first issue in 1883. They've still got the original wooden type in the back room, a refreshing change from my old newspaper, which changed its nameplate three times in five years in the late 1970s when it was going through an identity crisis. Professional designers would disapprove of the serif masthead clashing with the serif headline dress, but there is an unschooled, down-home feel to the *Equity* that seems to match it to its community. This paper does not shout: few headlines run larger than thirty-six points, few pictures wider than three columns. But the stories run on and on, in great rivers of columns that spill down the front page and turn to others inside, sometimes turning a second or third time. In fact, the paper seems to read inward from both ends—the back-page Social Notes turns inside as well, so that some pages in the middle are filled with just the tail-ends of stories from fore or aft. Here is the full blow-by-blow of community events, and this primacy of the printed word makes perfect sense. For the type of news the *Equity* prints, there is no competition from television.

Richard has cleared a desk for me beside his own. It belongs to the paper's only reporter, Colette Blain, who has been temporarily moved around a partition into a cramped area of the office that is only twenty feet long and twelve feet wide but serves as the home for all the other departments of the paper; display advertising; job printing; financial services; the paste-up and film-drying area for the darkroom; and the haven where the whole staff of ten gathers twice every day for coffee break and gossip. Besides Richard and Colette, the editorial department has a third employee, Jean Smith, who typesets the correspondents' copy, the letters to the editor and the council minutes from fifteen surrounding municipalities on the newspaper's Macintosh desktop system. Her job requires special skills that she alone possesses. Jean has lived in Shawville all her life and is a student of handwriting, so when one of the Social Note correspondents like Hermonie Sharpe or Phoebe McCord files her copy in rough longhand on the back of an envelope, looking like maybe they scribbled it there while driving along Highway 148 or watching "Coronation Street" on the TV, Jean alone is able to decipher what they write, what they spell wrong and even what they mean to say. It is said that Jean Smith knows everyone and everything in Pontiac County.

Colette dashes by and introduces herself. She is an attractive redhead in her early thirties who lives upstairs in an apartment whose back door is up a staircase near the editor's desk and through a thin trap door. I can hear kids crying up there. Colette is separated from her husband, who is an electrician in town, and dashes off her stories when her two pre-school daughters are napping or she can arrange for a babysitter. Sometimes Richard looks out for them, and they sort of share the editorial helm in a kind of tag-team. He looks at me disapprovingly when I say rather offhandedly and insensitively to Colette that if she needs any coaching on her writing, well, I am after all a teacher and just drop by. I've noticed, from reading back copies, that Colette has an awkward way of backing into her stories. But I've clearly got off on the wrong foot with her, not realizing that when you're going through a life crisis, with two dependent kids and no money, when you have no formal training in journalism and you're the only reporter on a newspaper that needs to come out every week full of stories about everything that's happening in the entire county around you, the priority isn't journalistic excellence, it's getting it all done.

Much about the *Equity*, in fact, has that same homemade, seat-of-the-pants quality. Only one employee has previous working experience in his or her job. Before they were hired here, the head pressman had never handled type, and the advertising manager worked in a lumber camp. Even the publisher, Heather Dickson, is learning on the job. Although a member of the family that has owned the paper for forty years, she had no experience in managing, marketing, editing or writing, even though she now does all four. Claire Lunam is called the circulation manager, although what she really does is answer the phone and talk to her neighbours. So she can casually joke with someone that, by the way, his subscription is two weeks overdue but, "don't worry Dale, I'm not going to cut you off," and that person can joke back that he's glad his newspaper doesn't behave like his wife. This kind of personal service builds loyalty and trust. Anne Taylor, who keeps track of the *Equity's* accounts, remembers a customer who used to pay his subscription with two fifty-pound sacks of potatoes. She thinks for a moment and says the paper would probably accept the same deal today. "As long as we keep up to the potatoes, I guess people will think we're fair value."

A newspaper with a circulation department that accepts someone's garden products does a lot of things for a community. In Shawville, the *Equity* is as vital a public service as the hydro and running water. If someone wants to know why her tax bill is late, she doesn't call Town Hall; she stops Richard on Main Street. If there's a noxious stink coming from Shaw-Consolidated, the newspaper may hear about it before the paper mill. "I'd say more than 50 percent of our news comes through the door at us," Heather says. The paper's motto might as well be: *Tell the Equity. The Equity will find out. It's on your side.* Somehow, we stopped using daily newspapers that way. They've become too big, too hard to reach, too obsessed with the bottom line and too concerned with what they have always seen as news: looking for what's wrong rather than following through and finding ways to put it right. This distances them from us in a way that has never happened to the *Equity* and its readers. While dailies are struggling to reflect their communities better, this paper is busy helping to create a *sense* of community among its readers, who include virtually all the literate adult souls in Pontiac County.

This kind of journalism was imported here by Rosaleen Dickson, who bought the *Equity* in 1953 when it was just a Linotype, an old Heidelberg press and some moveable type in a shed in a town she'd never been to. "When we moved out six months later, they moved some ponies in and it was a shed again," she remembers. Using a small inheritance from her mother, whose husband was the poet Kenneth Leslie and whose father had founded Moir's chocolates, Rosaleen Dickson, at the age of thirty and with four small kids, bought a building and set about learning the newspaper business from a collection of fifty-year-old journalism textbooks and a drunken tramp printer, who taught her how to hand-set a page, letter by letter. She put out the paper for thirty years while her husband David did the books. She was a one-woman dynamo, selling ads, gathering the news, writing editorials and finally getting so impatient for change that she got elected to Shawville council, the first woman ever. She built housing for senior citizens, established a community radio station and served as chair of the tourist association. Ten years ago, she turned the paper over to her son Ross and daughter-in-law Heather and moved back to Ottawa, but they still remember "Miz Dickson" in Shawville, and her textbook ethic—to tell the truth and look out for the Pontiac—still governs how this paper covers the news. Ross Dickson, who holds a PhD in chemistry from Cambridge University, is not your typical community newspaper publisher, but he and Heather have carried on the tradition, building up enough equity in the *Equity* to establish two other community papers in Ottawa. Although the couple recently separated, they still collaborate in business, and Ross offers to let me use a spare bedroom in his house a block away from the paper: "Walk right in if I'm not home. I never lock the door."

In the pantheon of Canada's community press, there is and has only ever been one newspaper called the *Equity*. There are Timeses and Newses and Echos almost everywhere, and the list of 683 English language papers belonging to the Canadian Community Newspaper Association includes at least two Driftwoods, but most are wonderfully one-of-a-kind, reflecting a rough-hewn independence and personality that I admire. Among them: the *Similkameen Spotlight;* the *Whistler Question;* the *Banff Crag & Canyon;* the *Jasper Booster;* the Sundre, Alberta *Round-up;* the *Swan Hills Grizzly Gazette;* the somewhat optimistically titled *World Spectator* published in Moosomia, Saskatchewan (circulation 3,517); the *Rose Valley View From Here;* the *Spirit* of Bothwell, Ontario (circulation 365); the *Hornepayne Bear News;* the Milton *Canadian Champion;* the *Miramichi Headwater;* the Antigonish *Casket* (dying to get it?); and, my favourite, the *Low Down to Hull and Back News*, published, it so happens, in nearby Wakefield, Quebec. The *Equity*, too, stands proudly among the originals.

In its inaugural issue of June 7, 1883, the newspaper explained its unique name and, in a gesture that foreshadowed modern marketing techniques, threw itself at the feet of its readers:

> Equity [is] that virtue which treats all persons according to the rules of reason and justice—an adherence to which, it must be admitted, is no very easy task; and, if through misjudgment or indiscretion, our efforts

to do so prove futile, the indulgence of a discerning public is solicited.

It's good that they added this, since the second issue did not appear as scheduled on June 14. The following week the paper said with refreshing honesty: "Our readers will pardon us, we trust .... The amount of work was more than we could accomplish."

Such honesty has become part of the paper's tradition. At a public meeting I cover two months later, I watch a farmer insist over and over again to a Quebec government traffic inspector that something he just said can't possibly be true because the *Equity* published a story saying the opposite. The farmer does not believe the inspector when he suggests the newspaper may have got it wrong, which as a matter of fact it did. This bond with readers does not occur anymore at dailies, whose journalism often seems to be suspect even when it's right. Why, I wonder, did people stop thinking of the daily newspaper with the same degree of ownership as that with which Shawville people still regard "their" *Equity*?

Part of the answer is found in Richard's superb editorials. His voice in them is "we, the people," and his viewpoint is bolstered by historical examples and is always solidly on the side of the people of Pontiac County. He will, for instance, acknowledge the heavy workload of being a volunteer on a local fair board, but will also editorialize in favour of greater community involvement because "a larger pool of labour, skilled or otherwise, would ease the burden upon those who take the welfare of their community seriously." He will tackle the difficult issue of small-town gossip by pointing out that a flurry of inaccurate "eyewitness" accounts of police busts on Main Street ruin hard-won local reputations and make citizens "believe the worst about each other," yet he will carefully avoid mentioning that the rumours involve drugs (which would be tantamount to spreading the rumours further; and the *Equity*, he writes, "does not deal in rumour"). He will skewer the Quebec government's reasons for slapping a surcharge on Pontiac residents for regional transportation services that they never use by pointing out the county "pays more for less" for too many other local government services lost in the interests of centralization.

His almost organic link to the community surprises me because, as I listen to Richard, I realize he is not native to Pontiac County, or even the Ottawa Valley. He does not talk with that distinctive lilting Irish, front-of-the-palate Valley twang that causes declarative sentences to unexpectedly soar at the ends, where Campbells become Kombles, where "coos, harses and pegs" are kept in the "bairn," where if you're truly native you might know someone who lives "vivdeen moyles narth o' th' toon loin," and where all real music is played on a fiddle. Richard plays the drums and comes from Kentucky. He speaks in a reconditioned drawl, with a pauseless and even monotone that reflects the relentless sense of certainty you find in many midwest Americans. "Richard's one of those draft dodgers settled in the hills," the advertising manager, Brent Horner, tells me later.

But Richard doesn't tell me that. All he says is that he moved here because of the cheap land, and newspapering runs in his family. His father owned a weekly paper and one of his brothers edits a weekly in Metropolis, Missouri, about 150 miles southeast of St. Louis. "Look at this," he says proudly, holding up the front page his brother sent him. Across the top is a black armband with the distinctive Superman logo on it. The comic strip had just declared Superman dead, and the namesake hometown was in mourning. At that moment, Richard looks like all newspaper people look when they admire the work of others: you wish you could have thought of it, something refreshingly original to float on the sea of mundane. Ideas like that, they take your breath away.

"I'll do anything, anything at all," I tell Richard. "Only I may be a bit rusty."

"You may see things we don't," he says, "because you're new."

Since the town hall is right next door, and there's a council meeting tonight, I suggest I look in. Richard gives me a quizzical look. The *Equity*, he says, doesn't cover a lot of municipal government meetings, just ones at which there is some likelihood of news happening that would make the effort worthwhile. With only one reporter, the paper cannot possibly cover the fifteen councils that meet on the same night in its circulation area. If something's going to happen, Richard is almost invariably tipped to it.

Still, elected officials should be watched, and with nothing better to do I drop in on the official monthly meeting of Shawville town council. When I walk in, seven heads jerk up as if I've disturbed them doing something naughty. I am the only spectator—a far cry from the raucous days 150 years ago when council meetings had to be moved out of town, "at least one mile distant from Robin McDowell's Tavern," because they often degenerated into drunken brawls. Now, Mayor Albert Armstrong patiently waits for councillors to finish discussing a resident's request for a culvert, then declares that there is a visitor in the hall tonight and will I please state my business. I mumble something about my internship and how I'm just looking on to see how the town works. There are tight smiles all around, and they go back to reviewing the town's monthly receipts, one by one, with the mayor asking secretary-treasurer Charlie Dale things like, "Now this bill for $31.27, Charlie, what was that for?" Richard is right. I've spent two hours taking notes and can't for the life of me think of anything worth writing for the paper, unless the purchase of a new clutch for the town sander qualifies as news.

The next evening I find myself in the Ed and Ellen Place Motel, in a windowless room filled with smoke and an H-shaped wooden table bristling with brown empties, for the annual meeting of the Shawville and District Snowmobile Club. Richard says there may be news in it, but obviously not enough to bring him out on a cold night in the middle of the week. The main task of the meeting is to plan the club's annual Poker Rally, a seventy-five-mile dash between seven of Pontiac County's most popular taverns. The reason it's called a poker rally is that participants are given a card at each stop, and the highest hand wins. Last year, it was three of a kind, not bad at all, considering many snowmobilers found ways to avoid finishing the course in the -20 degrees Celsius cold and with all those frothy distractions.

I immediately grasp two things: first, that snowmobiling was invented to get from bar to bar in the winter as quickly as possible; and second, that there isn't much in the way to stop that from happening. Nowhere, in thirty pages of Quebec government regulations governing the sport, is there any mention of a speed limit. You can go as fast as you want, it seems, as long as you're able to stop your snowmobile in eleven metres. Club president Bob Bradford, a hulking, gravel-voiced man in a plaid shirt left out at the tail, passes around a letter from a Catholic priest, a lifelong snowmobiler who solicited the club's financial support for a marathon trek to Alaska. His letter describes the most exhilarating moment, a hell-bent, white-knuckle freefall at Tumbler Ridge, B.C., when "we came down the chute from 7,000 feet to 2,000 feet in less than half a minute, going over 80 miles an hour with the brakes on. It doesn't get any better than that!" Yvon Levesque, the priest who did that and lived to write about it, is seventy-six years old.

The meeting lasts over three hours, much of that time being spent devising the rules for the Miss Snow Queen contest. Bob leans over at one point and asks me to be a judge, but the rules sound as complicated as the formula used to judge synchronized swimming in the Olympics. I politely decline, on grounds of journalistic objectivity. Ten points are given for an essay entitled "What do you think snowmobiling can do for tourism in the Pontiac?" and they hope it will be published in the *Equity*.

The next morning, I warn Richard what's coming.

"What about the meeting?" he asks.

"Oh, no news happened," I said. "Nothing to write about at all."

Now, there is a particular look editors give you when they seriously doubt your ability. It's like a double take, only with the eyes half-lidded with scepticism and the mouth slightly agape. When I used to inflict it on reporters, they called it Miller's Dead Fish Look. It says, "I don't fucking believe this, I send you out on a story, it happens right in front of you, you waste three hours of the paper's time, and have nothing to show for it? What am I going to fill the paper with?" On a staff with only two reporters, Richard may have a point, although he's too polite to come right out and say it. But he has another valuable editor's quality that I once possessed too—the ability to make others feel guilty without uttering a word. He is wondering how reliable I am, I think, and I begin to see him in a new light, as someone who has probably never come up empty from a meeting that he has taken the time to sit through. Perhaps only veteran community newspaper editors can attain such a high degree of productivity.

He casually suggests I tag along with Colette to an important meeting of the Quyon Fair Board. *Tag along with Colette?* I think. My God, he's double teaming us. I'm beginning to think my big-city concept of news is not serving me very well here. Although Richard doesn't expect me to write anything, just watch Colette, I feel a nervous fluttering in my stomach, exactly the way I used to feel the first few years I worked at the *Toronto Star*. It'll be okay, I think. Just try harder.

The Women's Institute Hall in Quyon is dark when we arrive, but the parking lot is a hive of activity. Farmers have paired off to socialize in steamed-up cars with their engines running against the cold. The mayor of Bristol is late with the keys to the front door. When he arrives, Jack Graham brings five dozen doughnuts and runs the annual meeting as if he's in a hurry to get to them before folks decide to drift away. Agricultural fairs are important community events in small towns but are usually too marginally profitable to afford paid staff. So Jack Graham knows nothing will get organized unless he signs up lots of volunteers. The twenty-two men and three women sitting on tin chairs in this drafty hall are all about to become directors and councillors of the Quyon Fair.

On the drive over, Colette says the spirit of volunteerism keeps Pontiac County running, and lets it slip that she judged the Miss Snow Queen contest last year.

Jack Graham's list—innocently entitled "Individuals who have shown an interest: Potential Directors and Councillors"—contains thirty-four names: Carmen and Duck Trudeau; Waverly Greer; Minor Chevalier; and Richard McAra, the night watchman at the fairgrounds, who is dressed in a suit and tie and carrying his little sure-shot camera because he's down for re-election to the board. While some might think that this marks him as a man who, as they say up the Valley, "tends to fart a little higher than his arse," you should know that no one who's a farmer in the township will *not* be elected to something before Jack offers up the doughnuts.

The Quyon Fair is a triumph of Jack's organization. He's a big turtle of a man, with alert eyes and a chin that seems about to disappear down the front of his collar. He farms a bit and sells insurance. When he's inspired with new ideas for the Fair, which he is often, he waves his hands in big chopping motions and talks about how pig wrestling and dainty dog shows could pull in the city folks. Last year the fair lost $2,000 on one rash new idea—pari-mutuel horse racing—and then there was that mix-up when *two* midway operators arrived with their identical truckloads of pipes, tracks, gondolas, generators and carnies. Jack sorted that one out nicely: he allowed both midways to set up, then let them fight it out in court for a year to collect the fee. Despite those setbacks, the fair attracted 20,000 visitors and showed an over-all profit of $3,360. One of Jack's secrets is good timing. He schedules the fair within a day or two of the turn of the month. "If July 1 gets a little away from us," he says, "the welfare cheques aren't in, or else they're spent, and revenues drop off too much."

This is a sound theory and one that seems to dictate the timing of major social events throughout Pontiac County. Bake sales, bingos, church socials, Lion's Club fundraising euchres and agricultural exhibitions all seem to cluster at month's end, where they end up competing for three of the county's most important sources of currency: the welfare, the baby bonus and the unemployment. The Pontiac has an unemployment rate of more than 16 percent, and there are pockets where it approaches 50 percent.

There's one outstanding bill from last year's fair—$50 listed for the services of a translator. This area was settled in the early 1800s by Irish loggers, and the land agent awarded land only to Protestants, so the Quyon Fair Board today is made up of unilingual English farmers. Someone who speaks French is always hired to ride linguistic shotgun with the government of Quebec.

"Money well spent," Jack says, letting it slip that the salary for the translator was a bottle of Courvoisier. "I wouldn't like to see that written up in the *Equity*," he says, looking sharply at us. Colette stops taking notes.

"Better call it something," a farmer says. "Refreshments? Honorarium?"

"Someone second that?" Jack jumps in. "Fifty bucks for the cognac? All in favour? Good. I never want to hear about this again."

He yields the chair to Vince McConnell, area representative for the ministry of agriculture, who calls for nominations for the board of directors. "Don't be shy," he says. "If I'm going too fast or doing something wrong, stop me. But we can all get home faster if we only nominate nine." That's the minimum number of directors specified for agricultural fairs. Nine are nominated and duly acclaimed without hurting anyone's feelings.

Jack moves that all the other people present, plus another ten or twelve names left on his list, be acclaimed as councillors. "Not too many left to put on," someone says. "Nearly everyone's here who's a farmer." Jack suggests: "Maybe we could double up by adding the wives." The Proulx boys, who earlier added their father's name, allow that their mother might be similarly proud to serve. Finally, Jack has forty names. Vince McConnell suggests a round of applause for the new executive, and of course everyone joins in.

It's not until the very end that Jack, looking sheepish for the first time all night, refers to a slight "technicality." No one may vote or stand for the executive of a fair board in Quebec unless he or she is a paid and current member, and new memberships are supposed to be cut off an hour before the meeting. Everyone forgot, and there is an awkward moment when the momentum of the evening threatens to crash to a halt. Some look to the Quebec ministry of agriculture representative for guidance, but he buries himself in his notebook. Like so much else, it's left to Jack, and again he comes through for the fair. "Don't put this in the *Equity* but I think we should get legal," he says, reaching in his pocket. "If you got five bucks, drop it on the table. Doughnuts is served."

Driving home, Colette says Richard once came to cover a fair board meeting and got elected to the executive because he forgot to avoid eye contact with Jack. He served the full three-year term.

Had Richard asked me to write a story on the fair board meeting, I don't think I could have obliged, since nothing had happened that matched any of the criteria for news that I was familiar with, such as significance, impact, surprise, and celebrity. But Colette's twelve-paragraph story is destined to start on page one, and it begins: "The Quyon Fair Board held its annual general meeting on Monday, January 11th, at the Women's Institute Hall in Quyon. Elected to the executive were ...."

Tagging along with Colette has been instructive and leads me to draw an important conclusion: news that binds readers to their community, and therefore to their newspaper, is not necessarily news that surprises them. It's often news that confirms what they already know, but explains why or how it happened, what it means and what may be coming next. It's news that spotlights their achievements, not just their tragedies. It's news that encourages them to participate in finding solutions, not just to sit back and let someone else deal with it. In these ways and others, community papers tend to activate their readers' social consciousness, whereas dailies, with their emphasis on "official" news and aberrant behaviour, tend to deaden it. Such news isn't always found in the places where daily newspapers look for it, in legislatures, in police stations, in courthouses, at press conferences or—increasingly, with the downsizing of newsrooms—over the phone. It happens around the corner, and you have to be there. Since I have no desire to spend my time in Shawville writing a bunch of "meeting-was-held" stories, I decide to look for news in other places, operating like something of a foreign correspondent just landed in a strange country; I will roam around with my curiosity aroused and write in depth and detail about what seems to affect ordinary people in the community.

Eugene Roberts, one of the grandees of U.S. journalism who just retired as managing editor of the *New York Times*, says that the most memorable work he ever did was when he first started out writing for a tiny paper in North Carolina. His editor gave him the farm column and told him to drive the back concessions and write about what he found. He did stories about sweet potatoes that looked like Charles de Gaulle, but also about how hailstorms can wipe out a farmer's inheritance. Ten years later, when he was a war correspondent in Vietnam covering the Tet offensive, he learned a powerful lesson about the impact those stories can have on readers. He found himself once in a dark bunker in Hue, interviewing American soldiers who had been trapped behind North Vietnamese lines for two weeks. When he introduced himself as a reporter for the *New York Times*, one of the soldiers said: "Hey, did you ever write the 'Rambling in Rural Wayne' column for the *Goldsboro News-Argus*?" From that, Roberts says today:

> I learned never to underestimate readers. They can laugh with you at the Charles de Gaulle sweet potatoes, but they expect depth when stories arise that are important to them. If tobacco prices are going up or down there is no limit to their demand for detail. I wish some of today's publishing executives had been out in the tobacco rows with

me. They would have learned that formula and slickness cannot substitute for substantive news coverage.[3]

Knowing what's important to your readers is one of the lost arts of daily journalism, where news values are determined largely by scheduled events, legislative routine, the press release or the police radio. Most reporters know what their assignment is before they leave the office, and very often what they write is predictable—yet another delay in this, a further development in that, reaction to something else, news of another tragedy. That is the way they've been conditioned to look for news, and that is what their editors expect them to report. The voice of the reader, saying this is not enough for us, is seldom heard.

What kind of news would a newspaper cover, I asked myself, if it unhitched itself from an agenda set largely by others and devoted significant resources to finding detailed answers to two simple questions: First, what are people talking about? And second, what *should* they be talking about?

The most interesting thing I've heard since I came to Shawville is that one of its most prominent citizens, the president of the local fair board, has been diagnosed with inoperable cancer. One or two other recent cases of cancer are mentioned during the morning coffee ritual at the *Equity*, when everyone on staff gets together to gossip. Someone says it's probably "that Chalk River thing again." It's one of the oldest myths of the Ottawa Valley: that a leak of radioactive material in the 1960s from the nuclear generating station at Chalk River, one hundred miles upstream, was causing health problems and genetic mutations. I remember catching five-legged frogs in Buckam's Bay near Ottawa forty years ago and believing that those leaked isotopes had somehow unleashed a secret and deadly plague on all living things. Any link to Shawville, which is seven kilometres from the Ottawa River, may be rather far-fetched, but I'm desperate. The first issue of the *Equity* since my arrival is coming out in two days, and I haven't one story to offer for it. I ask Richard where I can get my hands on some health statistics. "Here," he says, tossing over a thick, unpublished report by the Community Health Department of the Outaouais Region analyzing causes of death in Pontiac County for the last twenty years. "It came in last month, and nobody's had time to go through it." With an investigative reporter's zeal, I spend three hours, missing lunch and poring over every page until I manage to isolate some statistics that show mildly higher death rates for cancer in the past five years. I eagerly rehearse the order of my probing questions and arrange an interview with Dr. Pierre Roberge who, besides being director of professional services at the Pontiac Community Hospital, is the county's chief coroner.

Dr. Roberge is a slight, balding and heavily bearded man whose ponderous, bureaucratic way of speaking makes me suspect one of three things: (a) that he knows nothing about my Chalk River theory; (b) that he knows something, but I'm never going to find out what; or (c) I've wasted three hours and lunch, and am going to lose a hell of a lot of the rest of the afternoon before I can break away and turn my efforts to something that might produce a column inch or two for the paper.

My eyes begin to glaze over as he begins to explain how the Quebec health system is different from that of Ontario and how epidemiology (the study of the incidence of disease) really isn't his field, and that yes, more people are being diagnosed with cancer, but that's probably because there are more cancer specialists at the hospital now who can detect it. While I'm here, would I like a tour of the hospital perhaps? It's not often we have a reporter stop by.

I get up and begin to slip on my coat. He stays seated, talking about how this area is often ignored by government officials in Quebec, but that he and other doctors are specializing in the important but neglected field of rural medicine. I'm slipping my gloves on now. I've been in his office an hour and have nothing to show for it. I'm wondering how Richard will react to my Chalk River scoop falling through. "So," I ask Dr. Roberge, almost in desperation to get out, "is there anything else going on here that our readers should know about?" He thinks for a moment and fishes under the clutter on his desk to find a brochure. I might be interested in a course that some of the doctors are putting on in April. I glance at it and do a double take. The brochure is from McGill University in Montreal. Ten doctors and staff from the tiny community hospital located in Shawville are organizing the country's first conference for rural doctors, and McGill—Canada's most prestigious university—is hosting it.

"I'm impressed," Richard says, after I hand over my story, based on interviews with the doctors who organized the course and were able to sell the idea to McGill. He makes it the lead story in the paper. Colette is now an avid fan of what she thinks is my big-city investigative journalism technique. "I wouldn't have got that story," she says. I neglect to tell her that I almost didn't have the patience to get it either. Maybe there are other good stories to be had by not making my mind up in advance.

The *Equity*, it turns out, is designed around one principle: get all the copy in. There are no page dummies, those miniature sketches that allow an editor to make a page attractive to the reader. Copy is slapped down according to where—and how—it fits. And by anyone. It's not unusual to hear the display advertising manager shouting "I need 4 inches!" as he puzzles over how to fill the rest of the pages with stuff that's *not* for sale.

At 1:45 p.m. on this first production day, a disembodied voice crackles over a two-way radio: "Neil, there's a fire near the Norval place ... chimley fire, looks like." And Neil Sharpe, the typesetter, puts on his hockey jacket and dashes out. He's chief of the volunteer firefighters. So production of the two sports pages, filled largely with minor hockey reports, falls to Brent Horner. The hockey copy falls a little light, and he manages to jam a two-column headline on the best story in the paper: three legs of type about a nineteen-year-old dog that wears funny hats and eats spaghetti and lives with a priest. But that's okay. The third leg falls under a neighbouring headline that says Clarendon Municipal Council Minutes. It is not unusual for stories to get a little mixed up like that, or even for them to turn from page to page inside the paper. Once a headline continued over a turn too. I did not see a picture do so, but no one could swear it would never happen.

Next day, Jean Smith takes one look at the paper and utters an expletive we all think her incapable of. "Those *bastards*," she hisses. She's got her finger on an advertisement for Killarney's bar, which is letting everyone know about its Beach Party Night on Saturday. That's the same night as the snowmobile club's poker rally, which starts at Killarney's but is supposed to finish with a party at the nearby R.A. Hall. Jean, who happens to be treasurer of the snowmobile club, is not pleased. "We chose them as the starting point because we wanted to do them a favour," Jean says. "Now this!"

There's no doubt that the conflict in dates will affect the turnout at the poker rally. Some people just won't get out of Killarney's, and many who do may short-cut back there to catch the featured band from Toronto: Hank Sinatra and the Honky Tonk Nightmare. Jean is concerned that the club won't cover its costs and that Miss Snow Queen will be crowned to an empty house. Given the arduous scoring system, that may happen even without competition from Killarney's.

"I do hope we aren't covering this," Jean tells Richard, pointing to the bar ad. Richard and I say nothing, possibly because he's just told me he's been asked to fill in on drums that night for Hank Sinatra's band. He keeps his outside activities pretty much to himself, so Jean probably doesn't know this. Suddenly, it seems, all the conflicts inherent in contemporary journalism have been visited upon us: self-interest versus community good; the quest for profits versus public service; journalistic independence versus perceived or actual conflict of interest; hidden agenda versus full disclosure to your readers; not to mention the career-shortening mistake of pissing off the person who sets your type.

I try not to imagine what might happen to editorial peace at the *Equity* if things escalate to violence on Saturday, and a nylon-swishing herd of hard-core snowmobilers decide to storm down Main Street towards Killarney's, with Jean Smith in the lead carrying a torch. Out of the bar spill all these loutish, loud-shirted Texas country-rock enthusiasts in shades, Richard among them with his drumsticks, and their eyes meet in the torchlight ....

It's not easy being the editor of anything today. But at least on a small-town weekly, when things start to go wrong, you hear about it.

## Notes

Affairs.
3.  "Nothing Succeeds Like Substance," by Eugene Roberts, *American Journalism Review*, December 1993, page 3.

# CHAPTER EIGHT

# Coaster Cone's Complaint

Perhaps you need to work in a small town for a while to understand just how close journalism can be to its community, and how far away most of it stands. Unlike other people who consider themselves professionals, such as doctors and lawyers, big-city journalists seldom open their doors to explain themselves to the people they serve. So while you can visit a doctor to find out why it hurts and how to make it better, newspaper people seem to discourage human contact. Their office lobbies are staffed by security guards, not receptionists, and reporters and editors are often abrupt, defensive or inarticulate on the rare occasions when they are asked to explain something they've put in the paper. The difficult but legitimate questions the public might ask go unanswered: Why do you always cover what goes wrong, but seldom what goes right? Who are you accountable to anyway? Why didn't you check that information with me before you published it?

We tend not to trust institutions that we do not understand, and newspapers have paid the price for their own lack of accountability. How to win back the trust of their readers is a question that has troubled newspaper editors ever since daily circulation began plunging in 1990. Few have found any solutions, as we can see from the fact that only 10 of Canada's 105 daily newspapers have actually increased their circulation in this decade.[1] But on my third week in Shawville, a chap by the name of Lloyd Cone teaches me the lesson that, if newspapers are going to survive, a new contract needs to be written between them and their customers.

I meet Lloyd through the *Equity's* classified advertising pages, where he placed a two-column notice that says: "After almost forty-four years in the taxi business, I have retired. From the bottom of my heart, I want to thank my many friends and customers who have made it possible for me to earn my living in such a pleasant and agreeable way. I have enjoyed it immensely. Now, my taxi business is for sale."

I mention this to Katherine Hynes, the *Equity's* advertising salesperson. "Lloyd Cone's retiring?" She rolls her eyes. She and Anne Taylor exchange knowing glances, and giggle, as if to say: "Now why would you be wanting to do a story on crazy old Lloyd?" The memoirs of a small-town taxi driver, who has seen the life of the town through his rear-view mirror for more than four decades, seems like a wonderful story to me. It's the kind that newspapers often have too little time to tell but that readers find compelling, one that recounts the achievements of an ordinary life and, through it, how a community has changed around us.

When I phone him, he is reluctant, but I tell him that a story might help him sell his cab. "Now that I'm off the list, my time isn't too taken," he finally allows. He has no address because there's no number on his two-storey house on upper Centre Street, but it's right beside the firehall. I should call at the back door, he says. Only his father's barber shop customers ever come to the front.

So I go through the ritual of knocking on the back door, and Lloyd Cone shyly smiles and takes me straight to the front room. It's a barber shop all right. Along one entire wall is a carved oak barber shop mirror and cabinet, the kind with the veined marble top. The only other furniture is a seven-seater bench, which I take, and an ornate, old-time swivel barber's chair made by the Koken Companies, St. Louis. That's where Lloyd sits. He has a mane of white hair that would favour a cut and a strong, trusting face; he's wearing a cardigan and tie. There's a similarly dated feel about the place. A yellowed cardboard poster hangs on the wall showing the Prime Ministers of Canada, ending with Lester Pearson in 1967; there's a whisk like the kind barbers used to swish the hair off your shoulders; there's a shaving mug and brush; and there's a small case of hair ointment bottles with labels like Luxo Oriental Bouquet and Wildroot. Lloyd has kept the most important room in his house exactly like this ever since his father died, nineteen years ago.

I turn on the tape recorder, but Lloyd stops me. "Some things we should discuss first," he says. "I wouldn't want it written that I'm being forced to retire." In Quebec, no one can hold a commercial driver's license after they turn seventy, but that won't happen to Lloyd until March 6th. He's being forced to retire now, two months early, because he failed a medical. He needs an operation on his right eye and has been declared unfit to drive. He doesn't want people in town to know. The registered letter he got from the government said that he had to relinquish his license on January 3rd, so he drove his taxi until midnight on the 2nd, then walked down to the post office in the morning and mailed them his life.

Around town, they say Lloyd is the closest thing to a buck since Her Majesty, the Queen. I begin to suspect they're right. He knows exactly how much he paid for his first car, a second-hand 1946 Chevrolet ("$1,250—you'd pay more in taxes now than I paid for the car then"), and for all of the twelve cars he's used since. He knows he paid $1 per hundredweight for his taxi licence, the sale of which today would net him maybe $20,000. Lloyd doesn't need the money, though; he says he earns more through investments now than he did through the taxi business. Townspeople whom I interview emphasize his extreme thrift. He earned the nickname "Coaster Cone" because he used to shift his cab to neutral to save wear and tear on the engine by coasting down hills. When a bus pulled into town, he'd walk the two blocks from home to see if anyone wanted a taxi rather than waste fuel to find out.

Lloyd's memory is amazing. He remembers that his very first fare was to take two young people the five miles out to Green Lake and back. He charged them fifteen cents a mile. Today, that's gone up to one dollar per kilometre. He's always charged by the mileage, and never had a metre in his car. He rhymes off all of the thirteen cars he's owned over the years, mostly Chevs and Pontiacs, bought from his brother. "I liked to drive" is his only explanation for choosing a career that seems unusual to an outsider, especially since there were already two taxis operating in tiny Shawville when he set up in June of 1949.

Lloyd seems unusually proud of two things. First, "I've driven in six decades, the 40s, 50s, 60s, 70s, 80s and 90s, and I've never been involved in an accident where anyone got a scratch. I've been lucky. A few fender benders, maybe, but never a personal injury." Second, and this amazes me, "I stayed with it. I think in all the years I was in the taxi business, I took one day. My brother persuaded me on the first of July, 1967, to go to a hunt and fish club they had up in Lake Brûlé. It's the only day off I ever took."

He took loads of teens up to the Bryson Theatre. Then he spent Sundays chauffeuring the United Church minister around to his four rural churches because the Rev. George Hislop had no car. Did that for seven years, until the reverend retired, then switched to the Anglicans. The school nurse, Mrs. Frances Rice, hired Lloyd almost daily for twenty-two years to travel to her thirty-eight rural Protestant schools. Someone wanted to go to Montreal or Toronto, that was fine. He drove one Shawville man 400 kilometres to visit his sister in Hamilton. "Fella died two weeks later. Must have known his end was near." Along the way, he gave credit and occasionally lent money to his fares. His Grade 3, 5 and 8 teachers still get him to do all their taxi work. He always hauls their groceries, and sounds offended when you express surprise. "That's part of the business," he says. "You deliver the customers, you deliver their groceries in. One couple used to live for a while at the old Pontiac Hotel, and I'd carry their groceries up the three floors .... I thought everybody did that."

Lloyd became a familiar figure around Shawville because he always wore one of those old-time taxi uniforms. The hat eventually became so worn that the peak fell off, but he's replaced it, and he disappears upstairs to change into it one last time for a picture I want to take. I notice he's got an ancient Underwood on a little table in the barber shop, and he's typed out poems and sayings that he's heard on the radio, like someone would do if they had a lot of time on their hands. One says:

*I once thought a lot of a friend*
*Who turned out to be in the end*

*As I'd feared at the start*
*The most southerly part*
*Of a horse with a northerly trend.*

He reappears in a crisp blue suit with "Cone Taxi" emblazoned on the breast and on the front of his hat. He says that the only real change that he made in the business in forty-four years occurred in 1980, when a new law requiring unilingual French signs in Quebec required him to get rid of the apostrophe-s in the name of his company. So today it's Cone. Cone's would have been illegal. Lloyd prides himself on always obeying the law, even the one which is making him retire.

He looks almost lost as he sits in the barber chair in his taxi uniform and gazes wistfully out the window. He truly does not know what to make of retirement; he's worked those forty-four years with only one day off. But then he surprises me.

"You said you were born in 1943. When's your birthday?"

"The 19th of March," I say.

There is only the slightest of pauses.

"That would have been a Friday. Did you know you were born on a Friday?"

"What?"

"A Friday for sure."

"I don't remember. How do you know that?"

"Let's look," he says, rushing to another room and returning with a perpetual calendar. Sure enough, March 19, in 1943, was a Friday.

"How did you know that?" I repeat.

"Good memory," he says. "Drive a taxi and you need a good memory. Time was, I knew everyone's phone number in town. Every license plate too."

I thank him and drive back to the office. It takes maybe two minutes, but there's a message waiting from him, that he forgot to tell me something.

The coffee break crowd is bursting with curiosity. What did I think of him? Was he as eccentric as everyone says? Did he show you the barber shop? I show around the 1949 picture that Lloyd found for me. He's posing in his taxi uniform with his first car, the '46 Chev, and the three Fraser brothers. Neil Sharpe looks at the picture and names everyone in it, including the year and model of the car. "So old Dagwood's retiring, eh?" I ask why they call him Dagwood, and the women chuckle. Dave finally whispers, "The rumour is that he's supposed to have an appendage fifteen inches long." Someone once spray-painted the words "Cone-15" on the side of the Bank of Montreal building, which to a visitor like me might have appeared as unremarkable as the subway graffiti in New York that says things like "Zero-110," meaning someone nicknamed Zero who lives around 110th Street. But I guess things are different in small towns.

In small towns, there is much speculation about bachelors. They somehow do not fit in. I remember as a kid when my gang, if there was nothing to do, would go visit Old Mister Roach, a retired bachelor farmer who lived in a house that smelled of old age and mothballs. Mr. Roach was so glad to get company and tell us stories that he gave us each five cents to buy an ice cream cone. We never told our parents. It was somehow forbidden for ten-year-olds to visit a bachelor. Is that what was at work here? Lloyd Cone hadn't married like normal folk, so he must be eccentric, perhaps even a self-abuser.

When I phone Lloyd, he says what he forgot to tell me. "You know that ad I placed in the *Equity*? When I first started, I bought an ad in the paper every week about the same size, and that helped me get off the ground." When I ask, somewhat playfully to test his prodigious memory, if he recalls what the ad cost back then, he scarcely pauses. "Dollar fifty," he says. "This one was $35.61, including the tax." There's a short pause. "One other thing, too .... Those fellas I drove up to Green Lake, back in '49, my first fare? That would be Emerson Riley and Earnest Tippins."

Now I am a man who needs a list to remember to pick up my dry cleaning. I think I still have all my faculties, but I can't for the life of me remember what I wrote my first piece of journalism about, or how I earned my first dollar, or how many papers I delivered when I was twelve. Whatever would I say if I was interviewed by some rookie community newspaper reporter, who was interested in my life story? Lloyd Cone, this man with undeniable intelligence and a remarkable memory who spent his life serving his townspeople, making sure they were preached to, and nursed, and taken wherever they had a notion to go, often extending them credit or lending them money, carrying their groceries right into their homes, finally being forced to retire under circumstances he didn't want known ... and all this without winning the respect of every last person in Shawville ... somehow it didn't rest well with me. I wanted someone to tell me it wasn't so.

There is one unbreakable rule in journalism about writing profiles. You never just interview the subject; you are supposed to get a few comments from someone who knows that person. That someone just had to be Orla Mee. Lloyd mentioned that one of his long-time passengers was the woman who taught him in Grade 5, and I find her name in the phone book. She is in her late 80s and taught school in town for more than thirty-seven years. If Lloyd is particular about details, Orla Mee is obsessive. "Reliable and obliging," she says, when I ask what qualities Lloyd has that make him a good taxi driver. "Was he that way in school?" I ask. A simple question, but she takes, quite literally, five days to answer. She wants more time to compose her thoughts. Do I need to use her name? I persist, and there is a long pause while she considers my request for a snap assessment of Lloyd's character. "He was the kind that, you know how some students are mischievous? Well, he wasn't that kind."

But this is clearly not complete enough. Can she call me back, perhaps Monday? Weekly newspapers can afford such indulgences, so I agree. She calls me back in half an hour ready to dictate a precise paragraph. She calls back the next day when I'm out with an addition, then on the following Tuesday to make sure I got the revision. "I appreciate the opportunity to finalize my remarks, young man .... Lloyd deserves the best."

That did it for me. The article appears on page one, under the heading COASTER CONE RETIRES AFTER 44 YEARS and is accompanied by my picture of him in the barber chair with his taxi driver's uniform on. We also reproduce that old picture of Lloyd on the outing he had in 1949 with the Fraser boys. One of them, Earl, is making a bunny ears sign behind his brother's head, and Lloyd is standing to the right with his taxi driver's hat on and with his foot up on the bumper of his 1946 Chev.

The next day I get a call from the district reporter for the *Ottawa Citizen*, long distance. "John? I was just blown away by your story. Coaster Cone! It's a natural! Can you give me his phone number?" Flattery is an important investigative tool in journalism—and so is stealing another paper's ideas. This guy gets most of his stories by reading the community press, so he was oozing with compliments. "You must be just new there, I haven't seen your name before." Yes, I said, just started. "Well, you're probably going to get TV cameras up there on this one. What a story!" When he hangs up, I phone Lloyd to warn him that he may become the object of pack journalism. His voice seems cool. I suspect there's a problem with the story. Did I get something drastically wrong?

A week or so later, I experience that awful moment of truth that, luckily or unluckily, only reporters in small towns have to endure: I run into Lloyd on Main Street. By this time, the rival *Pontiac Journal* has appeared with its own version of his story. He appears not to recognize me, which I know is a put-on because he remembers people he only saw in a rear-view mirror forty-four years ago. "You had a problem with my story, didn't you?" I ask him point-blank. He furrows his brow, as if this is painful for him, too. He says he wanted something he could send to his relatives, and he couldn't possibly send the piece I wrote. He objected to my use of his nickname. "None of my friends would have told you that," he said. "I was raised to believe there was something not right about nicknames. I don't blame you. Some people I guess conned you into using that. You should have checked with me first." And if I had, I ask? "I don't like the name Coaster. Never did."

Lloyd thinks the article should have been written for him, not for anyone else. After all, it's his story. He certainly didn't give up his privacy to be ridiculed or embarrassed. I can see he's quite stung by the idea that he's regarded as a figure of some mirth in the same community that he's served so diligently all these years. It's a humbling experience, since I felt my profile of Lloyd was sympathetic and I never thought twice about using the nickname, which is what people still call him and which seems more endearing and colourful than pejorative. Indeed, I think the piece may do Lloyd some good in town. But my explanations sound hollow, self-serving and contrived. "I guess that newspapers have a hard time getting things right," Lloyd says finally, shaking his head.

Lloyd is saying he doesn't trust me any more. He's not sure he trusts any journalist to get his story right. He had a run-in with the *Journal* about their article on him too. "I asked the lady to let me see a copy of the article before it appeared, but she said that's not done. She said, 'Just trust me.'" I said if it's a true and accurate account, then I'll be writing a letter to the editor next issue saying this was a fine example of responsible journalism." He shakes his head again. "She got my birthday wrong. You got that part right. So I can't send that article to my relatives either." He pauses for a moment. "You don't have the number of that *Ottawa Citizen* reporter, do you? He hasn't called yet."

It reminds me of something Joann Byrd once said. The respected former readers' representative of the *Washington Post*, whose job was to handle reader complaints, observed that falling circulation should alarm journalists more than it does because it means they have failed to prove to the public that they are working in the public's interest. In a 1992 lecture on ethics she said, "When people don't know why we're doing things, and we stonewall them with declarations about a free press, they don't have to be malicious to conclude the more familiar motivation: that we are serving ourselves."[2]

What's needed by both the newspapers and the pubic is a more transparent affirmation of the role of newspapers in society. The public needs to know why journalists do what they do. Freedom of the press should be more than a convenient excuse for journalists who want to get the public out of their hair so that they can get on with the job. It should represent a constantly reinforced contract between journalist and reader, in which each of the parties gives up something in order to gain something greater. As citizens, we give up part of our privacy in order to participate in a public dialogue that can enrich our community. In return, we expect the press to respect our sacrifice, treat us fairly and put this public service ahead of its own commercial gain. The contract is broken if one side just takes, and newspapers, arrogantly and for the sake of profit, too often give nothing in return—not even an explanation.

Journalists are actually trained not to respect other people's privacy. The whole process of gathering news depends on reporters and photographers intruding into other people's activities. After any tragedy, they can be seen with their microphones, cameras and tape recorders camped on the front lawn of a victim's family. They attend funerals. They ask your neighbours what kind of person you are. They quote people who may have reason to dislike you. And when this appears in the paper, they are quick to defend their actions on the grounds that "the public has a right to know." Even as they say it, they know they have no right to speak on behalf of the public, who have never been consulted on such matters. In fact, the editors probably know that if they ever spelled out what they mean by the so-called "right to know," most of their readers would disagree with them.

A good example of this appeared in the *Montreal Gazette* in 1992, when the paper invited its readers to play editor for a day and say how they'd handle ten cases of news judgment based on real-life examples. The cases involved such issues as whether to publish photographs that might invade someone's privacy or be in bad taste, and whether reporters should accept free trips to cover news events or print information that might put victims of crime at risk. In half of the cases, readers voted against using information that editors said they'd publish. In another case, the paper's managing editor, Alan Allnutt, parted company with both his newsroom and his readers. He said he'd publish a story saying that a candidate for the provincial legislature has tested positive for the HIV virus believed to cause AIDS. Eighty-three percent of editors and 70 percent of readers said they wouldn't run the story because the man's health is his own business, but Allnutt (since promoted to editor-in-chief) said "people running for public office surrender a large part of their privacy when they accept a nomination."[3]

Coaster Cone's complaint is that he doesn't understand why his nickname should be considered public property. He deserves a good answer, but there is no guidance for him in the Canadian daily newspaper industry's Statement of Principles, which mentions only that "the inevitable conflict between privacy and the public good should be judged in the light of common sense and with decency." This implies a dialogue somewhere along the way between editors and readers over what is appropriate and what is not. The committee that rewrote the statement in 1995 generalized the guidelines in the expectation that individual newspapers would have their own, more specific, codes of conduct. But only a handful of Canadian dailies have such documents, and few of them publish their standards so that readers can know what they are.

Clearly, specific standards need to be articulated in Canada to cover all contentious areas of news coverage, such as what it means to be fair, where the line should be drawn to respect personal privacy, how confidential sources should be used, when race or religion is relevant in covering crime, whether misrepresentation or deception on the part of journalists is ever justified and how journalists should stand accountable to their readers. It's time for Canadian newspapers to emulate such professional bodies as the Society of Professional Journalists in the United States, whose 1996 ethics code cautions that journalists should "be sensitive when seeking or using interviews or photographs of those affected by tragedy or grief" and that "only an overriding public need can justify intrusion into anyone's privacy." It also says that journalists should clarify and explain news coverage and invite the public to discuss journalistic conduct.

The sad fact in this country is that neither newspapers nor professional groups like the Canadian Association of Journalists will willingly impose standards. The last time a journalist's code of conduct was suggested on the CAJ's on-line discussion list, it was roundly dismissed as "patronizing." For this reason, the public must demand that they do it. Author and thinker John Ralston Saul has observed that the citizen has been steadily marginalized in our society, shoved aside by the forces of corporatism, profit and efficiency. It's time for us to win back our central role in democracy. We must realize, Saul says, that whenever we are presented with a crisis-laden inevitability, we are being tricked and it is our duty to step forward and slow down the process. "Being mulish will give us the time to think about where we want our society to go, what it is we want to save, what it is we are willing to give up, and what it is that we expect."[4]

How this applies to the press was articulated most recently by Alison Redford, chair of the Alberta Press Council, who said that communities get the newspapers they deserve and that readers need to be more active in demanding that members of the press operate responsibly and in the public's interest. Having standards to live up to needs to be part of the reader-newspaper contract. The good news is that circulation has drifted so low and our lack of trust in how newspapers do their job has been documented for publishers so thoroughly that now might be a rewarding time to act. We need to persuade Canada's newspaper executives that their future depends on letting us into their affairs in three important ways: public accountability, public trust and public participation.

## Public accountability

At a special symposium organized in 1993 called "Public Perceptions of the Press," the *American Journalism Review* asked a panel of journalists and non-journalists to consider why the public seems to trust the press less. One of the participants was a police detective from Maryland who said: "I *have* to be trusted. I can think of a thousand instances where had I not been regulated by law, I would have done things differently .... Who does the media have to take an oath to?" None of the journalists on the panel had an answer. Nor were they comfortable with any kind of accountability beyond the competitive pressures of the marketplace—in effect, if you don't like us, go somewhere else. The moderator, journalist Hodding Carter, said: "We are the only business that we would allow to get away with saying, 'Trust us.'"

Freedom of the press—the right of everyone to receive information—is recognized internationally as a basic human right. This freedom cannot exist whenever improper influence—on the part of government, business, labour or an individual—is allowed to distort, alter or influence the free flow of information to the people. It is not a special privilege given publishers to print what they like or to exempt them from being accountable to the people whom they are in business to serve. Joann Byrd says that accountability "means we are open about our rationale and our processes and willing to respect a different view of how we are carrying out our responsibilities. Accountability means a conversation with our public—a two-way conversation."[5]

Journalists should realize how much they gain by claiming to work for the public: they have regular access to government leaders and the captains of industry; they can step inside police lines at the scene of the crime or stay in courtrooms to hear evidence that even juries can't hear; they have the right to insist that public decision-making bodies conduct their business in public; and they claim the duty to scrutinize every other important institution in society except themselves. It's time for them to realize that they owe something back. It's time for them to honour the other half of the bargain. At the very minimum, this involves an explanation to the public whenever they choose to print something controversial. Journalists generally debate the pros and cons of news judgment in the newsroom, but very seldom let the public in on it. We need to be told that the picture of a drowning victim was put on the front page to raise public awareness of the danger of swimming alone, not just because the paper thought sensationalism might sell extra copies. Editors will win more public trust if we know that they've considered the possible consequences of their actions. Take the case of the *Montreal Gazette's* ethical dilemma of the prospective politician who's tested HIV positive. Suppose the managing editor had felt obliged, before publishing such information, to write a story explaining why it is relevant to the election? Would he have been able to justify it? Might he have considered taking action to soften the blow, either by asking the politician whether he thinks his condition will make him less effective in public office or by making the news a lesser part of the story?

It would be healthier if newspapers decided to do that all by themselves. Chair Willard Estey wrote in the Ontario Press Council's 1992 annual report that "a free press is vital to a free community, but the worth of that institution to that community will depend on the self-regulated response of the free press to the needs and aspirations of the community it serves." Canada's daily newspapers have the potential to be the most accountable of any in the world, given the network of publicly controlled press councils, which include every province but Saskatchewan. As we've already seen in Chapter Two, the performance of both the press and the press councils in Canada leaves a lot to be desired. Thoughtful journalists recognize the need to change but don't know how to. Almost everyone else in newsrooms is too busy getting tomorrow's paper out to bother, and they get it out the old-fashioned way, by themselves. Asked to identify the biggest single obstacle to changing newspapers to ensure their healthy future, 70 percent of managing editors surveyed by the author in 1993 answered: journalists.[6] Self-regulation may need a firmer kick in the pants.

Making newspapers accountable to their communities takes on new urgency when so many of them are controlled by one man, Conrad Black, who chooses to live so far from his readers. Not only does this make the owner ignorant of the concerns of his community, it shortens the leash on his editors. Peter Calamai, who quickly lost his job as editorial page editor when Black took control of the *Ottawa Citizen*, figures that

> people who occupy the editor's chair at major metropolitan papers in this country only have a life expectancy of three to five years, maximum, because they're sucking up arrows and wounds most of the

time no matter who they work for, but particularly now if they work for
Black and Hollinger.[7]

The magnitude of this problem was not fully contemplated by the 1981 royal
commission on newspapers, but Tom Kent's following recommendation might
be worth embracing nevertheless. To ensure that absentee owners serve the
public good, he proposed that they should draw up written contracts with their
editors, promising them full control of all content, including the ability to
comment freely on any aspect of the publisher's business. Each contract would
be for a term of three to five years, and would be reviewed at year's end by an
advisory committee made up of two members appointed by the owner, two
elected from the newsroom and three elected from the community. The editor's
annual report to readers would be published, along with any comments offered
by the advisory committee. Such contracts would do a lot to tilt the balance of
accountability away from shareholders and back towards the public, where it
belongs. As Kent said in his report, the responsibility of the press is to provide
the information that is significant to the lives of Canadians in as comprehensive,
balanced, fair and understandable a way as is humanly possible. "We cannot
allow it to be tainted or subverted by commercial, any more than by political,
interests and ambitions."[8] As the beneficiaries of that information, it is our right
and our duty to safeguard it.

How then can we make individual journalists accountable to their readers?
We should pressure individual newspapers to draw up their own codes of
professional practice and publish them. These could become conditions of
employment, and any severe or continued violations would jeopardize a
journalist's employment. Such codes could be written into union contracts and
used by press councils to adjudicate complaints registered against those papers
by members of the public.[9] The present convention of judging press council
complaints solely on a case by case basis and not naming the individual
journalists involved would be discontinued in the interest of fuller public
accountability. Every newspaper would be required to publicize its membership
in a press council and to provide a guide telling its readers how to complain.
Adjudication hearings would be open to the public and publicized in advance,
so that everyone who wishes to can see the newspaper held to account for
disputes it cannot resolve with its readers. Since every press council in Canada
has a majority of public members (as opposed to members appointed from the
staff of member newspapers), it should be relatively easy for them to achieve
this change. They should take as their marching order the warning delivered in
1970 by the Special Senate Committee on Mass Media, which found the
concentration of ownership to be so far advanced that someday the public could
very well be silenced by its own press:

A much more immediate danger, we believe, is the familiar one of apathy. A public that doesn't care about the media, a public that is given additional reasons every day to be distrustful, resentful or—worst of all—bored by the media, is a public that doesn't prize its freedom as highly as it should.[10]

Public pressure could also persuade newspaper owners to take more responsibility for the education and training of journalists. They now are doing virtually nothing, either to ensure that the next generation of journalists is prepared for the task ahead or to provide mid-career retraining for their present staff. The fact that there are no standards for the training of journalists in this country is perhaps the largest single failing of the newspaper industry, and it acts as a barrier to earning the public respect that most self-regulating professions such as medicine, law and engineering enjoy. Canada's journalism schools should take the lead by inviting publishers and editors to sit on academic bodies such as curriculum and search committees, thus ensuring that the instruction and the instructors are professionally as well as academically qualified. Professional organizations such as the Canadian Association of Journalists and the Canadian Newspaper Association should make mid-career training a priority for the industry and find a way to fund it. Lessons can be learned from New Zealand, where the Industry Training Act of 1992 gave all industries the power to set standards of knowledge and skills for workers. The idea was to lift skills levels generally to allow New Zealand to be competitive in world markets. An industry council, aided by training grants from the government, accredits journalism programs and administers annual tests for graduates. If the public interest is going to be served by the press in Canada, we need reporters and editors who are even better prepared than they are now to understand and explain our complex society. And an industry that takes in $3 billion a year in revenue certainly can afford to invest in its own future. We, the public, can do our part by meeting with editors, writing letters and supporting media watch organizations that hold the press to public account.

Public agitation is a time-honoured tradition in democratic society, and it happens to be enshrined as a worthy mission for journalists on the masthead of our first national newspaper, the *Globe and Mail*: "The subject who is truly loyal to the Chief Magistrate will neither advise nor submit to arbitrary measures." The quotation is attributed to "Junius," the pseudonym of a writer who published many letters in the *London Public Advertiser* in England in the late 1700s. The particular letter from which it was taken objects to a member of Parliament's expulsion by supporters of King George III, and declares: "At such a moment, no honest man will remain silent or inactive." Junius' action was based on a sound democratic principle, and it is one that could certainly be usefully applied to our daily press. We need only first determine the basis of a modern-day crusade for the public accountability of newspapers in Canada.

# Public trust

"How do I find out about the freedom of the press and what my obligations are?" Too few newspaper proprietors today bother to ask this question, which Henry Luce, editor-in-chief of Time Inc., posed to the young American educator Robert Maynard Hutchins in 1942. Hutchins said he didn't know. Luce, a visionary whose understanding of the shortcomings of daily journalism applies even today, asked Hutchins to assemble a panel of experts to analyze the rights and duties of the press and, having secured Hutchins' aid, put up $200,000 to fund what came to be known as the Commission on Freedom of the Press. The thirteen-member committee included Hutchins, who became president of the University of Chicago at the age of thirty; theologian Reinhold Niebuhr; poet Archibald MacLeish; and Harvard historian Arthur Schlesinger. Their report, published in 1947, clearly spelled out the "social responsibility" of the press to provide the information to make democracy work.

Incredibly, the three reasons that the Hutchins commission gave for asserting that freedom of the press was in danger still apply today: first, access to its pages by diverse and dispossessed groups has decreased even as its reach across society has increased; second, those few who control the press have not provided a service equal to the needs of our society; and, third, the behaviour and practice of the press are often condemned by society and, if this continues, society will have to regulate it. Hutchins and his twelve academic colleagues nevertheless declared that "freedom of the press is essential to political liberty. Where men cannot freely convey their thoughts to one another, no freedom is secure."

The Hutchins commission was alert to the growing power of the mass press and insisted that it shoulder the following special responsibilities in return for the freedom conferred on it by the state. The press should train its reporters and editors to sort out truth from falsehood; report not only the facts but the truth about the facts, and do so in a context that gives them meaning; act as a forum for the exchange of a wide range of opinion; print a representative picture of the society it serves; and serve as an educator "in stating and clarifying the ideals toward which the community should strive." These simple yardsticks stand the test of time well, and it is humbling to measure today's troubled metropolitan newspapers against them. Although the press is undoubtedly more professional and accurate than it was in Hutchins' day, it is not performing its broader public duties appreciably better. Furthermore, when it is challenged by doubting readers, judges or critics, it is unable to muster the kind of clear, impassioned logic that the Hutchins commission used nearly half a century ago when it concluded:

> A free press is not a passing goal of human society; it is a necessary goal. For the press, taken in sum, is the swift self-expression of the

experience of each moment of history; and this expression ought to be true. Much of the press is intended solely for its own day; and the journalist sometimes reflects that his art is one of improvisation, and that its products, being destined to pass with the interest of the moment, require no great care in their workmanship. Yet, just because it is the day's report of itself, it is the permanent word of that day to all other days. The press must be free because its freedom is a condition of its veracity, and its veracity is its good faith with the total record of the human spirit.[11]

Half a century later, the Hutchins report stands as the most comprehensive and inspiring statement of the role of the press in North American society. Yet no newspaper owner, editor or reporter whom I know in Canada has ever read it, and some would certainly disagree with it if they did. Proprietors like Peter White, a long-time associate of Conrad Black and chair of Hollinger's UniMedia division, even dispute the whole idea of the press as a public service. White stunned a meeting of the Inter-American Press Association in Toronto in 1994 when he quoted a 1925 *Wall Street Journal* editorial during a debate on press freedom. "A newspaper is a private enterprise, owing nothing whatever to the public, which grants it no franchise," the editorial said. "It is therefore affected with no public interest. It is emphatically the property of its owner, who is selling a manufactured product at his own risk." In other words, newspapers are plain business propositions.[12]

There is no public trust to be won back if newspaper owners adopt this attitude. In time, their properties may crumble under them, and we cannot allow this to happen. Perhaps newspapers and universities have common cause in this task. Freedom of expression is no less valued in the academy than it is in our daily newspaper offices. Where to draw the limits of its licence, and how to assess the responsibilities that must accompany it, could usefully engage the minds of Canada's great philosophers, historians, anthropologists and communications theorists, not to mention its law professors, civil libertarians and most respected journalists. The Hutchins commission contained no newspaper executives, but it cobbled together a philosophical consensus on press freedom that has served the United States well for nearly half a century. It took testimony and conducted interviews with a cross-section of society and tested its conclusions in public hearings. Paying for a similar undertaking today would not unduly stretch the pocketbooks of Canada's profitable newspaper chains, and much good could come from it. Hutchins made several specific suggestions that were adopted by the U.S. press, such as accreditation of journalism schools to ensure proper training, and several that were not but remain good ideas, such as support for a new and independent agency to appraise and report annually on the performance of the press. A Canadian version of Hutchins would provide both the newspaper industry and its public with something even more valuable—a thoughtful rationale for the importance of a free press in our society.

## Public participation

How newspapers are written, organized and edited creates a barrier for readers at a time when every marketing principle says we should be urged to participate. This wasn't always so. When Alexis de Tocqueville visited the United States in 1831-32, he was struck by how actively Americans participated in their journalism, and he said that newspapers do more than guarantee liberty, they "maintain civilization." They did this, de Tocqueville believed, by making collective action possible. They permitted many people to think the same thoughts and feel the same impulses, simultaneously. They offered the forums where people, by arguing, discussing and exchanging, could participate in solutions. De Tocqueville would be disappointed if he were able to come back a century and a half later and to discover how newspapers have turned readers into spectators, not participants. American newspaper historian David Paul Nord says that "except in letters to the editor and op-ed essays, there is little democratic participation in the press—that is, sustained political discussion by the people, by the readers of the newspaper."[13] He believes that part of the reason is that newspapers prefer to report on official public events and write most of their stories based on brief factual interviews with sources such as politicians, business people, sports celebrities and police officers. Meanwhile, the popularity of opinionated radio talk programs and internet discussion groups suggests that "the people" are political and have something to say.

It's not hard to think of ways to encourage readers to write for newspapers again. The *Globe and Mail*, despite its image of being an elite paper targetted at entrepreneurs, probably does this better than any other. Two of its most popular features are the personal essay published every day on the Facts and Arguments page, and Collected Wisdom, a column in which readers answer questions posed by other readers, such as why are Canadian light switches "on" when they're up, while in Britain they're "on" when they're down. Other newspapers, particularly the *Kingston Whig-Standard* in the early 1980s, expanded the space devoted to letters to the editor and occasionally even invited people to write in to continue arguments. It's a small step from there to a newspaper some day publishing a free booklet to tell readers how to write such articles or holding evening writing workshops for those who'd like to participate in the press.

If such small steps can be successful, why do newspapers not take a larger one and invite readers to participate in their operations? Most newspapers routinely use focus groups to test prototypes for new products, and a few have set up so-called "readers' councils" to give them advice on other editorial matters. The *Ottawa Citizen*, at Peter Calamai's initiative, even invited a reader to serve as a guest editorial writer. But no newspaper in Canada has ever named a reader to its board of directors. None has ever hired a reader or any outsider to be its readers' representative. Readers are seldom admitted to daily newsroom meetings to discuss what stories will be played strongly in tomorrow's newspaper. On the few occasions that it has been done, editors find that the public has a wildly different perception of what's new and important.

If newsrooms are concerned that they've fallen out of touch with their communities, why doesn't one of them have an editor whose responsibility is bringing readers into the newsroom? Such a person, a "reader editor," would have an exciting and busy job. He or she could assemble a rotating committee of readers to regularly critique different sections of the paper, provide input on plans for new sections or beats and even dole out Readers' Choice awards for journalism that they found impressive. Using editorial interns provided by journalism schools, the reader editor could contact people who were affected by stories published by the paper to find out what information they found useful, how accurately they felt the story was and what information was missing. This could then be fed back to the newsroom.

The trust that such a project would earn could have important spinoffs. One might be a revolution in local coverage, freeing up staff reporters to do deeper, more analytical work. In the early 1990s, when a rival paper sprung up to challenge it, the *Press-Courier* in Oxnard, California (population 150,000), invited groups of readers in to talk about local coverage. The overwhelming theme that emerged was that they wanted to know more about their own neighbourhoods. They felt that their identity was getting lost as the paper focused on broader community issues. So the paper began a weekly Neighbor to Neighbor page, inviting community groups to submit news on crime patrols, school issues, neighbourhood achievements and notices of upcoming meetings. A map of the city shows where each neighbourhood report comes from, and the paper's community news editor provides information to help new community groups organize and contribute. The paper uses its own reporters to follow up on the many news tips that come from this network.

Groups of readers interested in participating in their newspaper could even organize a community advisory committee on their own and invite editors and reporters to participate. It may not be long before the group finds itself invited to meet regularly in the newspaper's boardroom and to take on a fuller role. Restoring trust is a two-way street. It requires concerted action by both publishers and readers. If one side gave the other a shove, a useful debate might occur about the whole question of what people in today's society *need* from their newspapers.

Pretend for a moment that newspapers actually have a social responsibility. What does it consist of? Does it stop at providing society with the basic raw information to make us informed citizens in a democracy? Does it extend to taking complexity out into the street and explaining it clearly and in context?

Does it extend further than that, into the realm of ensuring that everyone in society has equal access to this information? As our society matures and technology gets more sophisticated, scholars are warning about the potential for an "information underclass," and there is cause to worry about this. Only 37 percent of Canadian households have computers, and only a small number of those—usually higher-income households—have modems to hook them to the vast array of information available on the internet. Newspapers are central players in this trend towards information "haves" and "have-nots." Increasingly, they see the internet as the gateway to the future and are offering their information on-line, where it is consumed for free by the affluent few. At the same time, they are making economic decisions to limit the marketplace for their printed information. Advertisers don't want to pay to reach an audience that isn't likely or able to become customers. They are demanding that newspapers provide them with sophisticated demographic and psychographic information and are using it to "zone" their messages to hit the right audience in a cost-effective way. Newspapers, aware that advertising pays 75 percent of the bills, are trying to develop more of that desirable audience by focusing on niches of higher-income, better educated readers. Indeed, you can argue that the main reason Toronto is one of the very few North American cities with four healthy daily newspapers is that each of them appeals to a different class of reader. Driven by advertising demands, newspapers are ceasing to be a mass medium. This is exacerbated by their pricing strategies. Since advertising linage began to decline in 1989, newspapers have reacted by raising the cover prices. In a few short years, your twenty-five-cent daily became your seventy-five-center and, because of rising newsprint costs, it grew thinner, meaning you're getting far less for more money. People on uncertain incomes are deciding it's no longer worth subscribing.

Should newspapers, in pursuit of profitability, follow the lead of advertisers and focus on the affluent, the trendy, the younger and the better educated, and give up trying to reach all Canadians? Should they increasingly gear their content and distribution away from low-income or remote areas? Or, alternatively, should they start to explore the profitability of ensuring that everyone has access to the same basic information, and thereby contribute to a healthy, equitable, inclusive and informed society? Fulfilling this mission would require newspapers to make a whole different range of strategic decisions at a time when many of the bigger ones are making multi-million-dollar investments in new plants, new products and new technology. For example, the *Toronto Star* in 1997 launched what it called "the ultimate community newspaper" on the internet. CitySearch is a vast website of paid-for advertising that allows a browser (with the appropriate expensive computer) to choose a hotel, schedule a visit to the theatre, hook up with a real estate agent or browse a restaurant menu. Although it represents an investment of several million dollars, Rocco Rossi, the paper's vice-president of strategic planning, says: "We see this as a viable business proposition." But it's a service available only to the privileged few.

If this country's metropolitan daily newspapers were serious about getting closer to their communities and providing information to everyone, they wouldn't be housed where they are now—in inaccessible office towers, far from where their readers live and work. They would be spread out across the city in storefronts. These could function as public information kiosks, where citizens without the technology at home could drop in and access the newspaper's electronic news library or, for a fee, perhaps, get expert advice on how to find information on the internet. These storefronts, staffed with reporters, advertising sales representatives and district circulation managers, would bring the newspaper out into the streets to meet the people and would operate very much as a community resource centre. The merchant down the street could drop in at lunchtime and place an ad; the reader whose paper is habitually late could stop in and find out why; and anyone with news on her mind could talk about it with a reporter who knows the neighbourhood. Free services could be offered to draw in customers, such as event listings that are specific to each neighbourhood or "found" advertisements for lost pets.

It is surprising that no newspapers have thought of doing this. They now have the technology to separate their business and editorial offices from their production facilities and to communicate effectively using computer e-mail and the telephone. Yet whenever big newspapers plan new facilities, they invariably follow the same old model, which I believe is helping to distance them from their readers. Thus, when Pacific Press decided in 1997 to vacate its aging Granville Street megaplant, it spent $180 million for new presses and moved the rest of its operations into eight floors of an expensive office tower overlooking Gastown and Vancouver Harbour, thus ensuring that the editorial, advertising and circulation departments of the *Sun* and *Province* would be just as inaccessible to the public as they were before. And this at a time when Vancouver— demographically, culturally, economically and geographically—is changing dramatically around them.

The possibility of a two-tiered information economy should frighten us as a society. It should be a particular concern for newspapers, for if certain people, as a result of economic, cultural or geographic disadvantages, are denied information that might improve their education, health, happiness, sense of civic responsibility or income, then they will be poorer citizens and poorer customers. It's time for newspapers to take a leadership role in promoting what we might call "information equity." They are the principal information gatherers in our society. They have the technology at their disposal. They alone have the ability to literally give themselves back to their communities. If they are in every neighbourhood, facilitating society's hunger for information, being accountable instead of imperial and accessible instead of remote, they can begin to restore the trust we seem to have lost for them and learn to be essential to us once again. It works that way now at the *Equity*, where anyone can walk in and chat with the editor, and where a reporter can bump into a concerned reader like Lloyd Cone on Main Street and learn to be accountable.

## Notes

1. "Research Newsletter," Canadian Newspaper Association, November 1996. None of the newspapers that increased circulation from 1991 to 1996 sold more than 100,000 copies per day. Four of the ten were independent papers (Halifax's *Chronicle-Herald*, Montreal's *Le Devoir*, the *Amherst Daily News* and the *Caraquet L'Acadie Nouvelle*).
2. "Let's stop abusing the First Amendment," by Joann Byrd. The 1992-93 Ruhl Symposium on Ethics in Journalism, University of Oregon.
3. "You were the editor," *Montreal Gazette*, November 5, 1992, page A4.
4. John Ralston Saul delivered the Jackman Lecture at the Canadian Museum of Civilization, Ottawa, February 14, 1997.
5. Byrd also said: "Today we invite the public to see journalists as ever more distant, ever more arrogant people getting rich and famous by claiming to be something we're not. We invite people to tune us out and ask their own questions, to boo our performance and ignore our claim that we are only working for them."
6. "Newspapers and the future: A survey of Canadian managing editors," by John Miller, Ryerson Polytechnic University, Toronto, 1993, unpublished. Sixty-seven percent of the managing editors said that newspapers in the year 2000 will have to be "substantially different."
7. Interview with Peter Calamai, November 4, 1996.
8. *Royal Commission on Newspapers,* (Minister of Supply and Services Canada, 1982), op. cit., page 234.
9. The Alberta Press Council already does this, using a modification of the British Press Complaints Commission code. Larger press councils like that of Ontario have consistently refused to adopt formal codes, although from time to time complainants ask for them.
10. *The Uncertain Mirror: Report of the Special Senate Committee on Mass Media.* (Supply and Services Canada, 1970, Volume I), page 110. The report of the committee headed by Senator Keith Davey recommended the formation of provincial press councils and was instrumental in persuading a few Canadian newspapers to begin setting them up.
11. *A Free and Responsible Press*, edited by Robert D. Leigh, The Commission on Freedom of the Press, University of Chicago Press, Midway Reprint, 1974, page 132.
12. "Media censor themselves, journalists' conference told," by Antonia Zerbisias, *Toronto Star*, October 20, 1994, page E6.
13. "Readers love to argue about the news—but not in newspapers," by David Paul Nord, *ASNE Bulletin* (American Society of Newspaper Editors), April 1992.

# CHAPTER NINE

# The Brown Arm Ring Rule

Nothing defines a newspaper so indelibly as the way it chooses to usher its readers out of this world. Obituaries are the most intensely read stories a reporter ever writes, and there is little room for error. They are bound to be judged as either politely respectful or screamingly inappropriate, coldly reserved or wildly sentimental, fittingly complete or else scandalously selective. Gathering the information is difficult because the only sources happen to be dead or in a bad mood. And there are no follow-up stories on the deceased; you get everything right the first time, or else the slight burns forever in some survivor's memory. Since newspapers deal a lot in tragedy and loss, all of this is important.

The protocol for handling human death at the *Equity* is to wait until the family has quit grieving, and eventually someone will submit a tidy write-up of the dearly departed. This is an excellent way to ensure accuracy. It is also a good way to be really boring and late with the news. Reading six months of obituaries forces me to conclude that all of the old people in Shawville lived identical lives. They were married in the second paragraph, educated in the third, began work around the middle of the story, then quickly became predeceased, remembered fondly and survived by. The reason for this conformity is obvious: lacking journalistic skills, the families simply copy the format of previous obituaries. Wonderfully diverse lives thus become homogenized in much the same way as formula news-writing homogenizes events. So when the matriarch of the Hodgins clan turns 107 my third week in town, and dies five days later, I make a bold suggestion—that we interfere, and write something ourselves.

If Shawville has a royal family, its name is Hodgins. When the first white man walked inland from the Ottawa River to what is now Shawville in 1821, it was "Daddy Tom" Hodgins, a surveyor from Tipperary. He chose lot number eleven on the sixth range, and 175 years later his descendants still live on that land. Daddy Tom and the relatives he persuaded to come out from Ireland begat a long and colourful line of Hodgins. There was Big John of Thorne, Billy Dodger, Butty John, White Tom, Councillor Bill, Governor William, Richard of the Creek, Black Tom, Yankee George, Big Alex, Little Alex and Paddy George. Hodgins women in turn begat many of the other prominent families of Shawville, scores of Horners, Judds, McDowells, Daggs, Murrays, Tweedles and McQueens. The Shawville telephone directory currently lists sixty-six Hodgins. To put this in perspective, there are only forty-seven Smiths and one Jones. A Hodgins is head nurse at the hospital. One is head of the fair board. Another owns the family's hardware and dry goods store, which was established in its present location in 1857. There is a Hodgins Plaza, where the Loeb's grocery store is, and a Hodgins paint store, and a Hodgins electrician. A Hodgins is Left Supporter of the Vice Grand, Shawville Oddfellows Lodge No. 40. There are society Hodgins and Hodgins from the wrong side of the tracks, and nobody's quite sure how they're all related. All of them know one thing, though. When they pass on, their grave will probably be marked by a Hodgins product: Lloyd (Tombstone) Hodgins is the exclusive agent for Yolkowski Monuments, which he sells out of the back of his furniture store on Main Street.

The matriarch of the clan is Evaline May Hodgins, a remarkable woman who never lived more than half a mile from where she was born and, according to the *Equity's* coffee-break kibitzers, checked herself into the local nursing home at age 104 only because her son got married and she didn't feel like cooking for three. The day after she dies, Richard gives me permission to write a small obituary. I talk to her son, her nurse and her daughter-in-law and am treated to readings from the scrapbook that the old woman kept, a kind of personal history book that she was glad to share with countless school children doing projects. I write the following:

> Eva Hodgins lived the first 15 years of her life under the reign of Queen Victoria.
>
> The year she was born, Louis Riel was declared sane enough to hang. Gold was discovered in the Yukon, and the first transcontinental train reached British Columbia. One in every three babies born in Quebec that year didn't live long enough to celebrate a birthday. But Evaline M. (Elliott) Hodgins had other ideas in 1886. She got to celebrate 107 of them.
>
> And when she died last Wednesday, in a bed covered with a quilt she made herself, everyone remembered her as someone who was always looking forward to a better day.
>
> "If we could all be like her, the world would be a much happier place," said Donna St-Aubin, who nursed her for two years at the Pontiac Reception Centre. "When I get older, I want to be like her ... someone who doesn't expect others to do everything for them ... a person people would like to come to visit."
>
> People called her Eva. Even her son Stirling grew up not knowing that her middle initial stood for May. Her favourite activity at the

reception centre was playing a homemade trivia game with her younger sister Alice, who is 96. Not trivial facts from the past, like most of us play, but questions like how many hairs does the average human being have on his or her head.

She was seldom sick. In fact, the only birthday she ever had to celebrate in hospital was her last, the result of a stroke suffered 10 days before. Stirling Hodgins says she "pestered us and pestered us" to take her back to her room in the reception centre. A day and a half after they did, she died.

"I've had a good life," she was quoted as saying in 1988, on her 102nd birthday. "I've had some ups and downs, but I try not to pay attention to them."

Her memory was so good that children used to come to her for their school projects. Just the other day, she remembered for Stirling how, when she was 5, she and her brother would ride on the stone boat that drew the stumps for the fence built on the old Elliott farm in Yarm. The fence is still standing.

She moved from that farm to one just half a mile away when she was 23 and married Hurst Hodgins. That was 1909, the year J.A.D. McCurdy of Cape Breton made the first airplane flight in the British Empire. She was 32 before women in Canada got the right to vote, but things like politics didn't concern her. "Politics," she once said, "are all the same, and women's lib isn't for every woman. I was happy being a housewife."

Besides her son, she is survived by four grandchildren and eight great-grandchildren. It is a family blessed with long life. In 1988, the *Equity* published a picture captioned "640 years of experience." Eva Hodgins, 102, posed with two brothers, a sister and three cousins. Five of them were over 90.

People seem to be living longer, she said in 1986 on her 100th birthday. A sister, Harriett Glenn of Red Deer, Alberta, is 103 now, Alice is 96 and her brother Melbourne, also of Shawville, is 85.

She was born the eldest of nine children to Thomas Elliott and Catherine Smith. One of her earliest memories was being carried on her father's shoulder to the first St. Paul's Anglican Church in Shawville and being given a picture of Jesus holding a child. For years, she thought it was a picture of her and her father.

When she was 15, she drove by horse and buggy to attend the inaugural service at Holy Trinity Anglican at Radford. One of her last outings from the reception centre was to that church's 90th anniversary on June 16th, 1991. "She really thought that was something," recalls Donna St-Aubin. "Not many people can say they were able to go to their church's 90th anniversary service when they can remember going to the very first one."

She lived for 80 years at the Hodgins farm, doing chores, making quilts (the last one at age 100) and cooking turkey dinners for family gatherings at Christmas. Only at age 104, with her eyesight failing, did she decide to move to the reception centre. Typically, she threw a party for herself to celebrate.

Last Saturday, her funeral was held at Shawville United Church. The church was full, as places usually were when Eva Hodgins was being honoured.

On Monday, a plaque arrived a little late from the Prime Minister, commemorating her 107th birthday.

"That's politics for you," Eva Hodgins might have said.

Then she would have smiled.

The day after the paper appears, Stirling phones me at work.

"Mr. Miller," he says.

The man is 71. I'm thinking, if you got something wildly wrong here, John Miller, either you or the *Equity* is toast. It was hard to imagine anything in town standing up to a Hodgins advertising boycott.

"The family has discussed your article," he began ominously.

I had no experience in such matters. In the eighteen years that I worked for the *Toronto Star*, I never wrote an obituary and I never heard directly from anyone I had written about.

"We want you to know we don't believe we could have written the story better ourselves," Stirling Hodgins said with some emotion. "If you should ever need a recommendation, you can count on one from us."

For the rest of that day, I imagine myself as a young journalist a few months out of school, one of my students from last fall perhaps, getting praised for the first time for something he's written and beginning to consider the possibility of a better job somewhere else, perhaps in a bigger town than Shawville. So much of a journalist's life is spent covering unpleasant things; it is a joy to bask in the delight of a story written about good things, like the quiet courage of a person's 107 years or a wonderful philosophy of life that can inspire others— *always look forward to a better day.* Many daily newspapers no longer write about the achievements of ordinary people, and this distances them from us in much the same way that having a pompous or depressed friend discourages long conversations. Perhaps there's something here in Shawville for them to learn.

Hermonie Sharpe's theory is that you print what people want to see written down about themselves, which is news, and you don't print what hurts them, which is gossip. It's made her the most popular columnist at the *Equity,* more widely read than Ada Daley of Quyon or even Mrs. Verner Thrun of Ladysmith, and as a result she is anchored at the top left corner of the Social Notes page and paid double what the others earn—fifty cents an inch. She files her copy in the old-fashioned way, scribbled in longhand on the backs of old envelopes and on scraps of loose paper, and leaves it up to the redoubtable Jean Smith to turn it into legible type. She's a news gatherer, not a stylist, and her column each week might include the following: a little hard news—"There's a new edition to Clarence and Carol Tollman's family and her name is Crystal. Don't get excited, it is a Golden Retriever pup"; some investigative journalism—"I received a Christmas parcel this morning which was mailed from Kamloops, B.C., on November 30. This is January 18. It is not our post office because they are punctual so it was some place in between"; and commentary on the weather—

> You could write a diary on this winter and it would be sometimes a horror story to read, as so many people have bursted water pipes, cars that are too cold to start, even when they were plugged in. To break down on the road in such cold weather would be a real calamity. It sounds a great deal like winters away back. Cheer up, the first of February was this past Tuesday and once it is over, we can keep saying, it can't last much longer. It's a good time to have a hardy pot of vegetable soup on the go or how about good old stew.

One day I drive out to nearby Caldwell Corners to chat about news judgment with her. I find a tiny pepperpot of a woman of seventy-three who used to run a post office out of her front parlour while raising nine children; who has been widowed for a decade; who smokes incessantly despite bronchitis; and who almost never stops searching for news, whether it's by driving around in her ancient Pontiac, by people dropping in to chat or by using her busy cordless telephone. "Eh? I can't hear ya. Speak up," she says when a call interrupts us. "I know everyone in the county," she says, putting her hand over the receiver. "People call me quite a bit." Then she's off chatting up a storm with her friend May, giving out a little information, hopefully taking in more for the column she's written for nearly forty years. "It's the bronchials," she says into the receiver, coughing as she smokes. "I've got some infection ... doctor says I'll have to stop, but the good die young, so I'm safe. Yes .... Yes .... But May, how are we going to do it if I stop? You and I wouldn't be able to sit with our coffees anymore."

Hermonie not only cares deeply about the news she provides to readers— "If I miss a week, I feel guilty"—she cares about the *decency* of what she writes. She has seventeen grandchildren, and they all read her column. The daily newspaper she grew up with, the *Ottawa Journal*, was *decent*, she says, and after it was closed down in 1971 "it took me a long time to get used to the *Citizen*. ... Now they're looking for men for men and women for women in their ads. I couldn't get over that!" She sees her column as being nothing more than a social account of "our own little corner of the earth," and it occurs to me that, while every community paper has a Hermonie in it, not one daily newspaper in Canada does. The closest thing to it is a big-city gossip column, but that's usually about rich and powerful people and it's generally written in a catty fashion. There's nothing catty about Hermonie, and she assiduously guards the tone of what appears under her name. Ross Dickson remembers editing her, just once: "She phoned in and left a message to the effect, are you sure you still want me to write this column? So I went out and we drove around Clarendon for a while.... I think we stopped to pick some berries, and she made me some jam, and everything was okay."

Daily newspapers regard what Hermonie does as scarcely being journalism at all, but, as they struggle to get back in touch with their communities, that attitude is changing. The hottest new idea unveiled at the 1994 American Society of Newspaper Editors convention, and later at the annual meeting of the Canadian Daily Newspaper Association, was a prototype of a new daily section called "Celebrations." It was the result of a year of thinking by top editors of the *Chicago Tribune* and Thomson Newspapers; one executive called it both "radical" and "restorative" journalism. The section featured stories about weddings; people writing in about their best friends; new babies; good causes; and Our Proudest Moment, little blurbs on people winning awards and being promoted—anything that covered the rites and rituals of community living. Its creator, Colleen Dishon, who is senior editor of the *Chicago Tribune* and a member of the paper's crack Innovation Team, said this type of journalism may be an answer for readers who cry "Enough" when they read rivers of ink on how the world is disintegrating. "The reader's definition of news is broader than ours, so we must undergo a learning experience," Dishon said. "Journalists are trained to dig up facts that people do not want them to have. So what do they do about facts that people, by and large, want them to have? They package them ...[in] a powerful and personal new journalism." It turns out that this revolutionary answer, subsequently praised as innovative by daily editors across North America, is nothing more than what Hermonie Sharpe and the *Equity* have been offering their community for years.

It's undoubtedly true that people want to see their lives validated regularly in their newspapers. They like to see their names, their children's pictures, their achievements, the sum total of their community life—the good, not just the bad of things. It is a lesson that community newspaper editors have retained better than their daily counterparts. It would be unheard of for the *Equity* to fail to cover a Victoria Day parade, or the high school graduation, or the Santa Claus parade or the Shawville fair. But it is quite normal for a daily newspaper to pass up equivalent rites or rituals in its community. As U.S. newspaper editor Mary Wessling Harrington says:

> In our own way, we editors have made ourselves gods. We decide what is news and what isn't. That leads to cynicism and arrogance. We have to stop looking down at people and look at them straight on with

respect, or that distance between 'us' and 'them' may prove to be our undoing as an industry.

Still, in another way Hermonie is wrong. News is more than what people want to see written about themselves. Newspapers must also act as watchdogs, alert for wrongdoing or dishonesty on the part of public officials; harbingers for social change; and investigators of news that powerful interests want to keep hidden. Pursuing that type of news can often foster in reporters another kind of cynicism and arrogance that is directed towards the politician, the business person or the apathetic public that lets it all pass by. I think people today can detect these overtones. They show up between the lines and rob newspapers of the respect that should go to those who warn us of danger. It is in search of a Shawville equivalent for this type of news that I encounter Doc Rogers and learn about the Brown Arm Ring Rule.

My first conversation with Dr. Grant Rogers takes place at a quarter to five in the morning. If you want the town veterinarian, that's when you have to call him. Used to be you could reach him at eight o'clock, then it was seven o'clock, then six o'clock, but each year he gets busier. He answers the phone only until he gets twelve appointments, then he turns it off. This usually happens now by a little after five. I need to talk to him about Dale Crawford's cows. We have been tipped by the *Equity's* most reliable informant, circulation manager Claire Lunam's husband, who learns things by listening to the radio in his barn all day. This time he himself has dug something up: a mysterious virus has killed four of his neighbour's cattle. The *Equity* is hungry for farm stories.

Getting up at 4:45 a.m. is not easy when you don't have an alarm clock, and I tell Richard the story may be iffy. But I try an old student's trick: I visualize that time in my mind as I fall asleep, letting my subconscious do the work of digital electronics. It is so effective I wake up at 2 a.m., 3:15 a.m. and 4:25 a.m., then I read until a quarter to. Doc Rogers answers on the second ring. He says he's been up since four, stoking up the furnace with wood before the calls start. He's already half booked up.

Dale Crawford keeps ninety-six Ayrshire dairy cows two miles up the Otter Lake road above Campbell's Bay. Dale confirms to me that he now has only ninety-two, although, he says, "I don't know that I'd favour anything being put in the newspaper. We went as far away as California years ago to get some of the stock these cows come from. I been in Ayrshires since I was nine year old and I'm going on forty-nine .... It doesn't go down real smooth." Four of his best cows, including one he'd been offered $5,000 for, have been struck down by a mysterious infection shortly after calving. Dale says even Doc Rogers doesn't know what it is.

Sounds like a story to me. More than a quarter of the county's farms are into dairy, and a virus or bacterial infection could spread, especially if it's resisting antibiotics. Doc Rogers confirms this. Something is causing cows to hemorrhage just after calving, something he's never seen before. It's so severe and so lethal that the cows literally suffocate on their own blood. Only the latest broad spectrum antibiotic has been able to bring it under control. It's not infectious at this point, but he's still awaiting test results from Kemptville. Then he adds: "I don't know that this should be very newsworthy. It's not news. It's a personal and economic tragedy." Dale Crawford, who wakes up every day at three in the morning and sometimes works until eight or ten at night, does not make money farming. In Doc Rogers' mind, such a man deserves to be left alone. If word gets out that he had the infection on his farm, he might not be able to give his cows away. Even if word has already gotten out, why go out of our way to spread it further?

I consider this. I know how I would have answered if a student had raised it in class. I would have said our loyalties should go to the wider public interest. If there is a mysterious infection rampant in dairy country, we should warn people even if one farmer might suffer the consequences. But the quiet, determined, compassionate voice of the most respected vet in Pontiac County has given me pause. I decide to phone Dale Crawford again. "The virus could spread," I say. "A story in the newspaper would serve to warn the other farmers." "Oh," says Crawford, "Doc Rogers'll take care of that." I present it to Richard for a decision: I can write the story, I have all the information, but here's the argument against running it. When I tell him where the argument is coming from, he decides quickly. Let's hold off. Doc Rogers will handle it.

I have always believed journalism's job is to act as the earliest warning system for society. As Stuart Keate, the former publisher of the *Vancouver Sun*, once said, the basic duty of a reporter is "to dig for the truth, to write it in language people can understand, and to resist all impediments to its publication."[1] If someone gets hurt, so be it. It's not the newspaper's job to sort out all of the consequences; its job is to present the facts, as completely as it can, and to trust society to decide what to do about it. This role is best expressed in the motto of the Scripps-Howard chain of newspapers in the United States: "Give light, and the people will find their own way." Withholding a story that you know is true is the most serious decision a journalist can make. I am uncomfortable with Richard's decision because it runs so much against the grain of traditional newsroom thinking.

Yet I am also aware that the public is starting to place less value and trust in what journalists do. This is caused by several perceptions, which I think are mainly accurate: that journalism too often appears to lack a purpose serious enough to sustain it if its freedom ever came under threat; that it is more concerned with entertaining, titillating or pandering to readers than educating them; that so much of the news agenda is dictated by powerful vested interests; that journalists lack respect for the feelings of ordinary people, particularly in times of grief; and that they share an overriding cynicism that contributes to a negative and pessimistic view of the world. The stories that newspapers tell these days are so weighted towards horror and failure that readers may legitimately feel that there is no hope at all, no point in even trying to fix things that go wrong in society.

Whenever readers express this view of newspapers, they generally do so with a sense of regret rather than anger, as if they're mourning the loss of a friend. The *Calgary Herald* not long ago published a letter from a couple that was giving up its daily subscription. "We found that reading the *Herald* first thing in the morning left us feeling wound-up and negative before setting foot out the door," they wrote. "Do you have any solutions for us? We certainly miss the good aspects of the paper, but the peace of mind we have from not reading it certainly outweighs the daily subscription." The paper's readers' representative could offer no solution and complained about such an "ostrich-in-the-sand" attitude.[2]

I think that those readers deserve a better answer. They also deserve journalism that steers its main course somewhere between the shoals of *naïveté* and those of cynicism—perhaps something approaching healthy skepticism, which I take to mean staking out a hopeful watch over accepted belief. This type of journalism requires courage. It requires an ability to ask the questions that really need answering and to break away from what American editor Geneva Overholser once called self-censorship in the name of trying not to offend anyone:

> Let us embrace openness, with all its rough edges, all its individual inconveniencing. Let us concoct a rich stew of wide-openness, of good news, bad news, frightening news, news of hope and success, little victories and grand failures, humble news, high-flown news, tales of crime, tales of everyday lives, gossip of celebrities, inner workings of government.
>
> Let us brew a feisty mash from which good information will drive out the bad. Let us cease our self-censorship, quit worrying about being liked, and believe that the public can be trusted with information.[3]

Tempering this unvarnished truth-telling, however, must be compassion, an ability on the part of the press to gauge the consequences of its coverage, to distinguish between villains and innocent bystanders, to stop its practice of intruding clumsily and arrogantly into the sanctuary of private grief, such as showing up uninvited at funerals or gathering in some venomous herd on the front lawn of a family who has just lost a son or daughter to a murderer. Compassion does not mean any lessening of the drive towards truth-telling that fuels the best journalism, but it does require the press to approach the news with some consideration for the standards applied by the rest of the community. Most of us probably hold these kinds of ethical values: don't lie, cheat or steal; don't cause avoidable harm; help those in immediate need; treat all people as you'd want to be treated; keep promises; and respect people's dignity, privacy and autonomy unless they do something to forfeit it. Nobody gives newspaper people permission to operate outside those bounds, yet too often they do.

Courageous journalism, conducted with a sense of humanity and waged in the public's interest, can be a restoring force in our society, an advocate of hope rather than of despair, a watchdog as well as a builder. It should provoke and stimulate debate. It should be fearless in making sure our public officials are working for our benefit, not their own. Such journalism is so vital to democracy that its credo should be the antithesis of cynicism, which runs rampant in many newsrooms and is poisoning its product. The public deserves a press that brings the same, unwavering sense of honest decency and examination to everything it chooses to report, whether it be a police officer's statement, a politician's promise, a citizen's achievement ... or a town vet who says the problem is under control. The starting point for journalism should always be: don't assume; check it out. So I decide to spend some time with Doc Rogers.

I know nothing about farming, a deficiency I try to correct by picking up a copy of the *Valley Farmers' Forum*, published ten times a year. It's free to farmers but costs $12.84 a year if you have an urban address. For the uninitiated, it's as intimidating as opening an advanced computer manual. The *Farmers' Forum* features ads for such exotic things as Stihl chainsaws, Cargill Hot New Hybrid Seeds, Weagant Wide Mouth Slingers, Bush Hog Rotary Cutters, Forage King Grazers, Wifo Round Bale Grabbers, and Patz Open-Top Mixers. One notice reads: Fern Richer, "a farmer's friend. Will buy Crippled, Disabled and Down Cows. No antibiotics. Phone early." The *Forum* also features an advice column called Communicating With Your Cows. It is headlined: "Flipping the nipple, hair loss and gulping." Basically, you're supposed to check the corners of the eyes for iron deficiency, then phone the vet real quick.

Thus armed, I show up for a day on the road with Doc Rogers, who turns out to be a bear of a man in his early fifties with forearms the size of thighs and a quiet, almost deferential way of speaking, which indicates to humans that he's shy and which seems to comfort animals. He is wearing a thin beige coverall that looks as if he's been poured into it, and, underneath it, a white shirt and tie. "I've been wearing a tie for forty years," he says. "I find a lot of people tend to dress inappropriately, and I don't want to be one of them." Considering that most of his clients are three-quarter ton cows, he may be a tad overdressed, although the white shirt does yield the first clue that he might dig even deeper for his information than Hermonie Sharpe—a faint brown ring high on his right sleeve. I'm not sure what caused it, and there are certain things you don't ask a man of his size, but I can't help associating that mark somehow with the limits he put on my reporting of Dale Crawford's cows.

All you need to know about the decency of Doc Rogers is written in the Veterinarian's Oath that hangs on the wall of his office. It says, "I solemnly dedicate myself to the benefit of society, to the conservation of our livestock resources, and to the relief of suffering of animals. I will practice my profession conscientiously and with dignity."

He is beginning his twenty-fifth year in Shawville, and any one of his 225 clients is liable to call on any morning. He works about sixty hours a week, travels an average of 50,000 miles a year and seldom takes a vacation. He wears out a pair of heavy-duty rubber boots every sixty days. He makes farm calls Monday to Saturday all day long, and reserves evenings for pets. His wife Ann, who teaches French at the local high school, acts as his anesthetist. Doc Rogers hasn't managed to learn French; he'd like to, he has a lot of French customers, but then he doesn't say too much anyway, so what would be the point? He and Ann have four cats and a dog named Whiskey—all "rejects," animals whose owners didn't pick them up. I get the feeling that Doc Rogers can't really say no to anybody.

A few years ago, 340 farmers paid $15 each to attend an appreciation night for him in nearby Bryson. He stipulated that there be no gifts. "They came to me and wanted to know how to ask him," says Ann. "I said that's your first mistake. You have to tell him what you're going to do and that he had better show up. Otherwise it never would have happened." On appreciation night she recalled how she met him by approaching him at a dance when they were students at MacDonald College. "If you think he's quiet now," she told everyone, "you should have seen him then. But my Mom said, 'You hang onto that lad, Ann, he's a good boy.' And I did." Grant Rogers was touched by the affection of the people whose animals he mended, and this special bond between them exists to this day. He is without doubt the most respected citizen of Shawville.

When we get into his 1988 GMC Jimmy, I see it has 215,900 kilometres on the odometer. At that rate, he would have travelled more than a million miles up and down the back concessions of Pontiac County since 1968, when he first heard that there might be an opening for a vet since old Doc Armitage was moving on. Grant Rogers was the best student in his graduating class from the Ontario Agricultural College at Guelph, and when he came to Shawville, it reminded him of his native Lachute: a mainly English town in the province he loves and would never leave. He and Ann moved here two days after Christmas, and Doc Armitage moved out three days later, turning over his practice and selling them his house. "For ten or twelve years, farmers still called me Doc Armitage," he says. "They've stopped now."

The car smells of barnyard medicine. By the end of the day, my clothes do too, and I have to take them to the cleaners. The first stop is to the farm of Bob Younge, Grant's best friend, who has two hundred head of mixed Simmental and Charolais and is the second largest beef producer in the county. He looks a bit like an expectant father, since sixty of those cows will be calving in the next three weeks. They have to be checked every two or three hours around the clock. He's called the Doc in to do pregnancy tests.

Now this is not done like it's done with humans—putting a little urine in a plastic vial from the Shopper's Drug Mart, and waiting for the appropriate colour change. It is done by slipping on a giant plastic glove that goes nearly up to your shoulder, carefully lifting the tail of an animal that could kick you across the room and through the wall, and insinuating your entire arm up its backside. "A cow won't normally move around too much when you're in there," Doc Rogers says hopefully, shoving his defensive tackle's arm in up to the bicep ... or about where the permanent brown ring is branded on his white dress shirt.

"You start at the cervix, feel the size of the uterus," he says, explaining how he can pinpoint a pregnancy by touch. "If it isn't in calf, you can hold it in your hand. Remember, this uterus can grow to hold a 150-pound calf. If you can feel the fetal membranes through the wall of the uterus, and you do that very gently, then it's two to three months with calf. Bigger than that, the calf falls down on the floor of the cow's abdomen. Then you can feel the large buttons on the inside of the uterus, where the placenta attaches itself at about four months. Sometimes you can tell twins, but usually not." I ask why vets don't use ultrasound to detect a pregnancy, like human doctors do, and he gives me a long look. "It's fairly easy to notice in cows," he says.

A veterinarian surgically groping around for verifiable proof of a cow's pregnancy is a good metaphor for a reporter's search for the news. Both rely a lot on their training and experience, looking in dark places first for what is remarkable, then using observation and verification to determine its significance. But, above all, both get the opportunity to do their jobs effectively only if they have first established a basis of trust—the trust of the cow for a gentle arm up its backside, the trust of the farmer for the judgment of the vet and, in the case of the journalist, a trust that lies at the basis of all news reporting. It begins with the trust between a journalist and his sources of information and from there builds to the trust he is able to establish with his audience. Such trust is built the hard way, by editorial practices that establish a newspaper's reputation for courage, honesty and decency of purpose. "We will tell you the truth," a good newspaper should say to its readers. "We will tell you all of the truth you need to know to be good citizens, and we will do so for the benefit—not the vilification—of the community." When that trust with the public is present, the newspaper has a treasury of good will to draw on when it reports on controversial matters.

Readers know that the truth sometimes can be painful. It can leave marks on both a newspaper and its community. But like the mark on Grant Rogers' shirt, the line that defines how far a newspaper feels it should go to report the news needs to be carefully drawn. It should mark the precise point where courage should end and decency should begin, where benefit to the community begins to run into avoidable harm, where other people's privacy is invaded too much. I call it the Brown Arm Ring Rule, and it goes like this: If the number of folks who stand to be hurt by your story outnumber those it might help, don't print. Trust and courage are impossible unless the line is visible and consistently observed; and in much of journalism today, it is not.

At Archie Stanley's farm, the next stop, there's a problem. At least two of his cows, who calved yesterday, are toxic, meaning they have the same thing that's killing Dale Crawford's cows: a bacterial infection that damages the blood vessel walls and causes hemorrhaging. "It's a strange thing, and it's getting around," the Doc says. He lets it slip that he's found it on a third farm in the last day or so since we talked on the phone. He treats it with exinel, a powerful antibiotic administered intravenously. He doesn't tell any of this to Archie Stanley. Like "human doctors," as he calls them, Grant Rogers observes the niceties of patient confidentiality.

One of the cows he treats is Cheryl Stanley's 4-H Club championship cow, which she took to the Royal Winter Fair in Toronto in 1989. She's since completed her degree in agricultural business at the University of Guelph and may take over her father's farm. She hasn't quite decided yet. "Every time we've needed a vet, since I was little, it'd be Grant," she says. "If you have a sick animal, he'll come on his own, without you calling."

On the way to the next call, we happen to pass Vince McConnell, the Quebec agricultural ministry's rep in Shawville, who waves Grant over for a talk. He's just been up to Dale Crawford's, and asks Grant whether he'd like to get the Quebec authorities involved. His nose seems a touch out of joint because the carcass was sent to Ontario for testing. That wasn't done by Grant. He couldn't be reached that day, so Dale Crawford called in a vet from Renfrew. Grant sort of allows that we should be after the best help we can get. The two men are sparring with each other in the middle of the road, in the round-about way rural people sometimes have of dealing with touchy matters. Grant decides to pay a call to Dale Crawford, even though he's not on his list for today.

"I'm going to have to write this story now," I tell him on the way. He looks at me evenly. The bacterial infection is no longer an isolated incident; it's spreading, and all his skill hasn't been able to stop it. Other farmers need to be alerted. The Brown Arm Ring Rule still applies, but clearly the benefits of publishing now outweigh the harm. It's time for this information to be trusted to a public forum. Grant Rogers understands this, and even though my tagging along might put him in an awkward position with Dale Crawford, he nods.

If daily newspapers wish to practice what the public needs most today—courageous journalism, conducted with a sense of humanity and waged in the public's interest—they need to do more to allow people to understand the role of the sceptical reporter in society. Without that trust and understanding, a newspaper cannot hope to achieve any higher purpose, what Jack Fuller calls "the point of leverage from which it can move its world":

> The answer is that it has to set about building the platform long before it has occasion to use it. This is the most fundamental aspect of the relationship between a newspaper and its community because it

encompasses all the rest .... A paper known for taking cheap shots is not going to be effective campaigning against entrenched power or against the grain of its audience, because it simply will not be taken seriously.[4]

A newspaper can do that by engaging its readers in exactly the same kind of dialogue I had with Grant Rogers. Publishing news is an open act, and the consequences are there for everyone to see and evaluate. But too often the reasons for publishing are never made clear. And, of course, when newspapers choose *not* to publish—as they do often for reasons of taste, decency, avoidance of harm or fear of incitement—the public is told nothing at all. I've always thought this was wrong. Newspapers should lay the basis for courage and decency in journalism by consulting their readers in advance about if, when and under what conditions they will use controversial techniques such as anonymous sources and deception, to get the news; what issues most need the light of publicity shone on them; and even where the line should be drawn between privacy and the public interest. Kirk LaPointe understands this better than most Canadian journalists. Now the executive editor of Southam's new national paper, he thinks the press is abandoning its standards in the voracious competition for news. "It's not easy to turn off the cameras and put away the tape recorders, but I believe our readers are beginning to expect us to do that more often," he says. "We haven't taken to heart what our heart knows is right—that we are off track with our audience at the moment about fairness, values and morality."[5]

The elements of privacy and harm, inherent in the Brown Arm Ring Rule, get their final test at the farm of Dale Crawford. When I'm introduced, he says, "Oh yes, you're that bad reporter." I say, "I'm not a bad reporter. I'm a good one," but I can see he's on his guard. He has a perpetually worried look about him, and a way of leaning forward and tilting his head to one side with his mouth open, as if he's very busy and you're interrupting him. When I see a barn cat sleeping on top of a freshly born calf and want to take a picture, he says, "Well now, we're not supposed to have calves in with the cows ...." He lost another cow yesterday, and it's one that was treated with antibiotics. The Doc checks over several cows for him, and tells him the latest news from Kemptville. Still no word on what this is. We leave after twenty minutes. The Crawfords will receive no bill.

On the way home, I ask Doc Rogers how many farmers in the county make money just farming. He says that he doesn't know, but shrugs and nods agreement when I hold up the fingers of both hands. The Doc clearly doesn't do this job for the money either. I notice that the cream paint on his house is flaking off. If farmers can't pay his fees, well, it's okay if they drop by with a lamb or chicken or a couple of sacks of potatoes. Doc says he can't remember the last time he shopped for meat. Every summer on his only day off, Sunday, he hooks up a cutter to his tractor and grooms the fairgrounds across the street. Keeps it like a golf course, most people say. In 1988, when the Pontiac Agriculture Society honoured him with a silver plaque, the gift they gave was a new cutter. No one has offered to pay for his gas. He says he likes doing it for the relaxation, but I suspect it has more to do with the "benefit of society" stuff in the Vet's Oath. How will they ever replace him?

The Dale Crawford story turns out to be even stronger than I imagine. The bacterial infection spreads to other areas of Quebec and eventually kills thirty-one cows, baffling scientists in two provinces and several bordering U.S. states for months before they can devise an antidote, which they do largely with the help of Shawville's intrepid Doc Rogers.

A big-city daily newspaper would have investigated and reported this story quite differently. Four dead cows on a farm would hardly rank highly on the scale of local news events. If anything appeared at all, it would be a brief, probably gathered by phone and probably mentioning Dale Crawford's name. The story would have said, "Dr. Grant Rogers could not be reached for comment." And at least two people—the beleaguered farmer and the protective vet (in other words, the only two people mentioned in the story)—would be mad. They would not understand what values motivated the newspaper to invade their privacy and interfere with their business. And so all of the newspaper's sources for that story would dry up, and it would probably not bother with any follow-up. Newspapers, after all, are becoming marketing tools, increasingly intent on giving readers what they want. They do not fully appreciate that what people want most is thoroughness in reporting, news judgments exercised with human-ity, an honest dialogue with editors who make the decisions and, above all, a newspaper that tells *them* what's important. And what's most important to Pontiac County this week seems to be my cow story, until Claire Lunam walks over and asks matter-of-factly if we know anything about the body they found near Quyon.

The *body?* That delicious, fearful shiver common to all newspaper people alerts my spine. After twenty years as an editor and educator, I'm about to cover my first murder. Did murders actually happen in Pontiac County? Seems so—her husband's just heard it on the barn radio. So I bravely set off in my Ford Explorer for Quyon, twenty-two kilometres away, on the theory that the town is so small that any sign of police activity will be immediately obvious.

The lady at Morrissey's Gas Bar and Variety says, yes, there's been some excitement and hands me a copy of that morning's Ottawa French-language newspaper *Le Droit*. They have a picture of the body being taken out of the woods, and a story I can't fully translate, but I immediately sense that the paper I represent just might be a tad behind on this one. She gives me directions and I follow them out of town, but there's no sign of activity. I stop and ask a man who says I've taken the wrong turn, gives me elaborate "you can't really get there from here" directions, and ultimately offers to lead me there in his pick-up truck.

When we get to Cochrane Road, the police are long gone, but there's a well-packed trail sixty feet or so into the woods where I see some blood in the snow. Alertly, I take another of my many Pictures Without People In Them, and investigate the nearest house. A woman, who later introduces herself as Rose Guevremont, invites me in before her giant black mastiff learns how to stop barking and start biting. She is a small woman with a smoker's face, the kind of person you expect to see at bingo. Her husband Bernie is watching television soaps and smoking. It is three o'clock on a Thursday afternoon. The Guevremonts are entertaining at home. I ask if they know anything about the excitement here yesterday. "I was the one called the police," she says proudly.

"It wasn't me found it. That was Hilaire Drouin and his son. Hilaire, he lives up the road. He has a heart condition, you know, and he's out for a walk with his son? He's a hunter, eh, the son, and he seen some tracks heading into the woods, he seen little bits of blood, like paint, and he figured someone shot a deer. Well, he goes in and finds it was human. Then they come to us, say they found a body, and I phone the police."

All four returned to the bush to wait for the police to arrive. That's when Rose Guevremont got a good look. Bernie didn't, though, nor for that matter Hilaire. They just stayed out on the road, not having the stomach for it.

"You couldn't see the face," Rose says, "but it was wearing shorts like you wear in summer. No shoes, no socks. A dark blue T-shirt, nothing else."

I ask her why she couldn't see the face.

"It was covered with a plastic bag, clear plastic. With tape wrapped around it. Not clear tape—that thick cloth kind, all wound around like a mummy. There was blood on the head. You could see it through the bag."

She pauses, drags nervously on the cigarette, then focuses her eyes somewhere behind me, as if trying to remember something very important.

"The police," she says, "think there's been foul play."

Either that, I think to myself, or we've seen the world's most diabolically clever suicide. I thank them and drive into the Drouin place. It's like one of those old farmhouses you see from the highway and can't tell whether it's occupied. There isn't a speck of paint on it, and there's a tumble-down barn out back with a few head of cattle. No one's at home so I look around. There's a brand new Cadillac in the shed, a late-model red Fiero GT sports car buried in the snow outside, a couple of Chrysler sedans and a new-looking tractor. The farm must be more profitable than it looks. When I finally reach him by phone two days later, Hilaire Drouin asks again and again what an *Equity* is, and when he finally grasps it's a newspaper, he says the police promised him that his name wouldn't be used. He sounds a little scared, on account of the police not having made an arrest.

So, I think to myself, not *everyone* in Pontiac County is an *Equity* subscriber. An old man with a heart condition stumbling on a corpse in the woods is not a bad way to get into a story like this.

The police make an arrest three days later. The victim, a thirty-four-year-old unemployed welfare recipient from Hull, apparently got into a dispute with his landlord over unpaid rent. The landlord and his wife are charged. Foul play all round.

I decide that I don't need to use Hilaire Drouin's name. It has something to do with a mark on the sleeve of a good man's white shirt.

## Notes

1.  "The Press and the Public," proceedings of a conference of the Canadian Institute of Public Affairs (University of Toronto Press, 1962), page 22.
2.  "Shooting the messenger won't change reality," by Jim Stott, *Calgary Herald*, June 18, 1995, page A7. Another reader said "what a downer of an experience" it is reading the front-page headlines. "No wonder our civic, provincial and national psyches (not to mention economies) are in such negative, hang-dog states in the face of this never-ending water torture of negativism."
3.  "Toward Journalism's New Age of Hope," speech by Geneva Overholser, then editor of the *Des Moines Register*, University of California, Riverside, February 6, 1992.
4.  *News Values: Ideas for an Information Age*, Jack Fuller (University of Chicago Press, 1996), page 97. Fuller is a Pulitzer Prize-winning editorial writer and the publisher of the *Chicago Tribune*.
5.  LaPointe spoke on a panel entitled "Privacy and the Media" at the Canadian Newspaper Association's convention in Toronto on May 1, 1998.

CHAPTER TEN

# Epiphany
# in a $12 Room

R oom 6 of the Chapeau Hotel rents for $12 a night, double occupancy, in the high season. The high season in Chapeau is winter, on account of the fact that it's advisable to stay indoors as much as possible then. The room is ten feet long and nine feet wide and most of it is occupied by a brown metal double bed with a fleur-de-lis painted on the headboard and a mattress so slept-in that it creates consenting adults. If you're not good friends before you fall asleep, you are when you wake up.

Under a bare lightbulb in one corner sits a porcelain sink that serves the same temperature of water from both taps—tepid. For the rest of the facilities you have to go out into the hallway and turn hard right, twice. There are no pictures on the walls and the only furnishing is a three-drawer dresser with chipped handles. In the top drawer is a Government of Quebec Accommodation Guide that rates this hotel with a single star, which indicates "basic comfort." The guide seems to have missed the fact that, if you lie on the bed and try to go to sleep, you can hear the thunder of taped music through the floorboards from the bar downstairs until it closes at 3:35 a.m. The old Roy Rogers theme song, "Happy Trails To You," is always played last, followed of course by the rage of snowmobiles accelerating up Rue St. Jacques and diminishing into the night. Only then do you get to enjoy that restful one-star basic comfort.

I have come here because it is the only place in Pontiac County where I have some claim to belonging. It is an escape forty miles northwest from Shawville and from two months of feeling like an outsider there. I am starting to feel like all those daily newspapers in this country that have become increasingly alienated from their readers: too many are written and edited by people with no ties to their communities, and too many are owned by far-away conglomerates with no sense of the local history or traditions. Just like me in Shawville. People have been friendly enough, especially those at the *Equity*, but it is a town where the names in the phone book are the same ones you see on 150-year-old tombstones in the Village Cemetery. If you don't have the echo of those generations about you, you don't get invited in for dinner.

Nor does the Shawville nightlife offer much diversion. The town isn't big enough for a movie theatre or bowling alley, so there are only three places where an outsider can go to have fun after dark without an invitation: the curling rink, Killarney's or the arena. Mostly I go to the arena, where a chippy brand of hockey can be viewed from among huddles of parents sitting under blankets and sipping coffee in the frigid, drafty stands. If your chilblains act up, you can mix with Rotarians, Lions, Oddfellows, the mayor, the bank manager and high officers of the Shawville Fair Board at the curling rink, where the lobby is licensed as well as heated. The action there is more diverse—three ice surfaces instead of just the one. And if that isn't enough for you, just take a few steps and gaze down into the Shawville Squash Club's single court, which has been grafted onto the west side of the curling rink like the horizontal foot of some giant letter "L"; different sport, same demographics. The curling rink's been indoors for several years because folks finally got sick of the bumpy ice on the old outdoor rink, which had wind resistance and which sloped off too much on the hillside. Squash came to town with all the doctors. As for Killarney's, the only true bar in town, you go there if you want to be alone. The biggest crowd I ever found there on a weeknight was seven. The regulars are a couple of guys in feed hats watching an NHL game on TV, a couple of women playing Super Mario Brothers on the barside Nintendo and Bob Bowen trying for another perfect cribbage hand (for which he was honoured once on the front page of the *Equity*). But I believe it was at Killarney's that someone first mentioned Fred's to me. If I could go to Fred's hotel, up in the Chapeau, I'd be sure to have a good time.

Still, if it hadn't been for the letter from my mother, I wouldn't have gone there at all. She recognized some town names in a copy of the paper that I'd sent her out in Victoria, and she remembered a hotel she and Dad had stayed at during a weekend hiking trip across the Ottawa River from the army base at Petawawa, Ontario. Dad was stationed there, waiting to go overseas to fight in the Second World War. She sent old photos, and her handwriting on the back said "Chapeau, Quebec, 9th and 10th of May, 1942." Was the hotel still there? she wondered.

Fred's? Still there? I could read the sign "Hotel Chapeau" in the photo, and see a dapper man in a straw hat standing on the verandah, and the 1930s vintage car in the foreground. "Our room was on the second floor, front, at this end," Mom wrote. "It was hard for us to get any sleep, as you can imagine. I'll never forget the noise coming from that tavern below us!"

My first thought was that I was perhaps conceived there, but the arithmetic was off by about a month. It didn't matter; I knew I had to go and stay in that same room, to reclaim the two nights of my parents' heritage that had touched Pontiac County. I wrote for details, and Mom wrote back:

> Those early days of our marriage were marvellous. We made the most of every moment, wondering when the day would come when your Dad would be sent overseas. What fun for you to go and stay in the room we

had! Sorry to report that you were not conceived there that night, John. If you had been, that would have made this story complete, wouldn't it? Anyway, sweet dreams at the Chapeau Hotel .... There were a lot of burly loggers in the bar that night. I think we thought they were pretty rough characters since we had been used to better behavior at the officer's mess at Petawawa. Am I a snob?

The Chapeau Hotel is not a place that puts on airs for you, even though it is so important to the cultural history of the upper Ottawa River that, as a local history book says, "as long as you can still find a fiddler in the back room at Fred's, it will be a sign that Chapeau remains the way it was all over the Valley 150 years ago." The log booms that once filled the mighty river with pine, shore to shore, are no longer driven down to the great sawmills in springtime, but the regulars who drink in Fred's tap room on Saturday night still look like they might have worked on them: nimble legs conditioned to skitter over stiff-booms in calk boots now serve to keep the same lads approximately upright until closing time. Either that, or they're trained killers over from Petawawa with the Airborne Regiment, blowing off steam before postings as UN peacekeepers in Bosnia or Somalia. It's only a half-hour drive over the interprovincial bridge, so military personnel come for Fred's steaks, the best around, and early-morning drinking after the bars in Ontario close. Someone once asked Fred Meilleur how late he usually keeps serving, and he said: "The bair closes when y'uz goes ta bed."

My new partner Sandra thought it was romantic to stay where my parents once stayed, so she flew up from Toronto. I met her at the Ottawa airport and we drove one hundred kilometres up the Ontario side of the river, crossing over the bridge into Quebec near Desjardinsville, where my parents landed all that time ago on the steamer *W.L. Murphy* for a romantic weekend on Isle aux Allumettes. In fur-trading days, the island formed a natural plug in the Ottawa River and Indians used it as a toll station, exacting tributes from traders portaging past the rapids on either side. One visitor, in 1608, was the French explorer Samuel de Champlain, who turned back here in his futile quest for a passage to the Arctic Sea. The town of Chapeau, named for a hat-shaped rock in the river, sits on a hill at the northern tip of the island. Its 430 residents live around a Catholic church, an arena, two small stores and the Chapeau Hotel.

We meet the owner in his back room, around under the stairs and past a full coat rack. Fred Meilleur fills the small corridor—a man of 6-foot-3 and wide as a door, with a basketball-shaped stomach that testifies to the quality of his cuisine. His narrow, gaunt, wizened gray face looks like it belongs to some other body. His family is eating at little tables and watching cartoons on TV. "You're that newspaper lad from Shawville," he says, his hand making mine disappear, and I show him Mom's 1942 picture of his hotel and point to the room at the front right.

"That'll be Room 6," he says. "But I'm giving you Room 8 because it has a shower."

I say that's very nice, but, no, I want to stay in the same room as my parents. So he gives us both for the $12.

"I just turned 18," Fred says, almost wistfully, flipping through my yellowed pictures. "I was tending the bar."

It takes me a moment to realize he is talking about more than half a century ago. My parents were staying here, Mom who's now in her eighties and Dad, who's been dead for twenty-five years, *and this man here was serving them?*

"Like to keep this to show to my wife," he says, holding up a shot of my young Dad in his smart khaki Second World War artillery uniform. "He may look familiar."

The first thing I do when we get in the room is lie down on the bed and let my thoughts catch up to me. Same host, maybe the same bed, the same dresser, too …. I think, "My God. Mom and Dad were here when they had their whole lives ahead of them. Perhaps they tried to conceive me that night, and here I am six days away from my fiftieth birthday, here where they were …." Sandra says something more beautiful out loud: "It's as if they left love in this room fifty-one years ago, and we're here to pick it up again."

Epiphanies are those rare and wonderful moments when life's prism is taken away and, in a sudden, almost spiritual flood, the very essence of something is disclosed to you. My epiphany is not so much about coming face to face with my own mortality, although crossing my parents' path like this is gravely moving. Rather it's the metaphor that coming here suggests. My parents and I are outsiders. I have tried to prepare myself, I have read a history of the Pontiac and taken a six-month subscription to the *Equity*, but how can I presume to come here and write with any understanding about the people or their issues? I have never walked in their shoes. I have never held their good earth in my hands. Just as I am humbled by my unexpected meeting with the man who served my parents, I am humbled by my own inadequacy. And I think: just like me, many daily newspapers have become outsiders in their own communities—their staff unrepresentative of their readership, their ownership increasingly remote, their priorities profit not service, their voices without local tone, their ideas critical not constructive. Their hubris—that they still pretend to represent the public—might be part of their undoing. It strikes me then that they could learn a lesson or two by hearing about Fred Meilleur, a man who personifies the hopes, the yearnings and the warm kinship of the upper Pontiac as surely as the song heard so often in his back room and beyond—"The Chapeau Boys":

> *I'm a jolly young fellow*
> *Pat Gregg is my name*
> *I come from the Chapeau*
> *That village of fame*
> *For singing and dancing*
> *And all sorts of fun*

# Epiphany in a $12 Room

*The boys of the Chapeau*
*Cannot be outdone*

The song was written in 1884 by a young logger lad named Pat Gregg who lived just down the hill from the hotel. It tells the tale of adventurous young men who used to go back to the bush on logging expeditions. It echoes so faithfully with the roughshod rhythms of Ottawa Valley pioneers that folklorist Sheldon Posen wrote a book about it, calling it "the widest known, most imitated song relating to a specific Canadian locale other than *Red River Valley*." In this part of the valley, it's sung with all the enthusiasm and nostalgia of a modern-day legend, usually by someone standing up in a bar and saying, "Well, I can't sing, but I'll tell ya how it happened."

In Fred's dining room downstairs that night, I can feel the same spirit. The narrow room is filled with fifty or sixty people having a terrific time. Sandra and I ponder the one-page menu and note that the entrees are exclusively beef, a huge filet for $9, the kind of cut you'd pay twice as much for in Toronto. Fred wanders by holding a bottle of house wine by the neck and says, if only for our ears, "Ya can't go wrong with th' tenderloin." Steve, a guy from Pembroke at the next table, says we can order the tenderloin but we have to see the silver beaver.

"Hey, Rollie," he shouts to Fred's son, an equally large man in blue jeans with a changemaker strapped around his waist. "They want to see the silver beaver."

Fred, walking by again, says "Oh, they'll see it."

"And the Newfie chain saw," Steve says. "You see the silver beaver and the Newfie chain saw and then you see all the rest."

His companion, a woman with bare shoulders and spaghetti straps on her dress, says, "It's no good waiting for tomorrow either. It won't be the same tomorrow. You gotta see it tonight." She seems a little house-wined.

"Hey, that's it, okay?" Steve tells her seriously, drawing his finger across his throat. "Don't tell them any more."

"She'll ruin it for you," he tells us.

Behind a partition, the Chapeau Lion's Club is holding its annual dinner meeting. The Lion of the Year is announced and he gives a gracious acceptance speech, thanking everyone for their support. Fred takes time out to join them. A table of fourteen at the front of the dining room is celebrating a birthday. Fred keeps the glasses full. A hundred green and yellow balloons hang from the ceiling waiting for St. Patrick's Day. Fred says, "Someone asked me, 'How can a Frenchman celebrate St. Patrick's?' And I said, 'If you'd been married to an Irish girl for fifty years, you'd celebrate St. Patrick's Day too.'" For dessert, Rollie brings me a little cake with a candle in it, and he and the waitress sing happy birthday. Fred joins in at the end and we all enjoy ourselves, but none of us more than Fred.

He usually hangs around to last call but is there again the next morning,

Sunday, at eight o'clock, making sure our scrambled egg and six-inch ham is served hot, with lots of coffee refills. The price is $2 for the meal. He says it was 75 cents in 1942. When we finish eating, he brings the pictures and sits down for a chat.

His father, Edmonde, bought the hotel for $10,000 well before the Second World War, and Fred, a strapping lad, dropped out of school to help out. "How much education did I need? Beer was 25 cents a pint, ten was $2.50, a hunnert was $25. My figures was okay ...." Women weren't served in the bar then; they'd usually stay in the cars outside with the bottles of hard liquor. Saturday nights were when the loggers from Mellon's Boom would come to town for a drink or two, and Fred's back room would be filled with fiddlers, stepdancers and village people who knew the old shanty songs, and they'd drink and sing and sing and fight all night. Fred threw his share of customers out the door into Rue St. Jacques. A friend remembers him saying "So-and-so over there is going to have to take an airplane trip." And out he'd go.

He looks at the picture of Dad. "His face looks familiar, you know. I think I knew someone in the army who looked like him."

One man, and it may have been a soldier, got thrown out of the Chapeau Hotel twice the same night. He just sat on the step outside holding his bleeding head, Fred says, and when some American hunters came up and asked him about it, he said: "Jesus Christ." They asked him his name and where he lived and he said the same thing. Then he bet them a case of beer his real name was Jesus Christ. To prove it, he walked back into the hotel and Fred said, "Jesus Christ, you're back again." And one of the hunters said, "Give that man a case of beer."

He looks at Dad's picture again. "This really bugs me," he said. "If he came once, he probably came back." He goes to show it again to his wife, Helen, and comes back. "She thinks he chummed around with Lou Collier and them. You might ask your Mum."

I ask about the silver beaver. Fred says come on.

Fifty-one years in this bar, and Fred Meilleur has never taken a drink, but he knows what drinkers like. His bar is decorated with portraits of long-time customers, beer signs from around the world, an aircraft hanging from the ceiling fashioned from beer cans and a strange collection of conversation starters—goofy backwoods things like the Fur-Bearing Trout, the Newfie Chain Saw, and the Great White Jackalope. There's a nice story about the Jackalope, which is a stuffed animal in a glass case behind the bar. It has the body of a jackrabbit, and horns on it like an antelope. Rollie found it in Texas but ran afoul of Canada Customs, which wanted to charge him $35 in duty to bring it in. The customs officer asked him where he was taking it, and Rollie said a place near Pembroke, Ontario.

"Oh," said the Customs man. "When I was at Petawawa years ago we used to go over to a place named Fred's."

"I'm Fred's son," Rollie said.

# Epiphany in a $12 Room

Fred tells this story with a smile and waves a big hand, the way the customs agent waved his son through without having to pay a cent.

It's now about 11 a.m. on a Sunday, time for Mass, and the bar is filling up. Helen and their eldest daughter Anne, both of whom do the cooking, are at the corner table, near the Desert Storm commemorative plaque given to Fred by Petawawa. They introduce me to a man in a peak cap and hockey jacket named Elie Allard, who has written a little Irish ditty that goes like this, and sure but he'll sing it to you if you ask him twice:

> *They talk about Pembroke*
> *Chichester and Sheen*
> *They talk about places*
> *That I've never seen*
> *But there is a place*
> *Where I'm longing to be*
> *Freddy's hotel*
> *Is Heaven to me.*

We quickly find out that seeing the silver beaver admits a person to the innermost world of the righteous order of Fred's. It is an occasion Fred himself demands a respectful silence for, then leads us through the huge door into the refrigerator behind the bar. "From far and wide they come," he says, his breath like a mist in front of him in the sub-zero cooler and his huge fist pumping up and down. "And, behold, two—count 'em, two—genuine Canadian silver beavers." His hand comes down flat on a case of Molson Ex. And there they are: two shiny nickels, tails up, displaying their distinctive beaver emblems. The three of us, Sandra, me and Fred, burst out laughing at the old rube's shaggy dog joke, but Fred gets the last laugh. As we emerge into the light of the bar, the seventy-year-old grand old man of the Chapeau rings a large bell over the door, and everyone in the bar applauds our initiation. "If you had a good time, you'll come again," Fred says as we wave goodbye. "That's the best advertising there is."

The point is this, I think on the way back to Shawville: I have just been to a place where the proprietor is wonderfully at one with his customers. He has deep roots there, he shares their values, he respects and champions their culture, and he is an engaging enough host to rival the priest as a draw on a Sunday morning in a Catholic town. People see themselves reflected in Fred's hotel—and trust him for it—in a way that a growing number of readers no longer see themselves when they pick up their daily newspapers. If those papers could only learn to act a little more like Fred, I think they might begin to earn back some of what they've lost. If they could only learn to listen as well as they preach, identify with the best values of their communities instead of picking on the worst, and use their influence to campaign for the betterment of things instead of being detached observers of the status quo. But that would require them to search for answers in unlikely places, as I've done in coming to Shawville.

Community papers tend to act more like helpful neighbours than stern critics, and this binds them to their communities in ways that daily newspapers can only envy. If you asked the editor of a metropolitan paper what his mission is, he might say it's to be an opinion leader, or to set the news agenda, or to be a watchdog on behalf of the public. The job of the *Equity*, Richard once said in an editorial, is to act as "a town-hall meeting in progress." By that he means it should engage in a dialogue with its readers about the things that they care about. The editor should be a good listener who chairs the meeting and keeps the discussion going, not someone who dominates the discussion. "I think readers and editors stand more on the same level in a community paper than in a city daily," he told me once. "And maybe that's the essential difference between the 'town hall meeting' and the kind of forum the dailies provide. No one in a place like Pontiac can get away with being professionally pretentious for very long."

For a few years in the early 1990s, Hunter George was vice-president of Thomson Newspapers and oversaw editorial quality in the two hundred newspapers that the chain then owned in Canada and the United States. He is one of the few editors who appreciates what small newspapers might teach big ones. At a meeting of editors in 1994, he commented:

> All over America, newspapers large and small are re-evaluating their local news coverage—what they cover and how they cover it. In many cases, the big guys are trying to be more like the little guys. Small newspapers are better connected to their communities than big newspapers.[1]

When Thomson no longer felt it needed anyone at its Toronto head office to improve editorial quality at its newspapers, Hunter George found a job as editor of a paper in Lakeland, Florida, deliberately seeking out a smaller daily because "you can do more there." The reporting and editing staff is smaller and less difficult to turn around. Journalistic convention, with its lockstep arrogance, standoffish ethics and set way of doing things, is sometimes the great enemy of the revolutionary thinking that newspapers need to wage to connect to their communities.

Clearly, "being more like the little guys" requires new thinking about the ethics of reporting and editing, the kind of thinking that draws journalists away from standards of practice that justify detachment and towards those that permit involvement. This is a natural evolution. Katherine Fanning, former editor of the *Christian Science Monitor* and a past president of the American Society of Newspaper Editors, remembers her days as publisher of a struggling paper in Anchorage, Alaska, in the early 1970s, when she allowed her underpaid staff to take free trips with the oil companies and to advise political candidates. She wouldn't think of doing those things today. Newspapers have become more professional, and most have ethical rules against such conflicts of interest. That's good. By demonstrating that they're not in thrall to vested interests, newspapers are more likely to preserve their independence. What's bad about it is that this keep-your-distance ethic has separated papers from their communities. With circulation in decline, the smarter newspapers are realizing that something needs to change. Fanning says the pendulum has begun to swing back. "The important thing is that the paper have a relationship to the community. Without that connection we risk irrelevance, and all the high-mindedness in the world will not rescue us."[2]

The task facing newspapers today should be to fashion an ethic that allows their reporters and editors to put service to the community first in the value system of the newsroom. Fanning uses the analogy of a resuscitator, saying that newspapers need to start serving as a support system for public life:

> I think a good case can be made for this position because so many of the institutions journalism covers today are in trouble: the public schools, even the political system itself. As the only constitutionally protected business, the press can't avoid a special responsibility. If democracy falters, press freedom is sure to stumble too. So newspapers really do have to be more than informers; they must be citizens. And as citizens, they can't be aloof and distant.

What are the implications for journalistic ethics if newspapers were to take on a more activist role: if instead of detachment they sought dialogue; if instead of objectivity they practised engagement; and if instead of an elaborate and subjective web of rules to avoid conflicts of interest they had equally rigorous guidelines under which they could forge partnerships in their communities? How then could they still convince us that they are really independent and intent on serving us? It's probably not as difficult as critics imagine.

Take conflict of interest. In Canada, there was no publisher more absolutist than Beland Honderich, who ran the *Toronto Star* for more than twenty years as if he had personal instructions from its chief architect, Holy Joe Atkinson. Honderich's credo was to join nothing, and he expected his staff to do likewise. He saw his newspaper as an institution unto itself, demonstrably free of any possible taint to its independence. Thus, the *Star's* national editor, an otherwise fine citizen, agonized for days after his wife put up an election sign on their front lawn. Would he be in danger of being perceived a political partisan and therefore unable to fairly perform his job of assigning reporters to cover the election? Would he run afoul of Honderich's iron-clad ethic of non-involvement and thus jeopardize his career? Finally, he decided to add a tag saying "Hers" to his wife's sign and put up one labelled "His" right beside it. His sign was a blank piece of cardboard. He made sure he told the story enough times in the newsroom to guarantee that Honderich heard about it.

Such antics would be considered ridiculous and sycophantic in most newsrooms today, even at the *Star,* but the ethic of non-involvement remains strong. Most codes of journalistic conduct, and even some union contracts, contain a clause that says something like: "All employees shall refrain from any real or perceived conflicts of interest." Very often, what that means is not defined, leaving political reporters to decide if voting in an election falls under a perceived conflict or not, or whether marching in an anti-abortion demonstration might cause a legal affairs reporter to be disciplined. The reality is that the world has changed. Outdated ethical notions like this may actually be getting in the way of newspapers adequately covering their communities, and they certainly contribute to the feeling that newspapers now stand too much apart to be considered trusted citizens.

How journalists tend to tie themselves up in these ethical knots was demonstrated in a 1994 poll of American editors. (I regret having to cite American examples so often in this book, but I have little choice. In almost every case, no similar research has been done in Canada. That's because the people who own the press in this country do not believe in strong professional associations, and they do not fund any industry-wide research into editorial practices. Our universities, which have the expertise to do so, don't seem to have the interest. Thus, there is no professional impetus or forum to discuss new ways of doing things, the way there is in almost every region of the United States.) The American poll, conducted by the University of Kansas, showed that editors have a new attitude towards the role of newspapers in helping to solve problems for their communities. Eight out of ten of those polled said that they believe their papers should be among the most active and involved community leaders. There were two reasons: first, a widespread belief that the well-being of newspapers is closely linked to the health of their communities; and, second, a feeling that many of their communities are long on troubles but short on problem-solvers, especially people who are skilled at conflict resolution and consensus-building. More than four hundred editors responded from forty-eight states, and only 3 percent argued that a newspaper should never become involved as a leader in its community, on grounds that such involvement might lead to conflicts of interest and thus erode credibility.[3]

So what's standing in the way of these editors taking a more activist role in solving community problems? Seventy-five percent of them said that their newspapers had policies against community involvement. Among the activities prohibited were: being an officer of a charitable organization, United Way campaign or chamber of commerce; belonging to a hospital or school board; holding elected or appointed office in any capacity; operating a family business; being on the executive of a parent-teacher association; and signing petitions of any kind. Yet 71 percent of the editors said they were personally involved in community organizations, including half who'd either been an officer of a civic club or a charitable organization. This suggests that the traditional non-involvement doctrine of newspapers is being scoffed at and needs some refining.

Where to draw the ethical line should be the subject of constant debate in newsrooms. Instead, it often remains carved in stone and acts as a barrier to the community. Canadian editors tend to be even more traditional than their American colleagues, in part because the issue of community involvement hasn't been debated the way it has been in the United States. If they are serious about the need to reconnect with their communities and win back lost circulation, it is time for editors to develop an ethic that allows them to step into the void and provide more direct leadership. I suggest that it might be based on the following broad principles.

**Listening.** Community involvement by a newspaper should spring from a desire to listen more closely, not to preach louder. This suggests that any editorial position on civic improvement should be decided as a result of this involvement, not in advance of it, and that it should reflect the will of a substantial segment of the community.

**Enabling.** The newspaper should not seek to lead any cause but its own. Its primary role should be one of facilitation and support, allowing the community to come to grips with its problems, to explore a wide range of possible solutions and to have those solutions acted upon if they have merit. Once it supports a particular cause in its editorial columns, it can protect its credibility only if it stays free from any outside partisan involvement.

**Reflecting.** The newspaper should be open to any opinions from the community that disagree with its own. It should re-evaluate its position whenever new information comes to its attention. It should never allow a partisan editorial position to affect the evenhandedness of its news coverage. Besides being reflective *about* its coverage, it should reflect the community *in* its coverage.

**Disclosing.** Any community involvement or partnership, and the reasons for it, should be disclosed in the pages of the newspaper. Above all, it should hold itself accountable to readers for its actions.

It's not hard to see what kind of exciting journalistic experiments such an ethic of involvement might open up for Canada's daily newspapers. It would expand the scope of news coverage, for one thing. The problem with the old-fashioned definition of news is that it revolves almost exclusively around coverage of institutions and has little to do with how most people live their lives. Any attempt by a newspaper to "set the agenda" for its community is baffled at least in part by this limited view of the world and by the perception that newspapers are in business to support the status quo. This function is also limited by the declining reach of newspapers. As circulation has dropped during the 1990s, most daily newspapers are now unable to reach more than a bare majority of people in their communities. To reconnect themselves with their communities, newspapers need to explore news that hasn't yet made it onto somebody else's public agenda. To create the impetus for action and to muster the resources to investigate issues that need attention, they may need to form partnerships—perhaps by linking up with other media such as television and radio, or perhaps by enlisting the aid of polling firms, community groups and university researchers. They may need to take one step beyond just presenting the facts and letting someone else think of solutions. They may need to get the right people in the community together to address what needs to be done and connect them with those in authority who can do something about it. In other words, newspapers might be the best bet in our communities to take responsibility for helping people find solutions, not just adding to their list of problems. It's a job that some community newspapers perform well, and one that dailies need to learn.

The surest test of how committed a newspaper is to helping its community is to examine its editorials. How many address local concerns, as opposed to faraway issues of national or international dimension? How often are they supportive of ideas advanced by others, and how often are they dismissive? If they are against something, do they suggest an alternative solution? In 1993, I sat down with researcher Kimberly Prince to find out. We looked at editorials published in four large dailies (the *Vancouver Sun, Montreal Gazette, Winnipeg Free Press* and *Toronto Star*) and in two community papers (the *Haliburton County Echo* of Ontario, and the *Banff Crag and Canyon*). The results were revealing, and they suggest a critical, standoffish attitude on the part of big dailies, which may be alienating readers. Only 33 percent of the editorials in the four big papers (19 of 58) dealt with local matters, and three out of every four were critical rather than praiseworthy. By contrast, 86 percent of the community papers' editorials were local in nature (18 of 21), all but two of which were either supportive of local initiatives or else, if negative, offered other solutions. According to this survey, big daily newspapers do not tend to be activists in solving their communities' problems; as a matter of fact, they may even be getting in the way. The record gets worse if you look at smaller dailies, which presumably have less of a mandate than the *Vancouver Sun* or *Toronto Star* to offer their communities a world view. Only 14 percent of editorials we studied in four such papers (the *Peterborough Examiner, Kingston Whig-Standard, Saint John Evening Telegraph* and *Regina Leader-Post*) addressed local concerns (6 of 42). This represents an abrogation of local leadership that would be scandalous if it weren't so myopic. No wonder they're proving to be increasingly irrelevant to their readers.[4]

If I were editing a daily newspaper today, I would apply the same test to it that an editorial consultant for Thomson Newspapers once applied to that most-neglected of newspaper sections, the Lifestyle pages:

> Years in the future, a biographer begins research into the formative years of someone famous who came from your community. The author visits your newspaper, plugs into the electronic newspage files and calls up your lifestyles sections.
>
> He wants to get a feel for the way people lived in your town 35 years ago. What were their fears, hopes, joys? What were their interests? How did they dress? What were their financial priorities and worries? What ideas were they grappling with? Our author wants a sense of time and place; a feel for the texture of the society that molded his subject.
>
> Will he find what he's looking for? Will the stories tell what people cared about back then? Or will there be page after page of disjointed snippets about people long-dead and essentially forgotten? Will he find the threads but no fabric? Will he have to guess what the whole might have been?[5]

The same impulse—to have daily newspapers reflect the real life of their communities and help solve local problems—has led to some exciting experiments under the banner of what is called "public" or "civic" journalism. Although few papers in Canada have done such work, hundreds of these projects have been carried out in the United States, where the term "public journalism" was invented and developed, and where it has sparked a debate—between those who see it as a perversion of journalism's dearest traditions and those who see it as the beginning of a revolution that can some day transform newspapers. The debate is healthy, because it is a sign of an industry that cares about its future.

South of the border, public journalism has been nurtured, risked, tried, measured, evaluated and revised by journalists, academics and charitable foundations who share an interest in forging new roles for journalism. No such professional community exists in this country. Jay Rosen, a journalism professor at New York University, is generally credited with coining the term "public journalism" and outlining its philosophy, which he says starts from the realization that journalists and citizens have a common interest in finding solutions to society's problems. The time has passed for the press to act merely as a mirror. For one thing, it isn't a very reliable mirror, and, for another, citizens are retreating from public life and tuning out their daily need for news, threatening both democracy and the oxygen of democracy, the press. To stop this slide into apathy and drift, the press can't continue to sit on the sidelines, detached and seemingly disinterested.

Public journalism asks for a shift in emphasis, away from the machinations of insiders, the weekly chronicle of the power game .... It tries to put "what matters to citizens" and "the discussions that need to occur" in place of "what political professionals are telling and selling" or "who's up and who's down ...." [It] must include those problems that are just over the horizon or under the surface of daily life and thus less visible than they deserve to be. The press has a duty to make such territory visible, and this is where public journalism becomes a kind of investigative activity.[6]

Traditional journalism follows a script, identifying, decrying and demanding solutions to problems encountered by covering the other powerful vested interests in society. Frequently, it adds to society's confusion, hopping from one dose of bad news to another as if it were delivering bodies to what one editor calls the emergency room of the mind. "It arrives at our eyes and ears packaged in hopeless insolubility," says Davis (Buzz) Merritt, editor of the *Wichita Eagle* and author of *Public Journalism and Public Life.* "News is framed by both politicians and journalists as black-and-white contests, presented through the words of experts and absolutists. Each of the framers has a stake in continuing the argument; none has a stake in resolving it."[7]

Public journalists accept what they call a higher duty—to occasionally stimulate debate and *intervene* in public life in the interest of strengthening civic culture. Anticipating the objection of traditionalists, Merritt clarifies this point:

It does not mean becoming contestants. Rather, it means acting more as enabler, as referee and scorer: not dictating the strategy or outcome of the action, but acting as a fair-minded participant whose presence is necessary in order for outcomes to be fairly determined by the actual contestants. It also means providing hope and cultivating possibilities: that is, chronicling not only the problems but also the important news of successes, of alternatives to drift and despair.[8]

Although their methods are more sophisticated, what public journalists are really saying is that daily newspapers need to climb down from their podiums and act more like community newspapers, playing a role very much like the *Equity's* town hall meeting in progress; by doing so, they will reclaim the mantle of public service that has been lost in the headlong rush to maximize profits.

What kind of coverage has public journalism produced? It has turned political coverage from the traditional horse race into a lesson in civics. Instead of covering a municipal election by simply following the political candidates, the *London Free Press* decided in 1994 to commission a poll of voters to identify the issues that they wanted to be addressed and then made sure that the politicians dealt with them. It also launched a public education plan designed to improve voter turnout, which had averaged 33 percent for the past decade—a situation that editor Phil McLeod likened to letting a minority of shareholders decide the fate of a big corporation. The campaign showed impressive results: 42 percent of London voters cast ballots in the election, and the paper kept the public involved through phone lines and community meetings. Public journalism, although tentative so far in Canada, has encouraged traditional competitors for news to pool their resources and give their coverage added dimension and reach. When Premier Ralph Klein and his Conservatives began making massive cuts to Alberta's health, education and public services in 1994, all of the province's major news organizations decided to join forces to tell the stories of the impact such cuts would have. At the initiative of the University of Alberta, media groups including the CBC, the *Edmonton Journal*, the *Calgary Herald*, private radio stations and other institutions co-operated on research and gave plugs to coverage in rival media. The result was "Eyes on Alberta," a concentrated week of coverage that got behind political rhetoric and allowed the people affected to raise real concerns about the human cost of the cuts.

With a longer track record at these types of projects, American newspapers have discovered that public journalism can actually change some of the hoary traditions of daily news coverage, which is mostly reactive and superficial. Alarmed by an epidemic of child poverty, abuse and death, the *Detroit Free Press* launched "Children First," a campaign that it said would move the paper beyond its traditional journalistic role to assume a more active role in responding to a crucial need: saving the children. Stories involving children, from murders, to drownings and abuse, included information about prevention of such the tragedies, along with telephone numbers of helpful agencies. The paper convened a day-long conference on preventing abuse against children to which it invited the U.S. attorney-general. The result, according to the editor who directed the project, has been an important shift in focus: "I don't think we'll ever cover children's issues the same again. We tend to ask now, 'How can this be fixed.' I don't think we asked that before. We would write these moving scenarios and leave them hanging in midair."[9]

It is this advocacy role of public journalism, as well as the partnerships it encourages, that draws the most criticism from traditional journalists. Critics, like William Woo, former editor of the *St. Louis Post-Dispatch*, fear that newspapers are abandoning their principles too quickly in the quest for community activism. He asks some good questions:

> When the lion lies down with the lamb, when the editor and the real estate broker and the banker and the elected official form a team, whose ethics, whose culture prevails? ... It's not enough to say that our own traditional ethics will prevail when the pinch comes; for when the lions and lambs gather to decide what issues the community will confront, they will not get very far if one side adopts an attitude that the other perceives as holier-than-thou ....

> I am concerned about the question of where news and editorial decisions are made. Are they made in the newsroom or at the town hall meeting, within the deliberations of the editorial board or in the place where the editor sups with the civic coalition?[10]

Defenders counter that such criticism is disingenuous; public journalism does not require any newspaper to become an agent for those it covers, and no newspaper should allow that to happen. Indeed, it's traditional journalism, with its reliance on covering institutions, that often follows a script written by others. Public journalism allows a newspaper to expand the scope of the news it covers, to find out what's on the community's agenda and to choose to devote some of its reporting resources to covering and helping to resolve those issues. The four principles I mentioned earlier—listening, enabling, reflecting and disclosing—would help newspapers protect their credibility while they continue to experiment with journalism that serves society better.

A broader concern is that journalism in the United States remains more experimental and progressive than what we see in Canada. That may be part of the cost of allowing too much power to reside in too few hands. When the owner of more than half of this country's newspapers is not prepared to invest in editorial training, that can be bad for both journalism and society. In the United States there is a healthy interest in investing in the future. For example, the Pew Center for Civic Journalism, funded by the heirs to the Sun Oil fortune and based in Washington, provides something that no similar organization in Canada provides: seed money for interesting community-based journalism projects. In 1997, it supported thirteen wide-ranging projects, including a multi-media effort led by the *Seattle Times* to convene a "citizen's congress" to define an agenda for preserving Puget Sound, and an examination of why one million citizens of Oregon don't vote in elections and what would make them participate. More importantly, it tracks all of the projects it funds to assess what went right and what went wrong—something newspapers seem unable to do themselves. Still, the Pew Center realizes its efforts have limitations. Executive director Ed Fouhy, a former CBS correspondent, says: "Foundation funding is a meagre substitute for the dollars that owners and publishers ought to be spending to develop better educated people, stronger news values and innovative journalism techniques."[11]

In the United States, those who built giant press empires often established foundations to sustain the future of newspapering. More than two dozen still exist, vestiges of the Gannett, Knight-Ridder and *Chicago Tribune* fortunes, among others. The leading North American centre of professional development training for journalists, the Poynter Institute, is sustained by a bequest of stock from the late Nelson Poynter, who owned the *St. Petersburg Times*. It's a different story in Canada. None of the international newspaper barons who got their start here—the Beaverbrooks, Thomsons, Southams and Blacks—have set up foundations to invest in new solutions for what ails their industry. They do not support professional development, unless you count the Southam Fellowships, which allow three journalists a year to attend classes at the University of Toronto, and the Atkinson Fellowships, which enable up to two journalists a year to work on projects involving public policy. We simply have no tradition of newspapers reinvesting in and resuscitating their journalism.

With the proper nurturing, experiments like public journalism can establish new bridges with readers and a new role for newspapers in their communities. In early 1996, the Pew Center took the first measurement of what public journalism has achieved in the United States, and its findings are notable. Its researchers focused on four communities where public journalism experiments have been carried out and interviewed a cross-section of journalists, civic leaders and citizens to discover its impact. Nearly three-quarters of the citizens felt more positive towards the media, commenting that the reporting made them want to be more involved in their communities. In other words, the stories had their intended impact, and readers were quick to give credit to a more proactive form of reporting. According to one of these researchers, public journalism really involves a return to the basics of good reporting. "They got reporters back out onto the street talking and listening to citizens," said Prof. Lewis Friedland of the University of Wisconsin.[12] Ordinary people became the experts on what was important to them, instead of just examples used in illustrating stories defined by someone else.

When the Pew Center questioned journalists about public journalism, however, the reaction was more cynical. Most saw it as "a PR gimmick" ordered by management in an attempt to pander to readers. It is tempting to dismiss this as either poor newsroom communication or "bunkerism," an outdated belief that journalism is not unlike a list of commandments, worthwhile only when handed down to people on a stone tablet. But the center's findings are more worrisome than that. They show that the biggest impediments to producing journalism for the people may not be the people at all, but the journalists.

Some Canadian publishers, even those with editorial backgrounds, already understand this. "I don't want to be overly critical of journalists" says the *Ottawa Citizen's* Russ Mills. "But I think one of the biggest problems is with people in the newsroom who are not yet sufficiently focused on the needs of customers."[13] Journalists like to say "Here, read this. It's good for you, like vegetables," but readers often want to know about things that never appear on the newsroom's radar screen or that are working below the surface and may soon affect their daily lives.

Mills' counterpart in Kitchener, Ontario, publisher Wayne MacDonald, recently got a powerful and embarrassing lesson in how his paper is failing at community leadership. Three local citizens, a retired entrepreneur, a lawyer and a dry cleaner, began talking over coffee about gaps in the local health care system and how nobody was saying or doing anything about it. Faced with funding cutbacks from the Ontario government, the local health council had been working on a restructuring plan for two years, but people weren't being consulted and nothing was being written in the *Record* about what should be done. These three citizens decided to act. Soon they were poring over official reports, meeting doctors and local hospital administrators and talking with the people who needed care. What they found stunned them. Nobody was addressing the real problem: Waterloo Region was receiving 33 percent less in per capita health care funding than the Ontario average, yet its people were contributing more than their fair share of income taxes. It's the kind of reporting any good community-minded newspaper should be doing on a daily basis, yet Kitchener had to depend on unpaid private citizens to uncover the facts and launch a fight for more funding. When the "three musketeers" called a press conference to announce their findings, it was attended by all of the region's top politicians, representatives of three local hospitals and a reporter for the *Record*. "They did our work for us," MacDonald admits.

No revolution can be imposed from above or from outside. It must begin in Canada's newsrooms, where reporters need to return to their primary role—as society's storytellers—and editors need to be encouraged to provide as much spiritual leadership for their communities as Fred Meilleur's hotel does for the Ottawa Valley.

## Notes

1. "Fix local news or die," speech by Hunter George to the Associated Press Council of North Carolina, Chapel Hill, January 27, 1994.
2. "Connect with community or perish," by Katherine Fanning, *Nieman Reports* (Boston, Spring 1994), pages 61–62.
3. "Vacuum in community leadership is drawing more editors into activist roles," by John Ginn, *ASNE Bulletin* (American Society of Newspaper Editors, April/May 1994), pages 8–12.
4. Editorials in all ten newspapers were surveyed for a random six days in 1993. Dates chosen were April 14, May 20, July 9, August 16, September 25 and October 5. The community papers had a much higher propensity to encourage or approve of local initiatives, although their share of positive editorials was not excessive at 61 percent. It was merely much higher than the 26 percent of positive local editorials found in the large dailies and the 33 percent positive record of the smaller dailies. The research, which has not been published elsewhere, was done for this book.
5. "How well does your coverage reflect your community?" by Charles Gates, *The Editor* (Thomson Newspapers, June 1993), page 12.
6. "Public Journalism: First principles," by Jay Rosen, New York University, a discussion paper written in February 1994.
7. Quoted in "Are You Now, or Will You Ever Be, a Civic Journalist?" by Mike Hoyt, *Columbia Journalism Review* (New York, October 1995), page 28.
8. "Public Journalism: What it means, how it works," by Davis Merritt, a discussion paper issued in February 1994.

9. Jane Daugherty, quoted in "Arresting Crime," an article in *Presstime* (Newspaper Association of America, September 1993), page 32.
10. "As Old Gods Falter," a lecture by William Woo, the Press-Enterprise Lecture Series, delivered at the University of California, Riverside, February 13, 1995.
11. "Foundations: Nurturing Journalistic Values or Threatening Independence?" by Ed Fouhy, *Civic Catalyst,* (Pew Centre for Civic Journalism, January 1997), page 2.
12. "Civic Journalism: Surprising reach in communities, lukewarm acceptance in newsroom," article in *Civic Catalyst* (Pew Center for Civic Journalism, January 1997), page 1.
13. Interview with Russ Mills, November 5, 1996.

# CHAPTER ELEVEN

# King Billy and the 7-Up Pepsis

The first thing that you see when you walk into Loyal Orange Lodge No. 27 is a hand-printed sign that says: "We are not responsible for accidents occurring on these premises." Four old marching drums and several furled banners, relics of last year's Glorious Twelfth parade, sit on top of the rack where the farmers of Pontiac County are hanging their coats this night. Many act as if they've been here before. Inside the hall, long carved oak benches covered in red velvet defend the side walls, and four smaller thrones look down from a dais flanked by the Canadian and British flags. Orangemen favour strong colours and rigid thinking, the spirit in which a Father of Confederation, George Brown, editorialized in his *Globe* in 1853: "The principle of Orangeism is one of liberty and light because it is opposed to Popery, which is despotism and darkness."

Tonight, in the very Catholic province of Quebec, the uniformed and outnumbered forces of darkness are sitting nervously at a stacking table at the front with their heads down as the farmers and I fill up the hall. This is the first time the two men, Robert Bérubé and Pierre-André Cyr, have addressed a meeting in English.

Although the Orange Lodge dates back to 1836 in these parts, I did not know there was one still active in Shawville until Chris Judd told me about the problem of the 7-Ups. Judd is a town councillor and dairy farmer who is president of the local syndicate of the Quebec farmers union. His members are being hassled on the road by a new force of transport police called the Societé de l'assurance automobile du Quebec. Some farmers are being fined up to $600 on the spot because their horse trucks and cattle wagons have been suddenly deemed overweight. So Judd invited the men in the green uniforms and green and white cruisers to a meeting.

"I call them 7-Ups," Judd had said on the phone.

"Where's the meeting going to be?" I asked him.

"I booked the Orange Lodge."

"The Orange Lodge?" I replied. "Where is there an Orange Lodge around here?"

There was a pause.

"Are you calling from the *Equity*? Last time I looked, it was right out your front window."

Sure enough, across from the *Equity* is the funeral home, and across from the funeral home is the Wesleyan Methodist Church, and across from that is a squat white building that flies the Union Jack. Here at the intersection, I suddenly realized, are four plagues of the Canadian existence: unyielding religion, certain death, imported bigotry and a free press that sometimes misses the story right underneath its nose.

With that in mind, I sit down sedately on the red carved bench directly under the obligatory print of William of Orange charging across the Boyne in the year 1690 into the outnumbered flanks of the deposed and renegade Catholic, James II, and wait for something to happen.

The room is now full of about seventy men, most wearing workboots and, as I write later in my story, "still with the honest scent of the farmyard about them." There is something permanent about cow manure and disinfectant. Dairy farmers work around it for sixteen hours a day, and it stays with them, as if it's been inhaled into the soul, through hard showers, changes of clothes and, perhaps, generations. When an outsider is at a farm meeting, he sure knows it.

After brief introductions, Bérubé nervously clears his throat and says: "First we will discuss what is a farmer." Above me on the wall, I can almost hear King Billy snap to watchful attention. "If you want to be treated as a farmer hauling farm equipment under the Highway Safety Act," Bérubé says, "you need a slow-moving vehicle sign and you can't travel over forty kilometres an hour." He and Cyr look around to make sure the point has been received. "If you're going down the road at one hundred, you're not a farmer." Knowing glances are exchanged in the crowd.

This has been billed as an information meeting, but it quickly becomes apparent that Bérubé and Cyr aren't holding up their end of the bargain. Each has one year's experience patrolling the highways of Pontiac County enforcing the Highway Safety Act, and neither is a farmer. Their audience has maybe a thousand years of collective experience driving tractors and farm pick-ups in front of exotic equipment like liquid manure spreaders. They begin to ask questions that neither Bérubé nor Cyr can answer.

It's one of those times when a reporter needs to stop writing about what's said and concentrate on what's happening, to take one step out into the margin to get perspective and to find a way to make readers see what you see. It's a journalism lesson that I learned in 1974 when I was foreign editor of the *Toronto Star* and the biggest story in the world was the Watergate scandal. The paper had Bruce Garvey in Washington then, and he was an excellent reporter, filing every day or so on the White House's latest manoeuvre to avoid handing over the incriminating tapes that eventually proved U.S. president Nixon had covered up a burglary directed against his political opponents. As the editor in charge of the coverage, I wasn't reading any copy that captured the mood of Washington at this historic occasion, and I knew that Garvey, who'd been stationed there for a couple of years, didn't have the fresh eyes to see what I wanted readers to see. So I assigned myself to the story, not to analyze but to describe.

My story described how Nixon's secretary, Rose Mary Woods, walked her lawyer to the White House gate and had her picture snapped by a kid who asked, "Hey, are you anybody?" I noted that a red and white "Impeach Nixon" sign had been pasted over the marquee of the Watergate Hotel, where Nixon's troubles began when his White House spies broke into the Democratic national head-quarters. I looked through a telescope trained on the back door of the White House by a radical youth group that wanted to make sure "Dicky doesn't sneak out the back door to dispose of the tapes." The story concluded from the evidence that "the forces of impeachment will not wait much longer for Richard Milhous Nixon. The mood of Washington reflects this."

What I wrote was not a great piece of journalism, but it vividly transported readers to the scene of a momentous event and probably was more meaningful than the "news" of the day, which was yet another White House reaction to yet another request to hand over the tapes. Such descriptive stories are more powerful in print than on television, and they connect with the reader at a deeper, contextual and emotional level. Over the years, though, I began to see these stories appear less often in newspapers, perhaps because editors assumed television could tell them better with real pictures; perhaps because technical changes in the industry—web-width reductions to save newsprint and shorter stories to appeal to different demographics—were shortening readers' attention spans; perhaps because reporters lost their descriptive skills by being forced to gather most of the news by telephone. Whatever the reason, newspapers today "tell" more than they "show," and this has distanced readers from the medium that they used to regard as theirs because it spoke for them and took them places where they wanted to go. Stanley Woodward, the legendary sports editor of the old *New York Herald-Tribune*, described this function of newspapering best when he assigned a young Red Smith to cover his first World Series: "Get me the smell of the cabbage cooking in the halls."[1]

Whenever newspapers carry descriptive writing today, it stands out and is remarked upon. Ironically, this happened during the 1991 Gulf War, which is usually described as "the television war," but was anything but. Denied access to the war front, television journalists were reduced to talking heads on hotel balconies, describing what some general said at a briefing or introducing censored tape gathered by pool coverage. A few print reporters, notably Robert Fisk of the *Independent* in Britain and Kevin Donovan of the *Toronto Star*, set off across the desert in rented Toyotas and told readers what they saw and heard and smelled and touched. This was adventure! Television viewing soared but so did the circulations of daily newspapers. Readers were again being taken where they needed to go, and nobody else was offering that ride. An important lesson should have been learned by newspaper editors, but it wasn't. In my advanced editing class at Ryerson, we examined Fisk and Donovan stories fondly, as if they were museum pieces. After the war ended, I challenged my students for weeks with a scavenger hunt for examples of similar descriptive writing in any of the daily newspapers; no one could produce even one.

Now, inside the Orange Lodge in Shawville, as the information meeting turned into a vigorous grilling, I began to see a new way to tell the story. On one side, farmers began to cite outrage after outrage with the steady assurance of people who hold the secret of food in their hands and think they are getting screwed. On the other, Bérubé and Cyr were busily fanning through voluminous highway safety regulations, trying with little success to answer very specific questions about very unfamiliar farm machinery. One man asks a simple question—is it legal for a farm trailer equipped with reflectors to go on the road at night? Bérubé rifles through a manual, confers hurriedly with Cyr in French, and has to say: "That is a good question. We don't have anything in our books. We'll have to check and get back to you." Another man says, "You're new." Bérubé says yes, he is. "That's the problem," he's told. "You're new and we're new to this. Nobody tells us anything." It's not new regulations that are the problem, but the enforcement. Last year there was only one patroller operating in the Outaouais; since then thirteen more have been hired. Farmers are now being stopped for the first time and checked for regulations only a demented bureaucrat could fathom.

There are more than six hundred regulations in the Quebec Highway Safety Code. Many are printed only in French. They are so involved that the revisions to just one regulation—involving permits for trucks that haul big things like swimming pools and mobile homes—take up twelve pages of the Official Government Gazette.

As Bérubé starts to describe in detail the complicated system of figuring out whether a truck or trailer is overweight, he is asked a simple question:

"Where could you take a wagon to find out how much you can legally haul on it?"

This is asked by a farmer for whom a $600 fine would be a catastrophe.

"Call and make an appointment. We'll see if we can do it on the scales," Bérubé says.

There is a brief pause.

"What happens if you go up there and you're the wrong weight?" the farmer asks.

"You'll be fined," Bérubé says, smiling as everyone else recoils at his perverse Catch-22.

There is news from the meeting, and I could easily write a story that began: "Angered by a series of $600 roadside fines, local farm union leaders plan to lobby politicians in Quebec city to change provisions of the *Highway Safety Act,* which they say are unclear and discriminate against farmers. At a meeting this week...." That is the way most editors and journalism schools teach reporters to write news: the so-called Inverted Pyramid, which leads with the most important action taken and follows up with relevant details in descending order of importance. Instead, I decide to write it in a way that captures the meaning of the meeting rather than the news of it. Under the headline "Farmers learn why they get hassled," my story describes how the officers' lack of knowledge of both safety regulations and farm equipment slowly turned the audience against them, and how at the end they had to admit that they were only small cogs in the highway traffic act enforcement system, unable to explain the regulations that they had to enforce. The story struck a universal theme: a well-informed citizenry *can* stand up to bureaucracy and make it look foolish.

As I wrote it, I thought about Neil Postman. This American social critic outlined a compelling vision for the future of print journalism when he spoke to the International Federation of Newspaper Publishers in Copenhagen in 1990, and I have tried to incorporate it into my writing ever since. "You must alter your conception of what business you are in," he told them. "Up to now, you have been in the information business .... To survive in the long run, you must be in the meaning business." Readers, he said, are bombarded by a bewildering array of information that other forms of communication, such as television, fax machines and the internet, can deliver faster. He called it "information chaos," and said: "Your readers will know what happened. They need to know what it means." The worst thing you can do, Postman told the publishers, is "continue to represent the world as a series of discontinuous, historical, random events, which is the way television does its work."[2]

Despite being pressured as never before by declining circulation, rising costs, and speedier competitors, Canada's newspaper publishers and editors—with very few exceptions—have done nothing to reinvent the way in which they deliver information. One reason may be the lack of visionaries and revisionists in the top ranks of newspaper management. Another is the lack of any strong professional organization of journalists in this country. New ideas, if they poke their heads above the sand from time to time, are not nurtured or shared. Even if they were, newspaper proprietors have not demonstrated any interest in investing in the kind of journalism Postman is talking about.

One of the few publishers who has done much thinking about changing the editorial status quo is the *Ottawa Citizen's* Russell Mills. He regularly quotes Postman in his speeches and challenges journalists to a new way of thinking:

> Think of the volume of material that crosses your desk or reaches you at home each day. How much of it really adds value? Wouldn't you prefer less but better communication, material that adds understanding or insight instead of adding to the crushing burden of facts? I believe too many of our customers feel the same way about our products. To

them, we're part of the data-glut problem, not part of the solution.

In 1995, Mills wrote an unusual series of memos to his bosses at Southam after
he attended a five-day executive retreat at Emerald Lake Lodge in British
Columbia. His companions were the dean of business at University of Western
Ontario, a Swedish doctor who runs a clinic near the Arctic Circle, the president
of the Gestetner company in the U.S., a professor of psychology, and a senior
vice-president of an Alberta utility company. They hiked in the mountains, took
their shoes off and listened to Mozart, and talked for hours about the kind of
society that they'd like to live in. It was a rather elite group, and quite
surprisingly newspapers came up often as a topic for concern. Mills wrote: "I
was shocked by a view expressed by most of the rest of the group that the news
media seemed to get in the way of their ability to develop any real understanding
of what's happening in the world."

The discussion made Mills think of information as being on a rising chart
of values. At the low end is information that is highly useful but utterly
uninspiring, such as a manual on how to program a VCR. At the high end is
information that is inspiring but is of little practical value, like poetry. Newspapers provide information that falls at many places on this continuum but most,
Mills believes, is weighted towards the useful end—weather reports, sports
statistics, stock market listings, what the finance minister said in his budget
speech yesterday. This is what market research tells newspapers to do; and
although it is still an important part of their mission, it connects with readers only
on a superficial level. It is not giving them enough to forge unbreakable loyalty.
"They may want much more from us," Mills wrote Southam head office.

> They may be expecting the confusing world to make a little more sense.
> They may be expecting to have a bit clearer understanding of their
> place in it. They may be expecting a little more of the internal peace that
> should come with expanded understanding.

The future of newspapers, he said, may depend on providing such things as
knowledge, understanding and profound insight. Readers complain that they
have no time to read, yet they gobble up novels like *The Celestine Prophesy* and
*The Bridges of Madison County,* which connect with their deeper needs for
purpose and love. To win back readers, Mills says, newspapers "need to throw
a chain around their souls."[3]

This is a theory that could bear some fruit, but Mills was not encouraged to
develop it by the former Southam management. When I asked him how
newspapers can change themselves to start delivering this, he said, "I don't
know."[4] It is an answer too typical of newspaper executives in Canada today.
Many of them fear for the future but are beset by a kind of paralyzed thinking
that prevents them from taking any meaningful action to change. In Shawville,

I began to see what Postman and Mills were talking about and what kind of journalism might begin to make these deeper connections with readers. It is journalism that searches for meaning, that expands the scope of the news and that writes so that people will read.

## Searching for meaning

Much of journalism is stenography. The reporter or photographer adopts the guise of the detached observer and records what happens before him, often reproducing it uncritically. Thus many of the subtle and difficult issues of public life are reduced to statements and certainties, devoid of suspense, surprise, personality, doubt and meaning. When conflict is involved, as it often is with news, the reporter merely strives for balance by getting someone from the other side to dissent. Tomorrow, someone else weighs in with a different opinion. Stories deemed to be important get covered in little bits like this until some action is taken or it is time for the light of publicity to be shone elsewhere. There is little room for solutions, universal truths or even real understanding. So when I sat down to write my story on the farmers at the Orange Hall, I asked myself: Will I be serving my readers if I merely reproduce what everyone said? How could anyone who wasn't there connect with that? Since nothing was resolved, such a story would be about acrimony and stalemate. There's enough of that in the world already. Was it nothing more than a difference of opinion, or did I see something more remarkable?

Journalists are troubled by such simple questions about what they're up to. Nevertheless, answers are being demanded of them by readers who, quite rightfully, want to know what the payoff is for spending half an hour with their newspapers every day. The notion that journalists should try to *explain* the news for them, that it is a responsibility of the writer to make complicated events understandable and perhaps even to explore what's right and wrong about them runs counter to a half-century of journalistic tradition. The role of journalist as so-called objective observer was enunciated by American press commentator Walter Lippmann in the 1920s and has been more or less institutionalized as gospel in our newsrooms, even though its limitations are obvious. The trouble, James Carey points out, is that

> we have a journalism that is an early-warning system but it is one that keeps the public in a constant state of agitation or boredom. We have a journalism that reports the continuing stream of expert opinion but because there is no agreement among experts, it is more like observing talk-show gossip and petty manipulation than bearing witness to the truth.[5]

Objectivity is used by journalists these days as a kind of convenient excuse to justify to critics what they do: *How can you say I'm biased or inaccurate when I'm just taking down what happened?* This mind-set has outlasted dozens of attempts by journalists over the years to break away from the flat stenographic report. The New Journalism articulated by Tom Wolfe and others proved to be too loopy and personal for most newspaper editors, and seemed to put the writer in the way of the story too many times. "Investigative journalism" became the tool of avenging lords determined to root out evil in society, but this proved expensive and too often the evil lurked only in the reporter's mind. "Adversary journalism" passed out of favour almost as soon as editors began to worry about giving readers what they want, and they surely didn't want more bad news. Objectivity is still a convenient badge to pin on. It passes muster from the marketing people and is cheaper to produce.

But reporters are not any more objective than you or I. And readers don't always have time to wade through great heaps of raw information before considering what to think about complicated issues such as whether to pay down the national debt or dismantle medicare. What we have here is a profession in need of some more philosophical tools to do the job that society demands of it. There are clearly times when the press should not be impartial, when its journalism should reach conclusions based on the weight of evidence, when it should point the way towards specific solutions. Such journalism raises troublesome questions. What qualifies a reporter to undertake a project of this sort? How much time and research are needed? What oversight is required? How can the newspaper provide a forum for experts and readers who disagree with the conclusions? What effect will this type of work have on the credibility of the paper?

Objectivity does not really need its own code of conduct, because it is largely rooted in stenographic accuracy. Its downside is that it requires journalists to maintain an emotional and intellectual distance from the subjects that they cover. The kind of journalism that attempts to make sense of it all requires the courage of engagement, and this needs to be carefully spelled out. Certain newsroom values must change, owners must invest in newsroom resources and the basis must be established for a greater degree of trust from readers.

Perhaps the conditions under which this new kind of journalism is done should be written down as a kind of guideline and be subjected to public scrutiny. Such an exercise is well within the resources of most newspapers. One of the most effective was developed in the early 1990s by the Portland (Maine) *Press Herald* and could be modified for use by any Canadian paper. Its guidelines recognize the value of objectivity in reminding reporters not to let their stories be shaped by preconceived judgments, but they establish sound rules whereby writers can explore new levels of analysis, interpretation and judgment. The paper's editor at the time, Lou Ureneck, said that the initiative stemmed from asking a simple question: Does the press fail readers more often through timidity than bias?

If indeed readers would prefer a press that is more actively engaged in problem solving, or in explaining events and issues in terms that allow readers as citizens to understand and solve problems, then newspapers need to craft news reports that convey meaning as well as fact, insight as well as events .... And the one figure who is key to this kind of journalism is the well-informed reporter. A newspaper's decision to adopt a more interpretive approach to the news must be followed by a commitment to developing the research and analytical skills of reporters.[6]

Such journalism appears in Canadian papers from time to time, but too often it is undermined by insufficient time spent on research or conclusions that were decided in advance. Facts too often are gathered only to support a theory rather than to provide the rationale for one. Readers have the right to demand more. Whenever we do, we should ask newspaper editors things like: Do you have written guidelines for this type of journalism? What are the qualifications of this reporter to examine the topic in depth? How long was he or she given to work on it? What research help was provided? Why doesn't the paper provide a list of sources so that an interested reader can learn more? Why should I trust what you tell me?

What the Portland *Press Herald* calls "expert journalism" is only one of the antidotes to what another American editor, Maxwell King of the *Philadelphia Inquirer*, has famously called "the vomit school of journalism"—here are all the facts, we're dumping them in your lap and good luck trying to figure out what they mean.[7] Readers are saying that they want more than the surface facts, whether it's about public policy or controversial public figures. "Meaning" journalism is certainly not elitist. People still want to read about Tonya Harding and Princess Diana, but they don't want it only for the salacious gossip value; they want to know what it tells us about good and evil, fidelity and infidelity, charity and selfishness. And that's the dimension—the wider context—that newspapers have to start giving to their readers. There is a hunger for insight, depth and an examination of the weird human psyche even in stories about an ambitious figure skater, a loveless princess .... or a bunch of farmers duking it out with bureaucracy in an Orange Lodge in Quebec. News events become parables that lead us to wider bands of meaning in our society.

Postman best captured this idea when he said that newspapers should stop tailoring their news coverage to institutions and begin focusing on values and ideas. Instead of assigning writers to cover "beats" such as the courts, the legislatures and the stock market, why not place stories under such headings as greed, lust, altruism, stupidity, devotion, creativity and trivia? Getting into the "meaning" business, he says, means making those connections for readers. Some thoughtful journalists like Bill Kovach, former editor of the *Atlanta Journal* and now curator of the Nieman Fellowships at Harvard University, see this as a natural evolution for newspapers at the end of the twentieth century. He told a convention of journalism educators in Montreal in 1992:

> The value journalism has brought into the information system, is that it has been an institution of public understanding and participation. Journalists impose some order on chaos by selecting from all the information available at a given time that which is most useful and important to the audience, and presenting it in a context that makes it understandable and its importance obvious.[8]

To do that, newspapers need to redefine what they cover and how they cover it.

## Expanding the scope of the news

The transformation of the *Globe and Mail* in the early 1990s is one of the rare occasions in Canadian journalism where an idealistic and restless publisher teamed with an innovative editor to turn a dull newspaper of record into a forum for journalistic experimentation. Roy Megarry came to realize earlier than most that declining circulation was not a marketing problem; it was rooted in reader dissatisfaction with what newspapers were covering. As publisher, he cleaned editorial house, firing Norman Webster and Geoffrey Stevens, his traditionalist editor-in-chief and managing editor, and conferring the editorship of the country's most influential newspaper on William Thorsell, an editorial writer who had never worked as a reporter or editor. It proved to be an inspired move. Megarry declared, "We are publishing newspapers for another era, an era that has passed us by," and said the key to the future lies in "invention and innovation—we have to be prepared to take risks with editorial content by doing new things."[9] One of his first moves was to make Thorsell responsible for circulation development. His job was not to sell subscriptions but "to buy a half hour of the reader's time."

Megarry and Thorsell recognized the core of the problem, not just its symptom: that newspapers, in the previous twenty-five years of declining household penetration, had been loath to change even the most basic form of their product—the type of news they cover and the way it's written. No other institution in society, probably, could afford to ignore such a revolution in the way its raw material—in this case, information—was distributed and used. Television replaced newspapers as the primary source of news for most Canadians; the photocopier, fax and computer began to give people raw information faster and more completely; and our population became better educated, more sophisticated and increasingly cosmopolitan. The "bunkerism" of newspapers, their refusal to change, became the biggest threat to the financial well-being and social importance of the press in our society. What Megarry and Thorsell began at the *Globe* was nothing less than a revolution.

Thorsell translated Megarry's musings into journalism. He began by redefining the scope of news coverage and making sure that interesting experiments found their way into print. When he was asked to give the 1990 Clissold Lecture to journalism students at the University of Western Ontario, he used his platform to dismiss traditional newsgathering methods as lazy. "I believe we need to create new thematic beats of high status that focus on education but virtually ignore school board meetings, which cover technology, religion, social trends, Third World development, multiculturalism, ethics, architecture and families without easy, passive dependence on other people's meetings for our reports." Although Thorsell had detractors in his own newsroom, soon the *Globe* was bristling with audacious new ideas. The paper began to show the unmistakable evidence of being edited with flair, with intelligence and with a purpose beyond simply providing information. Thorsell called it "adult education—map-making in an increasingly complex landscape of issues and events." It slowly began to catch on with readers, who demonstrated that they were prepared to pay a premium for higher-quality information. The flagship Saturday *Globe* beefed up its content and raised its price gradually to $2 a copy, a record for any Canadian newspaper. By February 1997, Thorsell could boast that the past year's circulation had increased by 23,000 to reach 382,000.

If journalism were a true profession in Canada, bolstered by owners who believe in spending money on editorial research and development and in strong industry associations where new ideas might be shared and debated, perhaps the *Globe and Mail's* revolution would have inspired others and prompted newspaper journalism in this country to reinvent itself. It's not hard to imagine several exciting new roles that newspapers could take on. A newspaper as educator might start looking at how various levels of local government interact and tell us if services can be provided more efficiently. A newspaper as map-maker might add new layers to a story on a new municipal bylaw by referring readers to its website, which would contain background, a list of who voted for and against and links to related information and references. A newspaper that wishes to establish itself as a community forum might turn over a whole section to readers who wish to share ideas among themselves or contribute the product of their own research to current issues. A newspaper acting as conflict resolver might devote less space to covering a clash between a racial minority group and the police force and more to telling us what the underlying issues are and how such a conflict might be resolved. A newspaper that wishes to serve as a support system for public life would assign its municipal reporters to spend as much time out in the community as they do inside city hall. A newspaper serious about acting as a role model would write more about success stories and how people overcome adversity.[10] Whatever the competitive situations newspapers find themselves in, new technologies allow them—no, *require* them—to redefine what they cover and how it's approached. Otherwise, they may not survive.

Katherine Fulton, the founding editor of the *North Carolina Independent* and a 1992-93 Nieman Fellow, is one of the few journalists to think creatively about the opportunities, as opposed to the threats, for newspapers in the new information order.

> It is easy to imagine a future in which the newspaper won't be dropped on the front porch. The newspaper can become the community's front porch. New technologies will make it possible for people to gather, to gossip, to debate, to play a game together, because the newspaper has made it possible for them to find each other.
>
> Journalists will sit on the porch too, telling their stories and listening to peoples' reactions. Just behind the front porch, through the front door, will lie the world of information and ideas and people. The newspaper will help anyone who walks through in search of a fact or a service, whether they're looking for the most minute detail about the local sandlot league or about desert sands half a planet away.
>
> In this future, journalists can more often be perceived as raconteurs and bridge builders and researchers, not just cynical public prosecutors.[11]

Three things must change in newsrooms for this kind of reader-oriented journalism to happen. First, the hierarchical structure of top-down management must be blown up. This doesn't mean just reorganizing staff into "pods" or "clusters" with trendy theme names like "Applause" (a *London Free Press* team thrown together to cover both sports and entertainment), nor does it mean turning the editor into "general manager of the reader customer unit" (as the *Minneapolis Star Tribune* did briefly before it found it too cumbersome to explain). It means restructuring on the basis of the following three principles: (1) news coverage needs to better reflect the community and be useful and understandable to readers; (2) traditional newsroom organization, built on covering institutions, generally leads away from the interests of readers; and (3) news does not develop along the territorial boundaries that editors have established within their organizations.

Second, the news must be assessed using different methods. Most of it is now someone's "turf," gathered for sale at daily news meetings by editors with a vested interest in winning a prominent placement for it in the next day's paper. Anyone who has frequented such meetings knows that they are predictable, self-righteous, matter-of-fact, unimaginative and boring. Strangely enough, that's exactly how readers are describing the newspapers produced by these meetings: predictable, self-righteous, matter-of-fact, unimaginative and boring. What would happen if such meetings had a different agenda? What news would result if, in addition to asking what happened today, editors asked themselves which debates or discussions the community needs to be having? Answers could be prompted by consulting the people who matter most—the readers. Larger beats like business, family life or politics could have informal advisory boards of readers and professionals, who would meet with reporters and editors periodically to suggest and discuss issues that the newspaper should be paying attention to. Outsiders could even be invited into weekly news meetings or be hired as researchers.

Third, reporters must be assigned away from gathering the news, as they do now, largely at other people's invitation. Content would change radically if, instead of assigning traditional "beats" like business, politics, education, police and courts, the paper established thematic beats that more closely match how their readers actually spend their time. A short list might include: public safety (not just chasing police cruisers but examining crime trends and solutions); public health (examining issues such as sex education, medical research, the impact of hospital closings and preventive medicine); learning (what's happening in the classrooms rather than at school board meetings); public life (how governments spend our money, how we're taxed, how effective our politicians are); ethics and values (how business people, politicians, athletes, entertainers, doctors, lawyers and journalists make decisions); relationships (how do teenagers date in the age of AIDS, how do two-income households organize their time); getting around (why it takes so long to get downtown, why trucks have replaced railroads as deliverers of goods, what will the car of the future be like); workplace (looking at office politics, equal pay, downsizing, corporate profit-sharing); and diversity (how marginalized groups operate in society). Postman's "greed beat" is perhaps going too far, but why does no newspaper have a reporter covering the growing disparity of wealth in our society? Once a paper starts doing that, of course, it will have to find new ways to tell these stories.

## Writing so that people will read

In 1992, the *St. Petersburg Times* did something that no newspaper has done before or since: it took a chance by experimenting with different styles of writing the same story and asked readers which one they liked best. The result was dramatic. The so-called inverted pyramid style that has dominated newspaper writing for more than one hundred years does not work very well with readers. It communicates basic information quickly but is not enjoyable to read because it tells a story in reverse, starting with the conclusion. In the St. Petersburg experiment, it scored particularly poorly among younger and less frequent readers—precisely the folks newspapers must attract if they are to have a future.

This does not mean that all news should be told as narrative, the style that was preferred by most of the 1,174 readers polled. Using chronology, personality, examples, suspense and scene-setting to convey meaning clearly works for some stories and not others. But it is a powerful reminder that newspapers should use an arsenal of story forms and techniques and not rely solely on what has been called the Dracula of journalism—the inverted pyramid—which keeps rising from its coffin and sucking the lifeblood from newspaper writing, even though every rationale for its existence disappeared with the telegraph.[12] Even television doesn't tell stories in inverted pyramids anymore. Why should newspapers, which can't get there first, be wedded so eternally to a clunky style that seems to attract clunky, cliché-ridden writing, full of words like "spawned" and "triggered" and "amid," and other abominations of hackery like Suitcase Leads—first sentences that try to pack so much new information together that nothing has a chance to breathe?

"We live in a world of no narrative and no memory," says U.S. magazine editor Lewis Lapham, who criticizes television and newspapers for shortening people's attention spans. "The appeal is always to the emotion of the moment and not to the story so far. There's almost no historical perspective. Everything is taking place in the present at all times."[13]

American writing coach Paula LaRocque claims that newswriting has been deadened by other journalistic conventions as well: unnatural syntax, unnecessary qualification, clause-on-clause construction, sentences that back into themselves and foolish quotations foolishly fragmented.[14] Judging from the evidence of what appears in print, today's newsrooms seem to be filled with people who don't know how to make stories interesting, who write for their editors instead of readers, and who are so caught up in the daily grind that fresh and compelling approaches occur more by accident than by design. Maybe they learned to do it that way at bad journalism schools. A reader has only to delve back into library microfiche to discover the kind of journalism we once had, but lost. In 1890, for example, the Toronto *Globe* devoted most of its front page to a report written by a $17-a-week reporter by the name of Joseph Atkinson. He was sent to write about the hanging of a convicted murderer, and his story began:

> The murder of Frederick C. Benwell has been avenged. Reginald Birchall was executed on the scaffold in the yard of Woodstock gaol this morning at about 8.30. He died without confessing, without even alluding in public to his crime. He made no speech or remark of any kind after getting into the gaolyard save a casual one to the executioner. He maintained his nerve throughout, and but for a ghastly pallor gave no evidence of the emotion within his breast. From beginning to end he did not flinch or lose his self-possession. He died bravely, as he said he would die.[15]

One of the most dreadful executions in Canada's history was told with dispassion but with such attention to detail that the horror could never be erased from a reader's memory. The agony of the condemned man's last hours as the prison clock ticked down, Birchall still quietly maintaining his innocence to his wife, the brutal hangman sleeping peacefully one floor below—"I can carry it out as strict and stern as if I was shooting a dog"—these details left an indelible mark on the twenty-four-year-old Atkinson, too. He could never again condone the death penalty, and when he took over the *Star* and made it one of the country's great papers, he campaigned relentlessly for its abolition. His was journalism that stirred the mind, and he made sure that he always had writers on his paper who could do that for readers. Today's reporter, if allowed to witness such an event at all, might write something like this: "Amid a national debate on capital punishment that has split politicians and the country, Reginald Birchall, convicted murderer, was hanged today in what officials called a textbook execution."

Roy Peter Clark, a champion of good writing who co-ordinated the St. Petersburg experiment for the Poynter Institute, says the motto of a writer in journalism should be: I was there, and through my craft, you are there. "The most powerful journalistic writing, in almost every culture or language, derives from an attention to detail that allows you to both embrace the reality of the event and experience it in a vicarious way."[16]

Clark certainly practices what he preaches. In 1996, again for the *St. Petersburg Times*, Clark wrote one of the most powerful and talked-about pieces of journalism in years. It was a factual narrative account, using fiction-writing techniques such as internal monologue, reconstructed scenes, suspense and flashbacks, of what happened to a local family when a husband told his wife, "I have AIDS." The series, called "Three Little Words," ran every day for a month. Each one thousand-word account ended with a cliffhanger or some other foreshadowing device. The response from readers was remarkable. Circulation increased, and more than eight thousand readers called the paper's audiotext system to hear the author reading two-minute summaries of the story to date. Tourists called to find out how they could follow the story when they went home, so the paper offered reprints. A public forum after the series drew more than three hundred people, many of whom were affected by the HIV virus or were family or health workers. High school teachers assigned students to read the series and to write about their reactions. Clark says the skill of the writing wasn't what made an impact. It was the narrative form. "It may work in a special way in a newspaper, where readers can be encouraged to enter fully into the world of the story, day after day." Such writing, he says, involves deeper values such as empathy, understanding, tolerance and, ultimately, community.

No matter who owns the presses, journalism is, to a certain degree, public property. When the world changes and journalism is too hidebound or shallow to explain those changes for us, we complain or turn off. We as readers must encourage newspapers to invest in good writing by applauding it whenever it occurs. A phone call to the managing editor or publisher, a letter to the editor, a friendly personal note to the writer, would help build support for giving writers the time to tell it right. But newsrooms need to do more to give writers the *permission* to experiment. Writing coaches—editors who are teachers and good listeners and have no other line duties other than to encourage storytelling—are one answer, but only one Canadian newspaper (the *Edmonton Journal*) employs such a person. A better idea might be to publish a writing guide, so that reporters could choose from a variety of storytelling models, with guidelines for their proper use: the inverted pyramid, for short, newsmaking event reports; the list, for factual information that doesn't need explanation (such as what's open on Labour Day); the narrative, when atmosphere and time lines are important to reconstructing events; the descriptive story, when it's important for the reader to understand the scene; the extended interview, when the reporter tags along while some newsmaker goes about his or her job; the forum, where the reporter acts as a moderator rather than as a narrator and lets experts debate an issue directly; the mosaic or mapping technique, where the writer labels parts of a complicated story to help the reader understand such things as cause and effect; the analytical story, which requires the writer to take responsibility for weighing conflicting information and explaining what it means for people; and literary journalism, where the topic is so important or interesting that the reporter borrows from the novelist and, like Roy Peter Clark and his story on AIDS, takes us there and moves us profoundly. What interesting and compelling newspapers we'd have if we found writing there of this range every day.

The single most significant missing ingredient of daily journalism today is the well-told story. For the first time since rising newsprint prices shrunk the size of most newspapers, it's starting to come back. Conrad Black's better Southam papers have started to make room for long-form journalism in weekend magazines; and a few, such as the *Hamilton Spectator*, attempt to do it daily, with mixed results. This is important as never before because newspaper readers have changed. We want to know more. Our survival depends on it. Newspapers should know that it isn't enough anymore to tell us who said what. Minute-takers do that. Stenographers do that. Storytellers allow their readers to see, touch, taste and smell. They paint pictures for us. They show instead of tell. "Good writing," said George Orwell, "is like a window pane." It shows readers a world they cannot walk into by themselves.

For newspapers to encourage good storytelling, they need to invest in time (for it takes time to assemble the precise detail to tell stories well), they need to invest in skill (for a good story is a parable, touching on universal truths, and needs to be as delicately done as a painting), and they need to invest in space. They also need to invest in the basic intelligence of readers, which is perhaps the hardest investment of all for editors who seem to have spent a generation writing down to their audiences.

Barbara Amiel is not one of the great wizards of journalism, even though she holds the job of editorial vice-president of Hollinger Inc., the company her husband controls. But she stressed good writing as being key to the future of Canadian newspapers when she spoke to the CAJ's 1996 Women in the Media convention. "Newspaper owners now must take journalists very seriously," she said. "We are not simply the fodder between high yield classified ads. Our writing is the only ticket they have to survival."

My story on the 7-Ups generated two strong reactions in the community of Shawville, one emotional and one intellectual. The president of the fair board wrote in to object to my reference to "the honest scent of the farmyard," touching off an entertaining debate over whether farmers smelled any more than city people. And a reader from down the Valley, a professional man with no connection to farming, wrote to praise me for vividly showing an injustice. He said he hoped I was teaching my students at Ryerson to cover things that way.

## Notes

1. Quoted in *The Paper,* by Richard Kluger (Alfred A. Knopf, 1986), page 402.
2. "The future of newspapers," speech by Neil Postman to the International Federation of Newspaper Publishers, May 1990, Copenhagen, Denmark. "The second worst thing you can do," Postman added, "is to allow market research to continue to displace editorial judgment. That path leads away from the roots of journalism, makes news into a commodity like breakfast food and, by failure to respond to the deepest needs of citizens, insures, if not the obsolescence of newspapers, then their irrelevance."
3. Mills' memos in the summer of 1995 were addressed to Southam CEO Bill Ardell, vice-president Gordon Fisher and the publishers of the chain's other major papers. He concluded with a memo on August 31 in which he said: "Providing data or information is cheap. Supplying our customers with understanding or insight will require people with great breadth and depth of knowledge, the ability to communicate superbly and the time and resources to work at this level. Done well, this is likely to be expensive. Our long-term survival, however, may depend on this." Mills did not get a reply.
4. Interview with Russ Mills, November 5, 1996. Mills also said: "A lot of the kinds of stories we write are like walking in on the middle of a movie .... [We tell them] this is important to you, this is like your vegetables here, you should be reading this stuff, you should be following it, you should know about it. Well, a lot of people don't know, and we've got to find new ways to reach them."
5. "Expert Journalism," by Lou Ureneck, *Nieman Reports* (The Nieman Foundation, Winter 1994), page 9. Carey, a professor of journalism at Columbia University in New York, is quoted as saying that many of the evils of modern-day journalism stem from the acceptance of Lippmann's scientific-objective model.
6. Ibid. The guidelines developed by Lou Ureneck in Portland include the following:

> Expert reporting is a technique generally employed after a story has matured. It requires a reporter to master complex information for the purpose of reaching conclusions and to state those conclusions in clear and emphatic language. Expert reporting answers questions: Does this system work? Has this policy achieved its objectives? Is this organization being managed effectively, and in the public interest?
>
> 1. The effectiveness of expert reporting depends on thorough research .... This means becoming familiar with important information and significant interpre-

tations of this information before reaching conclusions.

2. The reporter should be able to draw conclusions based on an evaluation of information. They should be logical conclusions drawn from the information collected and analyzed. Discussions between reporters and editors are essential before conclusions are reached.

3. Arriving at conclusions and stating them clearly and forcefully are vital .... The evidence supporting these conclusions should be presented clearly and logically. The writer's goal should be to present a line of evidence that stands up to counter arguments.

4. Significant arguments against the conclusions of the expert reporter should be summarized, and evidence refuting these arguments should be presented.

5. The reporter should be careful not to allow stories to bog down in exchanges of opinion. The goal of expert reporting is to cut through the rhetoric and show readers where the weight of the evidence lies.

6. Expert reporting must be careful to preserve the distinction between conclusions and opinions. Generally conclusions are drawn from factual evidence; opinions are a mix of facts and the predispositions and values of the writer.

7.  "Sophisticated journalism can save newspapers," by Maxwell King, *The Editor* (Thomson Newspapers, December, 1992), page 15. The message of the Gulf War, King says, is that readers wanted "stories that offered context and perspective, that synthesized random streams of data and fact [and] above all, made sharp, conclusive and lucid sense of the blizzard of information TV was throwing at them."

8.  "Moving beyond Cold War journalism," speech by Bill Kovach to the Association for Education in Journalism and Mass Communications, Montreal, August 8, 1992.

9.  Speech by Roy Megarry at Ryerson Polytechnical Institute's School of Journalism, December 3, 1990. He said: "While it is necessary and interesting to know what happened yesterday ... increasingly I see us doing more to prepare our readers for the future; helping them cope in an increasingly complex environment; exploring a range of solutions to current problems .... Such an approach would make us more valuable, more necessary to the reader, and it would certainly set us apart from any other newspaper or communications medium."

10. This can be done in small ways. The *Calgary Herald,* for instance, began a daily feature called "Act of Kindness" in 1995. The paper set up a call line and invited its readers to suggest examples of small acts of kindness that might otherwise go unnoticed. It regularly surpassed its limit of 120 calls per day and attracted national media attention. Readers applauded the small bow in the direction of so-called "good" news.

11. "A new agenda for journalism," by Katherine Fulton, *Nieman Reports* (The Nieman Foundation, Spring 1994), page 17.

12. In the St. Petersburg experiment, four reporters wrote the same story, each in a different way; the stories were published in four adjacent zones at the same length, in the same position, under the same headline. Each was a typical one-day story on one of the following topics: people returning gift pets after Christmas, the extension of a recreation trail, a new campus for a local college, and the rejection of a proposal for a marina. Readers ranked the narrative form of each story ahead of the inverted pyramid, the point of view and the fact-box style.

13. "A voice that is forever questioning," by Antonia Zerbisias, *Toronto Star*, February 22, 1997, page K8.
14. "The Pyramid and storytelling," by Paula LaRocque, APME *Report* (Associated Press Managing Editors, January/February 1994), page 18.
15. *J.E. Atkinson of The Star,* by Ross Harkness (University of Toronto Press, 1963), page 12.
16. "More than one way," by Rebecca Ross Albers, *Presstime* (National Newspaper Association, October 1993), page 36.

# Chapter Twelve

# Restoring the Messenger

When I finally manage to stumble onto Shawville's dirty little secret, I wonder if I'm about to discover the third of life's three great truths: never eat at a place called Mom's, never play cards with a guy named Doc, and never write about the arena in a small town.

There's something almost sacrosanct about hockey arenas in small Canadian towns, even though Shawville's wasn't built to be a rink at all, but rather to show off healthy rutabagas and fine hand needlework for the annual Shawville Fair. The fair board just started freezing the floor so that it could be used in winter. Although the unheated corrugated steel exhibit hall has no insulation and is uncomfortable for spectators, it's where two National Hockey League coaches (brothers Terry and Bryan Murray) got their start on blades. Superstar Steve Yzerman played here in a midget tournament. This is where a young man who skates can, if he's noticed by the scouts, still find the surest ticket out of the Pontiac.

The tough brand of hockey played here is legendary throughout the Ottawa Valley, which served as the very cradle of the sport for nearly half a century. Rare was the team anywhere in Canada, amateur or professional, between 1880 and 1930, that was without a few Valley boys, including greats such as Newsy Lalonde, Frank Nighbor, Cy Denneny, Bill Cowley, Harvey Pulford, Syd Howe and Punch Broadbent. The best from right around here was Frank Finnigan, the "Shawville Express," who won Stanley Cups with the Ottawa Senators (1924 and 1927) and the Toronto Maple Leafs (1933) and who is now enshrined in the Hall of Fame. Fans used to bundle up in open sleighs, with hot bricks to keep their feet warm, and ride across the ice of the Ottawa River to follow their heroes. Sometimes a drink or two was had on the way. Every little town had a rink, and intense local rivalries grew up because, as Finnigan recalled shortly before he died, league size was limited by the number of miles a horse could travel per hour. He once told about taking a sleigh trip two miles across the frozen river to a hockey game when he was thirteen:

The worst part on a cold winter's night was the return journey after a game. You'd work up a real sweat during the game—remember in those days we were all Sixty Minute Men, we had no subs—and then you'd get on the sleigh in wet, damp, sweaty clothes, and your teeth would start to chatter and you'd start to shake, and the chills would set in and, even worn out from playing a whole game, the only way to survive was to get off and run behind the sleigh for warmth. Sometimes there were buffalo robes and you'd crawl under those and continue shivering. I often wonder how we didn't die of pneumonia .... That was my first "away" game.[1]

The timber barons who established world-beating teams in little places like Renfrew and Pembroke at the turn of the century have given way to their modern-day equivalents—elected town councillors who freeze the ice and fix the boards, Kiwanis Club volunteers who coach and public-spirited merchants like Chugg Electric who sponsor sweaters. But other things haven't changed at all. You can see the fans all hunkered down in blankets under hanging electric heaters that glow red but are of little use because the heat dissipates upwards with the vapour from the crowd whenever it cheers a Shawville goal. It's often -35 degrees Celsius at game time, inside, and you can tell how fast the ice is by how white the back wall turns.

The cold encourages a chippy brand of hockey played at a wickedly fast pace, the players flitting across bluelines like waterbugs, unleashing wild slapshots that thunder against the backboards and intimidate visiting goaltenders. Games are usually lengthy wars, prolonged by slashing, spearing, high-sticking, boarding, cross-checking and robust fighting. This, too, can be blamed on the climate, since the only place they heat inside the arena is the penalty box. During one Junior B game on a particularly cold night, I watch as the referee almost causes a stampede by asking the visiting team to volunteer a player to serve a bench penalty in the third period.

The only respite for spectators is the glassed-in snack bar area at the south end, which echoes between periods with the whump-whump of people beating their mitts against their sides to get their blood circulating again. Perhaps because it's warm, a stricter decorum is enforced here than on the ice. A sign from "The Management" spells out the Arena Lobby Rules:

1. No running.
2. No playing hockey.
3. Parents look after your kids!
4. No alcoholic beverages.
5. Kids not to be left unattended.
6. NO PETS.

The town of Shawville maintains the rink for the fair board on a lease of $1,000 per year, and it's a money-loser, costing taxpayers about $20,000 every season. This makes it unlikely that the place will ever get insulated, and there are diehards who think insulation would slow the game down too much for the players anyway.

Small-town arenas have a certain Spartan romance about them. The old one in Kinmount, Ontario, for example, is nothing more than a Quonset hut built exactly the width of the ice surface, so that boards were painted directly on the corrugated steel sides and doors were cut out so that home and visiting teams could park their heated RVs outside and use them to accommodate spare players between shifts, often learning the score only by hearsay. The imperfections of Shawville's arena did not strike me as remarkable until one day, almost two months into my internship at the *Equity*, I finally read the sign beside the Town Hall steps. It looks like one of those United Way thermometer charts, measuring the generosity of local charitable donors. Only this one is labelled "Shawville Community Centre Renewal Fund" and shows that nearly $100,000 has been pledged to fix up the arena. The sign adds, somewhat prophetically: "Every improvement has its price." Where, I wonder, has all that money gone?

Now there is a myth, perpetuated mostly by big-city editors, that nowhere is journalism so cowering and insipid as in a small town, where the advertiser up the street pays most of your bills and where friendships are more closely tied to consistent, favourable coverage. I know enough about Shawville to know that, if that money's gone astray, some of the community's most influential forces are involved. Both the town and the fair board do most of their printing and advertising with the *Equity*; both are right up there on the social scale, since election to public office and a position on the fair board are sure ways to get your picture in the paper often; and just about every parent in town takes a son or daughter to skate at the arena. A quick check with Richard confirms that the paper hasn't written a word about it. I'm about to get a powerful lesson in the vital role newspapers need to play in our society, and how all of us—readers, critics, publishers, journalists and government alike—have a duty to help them fulfill it.

A good place to start seems to be the Shawville town council, which will meet that Tuesday as usual, under the familiar old bleached portrait of the Queen and beside the municipal vault—seven men and a Hodgins woman who, once again, seem startled by a visitor. By now I have a nodding acquaintance and know them as the town grocer, the cab driver, the high school teacher, the part-time telemarketer, the hydro linesman, the dairy farmer, the mill worker and Charlie Dale, the impish and efficient secretary-treasurer who inherited the real running of the town from his mother. Just my luck, they're talking hockey. Seems that they called for tenders on the arena's superannuated Zamboni but no one expressed any interest, and now they have a storage problem. Also it seems that they were overcharged for repairs to the two nets, possibly because the repairman paid $200 to get his son into minor hockey, only to see him sit on the bench all season. There's a motion and they vote to pay half. When I finally get to Charlie to ask about the sign outside, the councillors have adjourned and left, and Charlie says I should have asked Donny Stevens when he was here, because he's the town's representative on the renewal committee.

"Is there any town money pledged to fix up the rink?" I ask him. "Lots," he says. "Gave $17,000 two years ago. Last year another $17,000 was set aside but held back because there was some hassle going on over there. Donny'd likely tell all about it." Charlie rolls his eyes and looks away, as if the whole thing is so … well, inefficient. I like Charlie a lot. He knows, without looking it up, exactly how much the town paid for everything it owns, including bolts for the stop signs. He has a fierce, protective pride about his work, probably because one of his ancestors, John Dale, discovered the townsite with old Tom Hodgins in 1821 and another was its first mayor. Whenever I quote him in a story, Charlie lets me know what he thinks of it. "I didn't mind that," is his highest praise. But when he dislikes something, he doesn't tell you anything; he just phones the *Equity* and asks if you can step next door for a chat. All the way over through the slush and snow, you think about what you've done to upset Charlie.

Donny Stevens is just like Charlie but without the edge. He is one of Shawville's leading volunteers. So when a whole section of the arena boards collapsed during a hockey tournament, he ran around and got braces made so the games could go on. When the electrical inspectors threatened to close the arena down as a fire hazard, he stepped in to get the main panel replaced. But more, much more needs to be done—insulation, for one thing, and showers! Imagine what a midget hockey tournament smells like when three hundred teenagers can't take a shower for three days! The town is in a bind because the fair board owns the arena and can't afford to improve it; if the town exerts too much pressure, the fair board might just decide to let it shut down. So two years ago Stevens, as a town councillor, stepped in to provide leadership. He worked out a fundraising campaign and a way of getting matching renovation funds from the Quebec government. There was only one catch: everyone—the town, the fair board and the hockey parents—had to agree to work together.

At first, everyone did. A partnership between the fair board and citizens who wanted a better arena seemed to make good sense. An agricultural exhibit building next to the arena at the Shawville fairgrounds had burned down the previous year, and there wasn't enough money from the insurance to rebuild it. By linking it up to the arena and sharing the new washrooms, the fair board could tap into the new money and the hockey people could free up valuable space in the arena for more dressing rooms. Stevens, who was chosen as chair of the arena renewal committee, put together a proposal that secured $265,000 in funding from the Quebec government for three specific projects—$50,000 for new boards, $65,000 for new washrooms and showers, and $150,000 to remodel the arena lobby and insulate the rink. This took care of 40 percent of the total costs.

The community had to find the other 60 percent. To do that, Stevens directed a volunteer fundraising effort that got off to a remarkable start. A total of $98,977.87 was collected from townspeople within a year. Part of this money was used to buy the new boards, which were installed using volunteer labour. But then differences arose between Stevens and the fair board, work on the arena came to a halt, Stevens resigned, and the renewal committee hadn't met in seven months. "I think a story is what people need to get things sorted out," Stevens says when I phone him. But he refuses to hand over any documents; I'll have to get them from the fair board.

Luckily, we'd already met. Two weeks before, I had stood on a tippy stacking chair in the cafeteria of S.E. McDowell Elementary School as all fifteen members of the newly installed Shawville fair board smiled up at me through the viewfinder of my untested Black's Insight Zoom 105. It was the town's most important society shot of the year, and there I was with no photographic experience and a lousy snapshot camera. For years, I'd been arguing that Ryerson's journalism program didn't need formal instruction in photography. "We don't teach typing," I always said. "We expect kids to know it. If people want to take pictures, they'll learn how to take pictures." Now those words came back to haunt me. In my twenty years in newspapers, I had directed coverage of several wars, the resignation of a U.S. president, Pierre Trudeau's abdication and the Montreal Olympics. I just knew what to do in those situations. But I didn't know how to make sure that fifteen strangers all had their eyes open when I pressed the button. I took about ten frames to make sure, then smiled with relief as they began to disperse.

That's when I experienced severe clong. Clong is a condition I believe only journalists suffer from, and it amounts to a sudden rush of shit to the heart. Ohmigawd, I thought. I've forgotten to get their *names!*

Getting accurate cutline information is one of the lost skills of my trade, something like the thirty-foot wrist shot in hockey. You just don't see it done much anymore. There is no one proven way to do it, and no journalism school in creation, I'm sure, teaches the first thing about it. Yet miss one name or get one wrong, and everyone in town knows it. The *Equity* puts great stock in accurate cutlines, since it runs so many pictures of people. So I had to call everyone on the fair board back, see if they remembered who they were standing next to, and take 10 minutes to copy down every name, left to right, and check spellings. I felt like a raw rookie on his first assignment and was vaguely resentful that Richard or Collette could have just taken the picture and run; they know all of these people by sight.

The ultimate test of cutline gathering, Richard explained later, was when the paper took a picture of the entire population of Shawville, gathered out there on the hill below the hospital, to commemorate Canada's 125th birthday in 1992. The cutline, with everyone's name, maybe 1,700 of them, took up more than half a page of the paper. The way they did that, I was told, is they laid string in rows across the hill, made everyone stand on the string, and passed notebooks across each row from the left so that each person could write his or her name in it.

Colette held the more recent everyday record—a picture of twenty-seven people the previous week. I asked what her cutline methodology was. "Oh, simple," she said. The people were getting achievement awards and the certificates were laid out on a table beforehand. So Collette copied down the names as written. "Then, as each one came up to receive an award, I made little notes about how they looked—drew little pictures of some of them in my notebook. That was just for back-up, though. When they lined up for my picture, I asked them to shout out their initials. I'd checked from the certificates—no two people had the same initials. So I just copied the initials down, left to right, and matched them later against the names. It was all done in a couple of minutes."

It was brilliant. I felt like hiring her on the spot to teach the new Ryerson course, Basic Cutline Techniques. But out of curiosity, a few days later, I examined her picture more closely: twenty-seven happy faces ... and twenty-eight names. Oops.

Reluctantly, I put the great arena scandal on the back burner for a couple of days while I cover more urgent news—Kenny Trudeau winning the biggest pike award (6 pounds, 4 ounces) at the ice fishing derby and a performance of the Lion, the Witch and the Wardrobe at the elementary school. Then at coffee break one day, Kathy Hynes, who sits on the fair board, mentions that there's some meeting about the arena project scheduled for that evening at the school. Something to do with an unpaid bill.

There are two smart rules for getting in to a meeting you aren't supposed to know about. First, you show up early, before there's enough of a quorum to tell you to leave. Second, you act like someone invited you. It's best if you're vague about who. Try to blend into the woodwork. Becoming invisible is a splendid journalistic technique. When you do that, Joan Didion once said, "People tend to forget that my presence runs counter to their best interests." And as the two warring sides of the arena fund sit down at the table, that's exactly what I do. Each side thinks the other invited me, and no one is rude enough to ask me to leave.

At issue is a $31,000 electrical bill for a set of new lights that Frank Lacourse installed in the arena. He has been trying to get someone to pay up for nearly three months. It quickly becomes clear that the arena renewal project has gone badly off track. The farmers and the townspeople are badly split, and most of the money raised has been used for other things. Judging from some handwritten figures on a sheet of foolscap that fair board president Ron Hodgins passes around the meeting, most has gone to the fair board to rebuild the adjacent exhibit halls for the Shawville Fair. Hodgins finally admits that $233,000 has been spent erecting the shell of a building that will house the long-awaited showers and washrooms, but the fair board can't afford to put in the plumbing or connect it to the arena. Even one of his own colleagues appears shocked at the overspending and lack of accountability. The meeting quickly breaks down in acrimony, with Lacourse's bill being the furthest thing from anyone's mind, including mine. What concerns me now is, will the *Equity* print my story?

Several more days of digging confirm everything that was said at the meeting—and there is a revealing moment when Ron Hodgins, showing me through the uncompleted exhibit hall, questions the whole idea of sharing washrooms with the arena. Imagine, he says, being a guest at a wedding and going to the bathroom dressed in a tuxedo, "having to whiz next to someone in hockey gear!" My story blames the impasse on two years of squabbling, changing priorities and lack of communication, and gives readers their first full accounting of what has happened to their money.

Now I have always regarded the operation of a newspaper as a public trust, with editors owing an overriding responsibility to the general good of society. The *Equity's* job, it seems to me, is to serve the people who raised the money to fix up their arena and who deserve to know how it has been spent. This so-called "watchdog role" of the press is not written down in our constitution, but the shopworn term by which you sometimes hear the press call itself—the Fourth Estate—implies that it is an important part of the self-governing process of a democratic society. The press provides the information that we need to make decisions—who shall govern us and how, which laws and values we should live by, how we face up to the challenges ahead—and it keeps tabs afterwards on how well our institutions are carrying them out. This responsibility of the press carries with it a great power that must not be abused. Thus it is wrong for a publisher to ignore news just because an advertiser wishes it or for an editor to ignore sloppy practices in local government just because your friends sit on council. It is wrong to use the press as a bully pulpit against your enemies, just as it's wrong to patronize those whose favour you seek. It's wrong to jeopardize the search for truth with shoddy or irresponsible reporting or questionable ethics. Every day, many newspapers in Canada quietly perform this vital job for democracy, but too few of us—within newspapers and among the reading public—fully appreciate the courage it requires, the good it does and the fragility that characterizes it.

Newspapers serve us best when they are leaders, when they stand up on behalf of readers and tell us what we need to know. To my surprise and gratification, the *Equity* knows this, and prints my story, even though a last-minute delegation from the fair board pleads with us to keep the whole mess quiet. As Heather Dickson says, you've got to have faith in your community. Strong communities, properly informed, can draw together and do the right thing. The paper's role here is to lay out the facts, without fear or favour, and let the community work. Not everyone in the office is as sure of this, however. "Boy, you'll hear about this in the morning," Kathy Hynes says, staying late after the paper is printed to read a copy of my story. "Hope you've got your bags packed."

The next morning, the paper sells out. Someone pins up my article at the arena and asks Dave Moore, who took his kids to an early hockey practice, "Who's that John Miller lad?" Over their morning coffee on Main Street, folks begin to debate what should be done now, somewhat relieved that things are out in the open at last. I run into the mayor and he shakes my hand and thanks me for doing the town a good turn. The other side weighs in a little later in the day, and the town quickly splits in two. There is talk of calling me before a special meeting of the fair board to justify my story. Although no one disputes the substance of my facts, the paper is being pressed to take a stand, and it occurs to me that this is the very same nightmare that keeps the new breed of daily newspaper publishers awake now across the country: the fear of hostile public reaction to something their paper prints. Trained in marketing and the bottom line, they simply want their editors to find out what readers want and give it to them, not realizing that this is precisely the way to hasten their demise. Again, the *Equity* strikes a blow for leadership and reasoned debate. Richard's editorial, "In the public arena," says that my story has unravelled a tale of misdirected energy and lack of communication and that its publication opens the whole issue to greater public scrutiny, which is a good thing. "Ultimately," the editorial says, "it will produce a better result: a community that builds upon its assets with all eyes open and all shoulders to the wheel."

That's the way newspapers *should* operate in society. If they often fail to do so, it's because several factors are making us question their role: the increasing concentration of ownership, the swing towards profit and away from public service, the pandering to popular tastes brought on by an emphasis on marketing, the lack of accountability or dialogue with readers, the failure of content, unethical or sensationalist reporting, competition from television, the abandonment of the mass audience and the inability of the craft to take on even a few of the trappings of a profession. Our trust has been rendered fragile and it hangs in the balance. If we still want the press to matter to us, if we see it surviving as our chief provider of information into the next century, then we must act now.

The biggest danger if we don't is that we may squander the hard-won libertarian concept of the press best described by Walter Lippmann as "the beam of a searchlight that moved restlessly about bringing one episode and then another out of the darkness into vision." On the whole, this philosophy has served us well, allowing the media to operate as a kind of watchdog over our important institutions by putting few barriers in the way of the free flow of information. Few Canadians would ideally want the government, or any other vested interest, to control the information that they receive each day. But in arguing that the state should have no business in the newsrooms of the nation, those who control the media have demanded special rights for themselves—for instance, an immunity on reporters being forced to turn over their notes or videotape as evidence in court, on grounds that this might turn them into virtual law enforcement agents of the state. Editors have also consistently argued before the courts that there should be no infringement on their absolute right to decide what appears in their publications. Critics like David Lepofsky have begun to argue that this is self-serving and needs to be re-evaluated.

In a little-noted paper, which he wrote in 1991, Lepofsky, then as now a constitutional lawyer with the Ontario attorney-general's office, spelled out an alternative view of the press. Section 2(b) of the *Charter of Rights,* he pointed out, guarantees freedom of the press to everyone, not just to those who own the media. He said courts may decide that

> People must be afforded a reasonable opportunity to secure space in the press or time on the airwaves to express diverse or competing viewpoints, so that the marketplace of ideas in Canada is not monopolized by the few wealthy, closely held and highly concentrated corporations which own much of the news disseminating capacity in Canada. This approach sees the prevailing corporate concentration in the mass media as a serious threat to the achievement of the goals of Section 2(b) of the *Charter.* These goals include the search for truth, the promotion of social and political participation, the fostering of democracy and the furtherance of individual autonomy and development, to name a few.[2]

Relying on journalistic ethics instead of the law to curb the excesses of the media does not work, according to Lepofsky, because there is little agreement among journalists on proper standards of conduct and because there is no professional organization to ensure that those who call themselves journalists are qualified for the job or held accountable for their actions. "At present," Lepofsky continues, quite convincingly, "journalistic ethics are too amorphous, too underdeveloped, too unenforceable and too susceptible to controversy to provide an adequate means of accountability. Moreover, they are usually implemented behind closed journalistic doors." Lepofsky calls for a public debate, one which he says is long overdue, on the way news outlets gather and report information to the public, the interests they actually serve in doing so and the impact of their activities on members of the public.

It's a good place to start. Concentration of newspaper ownership is irreversible in this country, and setting the threshold even higher would be an empty gesture. The failures of the Davey and Kent inquiries suggest that there may never again be the political will to appoint another royal commission into press ownership, and it wouldn't do much good anyway. The need for a much wider debate—into why our faith in newspapers is declining and what needs to be done to restore it—has been signalled again and again to those who own the press, and it's time that they listened. When an overwhelming majority of Canadians say in a poll that they favour various government limits on the press—to protect military secrets, for example, or to censor portrayals of unnecessary violence—newspaper owners should be worried that their privileged franchise is at risk. Their readers are looking for a much more equitable relationship.[3]

Some feel print journalism is in a liminal moment, an uncertain, transitional time somewhere between yesterday and tomorrow. We're not sure if the light at the end of the tunnel is a freight train coming toward us, heralding the destruction of newspapers, or the reflection of a shining new world of converging technologies and customized news, in which newspapers will play a pivotal role. Tom Rosenstiel, former media critic for the *Los Angeles Times*, says newspapers are too resistant to change to find their way out of the tunnel alone and need the public's help in drawing up a map for their future travels together. He says a newspaper's real product is not its expertise or its technology, but its relationship with its readers; and any good relationship, like any good map, is built on good information and trust:

> If you make your newspaper too sensational, it's like making one of those maps from ancient times, where England is the size of Greenland, and on the other side of the world we sketch in sea monsters because we don't know what's really over there. If you watch local TV there are a lot of sea monsters and if you fill up your newspaper with what you think rather than what you know, with a lot of interpretation and analysis rather than real information, the map may be pretty but it doesn't actually show all the roads. It's got a lot of colors on it but it's not as helpful as a navigational tool. And if you cut your newshole too much, the map doesn't get you very far.[4]

The denial of Canadian publishers about the perilous future of newspapers is breathtaking. Even as the dark buzzards circle menacingly overhead, most of them keep their dwindling herds running hard and feed them on the thinnest rations. Meanwhile in the United States, where conditions are far less ominous, the newspaper industry is reacting as if all of its livestock is at risk. Several professional and charitable organizations, prodded on by media critics, unfavourable polls and owners who seem to be more concerned than their Canadian counterparts about the long-term health of their franchises, are spending millions of dollars to find out what's wrong and how it can be fixed. Rosenstiel has been hired by the Pew Charitable Trusts to develop an institute that will study and improve journalistic standards, a move that is unheard-of in Canada, where such press critics are viewed as lepers or know-nothings. The Newspaper Association of America, the main professional body to which most U.S. publishers belong, is launching a $6 million advertising campaign aimed at shoring up the reputation of the daily press. And the American Society of Newspaper Editors has launched a three-year project to identify and address the causes of journalism's dwindling credibility. Its president, Sandra Mims Rowe, said it's time for newspapers to look beyond the quick fix. "If we really believe something must be done beyond hand-wringing ... this problem will not be solved, trust will not be built, in a year or two."

That's real leadership. Unfortunately, the only equivalent professional group in Canada is the Canadian Newspaper Association, and self-examination and angst about the future are the furthest things from its mandate. Its job is to whistle a lively, upbeat tune and lead all of the unsightly rats away from Main Street. Its national advertising campaign, based on the slogan "Grow your mind. Read a newspaper," attempts to make people feel ignorant or guilty for not reading one every day. The CNA was cobbled together in 1996 by owners who felt that they were spending too much money on professional associations and who wanted one that was more narrowly focused on marketing and lobbying, not on making their product better.[5] Although the CNA has an editorial committee, it has no budget nor clearly defined role, and it was forced to abandon what it was best at—editorial training and research—because big owners like Southam and Thomson didn't want to share their expertise. Altogether, the CNA is not the representation that an industry in trouble needs. Any doubts about that were dispelled at its first annual meeting in Toronto, where the entire morning's agenda was disposed of by shortly after 10 a.m., leaving organizers scrambling to fill the two hours until lunch. There were only twenty-two publishers present, and no one offered a question or substantial comment the whole day, even when I provocatively suggested in a panel discussion that some daily newspapers could start closing in Canada because no one is spending money to make them better. It's perhaps telling that three of the top four executives in the CNA at that time had no background in the newspaper industry. One was hired from government, one from television, and a third from the Canadian restaurant association.

Public pressure, and perhaps even political action, are needed to force the industry to address its perilous hold on the public's trust. If we believe the reliability and diversity of information is an important part of what makes our democracy work, we must ensure that our newspapers are operated in the public interest. A piecemeal approach, narrowly focused on concentration of ownership or the quality of individual newspapers, is not good enough. For example, the Council of Canadians campaigned for legislation to limit Conrad Black's newspaper holdings, but its efforts were ineffectual, narrowly based and late, particularly its unsuccessful attempt to challenge Black's takeover of Southam in court. Although funded by such groups as the Canadian Labour Federation and the Assembly of First Nations, the council had to rent a crowd of street performers to stage its largest public event outside Hollinger's 1997 annual meeting in Toronto. But at least someone is trying, and Black's public derision for the council and its chairperson, Maude Barlow, indicates that they're scraping some raw nerves.

What's needed is a broader effort, perhaps enlisting the support of the

Canadian Journalism Foundation, an organization of business people and media executives who want to foster a public dialogue about the role of the media in society but so far have failed to excite anyone about it and, in fact, usually meet in private. What the foundation has is access to serious money—more than enough to fund what might be called a People's Commission on the Free Press, headed by prominent citizens from various fields, supported by the newspaper industry and charged with working out a new consensus of the role of the press in our society. Such a project might attract some government funding but would avoid the limitations of a royal commission, which usually looks to government to work out its solutions. Government, like all of us, has an interest in promoting the freest press possible and one that is seen to be reliable and independent. And only government has the clout to get reluctant owners to pay attention. Imagine how quickly Conrad Black's interest would be engaged if the federal industry minister initiated a review of foreign ownership restrictions, coupled with a study of what other countries do to limit concentration of media ownership and how appropriate that might be in Canada.

Canada is virtually alone in not having any means to stop one company from owning a majority of newspapers. In France, for instance, the government has rules against any group controlling more than 30 percent of the press, and that figure drops to 10 percent if the group also has substantial broadcast holdings. Sweden has perhaps the most diverse and accountable press in the Western world, thanks largely to government subsidies designed to preserve smaller, independent publishers and an official press readers' representative who can fine newspapers if they violate a code of conduct. Sweden's population of nine million is less than one-third of Canada's, but it has as many newspapers and several times the number of publishers. In Germany, any mergers that allow a company to control a specific press market or strengthen an already dominant position are overruled by the country's cartel office. Britain empowers its Monopolies and Mergers Commission to assess any proposed newspaper sale for its impact on the accurate presentation of news and free expression of opinion. That's something Canada's competition bureau is specifically forbidden from doing.

The Council of Canadians argues that freedom of the press is not just a proprietary right of owners to do as they see fit but a right specifically granted to all Canadians. It says that legislation should support the following suggestions: no company or individual be allowed to control more than 25 percent of the daily newspapers in the country, or more than half of all media in a local area; federal tax inducements and interest-free loans be made available to community groups and non-profit organizations that wish to establish their own newspapers; and a code of professional practice be enacted to protect journalists from meddling owners. Many of its suggestions are overzealous and poorly drafted, but at least the Council of Canadians has flushed Conrad Black out of the closet so that even he seems to recognize the need for limits on one-person ownership of the media. Although he says that it's "unimaginably absurd" for anyone to suggest that his control of 60 percent of Canada's newspapers constitutes any threat, Black would support a 20 percent limit on ownership of all print, electronic and broadcast media.[6] That sets the bar a little lower than most of us would be comfortable with, but nevertheless a point of sorts has been conceded; ownership should be carefully monitored, because of the media's potential influence over public opinion.

A People's Commission on the Free Press would draw together a cross-section of interested groups—labour, business, newspapers, press councils, universities and readers. Public hearings could be held across Canada to find out what people think of the current press and how it's living up to its own statement of principles. These rules of journalistic conduct could be redrafted, if necessary, to reflect a consensus on the role and responsibilities of the free press. Recommendations could be made for making newspapers more accountable to the public, either by strengthening the mandate of existing press councils—allowing them, for instance, to fine newspapers that don't live up to the new standards—or by creating a Swedish-style national readers' representative who has the power to investigate and report to the public on shortcomings or abuses of the free press. This would start print journalism along the road to becoming a more professional activity.

A second task would be to encourage the press to change for the better. Groups of academics and newspaper executives could review the research on such things as credibility, accuracy and trust, and do new studies to fill in the gaps and sound out ideas for making newspapers better. Participating newspapers could then test out possible editorial solutions on their readers, then present and debate the results at the CNA's conventions. A good example of the kind of topic that could be tackled is crime coverage, which occupies a disproportionate amount of news space, mainly because it's cheap and easy to cover and because editors perceive that the public has an appetite for it. Researchers could illuminate other aspects of the case: that this emphasis may be contributing to public anxiety that violent crime is rising. Indeed the opposite is true. Although Statistics Canada reported decreased violent crime in 1996 for the fifth year in a row, a national poll by Angus Reid showed that 60 percent of Canadians felt that crime in their communities had gotten much worse in that period.[7] No newspaper really knows if it will lose or gain readers by cutting back or modifying its coverage of crime, and few are experimenting with ways to report crime in its proper social context. Nevertheless we should all feel a responsibility to ensure that our news reflects reality.

A People's Commission on the Free Press could also encourage more professionalism in journalism by examining how journalists should be trained. Unlike their counterparts, Canada's newspaper editors have taken no interest in how their future reporters and editors are taught. Journalism degree programs exist at seven Canadian universities and scores of community colleges but there is no formal system whereby industry can accredit curriculum (as there is in the United States), editors lay down no benchmarks of reporting and editing skills (as happens in New Zealand) and there is a trend to hire instructors more on their academic credentials than their knowledge of the newsroom. On the other hand, few universities bother to involve editors when they are rethinking curriculum. Three of them, Carleton, Concordia and Western, have amalgamated journalism with other programs, shifting the emphasis away from reporting and writing skills towards more theoretical or technical expertise. The University of British Columbia's new graduate school in journalism was funded by a publisher from Hong Kong and put together without any Canadian professional input. The training grounds exist, and more than three-quarters of all entry-level jobs in newsrooms are filled by these graduates. No one knows, however, if they're turning out people who are actually up to the task of transforming and revolutionizing print journalism.

For journalists in mid-career, there is precious little training at all. Canadian editors spend tens of thousands of dollars to send a few of their most promising people to the United States for professional development and have let the few Canadian initiatives, such as those at Ryerson and the Canadian Newspaper Association, wither and die. Because Canada's profitable newspapers have not funded a national newspaper training institute, our journalists are deprived of a Canadian version of the kind of short courses available at such industry-supported American facilities as the American Press Institute, the Poynter Institute for Media Studies and the Newspaper Management Center at Northwestern University. If anything, the situation is worse now than it was twenty-eight years ago, when Keith Davey's Special Senate Committee said that it was "astonished" that an industry so important, so prosperous and so intelligent has developed so little formal machinery for upgrading its personnel and its product. "If IBM had been as unconcerned about the kind of people it attracts and the conditions under which they work," the Davey report said, "it would still be making adding machines."[8] The opportunity for real collaboration between industry and universities is long overdue. Provincial governments can help by passing laws like that of the Parti Quebecois, which requires all Quebec companies to spend one percent of their payroll on training and development, or else have it taxed by the state.

Nearly a decade ago, Southam sent veteran editor Shirley Sharzer into newsrooms across the country to investigate the demand for mid-career training. After talking to more than three hundred journalists at sixteen papers, she said that there was such a strong demand for training, covering nearly every skill in the book, that the frustration almost exploded out at her. "Twenty-nine years as a journalist and I'm finally being asked about training programs?" one veteran reporter told her. "I should be *giving* them!" Writers, she found, had no idea what their editors thought about the stories they turned in. "There is no feedback," one said. "The only strokes here are cardiac arrest."[9] Sharzer urged

Southam to invest in training for strategic and economic reasons—to increase job satisfaction and performance and to make newsrooms more accepting of change. The company ignored almost all of her suggestions. Today, with Southam now under the arm of Conrad Black, the chances are nil that it will ever take training seriously or invest heavily in it.

If newspapers are to survive, they need to achieve a deeper level of sophistication. That means they need to finally heed all those warnings about superficiality and sensationalism that have come at them from readers and press critics for more than two decades. Otherwise, they risk devaluing the very nature of what they exist to deliver—the news. When the world's truth is treated as just another product to be sold, when its importance is fudged by its promotion or entertainment values, when we can no longer distinguish what Peter and Lloyd give us on the nightly news from what Oprah and Jerry serve up on their chat shows, when the front page of the *Toronto Sun* might just as easily be the front page of the *National Enquirer*, when the lurid and loopy take precedence over what's happening in Bosnia, it's not hard to predict the end of news as a commodity of public service. Perhaps the strongest such warning came in 1992 from a man who did more than his share to establish the noble role of the press as a powerful watchdog over our political institutions. Carl Bernstein broke the Watergate scandal for the *Washington Post* with his partner Bob Woodward, and their reporting led to the humiliating resignation of U.S. President Richard Nixon. Writing about the state of his country's press in terms that could equally apply to Canada's, Bernstein said:

> Increasingly, the America rendered today in the American media is illusionary and delusionary—disfigured, unreal, disconnected from the true context of our lives. In covering American life, the media break new ground in getting it wrong. The coverage is distorted by celebrity and the worship of celebrity; by the reduction of news to gossip, which is the lowest form of news; by sensationalism, which is always a turning away from a society's real condition; and by a political and social discourse that we—the press, the media, the politicians and the people—are turning into a sewer.[10]

I was astonished to hear a group of Canadian editors, who were participating in a rare brainstorming session on readership a few years ago, list "boring content" as their number one concern about newspapers. I mean, these were the people in charge of what went into their papers, and *they* were bored? Why shouldn't the rest of us be too? Asked what they thought people wanted to read, the editors compiled this list:

1. Scandal.
2. Drama.

3. Quality sleaze.
4. Shocking.
5. Human interest.

This is bankrupt thinking. It's the ultimate sin of modern journalism—the failure to treat readers as intelligent human beings, capable of having informed discussions about public affairs. There's just no charitable way to look at it, even if the list was only half serious or the product of editors who were self-conscious and unfamiliar with brainstorming together or, even worse, cynical about what motivates their readers. What is indisputable is that this flies in the face of history. In city after city, time after time, it's always the paper of substance and quality, the paper of subtlety and metaphor, the paper whose rich view of life sinks deep into the souls of its readers that survives and prospers in the long run. Only a very few Canadian editors appear to acknowledge this or have the resources to do anything about it, judging by the papers they publish every day. One of them is Neil Reynolds.

Now editor of Conrad Black's *Ottawa Citizen*, Reynolds earlier in his career made both the *Whig-Standard* and *Telegraph Journal* nationally respected newspapers. The real problem in journalism, he once said, is not that it fails to deliver what readers need most—what's true and what it all means—but that it doesn't even try to:

> As journalists, how can we communicate with our readers in any honest or authentic way if we don't go beyond the glib fact and ubiquitous statistic? If we don't go beyond the unexamined and unexplored statement? If we don't appreciate the difference between ideas and agendas? If we don't truly understand and articulate the essence of things?[11]

Reynolds was editor of the *Whig-Standard* when he wrote that, and he referred to a wire-service report that his paper had run about 100,000 university students raising their plaster statue of the "goddess of democracy" in Tiananmen Square just before China's dictatorial leaders crushed their revolt with tanks. The statue symbolized everything that they were fighting for, yet it wasn't mentioned until the fifteenth paragraph of a sixteen-paragraph report. "If ever historic, symbolic moments deserve literature from journalism, this moment was surely one," Reynolds wrote. "Rising from the waves onto a Pacific beach of historic significance, the west winds now a gale, the goddess of democracy meets her messenger, her story-teller, her guide—an unthinking and uncaring journalism, a journalism apparently capable neither of intelligent passion nor inspired observation."

People read newspapers to get the news, and the news is compelling when it is told with depth, detail, context, passion, symbolism and understanding. That must be restored to our newspapers, or they will surely perish in an age when other messengers can deliver simple information and entertainment much faster. I believe newspapers will prosper well into the next century if they learn to write about three things well: local news, which newspapers with their larger staffs are uniquely positioned to provide; explanatory journalism, written by people with specialized knowledge who can part the curtains and take people on a tour of the most fascinating ideas and developments of our time; and literary journalism, stories that really are stories because they tell parables and connect with readers on a deeper, visceral and emotional level.

To do that, newspapers will have to undergo a revolution. Those of us on the outside can encourage it to happen, by activism and public policy, but most of the toppling of icons must happen within newsrooms, where journalists, who have grown too comfortable at doing things the same way for too long and who bristle when confronted with evidence that it's not working, must literally reinvent their craft. The following is perhaps a way to start.

**Articulating a nobler mission.** Neil Reynolds says that newspapers should "celebrate, not lament, the seriousness of our purpose .... Our journalistic objective should be just that—solemn, meaning sober, deliberate and very important. Our writing should elicit thoughtful, reflective and, indeed, painful meditation."[12] Above all, he says, editors should never underestimate the intelligence of their readers by talking down to them. This means that newspapers must abandon their hopelessly flawed role of arrogant and imperial critic, able to cynically snipe at ideas put forward by others without having to defend any themselves or offer alternatives. For all of their good intentions, journalists have assumed a role that is not only beyond their abilities, it is ultimately anti-democratic and destructive. They need to rededicate themselves to the infinitely more difficult and important tasks of leading (not ingratiating), challenging (not pacifying), educating (not alarming) and explaining (not confusing). This can be done only by ensuring that our newspapers are run by strong editors who allow their reporters to engage in what Lewis Lapham calls "the imaginative labor of trying to tell the truth." By exploring a diversity of ideas, especially those that run against the grain of prevailing opinion, newspapers can invoke a sense of energy and hope, Lapham says,

> since the press in its multiple voices argues that the world of people and events can eventually be understood—not yet perhaps, not in time for tomorrow's deadline, but sooner or later, when enough people with enough access to better information have had an opportunity to expand the spheres of reference.[13]

**Serving the community.** Newspapers now know that the consequence of their imperial arrogance—public disinterest—will ultimately prove fatal to them.

The only answer is to restore the public service role of the press to a position of primacy. We as readers must demand it and newsrooms must respond by opening their doors and listening first, by engaging us in hopeful debate about our communities, by creating partnerships to brainstorm solutions, and by examining alternatives and empowering us to seek the best future for ourselves. It will be expensive, but the owners can afford it. Relinquishing some of their power will surely be threatening for journalists, but what they're covering now often does not serve us very well. As newspapers bind themselves closer to their communities, they must learn to stand more accountable by covering themselves at least as well as they now cover television, by telling us every day how and why they do things, by implementing hiring policies that reflect our diversity, and by rediscovering a version of Main Street, perhaps in the form of community councils that could help protect the independence of their editors against meddling and remote owners. Covering the agenda and pleasing the owner's friends and shareholders is easy, and it's cheap. But the harder job of journalism, the kind most needed in this age of corporate greed and sunny press agentry, is mucking about in the shade, shedding light on what's not obvious, exercising the courage to look out for the community first.

**Rediscovering the art of storytelling.** Reading a newspaper today is like getting served at a fast-food counter; most of it is bland, it comes off an assembly line, it's cheap and unsatisfying. You put up with it because you're in a hurry, and newspapers in turn seem to be in a hurry to get rid of you. They should be more like gourmet restaurants where they light you a candle and invite you to settle in and savour the steak. The very nature of news may need to be redefined to accomplish this. Just imagine if newspapers did for their written content what they did in the 1980s for their graphics. If the stories and headlines stirred a compelling emotion, or synthesized a series of events, or made us appreciate the *gray* of things instead of just the black and white. If newspapers continue as simple purveyors of information and entertainment, they'll go out of business tomorrow. If, on the other hand, they make a habit of rousing our higher instincts and emotions, and doing it with style and passion, we may value them as never before. They need to turn their writers loose, and let them take us to places we've never been.

**Anticipating change.** The marketplace hungers for the good and trusted editor, someone to guide us through a world of constant, threatening change. Peter Calamai, one of the smartest men in Canadian journalism, says that what's happening now, in real life and journalism, is similar to plate tectonics:

> All these geological plates are shifting around and no one knows where they're going to end up. What newspapers have been doing is adding to the problem, reporting the grinding sounds and the bits that break off

and the tremors, and not what's really happening.[14]

This deeper level of sophistication can be developed only by training; by hiring people who can actually synthesize ideas and who are not just good at stenography; by developing facilities for serious document research and computer-assisted analysis; and by editing the newspaper as if it was something more than a bulletin board, something approaching a journal of moral behaviour, perhaps, or an explainer of trends. It should tell us the "What's next?" as well as the "What happened?" This requires a revolution, an expensive revolution, but it's long overdue. It's hard to name any other $3 billion-a-year industry that spends as little as newspapers do on research and development.

**Experimenting.** Newsrooms tend to be dungeons of drudgery and habit where editors profess to know what readers want but really don't. That's what Christine Urban concluded after doing market research for nearly one hundred dailies in Canada and the United States. Her "10 Myths about Readers" put the lie to many of the following preconceptions used to edit newspapers today: stories must be short (Urban found that readers actually expect important stories to be long); newspapers must attract upscale readers (Urban found that working-class readers are often more loyal, and there are more of them); newspapers must be entertaining enough to compete with TV news (Urban found that news on TV actually whets the appetite for the fuller version in print); readers always demand more (Urban found that readers are "at risk" because they're dissatisfied with the quality of what's already there, not because of something that's missing).[15] Editors say two things that kill initiative and experimentation in newsrooms: "We never do it that way" and "We always do it that way." New subjects need to be covered, the stories need to be written in innovative ways and they need to appear in unexpected places in the paper. We should be surprised, challenged and engaged when we pick up our papers; we should never, ever be bored.

**Really sweating the loss of credibility.** Until the newspaper industry becomes more of a profession in Canada, it will not be able to address the lack of trust that's driving away readers. Hype and arrogance, ultimately, are suicidal. Covering events out of proportion to their significance, and doing so without effective accountability, tends to trivialize the institution doing the coverage. The last stand of journalism is to say that the public doesn't care about anything, so let's entertain, let's treat the news as spectacle, let's cover it cheaply and damn the torpedoes. Journalism desperately needs a dose of integrity, and it can get that only if it first rebuilds its professional institutions. Reporters and editors should have a commonly accepted set of ethical principles and a way of policing them; owners should help fund a strong national society of newspaper professionals and require their employees to belong to it; editors should open a dialogue with their communities about what they cover and how they do their jobs and they should have clear hiring standards, strong ties to journalism schools and a commitment to ongoing professional retraining. Jim Travers says: "What's important is that we raise the level of our information gathering to such a degree that people say, look, whatever form that this is in, these are the people I trust to bring it to me. These are the people with credibility. These are the people who give me insight. And we're a long way from that."[16] Newspapers need to get there soon, or they may be finished.

## Notes

1. *Old Scores New Goals*, by Joan Finnigan (Quarry Press, 1992), page 36.
2. "The Role of the Press in Freedom of the Press," by David Lepofsky, presented at the Cambridge lectures, Queen's College, Cambridge University, July 1991, page 16.
3. *Eight Nation Survey*, Times Mirror Center for the People and the Press, Washington, D.C., published on March 16, 1994. Sixty-seven percent of Canadians favoured restrictions on the press to protect military secrets, and 61 percent favoured restrictions to curb racial or ethnic insults—the highest percentage in any nation polled. The authors of the survey found these levels alarming.
4. *The Printed Newspaper: Its Future and Its Role*, report from the J. Montgomery Curtis Memorial Seminar, American Press Institute, September 24–26, 1996, page 18.
5. The CNA describes its mission as follows: "To represent the needs of its members and the public in the areas of public policy, marketing and professional affiliation. These areas permit the CNA to act on behalf of the industry in a proactive manner for the benefit of newspaper groups and independents alike, to raise the awareness of the benefits of newspapers to advertisers and readers and to monitor and analyze legislation potentially harmful to newspapers and freedom of the press."
6. Conrad Black talked about limits on concentration of ownership in a speech he gave to the Metropolitan Toronto Board of Trade on January 27, 1997.
7. "Homicides up; overall crime rate down," by Henry Hess, *Globe and Mail*, July 31, 1997, page A5.
8. *The Uncertain Mirror*, Report of the Special Senate Committee on Mass Media, Volume I (Minister of Supply and Services Canada, 1970), page 10.
9. *Professional Training in Southam Newsrooms: A Survey*, by Shirley Sharzer, for the Southam Newspaper Group, August 1989, page 26.
10. "A post-Watergate meditation on how the media blew it," by Carl Bernstein, *Globe and Mail*, May 30, 1992, page D1. He added: "The really significant trends in journalism have not been toward a commitment to the best and the most complex available version of the truth, not toward building a new journalism based on serious, thoughtful reporting." The media's obsession with the trivial and the bizarre, he says, represents "the triumph of the idiot culture."
11. "Journalism: The literature of the people," by Neil Reynolds, *The Whig-Standard* magazine, October 6, 1989.
12. Neil Reynolds spoke at Wordstock, a newspaper writing seminar at Ryerson

Polytechnic University, March 20, 1997.

13. From "The Mirror of the News," a speech that Lapham, the editor of *Harper's* magazine, delivered at the University of Oregon School of Journalism in 1985, as part of the tenth annual Ruhl Symposium on Ethics in Journalism.

14. Interview with Peter Calamai, November 4, 1996.

15. "10 Myths About Readers," by Christine Urban, ASNE *Bulletin*, July/August 1986, page 19. Urban is president of Urban & Associates of Sharon, Mass., and does market research and consulting for newspapers.

16. Interview with Jim Travers, November 7, 1996.

# Me and McRae

I haven't seen Earl McRae in fifteen years, but here he is rushing through the Ottawa airport with his customary pugnacious look, as if he's just waiting for some jerk to stop him and say, "Hey, aren't you that columnist?" It's a few days after my story on the missing arena money appeared in the *Equity*, splitting Shawville in two, and McRae has just touched off a storm of controversy up the entire Ottawa Valley by some comments he made about local hockey and its hick fans. So I decide to make his Sunday.

He seems relieved it is an old friend. Mayors of towns up and down the Valley have been calling for his scalp, ever since his column appeared in the *Ottawa Sun* ridiculing the fans of the Ottawa Senators who cheer every time the PA system plays "The Hockey Song" by Stompin' Tom Connors. The Canadian singer is a "thundering bumpkin" who makes McRae feel embarrassed to be a Canadian. Worse still, he wrote, the fans are from the "God-forsaken Ottawa Valley ... the bastion of yokeldom ... where inbreeding, wood-burning stoves, moonshine stills, outhouses, human manure on the boots and baying hounds in the night still reign supreme." McRae took it upon himself to apologize to visitors for "these bindlestiffs."

I recognized it as vintage McRae, but the mayor of Pembroke complained to the Ontario Press Council and threatened a class-action suit. Arnprior's mayor said she couldn't guarantee McRae's safety if he visited her town. Signs at the next home game said "Let's Stomp on Earl McRae."

McRae is a short, compact, sort of crazy-eyed throwback to the kind of journalists who, if they managed to acquire a column, thought their job was to antagonize people. He wears a trenchcoat and shows a lot of bottom lip. He looks like you imagine all of those sports phone-in hosts on the radio to look, with the kind of face a perfect stranger might walk up to and punch. Former Canadian heavyweight boxing champion George Chuvalo once shoved him up against a wall and threatened to rearrange his complexion. McRae actually used to do a radio sports phone-in show, but perhaps Chuvalo gave him an idea—that his face could provoke as much controversy as his writing—so he now does TSN. He has the type of mouth you imagine saying, "Yeah, well what makes you such an expert on hockey, pal?" He's perfect on TV, in the same way Don Cherry is perfect.

# Epilogue: Me and McRae

McRae's just in from a road trip with the Senators, who will establish an NHL record for losing forty-one games in other rinks this season while winning only one, and he asks what I'm doing in Ottawa. I explain about Shawville.

"Shawville," he says. "That's another place they don't like me. Went there to do a story about the Murrays after Bryan was fired as coach of the Washington Capitols and his brother Terry replaced him. It's a big deal in Shawville, right? The Murray brothers, and a reporter from Ottawa there."

The family must have let down its guard, sitting there in the Murray kitchen tossing back the odd beer with McRae scribbling down everything—including stuff about Terry's wife not being a loyal member of the family and probably having something to do with Bryan's demotion.

"I'm a reporter," McRae says. "Why wouldn't I put that in the story?"

I ask about his column, where he called the people of the Ottawa Valley "hayseeds" and "porkheads."

"Did it really happen just like you said, about the American hockey reporters in the press box cringing at the Ottawa yokels, or were you just being McRae?"

"No," he says. "I don't like Stompin' Tom, I think he's a hick, that part was true. I made up all the other stuff and put in the comments about the Valley just to get people stirred up. They hate it, you know, when an outsider sticks in the needle about inbreeding and shit on the galoshes."

I say I know.

"Glad to see you haven't changed, Earl."

When we worked at the *Toronto Star* together, in 1968, he was one of a talented crew of young reporters who were just beginning to challenge the conventions of their elders and write outside of the mold of inverted-pyramid journalism. They included Mark Starowicz, who was let go by the *Star* but went on to revolutionize CBC public affairs radio and television with programs like "As It Happens" and "The Journal"; and John Zaritsky, who later won international prizes for his film documentaries. McRae had enormous talent as a writer, but he also had a mischievous, unruly Hyde side to his Jeckyl-like talent, which the *Star* couldn't possibly satisfy. Once, he telephoned the ailing, competing evening newspaper, the *Telegram*, at a time when rumours had it up for sale. He did an uncanny, rather breathless impersonation of newspaper mogul Lord Thomson of Fleet to some unsuspecting veteran reporter in the newsroom and started a rumour that Tely owner John Basset had to publicly deny a few days later. McRae used to delight in playing the tape of that call during our drunken, fall weekend, football getaways to Buffalo, where he was once tossed out of a bar on Chipawa Street after squirting a stripper with a water pistol he'd filled with milk. I still remember the stripper stopping the music and pointing at him in the darkened bar: "That man there, he squirtin' me with somethin' through his coat!" Out he went, the buttonhole ambusher ambushed, and it became for me a metaphor for a kind of sneaky, mean-spirited, sniper style of journalism that is becoming too prevalent these days. Three cheers for a stripper with integrity!

What McRae does is rooted not in what he believes will benefit society but what he thinks will be read and be noticed: news as performance or entertainment. It is not my kind of journalism. It finds a large audience these days in those entertainment-news television shows, where nasty hosts use outrageous topics and flamboyant guests to try to arrest a fickle mass of channel-flippers. Until very recently, daily newspapers had no equivalent, but that too is changing as readership declines and newspaper companies are turning to people with MBAs for answers. More and more newspaper content is being decided not by journalists, whose goal is to inform, but by marketing experts, whose goal is to deliver the right audience to advertisers so that their companies can deliver the right dividends to shareholders. The decline of public-service journalism has depressed people like American editor Michael O'Neill, who says the corruption of journalism by tasteless, sensational entertainment is undermining public support for the legal protections that allow journalists to do their jobs; it's also irresponsible:

> The culture of entertainment is tuned to emotional stimulation rather than information. There is no journalistic tradition to guide the [journalistic] decision-makers and, in a climate of moral relativism, there are few scruples about perverting the public's view of society, government and the world beyond.[1]

McRae turns people's cranks the same way. Like the marketing executives, he peddles controversy and entertainment to the widest audience. A journalist's job, on the other hand, is to ring the bells of truth and warning for an informed citizenry. When we part, Earl McRae and I, it is with a certainty on my part that my journalism and his are light years apart in motive and tone. This, however, turns out to be one of those rash judgments to which our craft is all too prone to jump. I am due to be disappointed.

On the way back to Shawville, I stop in Quyon where they are celebrating St. Patrick's Day as only Gavan's Hotel can. The bar is the cradle of Irish music in the Outaouais region, even though it wasn't established until 1946. That's more of a tribute to its founder and his family than to its longevity. Lennox Gavan, besides being Fred Meilleur's brother-in-law, was the region's most famous singer of old shanty songs, which he rendered in the traditional way, without musical accompaniment and with a shillelagh in his hand tapping out the beat on a bar floor. His songs were learned in the oral tradition and passed on that way to his daughter, Gail, who is performing this night in an extravaganza that began at 2:30 p.m. and will go until closing time twelve hours later. Gavan's is so Irish that permanent shamrocks adorn the walls; so musical that it has named its French fries "Curleys" after one of the region's late, great Irish fiddlers, Dominic Curley; and so inexorably and commercially linked to the nearby snowmobile route that there is a closed-circuit monitor above the bar to show owners that their machine is safe and sound in the parking lot outside. When I arrive, there are maybe thirty-five snowmobiles on the screen, and so many people in snowmobile suits dancing that the swish of nylon competes with the wailing sound of the fiddles.

Gail Gavan is the master of ceremonies and has just finished thanking the Schwartz stepdancers when a chant starts in the crowd. "Do the Earl McRae song!" someone shouts. Gail Gavan, custodian of the legacy of Lennox and chief cultural curator of the whole museum of Irish shanty and folk music of the Valley, has written a song about my friend McRae.

> *G'day, G'day, Earl McRae*
> *Who you writin' 'bout today?*
> *Take your column to the U.S.A.*
> *And stick it where the Sun don't shine*
> *Oh, and stick it where the Sun don't shine.*

Her rendition gets thunderous applause, and I suspect McRae would interpret this as vindication of his journalistic ability. He's been noticed. They're talking about him out there. And if he were entrepreneurial enough to sell shares in himself, his stock would probably be rising.

Unfortunately, too many of Canada's major daily newspapers operate a lot like McRae. They talk a lot about getting in touch with their communities, but in their hearts they remain rude, callous, insensitive and smug. They address few of the issues that concern people most directly today; offer few surprises and no solutions; are almost impossibly deaf to new ideas and quick to take offence at any criticism; and shun conversation of any sort with anyone they deem less significant than themselves. They are the dinner guests from hell. And yet they always expect another invitation.

The next morning at work, Richard turns to me with a letter the *Equity* has just received. He delivers it like news of a death in the family. "You should see this," he says. "It's mostly about you." It is signed "Dismayed," and its main point seems to be that I write in a journalistic league that can only put me in the despicable company of people like ... Earl McRae.

> I'm writing to express my disappointment at the way your paper has handled the recent coverage and exploitations regarding the renewal of the Pontiac Agricultural Society buildings at the fairgrounds .... I am pleased, however, that Mr. Miller will be soon leaving the Pontiac to return to the renowned Ryerson to teach. When you were blowing Mr. Miller up (earlier in the year upon his blowing into town), I thought we could look forward to some interesting and unbiased stories. The *Equity* has only since become the "Weekly Crap on Millertime!!" Mr.

Miller and Earl McRae, of the *Ottawa Sun*, are in the League of Their Own!

The writer accuses me of unspecified inaccuracies and "sneaky antics," suggesting that I put up the copy of my story in the arena the night before the paper was distributed. More ominously, he or she also suggests that the agricultural association might go elsewhere for its printing needs. "That might bite to the tune of a few grand, eh? An eye for an eye." To the *Equity*, the letter said:

> When it's all said and done, no matter what allegations you print, Miller will be gone and Millertime will be terminated. When this uproar is over, hockey, figure skating, Canada Day celebrations, Shawville Fair and so on will continue in this town, but the damage John Miller initiated will last for a long, long time.

The paper is not used to getting such vindictive mail, and I try to keep my hurt feelings hidden. Me … and McRae! And I don't have McRae's advantage of having a thick skin. Still, being criticized does not bother me as much as something else: my realization that bad or vindictive journalism very often succeeds in driving out the good. It's just too easy to shoot the messenger these days. McRae's cheap screed against Ottawa Valley hicks has been used as a yardstick by a partisan critic to find my arena story mean-spirited. Like McRae, I am an outsider, and therefore not to be trusted. My careful documentation and my public service motive in writing it—to let people know what happened to the money that was supposed to fix up their arena—have been called into question, not by any challenge to my facts but by questioning my motive.

Again, the *Equity* knows how to react. Richard's next editorial challenges anyone to disprove the substance of my story and takes a swipe at people who don't have the courage to sign their names to personal attacks. In subsequent weeks, the paper urges the community to pull together to sort out its mess, encourages more citizens to get involved in reviving the fundraising campaign and manages to give things a nudge in the right direction by donating $1,000 to the fair board so that it can get on with the plumbing in the arena.

In a gracious editorial entitled "That John Miller Lad," Richard marks the end of my stay by observing that, as much as I've brought to the community in the way of an outsider's insight and an ability to see the extraordinary side of commonplace events, "it's possible the professor learned as much as he taught."

He's right about that, too. I learned how a journalism that lacks just about every resource except an abiding faith in its readers can exercise moral leadership and heal rifts and misunderstandings in its community. I learned how the fragile relationship between a reporter and his readers needs to be constantly tended to and how important it is to earn back any trust that's been lost. I learned that pandering—either to readers or to advertisers—will not achieve anything that lasts. And I learned that truth, the unvarnished truth, the sometimes hurtful, always elusive, incredibly important truth, can be delivered effectively only by a messenger who is known to be acting in the public interest.

The arena got fixed in the end. So, perhaps someday soon, can Canada's daily newspapers.

## Note

1.  "Who cares about the truth?" by Michael O'Neill, *Nieman Reports*, Spring 1994, page 1. O'Neill is former editor of the *New York Daily News* and a former president of the American Society of Newspaper Editors.

# Index

# Index

# About the Author

John Miller knows Canadian newspapers inside out. He worked as a reporter and editor on them for twenty years, including five as deputy managing editor of the *Toronto Star*. For ten years, he headed one of the country's leading journalism schools—at Ryerson Polytechnic University in Toronto. In 1995, he helped preserve and redraft the statement of principles that all of Canada's newspapers function by, and he is a former governor and judge of the National Newspaper Awards. Miller is now professor of newspaper journalism at Ryerson and lives in Hope Township, Ontario. This is his first book.